Yugoslavia in the 1980s

Westview Special Studies

The concept of Westview Special Studies is a response to the continuing crisis in academic and informational publishing. Library budgets are being diverted from the purchase of books and used for data banks, computers, micromedia, and other methods of information retrieval. Interlibrary loan structures further reduce the edition sizes required to satisfy the needs of the scholarly community. Economic pressures on university presses and the few private scholarly publishing companies have greatly limited the capacity of the industry to properly serve the academic and research communities. As a result, many manuscripts dealing with important subjects, often representing the highest level of scholarship, are no longer economically viable publishing projects-- or, if accepted for publication, are typically subject to lead times ranging from one to three years.

Westview Special Studies are our practical solution to the problem. As always, the selection criteria include the importance of the subject, the work's contribution to scholarship, and its insight, originality of thought, and excellence of exposition. We accept manuscripts in camera-ready form, typed, set, or word processed according to specifications laid out in our comprehensive manual, which contains straightforward instructions and sample pages. The responsibility for editing and proofreading lies with the author or sponsoring institution, but our editorial staff is always available to answer questions and provide guidance.

The result is a book printed on acid-free paper and bound in sturdy library-quality soft covers. We manufacture these books ourselves using equipment that does not require a lengthy make-ready process and that allows us to publish first editions of 300 to 1000 copies and to reprint even smaller quantities as needed. Thus, we can produce Special Studies quickly and can keep even very specialized books in print as long as there is a demand for them.

About the Book and Editor

The opening years of this decade have been difficult for Yugoslavia: Open revolt has occurred in Kosovo province and economic hardship has added to a general crisis of confidence. The system of self-management, once the pride of Yugoslav ideologists, has come increasingly under fire in post-Tito Yugoslavia as proponents of the system search for a new basis of political legitimacy. Yet for all the uncertainties since 1980, the collective leadership established by the late President Tito has continued to function, albeit ineffectively. Looking at the political debates, ethnic tensions, economic policy, religious organizations, gender relations, the media, the role of the Yugoslav National Army, dissidents, nonalignment, and relations with the Soviet Union, the contributors detail the complexity of changes affecting Yugoslavia today.

Pedro Ramet is an assistant professor in the Henry M. Jackson School of International Studies at the University of Washington. He is the author of Nationalism and Federalism in Yugoslavia, 1963-1983 (1984) and the editor of Religion and Nationalism in Soviet and East European Politics (1984).

For Bariša Krekić

Yugoslavia in the 1980s

edited by Pedro Ramet

Westview Press / Boulder and London

Westview Special Studies on the Soviet Union and Eastern Europe

Published in 1985 in the United States of America by Westview Press, Inc.; Frederick A. Praeger, Publisher; 5500 Central Avenue, Boulder, Colorado 80301

Library of Congress Cataloging in Publication Data
Ramet, Pedro, 1949-
   Yugoslavia in the 1980s.
   (Westview special studies on the Soviet Union and Eastern Europe)
   Includes index.
   1. Yugoslavia--History--1980-   . I. Title.
DR1307.R35 1985   949.7'024   84-20822
ISBN 0-8133-7012-4

Composition for this book was provided by the editor
Printed and bound in the United States of America

10 9 8 7 6 5 4 3 2

Contents

Tables

Acknowledgments

This book could not have been prepared for publication within any reasonable time frame without the assistance of Beverly Weiss, who, together with Gael Deviny and Kimberly Caulfield, typed much of the final manuscript. Her patience in the face of repeated editorial corrections and assistance with the proofreading are also very much appreciated.

I am also indebted to Russ Carr for showing me the ropes on the word processor so that I could do my share of the typing and for trouble-shooting when I ran into difficulties (which seemed to be constant, at first).

I am of course also grateful to <u>Problems of Communism</u> for permission to reprint the map of Yugoslavia, which originally appeared on page 50 of the March-April 1983 issue.

Finally, I would like to express my appreciation to my wife, Marilyn, for her unflagging patience and supportiveness during the work on this book.

One final note: at George Schöpflin's request, his chapter has not been "Americanized," and hence follows the British spelling conventions.

Pedro Ramet

About the Contributors

OTHMAR NIKOLA HABERL is Professor of Contemporary History of Eastern Europe, University of Essen, Federal Republic of Germany. Born in Sarajevo, he spent the first seven years of his life in Yugoslavia, and has visited Yugoslavia periodically since 1971. He was educated at the Free University of Berlin, receiving both undergraduate and doctoral degrees there. He is the author of Die Emanzipation der KP Jugoslawiens von der Kontrolle der Komintern/KPdSU (1974), Partei-organisation und nationale Frage in Jugoslavien (1976), and Die Abwanderung von Arbeitskraeften aus Jugoslawien (1978), and coeditor (with Lutz Niethammer) of Marshall-Plan und Europaeische Linke (1985) and (with Klaus-Detlev Grothusen and Wolfgang Höpken) of a two-volume study, Jugoslawien am Ende der Aera Tito (1983, 1985). His articles have appeared in Deutsche Studien, Osteuropa, Suedostforschungen, and other journals.

WOLFGANG HÖPKEN is Assistant Professor of Modern History of Eastern Europe and the Soviet Union, University of Hamburg, Federal Republic of Germany. Born in Oldenburg, Germany, he received his Ph.D. from the University of Hamburg in 1980. He spent nine months in Yugoslavia 1978-1979, mostly in Ljubljana and Belgrade, and has visited Yugoslavia annually since 1981. He is the author of Sozialismus und Pluralismus in Jugoslawien (1984) and edited Veljko Mičunović's Moskauer Tagebuecher for German publication (1982). He is coeditor (with Klaus-Detlev Grothusen and Othmar Nikola Haberl) of a two-volume study, Jugoslawien am Ende der Aera Tito (1983, 1985). His articles have appeared in Osteuropa, Politische Vierteljahresschrift, and Suedost-Europa.

ZACHARY T. IRWIN is Assistant Professor of Political Science, Behrend College, Pennsylvania State University. Born in Port Jervis, New York, he received his A.B. in History from Hamilton College, his M.A. in International Relations from Johns Hopkins University, and his Ph.D. in Political Science from the

Pennsylvania State University. He lived in Belgrade 1973-1974 on a Fulbright fellowship. He is coauthor of Introduction to Political Science (forthcoming) and has contributed chapters to Ethnic Separatism and World Politics (1984), Religion and Nationalism in Soviet and East European Politics (1984), and Threat Perception and the Regional Hegemons (forthcoming). His articles have appeared in the Canadian Journal of American Studies and East European Quarterly.

BARBARA JANCAR is Professor of Political Science, State University of New York, Brockport. Born in Keene Valley, New York, she received her A.B. in Comparative Literature from Smith College and her M.A. and Ph.D. in Political Science from Columbia University, with a certificate from the Institute for East Central Europe. She has visited Yugoslavia six times, most recently in 1984. She is the author of The Philosophy of Aristotle (1963), Czechoslovakia and the Absolute Monopoly of Power (1971), and Women under Communism (1978), and has contributed chapters to Soviet Society and Politics in Transition (1974), Soviet Foreign Policy in the Third World (1980), Female Soldiers: Combatants or Noncombatants (1982), and other books. Her articles have appeared in Problems of Communism, Signs, Studies in Comparative Communism, and other journals. She is currently completing a book on Women, Revolution, and Yugoslavia.

CHRIS MARTIN is a doctoral candidate of Economics at the University of California, Berkeley, and Research Associate at the Institute of Industrial Relations, UCB. Born in Ohio City, Ohio, he received his A.B. in English and Slavic Literature and his M.A. in Economics, both from the University of California, Berkeley, and is currently writing his doctoral dissertation there. He spent six months in Yugoslavia in 1983, mostly in Belgrade and Ljubljana.

PEDRO RAMET is Assistant Professor of International Studies, University of Washington. Born in London, England, he received his A.B. in Philosophy from Stanford University, his M.A. in International Relations from the University of Arkansas, and his Ph.D. in Political Science from UCLA. He visited Yugoslavia for the first time in 1978, lived in Belgrade for 10 months 1979-1980 on a Fulbright-Hayes fellowship, and made a subsequent visit to Yugoslavia in 1982. He is the author of Sadat and the Kremlin (1980) and Nationalism and Federalism in Yugoslavia, 1963-1983 (1984), and editor of Religion and Nationalism in Soviet and East European Politics (1984). He contributed a chapter to At the Brink of

War and Peace: the Tito-Stalin Split in a Historic Perspective (1982). His articles have appeared in _Problems of Communism_, _Religion in Communist Lands_, _World Politics_, and other journals.

ROBIN ALISON REMINGTON is Professor of Political Science, University of Missouri. Born in Boston, she received her B.A. in Political Science from Southwest Texas State College and her M.A. and Ph.D., also in Political Science, from Indiana University. She lived in Belgrade for 14 months 1970-1971 and again during 1981, on a Fulbright fellowship, and has made shorter trips to Yugoslavia in 1967, 1974, and 1982. She is the author of _The Warsaw Pact: Case Studies in Communist Conflict Resolution_ (1971), editor of _Winter in Prague: Czechoslovak Communism in Crisis_ (1969), and compiler of _The International Relations of Eastern Europe_, an annotated bibliography (1978). She has contributed chapters to _Eurocommunism between East and West_ (1981), _Communism in Eastern Europe_, 2nd ed. (1984), _Soviet Allies: the Warsaw Pact and the Issue of Reliability_ (1984), and other books. Her articles have appeared in _Orbis_, _Studies in Comparative Communism_, _Survey_, and other journals.

DENNISON RUSINOW is Associate of the Universities Field Staff International, based in Vienna. Born in Newark, New Jersey, he received his B.A. from Duke University and his M.A. and D. Phil. from Oxford University. He lived in Yugoslavia for ten years (Belgrade, 1963-1964; Zagreb, 1965-1966; Belgrade, 1967-1973), and has made frequent return visits since. He is the author of _Italy's Austrian Heritage, 1919-1946_ (1969), _The Yugoslav Experiment, 1948-1974_ (1977), and _The Institutional Framework of a Federally Structured Cyprus_ (1978). A regular contributor to the University Field Staff International reports, he has also contributed articles to _The Antioch Review_, _Europaeische Rundschau_, _Journal of International Affairs_, and other journals.

GEORGE SCHÖPFLIN is Joint Lecturer in the Political Institutions of Eastern Europe at the London School of Economics and the School of Slavonic and East European Studies, University of London. Born in Budapest, Hungary, he studied, from 1957 to 1962, at Glasgow University, where he graduated with M.A. and LL.D. degrees. After pursuing his studies at the College of Europe in Bruges, he joined the Royal Institute of International Affairs in London, moving to do work at the Central Research Unit of the BBC External Services in 1967. A regular contributor to _Soviet Analyst_, he is coauthor (with Stephen White) of _Communist Political_

Systems (1982), and editor of _The Soviet Union and Eastern Europe: a Handbook_ (1970) and _Censorship and Political Communication in Eastern Europe_ (1982). He contributed chapters to _Communist Power in Europe_ (1977) and _Opposition in Eastern Europe_ (1979). His articles have appeared in _Religion in Communist Lands, Suedost-Europa_, and _Survey_.

LAURA D'ANDREA TYSON is Associate Professor of Economics, University of California, Berkeley. Born in Dayonne, New Jersey, she received her B.A. from Smith College and her Ph.D. in Economics from M.I.T. She lived in Yugoslavia during 1972 and has returned there in 1981 and 1983. She is the author of _The Yugoslav Economic System and its Performance in the 1970s_ (1980) and coeditor (with Egon Neuberger) of _The Impact of Industrial Economic Disturbance on the Soviet Union and Eastern Europe_ (1980). Her articles have appeared in _The European Economic Review, Journal of Comparative Economics, Soviet Studies_, and other journals. She has also contributed to reports for the Joint Economic Committee of the US Congress.

SHARON ZUKIN is Professor of Sociology, Brooklyn College, City University of New York. Born in Philadelphia, she received her A.B. from Barnard College and her Ph.D. from Columbia University. She made her first visit to Yugoslavia in 1967 and spent extended periods in Belgrade in 1970-1971 and in 1979, and has returned to Yugoslavia periodically since. She is the author of _Beyond Marx and Tito: Theory and Practice in Yugoslav Socialism_ (1975) and _Left Living: Culture and Capital in Urban Change_ (1982), and editor of _Industrial Policy: Business and Politics in the United States and France_ (1985), and contributed a chapter to _The State in Socialist Society_ (1984). Her articles have appeared in _Politics and Society, Telos, Theory and Society_, and other journals. She is currently working on a book on deindustrialization in comparative perspective.

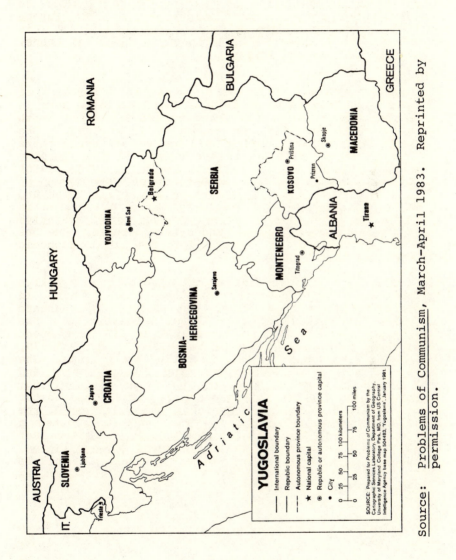

YUGOSLAVIA

— International boundary

| Republic boundary

--- Autonomous province boundary

★ National capital

◉ Republic or autonomous province capital

● City

| 0 | 25 | 50 | 75 | 100 kilometers |
| 0 | 25 | 50 | 75 | 100 miles |

SOURCE: Prepared for *Problems of Communism* by the
Cartographic Services Laboratory, Department of Geography,
University of Maryland College Park, MD, from US Central
Intelligence Agency base map 504483, "Yugoslavia", January 1981.

Source: Problems of Communism, March–April 1983. Reprinted by permission.

Introduction

1
Apocalypse Culture and Social Change in Yugoslavia

Pedro Ramet

A subtle change has taken place in Yugoslav society over the past few years. The buoyancy, confidence, and self-congratulation of the 1970s are gone--casualties of the now-general realization that 'self-managing socialism' has failed to live up to its promises. In their place, there are strains of pessimism, gloom, resignation, escapism of various kinds, and a feverish creativity associated with what might be called 'apocalypse culture.'

By 'apocalypse culture' I mean culture which is inward-looking, absorbed in a quest for meanings, and prepared to question the fundamental political and social values of the society. Associated with normlessness and anomie, it is therefore symptomatic of deep social insecurity, and is peculiar to developed societies in decay. Its openness to radically new formulas springs from the sense--whether a belief or (as more usually) merely a mood--that the system in question has arrived at a historical turning point, that it is, so to speak, the 'end of time.' Contributors to 'apocalypse culture' view themselves, thus, as social critics, voices warning of dangers ahead, even as prophets offering new visions and new formulas. There is a degree of this present in all modern societies. What defines 'apocalypse culture' is the peculiar intensity of this introspective brooding, and the centrality it comes to occupy in social debates.

I should like to emphasize at the outset that to identify an instance of apocalypse culture is not to suggest that the society in question is necessarily about to expire or to fall apart. What the presence of apocalypse culture reveals is merely that many people

*I am grateful to Peter F. Sugar and Sharon Zukin for comments on an earlier draft of this chapter.

in the country in question <u>fear</u> that their society is in fact disintegrating.

Apocalypse culture is thus associated with social crisis, more particularly with the disappearance of confidence on the part of the general population that current problems can be resolved using existing political formulas and social practices. But though the old solutions are seen as having lost their utility, the absence of consensus about new solutions creates an atmosphere of uncertainty. Yet by rivetting consciousness on the need for change, apocalypse culture is inherently regenerative--at least potentially. Apocalypse culture is, of course, only one of a number of possible responses to social crisis, but most of the responses (whether one thinks of peaceful change of leadership, internal reform, social chaos, revolution, civil war, the emergence of new social movements, or apocalypse culture itself) represent forms of pressure for change.

Apocalypse culture actually subsumes two distinct phenomena. First, there is the cultural sphere proper, where apocalyptic artists push the limits in terms of content, and sometimes also in terms of artistic form. Here one speaks above all of literature, though music and the plastic arts may also become vehicles for the expression of despair and social criticism. Because of the context in which it arises, apocalyptic art may contain features designed to provoke or outrage the spectator, and may display an absorption with decadence and the unseemly side of social existence. The apocalyptic artist tends toward nihilism, rejecting all social mores as vacuous. In contemporary Yugoslavia, apocalypse culture has embraced fiction reexamining the circumstances of the postwar imprisonment of thousands of suspected political opponents of Tito, poetry critical of Tito, nudity in theatrical performances, punk Naziism, and works taking a fresh look at the fascist Croatian <u>Ustaše</u> and Serbian Chetniks of World War Two, ethnic relations in postwar Yugoslavia, and other sensitive subjects. Second, one can speak of a related phenomenon in the political sphere, a kind of 'apocalypse politics', characterized by discontent so rampant that critical discussion cannot possibly be suppressed. Within this sphere sundry taboo alternatives may be openly broached and discussed.

Although apocalypse culture presumes a developed society, the higher the general level of cultural and educational attainment, the richer the phase of apocalypse culture is apt to be. In turn-of-the-century Vienna, for example, the level of attainment was already exceedingly high, and the resultant apocalypse culture (which embraced everything from the florid surrealism of the 'New Vienna School' to atonalism in music to the self-destructive irony of the young Viennese 'artist as art' who, in his final performance, hacked himself up, limb by limb, to drive home the point that he considered social existence without meaning) was correspondingly rich. In late Austria-Hungary as in Weimar, Germany, apocalypse culture also embraced a search for thorough-going political solutions to what was widely seen, in each case, as pressing social and political crisis.

What are the conditions in which apocalypse culture arises? To begin with, a nation must be at peace to experience a phase of apocalypse culture. In conditions of war, the energies of a society are necessarily too focused on the war effort to permit the emergence of soul-searching and self-doubt; and where such phenomena do emerge in wartime, as in tsarist Russia in the First World War, the system in question usually crumbles. The second precondition--which is in fact the key to apocalypse culture--is a pervasive crisis of confidence. This crisis of confidence may be stimulated by steady economic deterioration (which in Yugosalvia can be dated from mid-1979), though economic decay is not itself a precondition (as the example of turn-of-the century Austria illustrates). Third, changes in social classes and in social relations contribute to the sense of disequilibrium in which doubt and critical assessment arise. Fourth, the failure of the elite to provide generally acceptable solutions to pressing problems on the agenda is apt to fuel malaise and social criticism. When the political elite is itself seriously divided--as has been the case in Yugoslavia since Tito's death in May 1980--the absence of consensus is a foregone conclusion. And finally, whether because of stable, inherited liberalism or because of political relaxation or because of political weakness at the center, the possibility for self-expression must exist. In Yugoslavia, one encounters the curious example of a communist regime which, in the last several years, has repeatedly allowed its publishing houses to publish highly critical and controversial material, only to subject these same works to vilification in the press for anti-socialist views.

IS YUGOSLAVIA IN CRISIS?

There continue to be voices within the Yugoslav political establishment which deny that there is a crisis at all. A recent issue of _Socijalizam_, for example, published an article by Aleksandar Fira, denying that the system is in crisis, because, in his view, it is still capable of dealing with social "disturbances."(1) Similarly, the Belgrade weekly

magazine, <u>NIN</u>, urged in December 1983 that the steady
wave of complaints submitted to the party by ordinary
citizens (2,660 addressed to the Central Committee's
Commission for Appeals and Complaints, between July
1982 and June 1983) be seen as evidence of the "deep
faith" Yugoslav citizens still retained in the League
of Communists of Yugoslavia (LCY).(2)

Yet since early 1983, both LCY officials and
Western observers have explicitly described Yugoslavia
as in crisis.(3)   Moreover, the Yugoslav public itself
generally views the present predicament in terms of
crisis. The heart of the sense of crisis is economic:
with inflation racing, at the end of 1984, at an annual
rate of between 60 and 100 per cent, some lower class
Yugoslav families were having to spend 70 per cent of
their monthly income on food.(4)   It is now openly
conceded that "the average worker's household can no
longer make ends meet."(5)   In fact, a survey conducted
in late 1983 found that only 16 per cent of Yugoslavs
are able to cover cost of living expenses with their
regular incomes.(6) This may account, in part, for the
recent increase in smuggling operations, especially in
Slovenia.

The system's inability to assure stable supplies
of medicines, coffee, certain meats and fruit, and
other staples, and generally disappointing economic
performance during the last several years have shaken
popular confidence in the system per se. A September
1982 poll found that only 44 per cent of workers felt
positive about the system, while a public opinion poll
conducted in Belgrade in 1983 found that only 38 per
cent of respondents expressed confidence in the party
(as contrasted with 64 per cent in a 1974 survey), and
14 per cent declared that they had little or no respect
for the LCY (as contrasted with 2 per cent of
respondents in 1974).(7)   Another poll, conducted by
telephone among Yugoslavs in all eight federal units,
found that nearly half of the respondents were
uncertain if and when the current economic difficulties
would ever be resolved, with more than half (54 per
cent) blaming the federal units' slowness in reaching
accords for the government's inability to fashion an
effective economic policy. Another 21 per cent claimed
that political authorities lacked good ideas, while 8
per cent attributed the policy paralysis to sheer
governmental inefficiency.(8) Yugoslavs as a whole are
despondent about the economic situation, and doubt the
ability of the government to extricate the country from
that situation; the result is the shattering of the
mythology about the superiority of self-managing
socialism, and a strange feeling of being adrift
without a rudder.

The Yugoslav press has not shied away from the subject. The Belgrade youth periodical, Omladinske novine, charged in October 1983: "We know well what goals our Revolution set before itself. Our present-day results have absolutely nothing in common with what our battlers, headed by Comrade Tito, wanted."(9) Another periodical, Duga, asked in June 1984, "Who is to blame, or better, who is responsible for the crisis of Yugoslav society and self-management?" Duga's all-encompassing answer--"the whole society"--did not exempt the authorities from co-responsibility.(10) Interestingly enough, the usually more timid organ, Borba, went further in this respect. After blaming party leaders for "rarely sid[ing] with dissatisfied workers"--an extremely serious charge in any communist state--Borba went on to warn that the party was forcing workers into the role of passive observers, having no role in either the creation or the execution of policy.(11)

The political leadership has thus been forced to concede the seriousness of the crisis. Various officials have conceded that party principles and programs are regularly ignored or shortcircuited, that the workers have never been given a decisive voice in managing their enterprises (as promised by self-management), and that the League of Communists is often unable to resolve important conflicts of interest.(12) Jure Bilić, one of Croatia's three representatives in the LCY Central Committee Presidium, even declared that much of what has been standard practice in Yugoslavia has been based "on illusions and sometimes even on fantasy,"(13) though his solution--a thorough purge of party ranks--smacks of standard communist methods, rather than the breath of innovation. In October 1984, in a letter to the Republic Assembly of Bosnia-Herzegovina, the Yugoslav veterans of the Spanish Civil War wrote that the country could not wait until 1986 for the next regular party congress and that a special extraordinary congress should be called, without delay, to deal with the crisis.(14)

With its own self-confidence slipping, the party leadership took the novel step, at a "stormy" session of the Central Committee in June 1984, of agreeing to submit a long questionnaire about the party's role in society to its 70,000 grassroots party organizations.(15) What impact this might have remains to be seen, but there are very human reasons for resisting conclusions which threaten to shatter one's worldview or to undermine the premises of one's position. As sociologist Veljko Rus of Ljubljana noted recently, in an interview with a Belgrade magazine:

Every time I explained certain social
processes to the politicians a kind of

tension always emerged, which later became
nervousness and intolerance. This was not
because I was critical but because I
revealed certain new facts that would force
people to change their minds about
society.(16)

Moreover, according to General Gojko Nikoliš, when
answers to a recent survey conducted by <u>Komunist</u> among
sociologists, economists, and other trained
professionals on the question, 'what should be done?',
proved inconvenient, the survey was banned and its
initiators punished and suspended from their jobs.(17)

SOCIAL CHANGE AND THE SOURCES OF CRISIS

The most important vertices of social change which
have contributed to the emergence of a sense of general
crisis are: economic deterioration, political
paralysis, demographic changes affecting the ethnic
balance, and the breakdown of traditional society and
displacement of the old norms by a pervasive
relativism. In combination these have also excited
nationalist passions--which further complicates the
picture.

Several factors are responsible for the economic
mess. Among external (environmental) factors one might
mention the oil price increases after 1973 and the
world economic recession of the late 1970s. Among
domestic (policy) factors, the chief culprits were: the
autarkic desire of every republic to have its own steel
mill, its own automobile company, its own airline, and
so forth, regardless of the market, and a readiness in
at least some cases to subsidize inefficient
enterprises for strictly noneconomic reasons;
overborrowing from foreign sources, beginning in the
mid-1970s, to cover the costs of poorly coordinated
overinvestment; and the failure to transform the
southern regions of the country, especially Kosovo,
from economic drains into economic boons. With respect
to the last mentioned factor, Yugoslav decision-makers
seriously miscalculated by funnelling developmental
funds in Macedonia and Kosovo into capital-intensive
projects and extractive industries, rather than into
labor-intensive ones, and thus failed to make any
headway toward alleviating the unemployment problem in
the south.

Yugoslav overborrowing was clear already in the
late 1970s, when domestic earnings covered only 15 per
cent of investments, with the rest dependent on foreign
credits.(18) By 1984, Yugoslavia's debt to the West
exceeded $20 billion. Inflation hovered around 40 per
cent between 1980 and 1983, and then topped 60 per cent
in 1984. Unemployment has similarly climbed steadily,

nearing the one-million mark by the end of 1983, while among the employed, absenteeism has become an ever graver problem. On the positive side, industrial production rose 4.7 per cent during the first six months of 1984, while exports rose 6 per cent. But the accompanying policy of belt-tightening, which reduced consumption and retail trade in Yugoslavia, also undermined the standard of living, and in reflection of this, the number of strikes increased 80 per cent between 1982 and 1983 and has continued to rise since then.(19)

More troubling is the regime's inability to formulate a coherent economic strategy. Although the Krajgher commission for economic stabilization had been at work since 1981 and had submitted a set of detailed recommendations on the eve of the 12th party congress (held in June 1982), it was not until late June 1983 that the Federal Executive Council was to appoint a commission to carry out the recommendations of that commission, although the party was said to have endorsed the findings by an overwhelming (or in some accounts even "unanimous") vote of confidence. Moreover, even after this formal endorsement, the party failed to get the recommended measures carried out, because of obstruction by recalcitrant elements in the party.(20)

There is increasing recognition within the political establishment that the private sector has been the most productive, and more pragmatic officials have suggested that private agriculture and private businesses be supported and stimulated, rather than subjected to prejudicial taxation.(21) Party conservatives have opposed this, have criticized the International Monetary Fund (IMF) for imposing conditions for economic loans, as "interference" and have even demanded abrogation of Yugoslavia's agreement to adhere to IMF conditions.(22) The political elite is so factionalized that policy-making has been paralyzed. During 1983, for example, of 25 major laws due to be considered by the Federal Assembly, only eight were passed. The other 17 were shelved for reconsideration later.(23) The result is that the party has been unable to fashion a coherent strategy to halt the steady economic deterioration, and living standards continue to sink.

A second set of changes has been associated with the disappearance of traditional culture and traditional mores, especially in the cities, and has led to the social dislocations generally concomitant with modernization, viz., the diffraction of moral focus, the relativization of behavioral codes, the appearance of the generation gap as a constant in social life, and the steady secularization of society.

To take the last point first, the percentage of youth
claiming to be religious declined in samples from 40
per cent in 1969 to 26 per cent in 1983,(24) with
losses most severe among traditionally Orthodox
families. Modern 'hip' fashions have become popular
among urban youth,(25) divorces are climbing
steadily,(26) violent crime has only recently become a
matter of serious public concern,(27) and, since about
1981, drug addiction has assumed troublesome
proportions. There are about 10,000 registered drug
addicts in Yugoslavia today, though there may be two to
three times as many unregistered addicts.(28) Not
surprisingly, there have been critics on hand to
deplore the decline of morality in the country, and
especially among the younger generation.(29)

Within the context of the combined impact of
economic deterioration and the erosion of traditional
values, the demographic shifts recorded between the
1971 and 1981 censuses take on more ominous meanings.
The massive flight of Serbs and Montenegrins from
Kosovo has been a matter of party concern for well over
two years at this writing, while Croats have expressed
alarm at their numerical decline in both absolute and
relative terms. In Slovenia, the steady influx of non-
Slovenes (especially where Albanians are concerned) has
increasingly been viewed as a threat to the
preservation of Slovenian language and cultural
distinctiveness.(30) In every republic in Yugoslavia
today there are groups which feel threatened either
culturally-demographically or economically, or both;
the situation is most acute in Kosovo, the scene of
secessionist turmoil in 1981 and still unstable four
years later, where some 800 persons have been jailed
for irredentism between spring 1981 and autumn
1984.(31) Yet exclusivist nationalism has also become
more pronounced lately among Croats, Hungarians, Serbs,
and Bosnia's Muslims.(32)

In some cases, the nationalist backlash has
assumed extremist forms. Serbs, especially Serbian
students, have been reported singing Chetnik songs,
wearing Chetnik emblems, and assuming, as pseudonyms,
the names of leading Chetnik figures.(33) Croatian
youth in both Croatia and Bosnia have been reported to
have sung fascist Ustaše songs and to have greeted each
other by shouting "Heil Hitler!"(34) And a new
synthetic phenomenon, punk Naziism, has recently
emerged in parts of Slovenia and Vojvodina, while the
Dalmatian coastal town of Split has recently been the
scene of embarrassing "subversive" incidents.(35)

Given the party's obvious anxiety at the
resurgence of exclusivist nationalism,(36) one might
think it would take heart at the swelling of the ranks
of citizens declaring themselves "ethnically

uncommitted--Yugoslavs" in the census--1,219,024 in 1981, more than a fourfold increase from 1971's figure of barely 273,000. Yet, while some welcome this development, the suddenness of the increase makes other party elders uneasy. Croatian party Central Committee member Dušan Bilandžić, for instance, fretted in 1982: "I think that the phenomenon of Yugoslavism in the ethnic sense, especially its sudden growth, says that something is awry in society, for it is not an entirely normal social phenomenon."(37)

APOCALYPSE CULTURE

Between rapid secularization, economic deterioration, the resurgence of exclusivist nationalism, and the plummeting of confidence in the political system, Yugoslav society has experienced social trauma. All that remained, under these circumstances, to catalyze the frondescence of apocalypse culture, was political relaxation or weakness. The unresolved post-Tito factional rivalry in the party has assured a measure of both.

The literary scene has reflected the self-examination to which Yugoslavs are subjecting themselves. Nothing has been spared scrutiny--not Tito, not the party, not the Partisan war, not the mythology of 'brotherhood and unity'.

The cultural efflorescence began when playwright Dušan Jovanović, novelist Antonije Isaković, and other writers opened discussion of what had long been a taboo subject--the Goli Otok prison, northeast of Rab, where Tito had imprisoned his Stalinist opponents after the break with Moscow in 1948.

Jovanović's play, "The Karamazovs," which received its premiere performance in Slovenia in 1980 and opened in Zagreb in 1982, deals with the experiences of Svetozar Milić, a devoted communist who had learned to identify Tito's accomplishments with Stalin's inspiration. When the break came between Stalin and Tito, Milić wondered, in perplexity: "This has hit us overnight. [But] something which was always pure white cannot suddenly become black."(38) And Jovanović records how the Yugoslav Academy of Sciences continued for a while after the break to praise the leadership of Josef Stalin. But in changed political circumstances, old loyalties and new doubts were both liabilities, even offenses. Milić's "unreliability" was guilt enough, and he was sent to Goli Otok, where, with the aid of daily torture, he was trained to recite: "I am a bandit, a deserter, a scoundrel, without worth or honor, without pride, a chameleon, a sectarian, a provocateur, a stowaway on the ship of history of the Yugoslav people. I am a Cominform pig."(39) Milić, an honest man with honest doubts and uncertainties, was psychically broken at Goli Otok and died in prison. His judge, at the mock trial at which his fate was determined, went on to become a professor of philosophy. Jovanović's ironic touch draws attention to the absurdity of the situation.

Tren 2 (Moment 2), by Antonije Isaković, is perhaps the most controversial and best known of a series of novels dealing with the same theme. Isaković underlines the arbitrariness of the imprisonments, with large numbers of totally innocent (non-Stalinist) citizens arrested, along with Stalinists, and describes the severity of their treatment at Goli Otok. Tren 2 also includes an interesting added feature: a flashback to the Kronstadt rebellion of March 1921, in which Russian sailors repudiated the Bolshevik usurpation and demanded the fulfillment of the promises of the October Revolution and the establishment of a genuine workers' democracy. The Bolshevik Party instead suppressed the rebellion, massacred the rebels, banned factionalism, and consolidated the dictatorship. Isaković's recollection of this episode in Russian history suggests a parallel between Kronstadt and Goli Otok: perhaps each of these represents, in a different way, a 'wrong turn' in the revolution, a fateful derailing of a broadly based movement.

Another novel on the same theme, Branko Hofman's Noć do jutra (Night to Morning), proclaimed by many to be the best Yugoslav novel of 1981, prompted the youth organ Mladost to compare Goli Otok with Nazi concentration camps and Stalin's Gulag, and to ask that the party reexamine the episode.(40) Similar themes were taken up in Ferdo Godina's Molčeči orkester (The Dumb Orchestra), Jure Franičević-Pločar's Generalna proba (The General Trial), Žarko Komanin's Prestupna godina (Leapyear), and Slobodan Selenić's Pismo/glava (Letter/head). The importance of Goli Otok for these novels is that it represents the Yugoslav Republic's 'baptism by fire' and at the same time a fundamental inconsistency in the regime's albeit confused portrayal of its evolution from heroic Partisan war to early Stalinism to the 'progressive' break with Stalin to 'self-managing socialism'. The legitimacy of any system is closely bound up with the mythology surrounding its founding: founders are generally seen as exemplary if not brilliant individuals and the founding political principles as uniquely wise groundrules for just governance. By coming to grips with the rather brutal realities of the birth of Titoism, these sundry novelists shattered the mythology of the founding, and with it, the system's claim to peculiar beneficence. Equally, to wrestle with Goli Otok, is to wrestle with the conscience of the revolution, to fret about the primeval crimes upon which a political order is built. These novels struck a responsive chord with the public and the weekly magazine NIN began publishing a series of articles on the famous prison, including some allegedly hitherto unpublished documents. But the big question—whether a system born in repression was not critically flawed and thus intrinsically limited—has necessarily remained unanswered.

Other novels published since Tito's death have struck the Yugoslav public as more inspired by Serbian nationalism. Vuk Drašković's novel, Nož (The Knife), for example, hammers at the theme of Serbian suffering during the war and challenges the LCY's thesis that Bosnian Muslims are a discrete ethnic category, arguing instead that they are merely Serbs whose forefathers had abandoned Orthodoxy out of opportunism. Vojislav Lumbarda's novel, Anatema, is likewise inspired by Serbian nationalism, as is Milić Stanković's historical pamphlet, Sorabi, which takes up the argument that the Serbs are the oldest people in the Balkans.(41)

Nationalism was also the theme of the highly controversial play, Golubnjača (Pigeonhole), which opened in Novi Sad in October 1982, though treated more ambiguously. Written by 30-year old Jovan Radulović, the play is set in the Dalmatian hinterland of the 1960s and shows young Croatian and Serbian children still mired in the prejudices of the internecine struggle of World War Two, in which their parents faced each other as foes. The play seems to indict the LCY for failure to construct a society in which these prejudices could be overcome, yet at the same time complains more particularly that Serbian residents in Croatia are subjected to constant discrimination, whether by the Ustaše or by the communists.(42) The play created a sensation in Vojvodina and played to packed houses, it won a prize in Slovenia, and stirred up furor and confusion in party circles. Croatian observers were quick to condemn the play; others wondered whether the piece was nationalistic or, on the contrary, more truly anti-nationalist.(43) Eventually, the party decided the play was potentially dangerous and banned it from further production. The ban stirred a wave of protest from the public, especially from writers and students, and more particularly from the Serbian Writers' Association.(44)

The post-Tito theater has, in fact, been a paradigm of apocalypse culture. Marx himself has not been spared, and has been lampooned for his "boring" ideas.(45) Other plays, by Slobodan Šnajder and Dušan Kovačević, have reexamined the Ustaše episode and probed the reservoir of mutual denunciations and omnivorous distrust which were played out behind a facade of 'brotherhood and unity' in the late 1940s.(46) Similarly, poet Gojko Djogo earned notoriety in 1981, by publishing a collection of satirical poems apparently critical of Tito; his hubris brought him a one-year prison sentence.(47)

The apocalypse syndrome has also spread to the rock music scene. Some groups, such as the Serbian groups "The Crazies" (Šizike) and "Electric orgasm" (Električni orgazam), and the Slovenian groups "Rendezvous" and "Videosex," by and large avoid political themes, and are iconoclastic at most in the sense that their exaltation of sexual license clashes with traditional communist puritanism.(48) Other groups have provoked the authorities by singing nationalist songs or by contributing to the emergence of a rock "counterculture," which authorities view as inimical to "the peace of mind of our society."(49)

The Ljubljana group "Pankrti" seems to have been especially trying. In open mockery of the Partisan mythology, the group proposed to release an album showing a young man hugging a war monument. The producer intervened to require that the jacket not depict any monument from World War Two; so a monument from World War One was used instead. The group also hoped to call the album "The Pankrti in Collaboration with the State"--a title which would have drawn attention to the allegorical intention behind the picture. This too was disapproved, and the album was released with the title, "Favorites of the State"--a dubious claim indeed. Even with this "advice" from above, the album stirred controversy. In the song "Unanimous and Firm"--no doubt a play on the much touted "unity" of Yugoslav society--Pankrti sing:

> I am shocked that things can exist which
> consciously put our present moment in a
>   bad light and destroy our average.
> I protest, whoever is not for us is against us.
> I protest, whoever is not for him [Tito?] is
>   not one of us...
> I am shocked that we still put up with the
>   indecisive who are detracting from our
>   ability to act.
> Whoever thinks too much gets everything wrong.
> I am shocked at this critical moment.
> But if we are unanimous and firm,
>   we will be able to destroy them when
>   we come across them.(50)

Two songs by the Sarajevo rock group, "Smoking Forbidden" (Zabranjeno pušenje), were banned from radio programming in January 1985, because they compared present-day Yugoslavia unfavorably with Austria-Hungary and the interwar kingdom of Yugoslavia.(51) Still another group, a Slovenian punk rock ensemble, invited trouble by calling itself "4R" (the "Fourth Reich") and displaying swastikas at a concert. The School of Political Science of Ljubljana University subsequently organized a roundtable discussion of punk rock, to discuss such questions as whether "punk is Naziism writ small." The discussion was attended by the Slovenian Republic Secretary for Internal Affairs and representatives from the Ljubljana City Secretariat for Internal Affairs and the Supreme Court of Slovenia.

Finally, in a brazen display of their forebodings of the 'end of time', the Slovenian student paper Tribuna ran a front-page obituary for Yugoslavia in early 1984, observing, "We leave her with fond memories," and signing the notice, "all of her citizens,"(52) while the student literary monthly Vidici published a series of articles between 1980 and 1981, in which the key term "apocalypse" (apokalipsa) allegedly figured as code for "the definite collapse of the existing system."(53)

The new wave of politically engaged culture did not escape the notice of party conservatives, who attacked the avant-garde tendencies, in mid-1983, as stemming from obsession with Western-style liberalism and from "creative weakness."(54) Early in 1984, Croatian conservative Stipe Šuvar—who had earlier complained that "there are some people in Yugoslavia who specialize precisely in unearthing the errors of the past, i.e., the errors of the party"(55)—drew up, together with certain colleagues of his, a list of some 200 Yugoslav dramatists, novelists, poets, filmmakers, and other intellectuals who were said to be fomenting "cultural counterrevolution." The cardinal sins of which those listed were said to be guilty were the demystification of society, negativism toward socialism, and portrayal of the wartime Partisans as no better than the Chetniks or the Ustaše.(56)

What these sundry plays, novels, poems, and rock songs have in common is their critical reevaluation not merely of present policies and problems, but of the central underlying myths and heroes of the state. This is characteristic of apocalypse culture, and indicative of profound social stress.

APOCALYPSE POLITICS

If intellectuals and artists have been drawn into more critical paths in the cultural sphere, so too intellectuals and politicians have been engaged in an extremely lively and often daringly creative debate about political alternatives. Although this debate began shortly after Tito's death,(57) it seems to have grown more intense during 1983 and 1984.

Repeatedly, voices have warned that Yugoslavia has reached a political deadend and needs to strike out in a new direction. The Zagreb weekly, _Danas_, urged in 1982, "It is necessary to throw out the 'past' even though it was, in our case, even illustrious, and the view that the party has the right to manage society in the name of a triumphant revolution...[The party] must stop giving directives....The weaknesses of the LC arise from the inability to get started in this direction."(58) Milenko Marković made a similar plea for democratization in the pages of _Socijalizam_ in 1983, but couched it in terms of a return to an earlier truth. In his words, "there has been more talk in recent years about 'the development of the socialist state' and 'the strengthening of the national character of the state,' but ever less mention of the withering away of the state"(59)--a process which Yugoslav theoreticians once claimed was unfolding more quickly and more smoothly in Yugoslavia than anywhere else in the world.

The themes addressed in the cultural sphere have also been prominent in the political discussions. In the past five years, a large number of excellent studies of interwar, wartime, and early postwar Yugoslavia have been released by Yugoslav publishers, as well as scholarly treatments of more contemporary political issues. Many of these works, and especially those dealing with the wartime and early postwar periods, have been highly controversial. The best known example is Vladimir Dedijer's four-volume project, _Novi prilozi za biografiju Josipa Broza Tita_ (_New Contributions to the Biography of Josip Broz Tito_), of which the first three volumes had been published by the end of 1984. Dedijer's second volume created a stir by bringing Tito down to earth and allowing that Tito had important faults.(60)

Likewise, Marx and Marxism have taken a beating lately. The Belgrade publishing house 'Zapis' published a book by Ratko Milosavljević in 1982, for example, which admitted that Marx had made "great errors" and underlined the importance of his mistaken projections about food and population trends.(61) Subsequently, at a three-day symposium held in Novi Sad in December 1983, Serbian Professor Svetozar Stojanović exploded the myth that Marx's ideas are uniformly democratic. On the contrary, Stojanović observed, Marx's writings are characterized by unresolved contradictions and even weaknesses. Among the latter, Stojanović highlighted Marx's concept of the dictatorship of the proletariat, which Marx thought should have a clear "repressive" face and which, according to Stojanović, lent itself to the bolshevik adaptation. Indeed, "through the manner in which he built his theory, Marx created the possibility that Marxism would be bolshevized."(62) Stojanović upbraided Marx for having failed to anticipate that his ideas could just as easily lend themselves to a despotic adaptation, charged that Marx failed to subject his own theory to critical analysis, and concluded that the Marxist idea of the dictatorship of the proletariat was an "unfounded" and "dangerous" idea.(63)

Still other Yugoslav writers have variously stated that the communist party monopoly is incompatible with a prosperous economy,(64) that Yugoslavia's present difficulties are attributable to the institutions and practices established by the 1974 constitution,(65) and that socialism, once thought to be inevitable, is not inevitable at all.(66) Politicians of both liberal and conservative hues have been complaining for years that the devolution of power to the federal units has gone too far and that the federal government no longer has a real handle on policy (though it may be noted that party conservatives are apt to give more stress to this argument than party liberals). Moreover, few institutions in Yugoslavia have escaped party criticism in recent years, and the party itself has been taken to task for various failings, including mismanagement, corruption, factionalism, inefficiency, the loss of prestige among workers and youth, and an allegedly increasing tendency to exclude ordinary party members from party decision-making.(67) As if that were not enough, Presidium member Hamdija Pozderac told the 16th Plenum of the LCY Central Committee, in March 1985, that workers' self-management has not been properly implemented.(68)

These searing criticisms--which exceed anything previous in the history of communist Yugoslavia, in both scope and depth--have been accompanied by a series of bold proposals for radical political change. The frequency with which such proposals are being put forth is itself evidence of social stress and symptomatic of apocalypse culture.

Some critics have suggested changes in the party itself. As early as February 1981, Croatian journalist Antun Žvan suggested that 'democratic centralism' was an archaic concept and should cease to be a guideline for intra-party behavior, and that, on the contrary, party discipline should be relaxed.(69) In a similar vein, the former Partisan general Petko Dapčević told the 12th Party Congress in June 1982 that Leninism was outdated and that the idea of a dictatorship of the proletariat was incompatible with self-management.(70) Still another ranking party member, Professor Jovan Marjanović, revived an earlier suggestion that Yugoslavia be transformed into a nonparty system.(71)

Other critics have urged changes in the federal system—whether to strengthen the federal government, to strengthen the federal units, to diminish the autonomy of Kosovo and Vojvodina, or to grant Kosovo full republic status, as many Albanians in that autonomous province demand. A new federal 'Platform for Kosovo', unveiled in October 1984, would place Kosovo under the jurisdiction of the federal government (as a province of the entire federation) rather than under the government of the Serbian republic.(72)   A more radical idea, on the part of sociology professor Vojislav Šeselj, to abolish four of the eight federal units, turning Vojvodina, Kosovo and Montenegro over to Serbia, and dividing Bosnia between Croatia and Serbia, brought its author an eight-year prison sentence.(73)

The idea of multi-candidate elections for governmental and even party posts, tried out in local elections in the late 1960s, keeps reemerging. Pavle Nikolić, then president of the Serbian Commission for the Political System, opined in April 1980 that true democracy presumed a choice among a number of candidates, an idea seconded by Najdan Pašić, president of the Serbian Constitutional Court, in November of that year.(74)   The idea of multi-candidate elections was bandied about in 1982, at the time of the 12th Party Congress, but the issue remained unresolved. Party theorist Jovan Radovanović joined the fray in May 1983, rejecting the notion that democracy consisted in ratifying a predetermined list of "most qualified" persons and the corollary that electing the "less qualified" is undemocratic.(75)   In the next few months, others seconded Radovanović, including Croatian party official Dušan Bilandžić, party theorist Vladimir Goati, and the editorial board of <u>Vjesnik</u>.   Goati challenged the one-candidate-per-post principle head-on:

> On what basis should we know in advance
> whether a candidate is "generally accepted"
> while another is not? Which agency is
> entitled to make such a decision and on what
> basis? After all, does not such a
> procedure create a danger that such an
> agency might become a substitute for the
> voters, for the people in general, thus
> jeopardizing the democratic principles to
> which we all pay lip service?(76)

In early 1984, Slovenia let it be known that it intended to put forward three candidates for the republic's single seat in the collective presidency. But when the other republics made it clear that they meant to have only one candidate per post, Slovenia backed off and named, instead, only a single candidate, as always.(77)   The irrepressibility of the multi-candidate idea suggests that there is strong support for it in many parts of Yugoslav society.

But while talk of multi-candidate elections usually presumes that all candidates will be members of the communist party, some Yugoslavs have gone further yet and advocated establishment of a two-party system. That the party continues to permit publication of such proposals and their open debate may indicate the support the idea has in certain quarters. The usual form that the proposal takes is to transform the party's mobilization arm, the Socialist Alliance for Working People of Yugoslavia (SAWPY), into a second party, and in this form, the proposal can be dated to the late 1960s.(78) And it was in this form that Serbian political scientist Mihailo Popović presented it in spring 1984. Addressing a party symposium in Belgrade, Popović said that SAWPY "should assume the role of a second party in the country's one-party system, not competing with the League of Communists in trying to assume power in the country but rather becoming a kind of official socialist opposition." Whether any party could possibly find a way to make permanent 'loyal opposition' status a genuine role was left unanswered, but Popović hoped that SAWPY could become independent of the LCY and "in a certain sense a 'rival' to the League of Communists, [with] many more non-Communists included in SAWPY's leading agencies."(79)

Sociologist Miroslav Živković returned to this theme in early 1985, declaring that self-management could not solve the system's problems and calling for the establishment of a "social democracy," complete with regular multi-candidate elections.(80)

Two political scientists from Belgrade coauthored a book about postwar political development, which addressed the same theme indirectly. Recounting the methods by which the communist party consolidated its rule, they argued that the destruction of the democratic parties in the postwar coalition government proved injurious to Yugoslavia and suggested that a full-fledged multi-party system should be restored.(81) That this book could have been published at all is a clear sign of Yugoslavia's tangible openness. That the book was eventually prohibited and withdrawn is indicative of the regime's feelings of vulnerability and fear of encouraging challenges to its monopoly.

Almost as daring is a program outlined by Stojanović in April 1983, involving the incremental introduction of political pluralism:

> First, the LCY should undergo full democrati-
> zation, including secret ballots for all party
> posts, with several candidates for each and
> the right to form factions within the party

organization. Secondly, the Socialist
Alliance, the country's largest mass organization, should be separated from the party
and become a genuine independent political
organization based on voluntary membership;
it would participate in power while
recognizing the leading role of the LCY.
Thirdly, the trade unions should also be
separate from the party organization,
becoming genuinely independent and a vehicle
for the self-management system; strategic
and key sectors of the economy should remain
nationalized, while the rest should be a
mixed economy open to private initiative.
Finally, the federal structure should be
reformed and strengthened; administrative
and cultural concerns should remain under
the control of the republics, and various
federal agencies could even be transferred
from Belgrade to other republican centers,
but economic life should become fully
integrated.(82)
Finally, mention should be made of 'New Left'
currents in Yugoslavia which speak of a "second
revolution" to "complete" the democratization of
political life.(83) Both these advocates and some
establishment figures have spoken lately of the need to
"overthrow the bureaucracy" and end the pervasive
passivity and opportunism in the system. Croatian
party elder Jure Bilić himself warned recently, "We
have to change things; otherwise chaos will
prevail."(84)

CONCLUSION

Aleksa Djilas warned recently, that "an
ideological dictatorship creates an ideological
civilization, in which practical activity and action
are difficult to bring to fruition."(85) As a result,
according to the younger Djilas, even the
intelligentsia remains shackled by the premises and
thought patterns of the ideology. In conditions of
profound social stress, the edifice of political
culture crumbles and feverish creativity appears. But
the cost of transcending the crisis may be the
abandonment of a lot of old political baggage.
Apocalypse culture is by nature regenerative. It
negates the old in order to advance new perceptions,
ideas, and solutions. The incompatibility of many of
these solutions is merely the reverse side of the
richness of the current search for escape from the
present quandary. A product and symptom of social
stress, apocalypse culture is at the same time an

organic response by which a society strives to restore itself to health. It is, thus, in and of itself, a positive phenomenon. The direction in which an apocalyptic society eventually evolves is not predetermined. There are opposing forces in Yugoslavia for fragmentation and unity, devolution and centralization, liberality and repression, openness and closure, a multi-party system, a multi-candidate system, and continuance of the status quo, and writers offering rival views of the country's often turbulent and uncertain past. But by heightening people's awareness of both the problems and the alternatives, and by underlining the openendedness of political development, apocalypse culture provides a powerful impetus toward innovation and change.

NOTES

1. Aleksandar Fira, "Postoji li kriza političkog sistema socijalističkog samoupravljanja?", in _Socijalizam_, Vol. 26, No. 10 (October 1983), p. 1414.
2. _NIN_ (December 4, 1983), p. 20.
3. For an enumeration of those concerned, see Pedro Ramet, "Yugoslavia and the Threat of Internal and External Discontents," in _Orbis_, Vol. 28, No. 1 (Spring 1984), pp. 109, 120.
4. _The Economist_ (London, June 30, 1984), p. 45.
5. _Večernji list_ (Zagreb, March 4, 1984).
6. _NIN_ (October 30, 1983), trans. in Joint Publications Research Service (JPRS), _East Europe Report_, No. 84947 (December 14, 1983), p. 37.
7. _Ibid_, p. 39; and George Schöpflin, "The Yugoslav Crisis," in _Soviet Analyst_ (January 26, 1983), pp. 1-2.
8. _NIN_ (April 10, 1983), summarized in Foreign Broadcast Information Service (FBIS), _Daily Report_ (Eastern Europe), April 14, 1983, p. I9.
9. _Omladinske novine_ (Belgrade, October 30, 1983), trans. in JPRS, _East Europe Report_, No. EPS-84-006 (January 6, 1984), p. 216.
10. _Duga_ (June 2-16, 1984), p. 4.
11. _Borba_ (Belgrade, April 2/3, 1983), trans. in FBIS, _Daily Report_ (Eastern Europe), April 12, 1983, p. I5.
12. _Večernje novosti_ (Belgrade, February 27, 1983), cited in Slobodan Stanković, "Yugoslav CC Plenum: Party on the Ideological Offensive," _Radio Free Europe Research_ (March 11, 1983), p. 2; _Start_ (Zagreb, January 14, 1984), cited in Slobodan Stanković, "Yugoslav Discussion over Reform of the System Continues," _Radio Free Europe Research_ (February 21, 1984), p. 2; and _Vjesnik_ (Zagreb, May 10, 1984).
13. Quoted in _Vjesnik_ (July 27, 9183), as cited in Slobodan Stanković, "The Yugoslav Dilemma: How to Abandon the Illusions," _Radio Free Europe Research_ (August 8, 1983), p. 5.
14. Letter submitted by Yugoslav Veterans of the Spanish Civil War to the Republic Assembly of Bosnia-Herzegovina in Sarajevo (October 22, 1984), xerox of typescript, p. 3.
15. _The Economist_ (October 27, 1984), p. 51.
16. _Intervju_ (Belgrade, January 6, 1984), quoted in Slobodan Stanković, "Yugoslav Sociologist Blames Ideology for Social Failures," _Radio Free Europe Research_ (January 31, 1984), p. 2.

17. Gojko Nikoliš, "Govor na skupštini Udruženja španskih dobrovoljača" (Sarajevo, October 22, 1984), xerox of typescript, p. 6.

18. Francesco Gozzano, "La Jugoslavia fra Pressioni Esterne e 'Contraddizioni Dialettiche' Interne," in Affari Esteri , Vol. 11, No. 43 (July 1979), p. 324.

19. Corriere della sera (Milan, May 6, 1984); The Seattle Times (September 2, 1984); Studentski list (February 26, 1982); Christian Science Monitor (December 5, 1983); Tanjug (September 12, 1984), trans. in FBIS, Daily Report (Eastern Europe), September 13, 1984, p. Il; and The Economist (June 30, 1984), pp. 45-46.

20. Vjesnik (June 27, 1983); and Ekonomska politika (April 16, 1984), p. 12.

21. Slobodan Stanković, "Toward a Political 'Turning Point' in Yugoslavia?", Radio Free Europe Research (June 12, 1984), pp. 5-6. For a somewhat earlier discussion of private enterprise in Yugoslavia, see Der Spiegel (December 4, 1978), pp. 204-209.

22. Frankfurter Allgemeine (March 12, 1984), and (November 26, 1984).

23. Zdenko Antić, "Crisis and Dissent in Yugoslavia," Radio Free Europe Research (October 23, 1984), p. 18.

24. NIN (July 29, 1984), p. 18.

25. "Moda: Recite to majicom," in Danas (Zagreb), No. 128 (July 31, 1984), pp. 66-68; and Christian Science Monitor (September 10, 1984).

26. Borba (August 22, 1976), trans. into German under the title, "Sozialprobleme und Ehescheidungen in Jugoslawien," in Osteuropa, Vol. 27, No. 5 (May 1977), p. A305.

27. Večernji list (June 30-July 1, 1984).

28. NIN (December 13, 1981), p. 29; and New York Times (January 12, 1984).

29. NIN (November 28, 1982), trans. into German under the title, "Unmoral als Existenzvoraussetzung," in Osteuropa, Vol. 34, No. 2 (February 1984), p. A107; and Danas (December 6, 1983), pp. 21-22, trans. in JPRS, East Europe Report, No. EPS-84-016 (February 3, 1984), pp. 180-183.

30. Danas (July 24, 1982), trans. in JPRS, East Europe Report, No. 81989 (October 15, 1982), p. 92.

31. Frankfurter Allgeemine (October 13, 1984).

32. Tanjug (December 10, 1981), trans. in FBIS, Daily Report (Eastern Europe), December 16, 1981, p. I21; Politika (Belgrade, January 21, 1983); Die Welt (March 15, 1983), trans. into Croatian in Nova Hrvatska (London, April 10, 1983), p. 18; Borba (March 31, 1983), trans. in JPRS, East Europe Report, No. 83316 (April 22, 1983), p. 106;

24

and Zachary T. Irwin, "The Islamic Revival and the
Muslims of Bosnia-Hercegovina," in East European
Quarterly, Vol. 17, No. 4 (January 1984).

33. Borba (April 4, 1983), trans. in JPRS, East Europe
Report, No. 83409 (May 5, 1983), p. 56; and "Das
schwierige Zusammenleben der Voelker," in
Osteuropa, Vol. 34, No. 5 (May 1984), p. A257.

34. Politika (September 18, 1984), summarized in FBIS,
Daily Report (Eastern Europe), September 25, 1984,
p. I2; and Frankfurter Allgemeine (October 30,
1984).

35. For reports on Vojvodina, see Vjesnik (April 11,
1983); and Vjesnik--Sedam dana (April 16, 1983).
Re Split, see Vjesnik (February 7 and 21, 1985).

36. See Radovan Radonjić, "Antisocijalističke
tendencije i snage u našem društvu," in
Socijalizam, Vol. 26, No. 4 (April 1983), p. 595;
and Politika (September 13, 1984).

37. Vjesnik--Sedam dana (May 8, 1982).

38. Quoted in Leonore Scheffler, "Goli otok. Das Jahr
1948 in den jugoslawischen Gegenwartsliteraturen,"
in Suedost-Europa, Vol. 33, No. 6 (June 1984), p.
355.

39. Quoted in Ibid., p. 356.

40. Richard F. Staar (ed.), Yearbook on International
Communist Affairs 1982 [hereafter, YICA 1982]
(Stanford, Calif.: Hoover Institution Press,
1982), p. 502; and Robert Wesson (ed.), YICA 1983
(Stanford, Calif.: Hoover Institution Press,
1983), p. 372.

41. Zdenko Antić, "The Danger of Increasing Serbian
Nationalism," Radio Free Europe Research (March
24, 1983), p. 4.

42. Heinz Klunker, "Die Taubenschlucht oeffnet sich,"
in Theater Heute (September 1983), p. 20;
Kroatische Berichte, Vol. 8 (1983), No. 1, p. 7;
and Der Spiegel (January 24, 1983), pp. 109-110.

43. Christian Science Monitor (April 25, 1983); and
Vjesnik (January 15, 1983).

44. Radio Belgrade (December 22, 1982), trans. in
FBIS, Daily Report (Eastern Europe), December 27,
1982; p. I35; Neue Zuercher Zeitung (January 16-
17, 1983); and Vjesnik (February 19, 1983).

45. Profil (May 7, 1984), p. 53.

46. Klunker, "Die Taubenschlucht," pp. 22-23.

47. Reduced from the original two-year sentence. See
Tanjug (May 19, 1981), trans. in FBIS, Daily
Report (Eastern Europe), May 21, 1981, p. I9;
Oslobodjenje (Sarajevo, May 22, 1981); and
Politika (March 25, 1982), trans. in FBIS, Daily
Report (Eastern Europe), April 1, 1982, p. I11.

48. See Vjesnik (May 7, 1984); and Duga (June 2-16,
1984), p. 51.

49. <u>Vjesnik</u> (April 13, 1984). See also <u>NIN</u> (March 13, 1983), trans. in JPRS, <u>East Europe Report</u>, No. 83541 (May 25, 1983), p. 92.
50. Quoted in <u>NIN</u> (November 14, 1982), trans. in JPRS, <u>East Europe Report</u>, No. 82530 (December 27, 1982), p. 65.
51. <u>Vjesnik</u> (February 1, 1985).
52. <u>Oslobodjenje</u> (March 30, 1984). trans. in JPRS, <u>East Europe Report</u>, No. EPS-84-060 (May 9, 1984), p. 88.
53. Zdenko Antić, "Some Yugoslav Party Quarters Concerned about the Student Press," <u>Radio Free Europe Research</u> (February 8, 1982), p. 2. This case is discussed at greater length in chapter 5.
54. <u>Oslobodjenje</u> (July 7, 1983).
55. Quoted in <u>Die Welt</u> (November 7, 1980).
56. <u>Neue Zuercher Zeitung</u> (June 16, 1984), and (July 3, 1984).
57. See Pedro Ramet, "Yugoslavia's Debate over Democratization," in <u>Survey</u>, Vol. 25, No. 3 (Summer 1980), pp. 43-48.
58. <u>Danas</u> (August 10, 1982), trans. in JPRS, <u>East Europe Report</u>, No. 81738 (September 10, 1982), p. 57.
59. Milenko Marković, "Decentralizovani etatizam i medjunacionalni odnosi," in <u>Socijalizam</u> , Vol. 26, No. 6 (June 1983), p. 904.
60. Staar (ed.), <u>YICA 1982</u>, p. 497.
61. <u>NIN</u>, No. 1692 (June 5, 1983), trans. in JPRS, <u>East Europe Report</u>, No. 83937 (July 20, 1983), p. 43.
62. Svetozar Stojanović, "Marks i ideologizacija marksizma (kritika jedne predrasudne moći)," in <u>Gledišta</u>, Vol. 25, Nos. 1-2 (January-February 1984), p. 28.
63. <u>Ibid.</u>, pp. 32, 33, 30.
64. Slobodan Stanković, "Yugoslav Journal Praises 'the Budapest Style of Pluralism'," <u>Radio Free Europe Research</u> (May 17, 1984), p. 2.
65. Zdenko Antić, "Yugoslav Sociologists urge Genuine Democratic Reform," <u>Radio Free Europe Research</u> (December 29, 1983), p. 2.
66. <u>Intervju</u> (August 19, 1983), p. 31, as cited in Slobodan Stanković, "Yugoslav Theorists have Second Thoughts on Communism," <u>Radio Free Europe Research</u> (October 6, 1983), p. 1.
67. <u>Reporter</u> (July 8-15, 1982), p. 22; Slobodan Stanković, "Where are the Experts in Yugoslavia?," <u>Radio Free Europe Research</u> (August 24, 1984), pp. 2-3; <u>Danas</u> (August 28, 1984), p. 4; and <u>Neue Zuercher Zeitung</u> (September 30-October 1, 1984).
68. Slobodan Stanković, "CC Plenum Deplores Disunity," <u>Radio Free Europe Research</u> (March 28, 1985), p.11.

69. For more details, see Pedro Ramet, "Jugoslawien nach Tito--zerbrechliches Gleichgewicht und Drang nach Legitimation," in Osteuropa, Vol. 32. No. 4 (April 1982), p. 298.
70. Wesson (ed.) YICA 1983, p. 369.
71. Večernje novosti (October 7, 1982), as cited in Ibid., p. 371.
72. Christian Science Monitor (October 9, 1984).
73. The Economist (July 14, 1984), p. 48; Profil (July 16, 1984), p. 43; and Christian Science Monitor (August 7, 1984).
74. NIN (April 27, 1980), p. 22; and Borba (November 6, 1980), as cited in Zdenko Antić, "Yugoslav Leaders Disagree about Reforming the System," Radio Free Europe Research (April 22, 1983), p. 1.
75. Borba (May 11, 1983), as summarized in Slobodan Stanković, "Yugoslavia to Change its Electoral System?", Radio Free Europe Research (August 8, 1983), p. 2.
76. Politika (December 11, 1983), as quoted in Slobodan Stanković, "The Yugoslav Electoral System: A Race with a Single Horse," Radio Free Europe Research (December 30, 1983), p. 3.
77. The Economist (March 3, 1984), pp. 50-51.
78. See "Jugoslawischer Theoretiker fur Zweiparteiensystem," in Osteuropaeische Rundschau, Vol. 13 (December 1967), pp. 19-21.
79. Večernje novosti (June 2, 1984), as quoted in Slobodan Stanković, "Call for 'Official Opposition' in Yugoslavia," Radio Free Europe Research (June 28, 1984), p. 2.
80. Večernje novosti (April 16, 1985), as cited in Zdenko Antić, "Sociologists See Tension Rising in the Country," Radio Free Europe Research (April 22, 1985), p. 17.
81. Vojislav Koštunica and Kosta Čavoški, Stranački pluralizam ili monizam (Belgrade: Institute for Social Science, 1983).
82. Antić, "Crisis and Dissent," p. 8.
83. Die Welt (June 1, 1983), trans. into Croatian in Nova Hrvatska (June 19, 1983), p. 16.
84. Duga (April 6, 1985), quoted in Slobodan Stanković, "Strife and Disputes Continue," Radio Free Europe Research (April 22, 1985), p. 21.
85. Quoted in Robert F. Miller, "Yugoslav Socialism and the 'Democratic Alternative'," in Quadrant (July-August 1984), p. 103.

Part 1

Institutional Arenas

2
Party Monopoly and Political Change: The League of Communists Since Tito's Death

Wolfgang Höpken

The League of Communists of Yugoslavia (LCY) is not merely the representative of a specific Yugoslav model of socialism, with a different understanding of Marxism-Leninism from that in the other socialist countries, and whose central elements--self-management and nonalignment--differ fundamentally from the domestic and foreign policy configurations of the Soviet bloc states. It also presents a concept of the party which differs substantially from that of the Soviet bloc. In fact, one may trace the second Soviet-Yugoslav rift to the Yugoslav party program of 1958, with its theses about the role of the party. The idea that with the development of communism, not merely the state but the party as well would wither away, leaving the party over time ever more restricted to ideological and educational functions, earned the LCY approbation in the Soviet party program of 1961 for having evolved into "the most complete embodiment of revisionism."(1) This verdict overlooked the fact that the "revisionist" prognosis, under which "the leading role of the League of Communists of Yugoslavia will gradually disappear with the development of all-embracive forms of direct democracy,"(2) was considerably relativized by the allusion to the preservation of the control and protective functions of the party for an indefinite period.

Indeed, none of the theoretical elements of Yugoslav socialism have been subjected to such frequent shifts of emphasis as this definition of the role of the party. Yet to the present, the party continues to claim that the Yugoslav system differs from both the multi-party system of the West and the one-party system of the East. Self-management is in its essence a kind of "non-party democracy" in which even the LCY makes no claim to political monopoly and in which the party carries out its policy in dialogue with other organizations and institutions. The enduring powers of control and intervention enjoyed by the League of Communists, which are grounded in the Constitution of 1974,(3) are understood thus as solely a function of the necessary role that the party plays in protecting the socialist system from capitalist, bureaucratic, nationalist, and other "hostile tendencies." This role should diminish as self-management is further developed.

This theory of the party has of course an internal contradiction, viz. the need to reconcile the claim of democratic and direct self-management of the citizens with the party's claim to leadership. In practice, the question as to how the role of the League of Communists in Yugoslav society should be arranged has, in comparison with the ruling practices of other communist parties, led Western researchers to changing and contradictory judgments, oscillating between the thoughtless ascription to the Yugoslav party of a "totalitarian pattern" and a euphoria over Yugoslav pluralism. Carl J. Friedrich, on the one hand, expressed the opinion, in 1967, during what is generally recognized to have been the most liberal period of Yugoslav party rule, "that Yugoslavia has exhibited--at least until recently--all the characteristic features of totalitarian regimes."(4) On the other hand, M. George Zaninovich writing only two years later, saw Yugoslavia already on the way to becoming a "multiorganizational system,"(5) while for George Klein, party supremacy had been so thoroughly reduced that in view of the pervasive pluralism of the system, it was impossible "to fix with precision, where the true power lies or where key decisions are made."(6)

Even without wanting to revive the totalitarian model for Yugoslavia, one must see, in retrospect, that expectations of a "withering away from power" such as was outlined in the party program were overdrawn even for the late 1960s. Even in the years 1966-1971, reformist forces sought at most the broadening of the autonomy of other organizations and institutions, and not the division or abrogation of the power of the party.(7)

Now, with virtually steady deterioration of the economic situation of Yugoslavia since the beginning of the 1980s, the party has been flung into a new crisis, incrementally undermining party unity. Centrifugal tendencies have seized the LCY and in consequence, have tangibly transformed the role and character of the party monopoly. Meanwhile, in Yugoslavia itself the danger of the disintegration of the party is no longer contested. This process of gathering erosion of the League of Communists in the first five years since Tito's death will be examined from two perspectives in

the following pages: first, from the standpoint of
elite dissensus, probing thus the elements of consensus
and controversy involving the federal and republican
party organizations, and second, from the standpoint of
changes in the structure and inner-party life of the
LCY.

POLITICAL CHANGE AND PARTY DEVELOPMENT IN THE 1970s

The stabilization course adopted after the crises
of the early 1970s(8) was more than pure
"recentralization." It was founded on three concepts:
the expulsion of liberal leaders and the reaffirmation
of democratic centralism; the retention of a radical
federalism on the state level; and a decentralized
system of self-management. This system remained intact
in the last years of the Tito era. The years 1974-1980
were relatively quiet, and the Eleventh Party Congress
in 1978 demonstrated continuity and regained unity.(9)
Allusions to differences between the republican parties
and the center, for example in the question of changes
in party statutes, revealed that beneath the
administratively ordained party unity there was the
potential for latent centrifugal tendencies.(10)

A final change was introduced by Tito himself in
November 1978, when he addressed the Eighth Trade Union
Congress, and called for limiting the terms of state
and party chiefs, of chairmen of district committees,
and of republican and provincial party organizations to
one year, and the terms of secretaries to two years.
The trade union organizations themselves, as well as
most governmental organs, likewise adopted this "Tito
initiative,"(11) which was lauded as a measure directed
against the "leaderism" and "unhealthy ambitions" of
individuals.

THE SUCCESSION PERIOD, 1980-1982

Only a year after Tito's speech before the Eighth
Trade Union Congress, the projected succession
mechanisms were put to the test. The prescribed
transition to a collective leadership was accomplished
with ostensible success, and George Zaninovich called
the frictionless transition from the Tito era to the
post-Tito era a "unique experience among communist
systems," and a lesson for those Western social
scientists who were accustomed to seeing Yugoslavia
from the perspective of internal crisis.(12) Tito's
long illness doubtless eased the transition, and in
this exceptional situation, the federation, the
republics, party and state leaderships drew closer
together. Latent smouldering differences had to be
repressed in this time of uncertainty. Lazar

Koliševski, who took charge as vice president in the first weeks after Tito's death, confirmed that the party and state leaderships of the federation cooperated with the republican leaderships without any problems.

The routine turnover in party and state leadership positions since then has proven stable. Yet the impressive smoothness of leadership rotations should not obscure the fact that the radical federalization of the system has not sufficed to neutralize disintegrative tendencies. Indeed, in some respects, the institutional structures bequeathed by Tito have actually proven counterproductive.

The April riots in Kosovo and the deteriorating economic situation ensured, in tandem, that 1981 would be a year given over to the theme of <u>community</u>. Developments in Kosovo presented an occasion, in particular, for raising the question of the relationship of the federation to the federal units, and of the LCY to the republican parties.(13) Even the economic downturn and the helplessness with which the party leadership at first tried to cope with it were blamed, to a large extent, on the tendency toward "republican etatism," i.e., on the economic egoism of the respective federal units. High party functionaries themselves began to criticize the party, as of 1981, for its ever more evident inefficiency in dealing with the crisis. The greatest weakness in the party's work, however, was the lack of concrete action toward the realization of adopted decisions.(14)

While functionaries continued to pay lip service to democratic centralism, the republican parties were becoming ever more independent and self-regulating. And as the Twelfth Party Congress approached, there were calls even in the higher party echelons for an open debate about democratic centralism itself,(15) such as had not been conducted since 1969.

For most of 1981, theoretical essays appeared with a content ranging from a liberal view that democratic centralism was no longer relevant, to demands for recentralization. One must, however, keep in mind that these essays did not all reflect the same influence within the party leadership. Indeed, some of the more liberal proposals to come from intellectual or journalistic quarters amounted to more smoke than fire.

The most radical proposal in this debate suggested the replacement of democratic centralism with a principle of "democratic unity." The Zagreb journalist, Antun Žvan, who first suggested this concept, wanted thereby to transcend what he saw as an obsolete concept from Lenin's time and to provide a more modern concept, suitable to a pluralistic society with differentiated interests.(16)

Other proposals sought rather to provide essentially new definitions of democratic centralism or to base decision-making in the LCY on the principle of "democratic negotiation" (demokratsko dogovaranje) among the republican and provincial party organizations.(17) Such a demand amounted to a call for the sanctioning of what had long been the de facto practice of negotiation and consensus-building among the republican party organizations and the confederalization of the party along the lines of what had already been accomplished in the governmental structure. In short, this entailed transforming the LCY into an umbrella organization of fully autonomous regional parties.

The antagonists of these proposals wanted to prevent precisely such a result and sought to engineer a corrective to what they viewed as the danger of disintegration within the party. Such impulses came above all from Serbia--which is scarcely surprising after the revelations concerning the withholding of information by the Kosovar provincial party organization. Nenad Kecmanović, for instance, warned that the idea of letting democratic centralism operate only at the level of the republican party organizations and to make the Central Committee and Presidium of the LCY only forums for the republican parties would open the door to centrifugal tendencies and finally paralyze the party altogether.(18) Rade Končar, the chairman of the Novi Beograd party organization and member of the party committee of the city of Belgrade, went even further. In a spectacular performance at the Twelfth Party Congress, Končar proposed that the gathering disintegration of the party be remedied by total structural reorganization replacing the territorial principle with a production principle.(19)

It is difficult to assess the true weight of all these proposals for the formation of opinion in the upper echelons of the party. Until Končar stepped forward, most of the proposals came from intellectuals or journalists, who may enjoy open access to the media but whose influence on inner-party elites was probably slight. They are better seen as evidence of the relative openness of discussion at the time than as reform proposals with real chances of adoption. Certainly, no well known party functionary openly endorsed either the concept of "democratic unity" or the confederalization of the party under the rubric of "democratic negotiation." On the contrary, Žvan's concept of "democratic unity," which had the goal of a conceptual separation from democratic centralism, was sharply attacked from various sides. Fuad Muhić, the Sarajevo polemicist, reproached Žvan, absurdly accusing him of following the theoretical line of such contradictory political movements as the New Left of 1968, the Croatian mass movement of 1971, Kosovar irredentism, and even Eurocommunism.(20) At the same time, Franc Šetinc, a member of the Slovenian party leadership, made it crystal clear that Žvan's ideas were unacceptable even for the otherwise generally "liberal" Slovenian party.(21)

But there was no party consensus for recentralization, on the other hand. The then party chairman, Dušan Dragosavac, speaking at the Twelfth Party Congress in June 1982, condemned not merely "democratic unity" but also those "who under the cloak of concern for the unity of the LCY actually call into question the equality, independence, role, and responsibility of the republican and provincial party organizations, and strive thereby to transform the LCY into a monolithic party of the centralist type"(22)--an unmistakable sideswipe at Rade Končar.

After this distancing from the more radical proposals, one could expect from the Twelfth Party Congress at the most a "more precise" definition of democratic centralism, and hardly a really new definition. The proposals for the revision of the party statute proved to be only very slightly influenced by the debates preceding the Congress. In contrast to the public discussions, in which "liberal" positions were also represented, the principle of democratic centralism was not challenged by anyone within the Central Committee, and the party statute adopted at the Twelfth Party Congress actually broadened the scope of democratic centralism.

Otherwise, the Twelfth Party Congress ended with formless and still controversial compromises, aimed at achieving a middle path between the efforts of individual republican parties to secure their autonomy from the central party and the (above all Serbian) efforts to strengthen the central party organs. Thus, the propensity to make the members of the Central Committee answerable directly to the republican and provincial parties which elected them came to nothing. Indeed, such a regulation would have constituted a further step on the path to the confederalization of the party. Nor were there any traces in the new statutes of other proposals circulated before the Congress, such as the Montenegrin suggestion "that republican party organizations be divested of the power to elect members of the CC LCY and allowed only to nominate candidates to be picked at the regular Yugoslav party congresses."(23) Rather, the adoption in the new statute of the provision that every CC member is responsible to the CC itself and to the party Congress served to underline the CC member's duties to the party as a whole.

There were further differences of opinion regarding the regulation of relations between the CC and the party Presidium. As early as June 1980, the CC considered the proposal that the post of chairman of the CC Presidium be replaced with a post of chairman of the CC itself.(24) A regulation of that kind would doubtless have signified a tangible strengthening of the Central Committee. The idea was referred to the Twelfth Party Congress, which sought to achieve a compromise by leaving the post of Presidium chairman intact, while providing more detailed and concrete stipulations regarding the prerogatives of the Central Committee.

Whereas the Central Committee had more or less sunk, during Tito's time, to being an important producer of resolutions—this, at least after the party crisis of 1971-1972—its role as the party's highest organ between congresses and as the active shaper of party policy was once again given stronger emphasis. At the same time, the Presidium was more clearly defined, as the executive organ of the Central Committee. While Tito had "<u>led</u>" the work of the Central Committee, the Presidium was now said to "<u>organize</u>" the CC's work. The Presidium was expressly charged with making specific proposals to the CC, with cooperating actively with the republican Central Committees and the Provincial Committees of the provincial party organizations, and with bringing urgent business to the attention of the CC. In this way, the prerogatives of the CC vis-à-vis the Presidium were at least nominally broadened.

The effort to strengthen the Central Committee was linked with demands for multi-candidate elections to the committee and for a secret vote in the selection of its executive organs. The Party Congress was not prepared to acquiesce in the establishment of multi-candidate elections, though the secret ballot, in elections of executive organs, was for the first time allowed in the party statutes.

Whether both the strengthening of the Central Committee and the democratization of its election could really be seen as reforms brought about by a "liberal" wing of the party, as was given out at the time, does not seem so clear. Rather, it bespeaks a drive to "de-federalize" the upper echelons of the party. For, much as had happened with the collective State Presidency, the party Presidium had developed ever more clearly into a sounding board for the positions of the individual parties. Its actual task of functioning as the integrative leading organ of the party was thus pushed into the background.

Even with respect to Tito's call for one-year mandates in all executive organs, the Congress found itself divided. In particular, the Slovenian party opposed a proposed rule fixing the term of the chairman of the republican Central Committee at one year, preferring a two-year mandate for their party. The result was again a compromise, in which the one-year mandate was prescribed for chairmen of organs of the central party and a two-year mandate for secretaries of central party organs, while the republican parties were allowed to set their own rules regarding their respective officers.(25)

The first post-Tito party Congress thus failed to clear up the fundamental uncertainty in party development. It neither countered the de facto predominance of republican party organizations as against the federal organs of the party nor dared to sanction openly the already strongly confederal practices. Hence, it made a verbal reaffirmation of democratic centralism, but permitted actually no counterweight to the centrifugal tendencies.

FROM FEDERALIZATION TO DISINTEGRATION, 1982-1984

It was already clear from the first CC session after the party congress that, contrary to the optimistic prognoses of the time, the Twelfth Party Congress had failed to achieve unity of purpose within the party leadership. In the election to the CC Presidium—hitherto a formal act of ratification—one of the proposed candidates failed to receive the necessary number of votes.(26) Mitja Ribičič, the newly chosen party Chairman, conceded a few months later that this development, while in reality scarcely spectacular, had an alarming effect on party echelons.(27)

In the following months, the party center tried to get a grip on things. Contacts with the republican and provincial party organizations were intensified. And in early 1982, it was laid down explicitly that members of the Central Committee should not misconstrue themselves as representatives of their respective federal units.(28)

In practice, such appeals had little effect, and the party Presidium would concede a year later that despite repeated resolutions, words were not being translated into action.(29) In February 1984, the Twelfth Plenum of the Central Committee reviewed the lack of progress toward carrying out the earlier decisions and had to content itself with calling anew for their execution.(30) Where the policy of economic stabilization was concerned, there remained "different views within the very ranks" of the Central Committee, and after six meetings of the CC devoted to this subject within two years, the party organ Komunist conceded that democratic centralism was degenerating into "sterile repetitions of exactly the same resolutions, lack of adherence to these resolutions in practice, and the evasion of democratic debate."(31) Given this "semi-paralysis" of the LCY in economic policy, Croatian CC member Slavko Šajber could quite rightly claim that the party as such existed only for the duration of the party congress: between congresses, the LCY had long ago devolved into an umbrella organization for negotiations and compromises between the republican party organizations, and was capable of united action only when the republican party organizations reached a consensus autonomously.(32)

The undeniable centrifugal tendencies in both economic and political questions impelled the party leadership to make a new effort in summer 1984 to restore the efficacy of central party organs. In preparation for the Thirteenth Session of the Central Committee in June, the Presidium drew up a statement directing criticism above all at the relations between the central party organs and the republican and provincial party organizations. "Decisions adopted unanimously at the national level are being carried out only half-heartedly, and execution is largely limited to those aspects which suit the particular region at the moment," the report charged. "Under the slogan of 'concern' for one's own republic and nation, and for one's own working class," the independence of the republican and provincial parties was said to have been "one-sidedly" interpreted, while the right of the central party organs to exert "direct influence and supervision in the work of the organs of the CC of this or that republic or province" had been contested.(33)

On the basis of this criticism, a draft resolution was presented by the party Presidium for adoption at the Thirteenth CC Session. Discussions of this 14-page resolution, which contained some by no means concrete proposals for the improvement of party unity,(34) produced outspoken controversy, and Dimče Belovski, secretary of the Presidium, considered it necessary to deny speculation about an ostensible conflict between the party Presidium and the Central Committee.(35) Meanwhile, Spiro Galović, a CC member and member of the Serbian party Presidium, openly conceded that there had been differences over the draft resolution, in which "the real disagreements were cloaked in syntactically untenable idioms."(36) In fact, the Central Committee hesitated to pass the draft in the form in which it had been presented, because it was seen as too general. Instead, it decided to turn the document over to the roughly 70,000 basic organizations of the party for discussion, and to adopt it as the basis for the

Thirteenth Party Congress of 1986 only after those discussions.

But whether this recourse could serve to overcome the disintegrative tendencies within the party leadership was, from the beginning, open to question. Indeed, it seemed to figure more as an attempt to legitimate the party than as a real effort to solve the problems of the day. "The party debate," declared the Zagreb magazine _Danas_, "came at the last minute--at five minutes to 12--in the effort to win back popular trust in the party."(37)

Meanwhile, another no less explosive subject had become the occasion for lively controversy: the question of the eventual reform of the political system --a subject already broached at the Twelfth Party Congress in June 1982. CC member Najdan Pašić spoke out both at the Congress and later, in July 1982, at the Second Session of the Central Committee, calling for a review of the political system in order to lay hold of the political roots of the economic crisis. In a "Letter to the LCY Presidium" in September of that year, Pašić underpinned his demand with a probing critique of the efficiency of individual political institutions. Excessive decentralization and institutionalization of the system had, according to Pašić, rendered policy-making inefficient. And as a result of the "parcelization" of the system, the political institutions, including even the party, had increasingly forfeited their integrative capacity.(38) While certainly not a call for centralism, Pašić's critique was nonetheless inspired by the notion that a cautious recentralization on all levels could improve the efficiency of the system.

Taking up Pašić's initiative, the party set up a working group under the chairmanship of Tihomir Vlaškalić, to prepare an analysis of the political system much as the Krajgher Commission did in the economic sphere. The results of this analysis have, at this writing, not yet been made public, though it is clear that the extent of eventual change in the political system is highly controversial.

As Pašić's initiative had already suggested, the impulse to reform came above all from Serbia. Serbian economists and politicians criticized the federal decision-making practices more clearly than did people in other republics. Jovan Djordjević, one of the best known Yugoslav constitutional jurists and a co-author of the 1974 constitution, bemoaned the fact that through the one-sided stress on the competences and autonomy of the republics, the Yugoslav system had taken on strong overtones of a confederal system.(39)

After the events in Kosovo, Serbian politicians became even bolder in their criticism of the federal balance. Dragoslav Marković openly criticized the principle of consensus, as a mechanism for decision-making, in his address to the Fourteenth Session of the LCY Central Committee in October 1984. This principle had developed from a necessary guideline for certain critical policy questions into a modus operandi for any and every question.(40) As a result, important political measures had repeatedly failed to pass until it was too late or until they had been seriously watered down.(41) In November 1984, finally, the Serbian party leadership set forth a series of relatively concrete ideas for change in the political system, affecting basically three areas: workers' self-management, cadres policy, and, above all, the relations between the republic of Serbia and its two autonomous provinces, Vojvodina and Kosovo.

The Serbian party's proposals sought to improve the efficiency of the enterprises by strengthening the larger work organizations at the expense of the smaller "basic organizations of associated labor," through a reduction of the decision-making capacity of the enterprises, and through a diminution of the administrative costs which had been inflated by decentralization.

In the area of cadres policy, the Serbian party suggested replacing the practice of one-year mandates with two-year mandates, and allowing office-holders to be reelected once, thus permitting them to serve for a total of four years.(42)

The most sensitive proposals, of course, were those affecting the relations between Serbia and its autonomous provinces. On this score, Serbia had been dissatisfied long before the 1981 riots in Kosovo. As early as 1975, the Serbian party leadership had made its first attempt to trim back the extensive powers ceded to the provinces. At that time, a so-called "Blue Book" about the conflicts and jurisdictional disagreements between the Serbian republic and its provinces was issued, in order to shore up these demands. This book has never been released to the public. Now, in the wake of the riots, a working group under the chairmanship of Belgrade Professor Radoslav Ratković reached the conclusion that Serbia had become steadily more "federalized" ever since 1974. The republican government had become more and more a government only for "narrow Serbia," i.e., for the Serbian republic minus the autonomous provinces. Even in instances where the constitution empowered the republican government to take unilateral decisions affecting the entire republic, it had become customary to seek the agreement of the two provinces before taking action. Serbian intentions were unmistakably to restore the primacy of the republic over the provinces.

As a first step in this direction, Serbia demanded that it be allowed to transfer its economic assistance to Kosovo directly, rather than funnelling it through the federal fund for the underdeveloped regions (a mechanism which excluded any possibility of Serbian influence).(43)

It is thus no surprise that the Serbian proposals encountered open opposition in both autonomous provinces. The Provincial Committee of LC Vojvodina in particular let it be known that it could not accept what federal development since 1968 had called into question. Criticism from Kosovo was naturally even sharper. The Serbian reproach for exaggerated provincial autonomy was seen as "one-sided" and completely unacceptable, and Kosovo rejected any revision along the lines of the Serbian proposals. The provinces were annoyed, however, not merely with the content of the Serbian proposals but also with the circumstance that they were broached without prior consultation with the provincial organizations. Such a procedure--so complained Bajram Seljami, Kosovo's deputy in the CC LC Serbia--"creates an atmosphere which does not lead to the strengthening of mutual trust, unity, and community, but drags the complications before the public."(44) Only by adopting a text which, in the decisive points, was largely neutral and general was it possible for the Eighteenth Session of the Central Committee to achieve at least a superficial unity. In fact, however, the Session saw anything but a narrowing of differences.(45) At the next session of the Kosovar Provincial Committee, Iliaz Kurteshi, in a direct swipe at Serbian party chairman Ivan Stambolić, criticized those who wanted to make the provinces' place in the Yugoslav federation a matter of dispute.(46) Asem Vlasi, the party chief of Priština, followed suit, observing that "the specificity of Serbia consists in that it includes two provinces, and this is a social reality which one must recognize."(47)

There was more to the Serbian proposals, however, than the prescribed revisions in relations between the republic and the provinces. Just as Serbia insisted on greater jurisdiction vis-à-vis its provinces, it also called for more decision-making powers for federal organs and a scaling back of the principle of consensus.(48) With regard to the party, the Serbs revived a proposal which had emerged originally in 1981, under which members of the LCY Central Committee would no longer be designated by the republican parties but would be chosen at the LCY Congress from among a plurality of candidates--which amounted to a tangible effort to "de-federalize" the central organs.

The Serbs refused to be tainted with the brush of "unitarism." Slobodan Milošević, a member of the Central Committee of the Serbian party, asserted,

We must free ourselves of the complex of unitarism. Serbian communists have never been champions of unitarism. On the contrary, we have throttled every attempt at such a policy. The Serbian communists have long been saddled with a complex about unitarism, and unjustly so, and made to feel guilty for a relationship with the Serbian bourgeoisie.(49)

If, then, the Serbian proposals were not presented as a plea for centralism, they did aim, without question, at reducing the current powers of the republics.

So it was no surprise that the Serbian proposals evoked little appreciation in the other republics, let alone in Kosovo and Vojvodina. Especially in Slovenia, the Serbian suggestions were taken up with skepticism and open dismay. Slovenian-Serbian differences were publicly aired at the Fourteenth CC Plenum in October 1984, when Slovenian functionaries France Popit and Andrej Marinc inveighed against the manner in which Dragoslav Marković had called for reform. Marinc went so far as to aver that the discussion about change in the political system should no longer be conducted in public, since this could lead to "a political crisis, to a crisis of society."(50) Marinc, the current head of the Slovenian party, emphasized his disinclination to see substantial changes in the political system. With an unmistakable wink at the Serbian party, he rejected any linkage of the long-term program of economic stabilization and reforms in the political system.(51)

The Croats were only slightly more reserved in their response. Stipe Šuvar, in whose eyes the long-term program of economic stabilization itself could figure at most as a "fire brigade program," saw in the unfolding discussion about change in the political system a threat that Yugoslavia's entire evolution since 1972 might be undermined.(52)

Nor were representatives of the individual republics the only ones disturbed by this question. Functionaries of the federal organs were also drawn into the controversy. Politicians of the older generation, such as Mitja Ribičič and Aleksandar Grličkov, whose political standpoint can no longer be identified with the interests of a specific republic, warned against insisting on political ideas "which have not been confirmed in practice."(53) Similarly, Stane Dolanc, the Slovenian member of the collective Presidency, declared that the entire discussion was creating a climate "which is not necessary at the present time."(54)   Other members of the collective Presidency also expressed reservations.

There is little support for the idea of institutional change outside Serbia. At the most, the Serbian party might find an ally in the party organization of the Yugoslav People's Army (JNA). The Presidium of the JNA party organization appealed, for example, for greater unity from the party and the state, and signalled its readiness to see changes in the system, to the extent that they should prove necessary. At the same time, it wanted to avoid any attack on the core elements of the system and inveighed against the discussion up to then, which had only served to stir up "confusion among the population."(55) On the whole, thus, the army organization seemed to be closer to the defenders of the status quo than to the Serbian critics.

A reform of the political system which is more than cosmetic is not to be expected. Harmony among the republican parties is obviously restricted to marginal issues, such as the method of voting or the self-managing interest communities.(56)   Changes in the basic elements of the system, even where they might be well founded, are on the contrary not realizable. Neither attacks on the Basic Organizations of Associated Labor (BOALs) nor criticisms of the federal system can win consensus among the republican party organizations. The reform, which like the program of economic stabilization was supposed to help to contain the centrifugal tendencies in the system, has run aground on precisely these centrifugal tendencies. And just as in the case of the stabilization program, so too when it comes to proposals for political reform, the LCY is evidently not in the position to achieve consensus.

SOCIAL CHANGE AND INTRA-PARTY DEVELOPMENT

The contemporary crisis of the party is, however, not merely a crisis of its leading organs. Intra-party affairs have also been affected by unmistakable obstacles to development. Decision-making mechanisms and opportunities for participation in the party have failed to keep pace with the LCY's growth into a mass party.

The years 1966-1972 had been characterized not just by a stagnation but by an actual decline in party membership. In addition, there was a turnover in membership such as had been unknown in earlier years. In particular, the number of voluntary resignations reached 10,000-15,000 per year in this period, suggesting implicit criticism of the party but also signalling a sense of freedom to leave the party

Table 2-1

Party Membership, 1946-1984

1946	258,303	1975	1,302,843
1952	772,920	1976	1,460,267
1955	624,806	1977	1,623,612
1960	1,006,285	1978	1,774,624
1965	1,046,202	1979	1,884,475
1970	1,049,184	1980	2,041,299
1971	1,025,476	1981	2,117,083
1972	1,009,947	1982	2,154,000
1973	1,076,711	1983	2,200,627
1974	1,192,466	1984	2,500,000

Sources: Figures for 1946-1965, Miloš Nikolić (ed.),
SKJ u uslovima samoupravljanja (Beograd:
Komunist, 1967), p. 748; figures for 1970-
1979, Komunist (December 30, 1980); figures
for 1980-1981, "Membership in the League of
Communists of Yugoslavia," in Yugoslav
Survey, Vol. 23 (1982), No. 4, pp. 29, 31;
figures for 1982, 1984, Richard F. Staar,
"Checklist of Communist Parties in 1984," in
Problems of Communism, Vol. 34, No. 2 (March-
April 1985), pp. 91, 95; figure for 1983,
Richard F. Staar, "Checklist of Communist
Parties in 1983," in Problems of Communism,
Vol. 33, No. 2 (March-April 1984), p. 45.

without fear of sanctions. The party must have found
it particularly painful to see membership among the
workers decline. Between 1965 and 1972 the proportion
of party members drawn from the working class dropped
from 33.9 per cent to 28.3 per cent, dipping in
absolute numbers from 355,022 to 285,592.(57)
    The party began to worry about an impairment of
its overall social composition as it saw workers drop
out and technocratic and middle class elements take
their places.(58) After the purges of 1971-1972, the
party vigorously sought to recruit new members,
especially among workers and youth. Since 1973 at the
latest, the class criteria for selection, which had
been at least formally maintained, have been abandoned
in favor of a more or less open recruitment policy for
the party.
    As a result of this change in cadres policy, the
number of party members has more than doubled since
1972 (as the figures in Table 2-1 bear out).
Membership has grown about 9 per cent annually, with an
especially high growth of 200,000 new members in 1980,
the year of Tito's sickness and death. Today, one out

of every 10 Yugoslavs, or one out of every eight Yugoslavs over age 16, is a member of the party. On a per capita basis, this makes the LCY one of the strongest communist parties in Europe.

Dividing the membership by republics and provinces does not reveal any extreme distortions. A symetrical representation of the party in every republic could not be achieved, however, and the proportions of the membership drawn from Slovenia, Kosovo, and Croatia do not correspond to their overall demographic weight (see Table 2-2). In fact, the entry of new members has been lowest in Croatia during the decade 1972-1982.(59) With regard to the ethnic affiliation of party members there are likewise no great disproportions, though Serbs and Montenegrins continue to be overrepresented in the party (see Table 2-3). The Albanians are the most seriously underrepresented, but in this respect one must bear in mind that more than half of the Albanian population in Yugoslavia is younger than 19 years, and that the Albanians of Kosovo have traditionally been disinterested in party membership. Still, even in Priština, the capital of Kosovo, where Albanians number more than 70 per cent of the population, only 59 per cent of the city party organization was ethnically Albanian in 1981; by contrast, with 39.1 per cent of the Priština party membership, Serbs and Montenegrins were significantly overrepresented.(60)

While the party has failed to make any headway in increasing the proportion of its membership drawn from the working class and while the leading positions in the party continue to be monopolized by privileged social groups,(61) the party has succeeded in its efforts to attract more youth into its ranks. In 1970, 20 per cent of party members were youth; at the beginning of the 1980s, the figure was 31 per cent.(62) Most of these new entrants were students; young workers proved more difficult to draw into the party. For many of those who joined the party in the 1970s, membership was an expression of diffuse loyalty or even merely a short-term political calculation, rather than an expression of the will to long-term political commitment. Youth have not been able to obtain any tangible representation in the leading party organs, and only 1.2 per cent of the Central Committee members are young people.(63)

Between 1980 and 1983 the number of new entrants into the party fell off sharply, and in the first six months of 1983, the Slovenian party, for example, experienced almost no growth at all.(64) An inquiry in Niš came to the conclusion that "from year to year there are fewer and fewer admissions [to the

Table 2-2

Membership in the LCY by Republics and Provinces
(in %)

	1971 LCY[a]	1971 Population	1981 LCY	1981 Population
Bosnia-Herzegovina	13.7	18.3	18.3	18.4
Montenegro	3.8	2.6	3.5	2.6
Macedonia	6.6	8.0	6.8	8.6
Croatia	20.5	21.6	16.4	20.5
Slovenia	6.2	8.4	5.9	8.4
Serbia	42.5	41.2	42.7	41.5
Serbia proper	27.7	27.0	27.9	25.3
Vojvodina	10.5	9.5	10.5	9.1
Kosovo	4.3	6.1	4.3	7.1
Yugoslav People's Army	6.6	–	5.6	–
Federal Organs	b	–	0.7	–

(a) = 1972;   (b) = LC Organizations in Federal Organs were formed in 1973.

Sources: Membership in the League of Communists of Yugoslavia, in: Yugoslav Survey, Vol. 23, No. 4 (1982), p. 29; Statistički Godišnjak SFRJ, (Beograd: Savezni zavod za statistiku, 1976), p. 101; Statistički bilten broj 1239, (Beograd: Savezni zavod za statistiku, 1981), p. 11

party]."(65)   This trend reversed itself in 1984.(66) All the same, one may say that the economic misery and the incapacitation of the party have diminished the party's attractiveness in the eyes of potential target groups—especially workers and youth. Most recently, workers have been particularly difficult to recruit, and nowadays account for only 26 per cent of new registrations, as opposed to more than 30 per cent in the 1970s.(67)   Against this, the workers have displayed a marked proclivity to leave the party, and this tendency seems to be increasing.

A similar development showed itself also among the youth. In Croatia, the proportion of party membership under age 27 fell, during the 1970s, from 27 per cent to 21 per cent. This is not merely a factor of the aging process, but reflects to a greater extent the markedly narrower interest among youth in joining the party.(68) It reflects, as Gordan Radman, Chairman of the Youth Union openly conceded, a growing political distance between youth and the party and a decline in the prestige of the LCY.(69)   This conclusion is

Table 2-3

National Structure of LCY-Membership,1971-1981

1971

	% of Yugo-slav popu-lation	LCY-members	in %	% of LCY-members among the nation
Serbs	39.7	507 027	49.4	6.2
Croats	22.1	178 826	17.4	3.9
Slovenes	8.2	65 546	6.4	3.9
Montenegrins	2.5	69 079	6.7	13.6
Macedonians	5.8	63 848	6.2	5.3
Muslims	8.4	46 870	4.6	2.7
Albanians	6.4	35 174	3.4	2.7
Hungarians	2.3	10 973	1.1	2.3

Table 2-3 (cont.)

National Structure of LCY-Membership,1971-1981

1981

	% of Yugo-slav popu-lation	LCY-members	in %	% of LCY-members among the nation
Serbs	36.3	997 323	47.1	12.3
Croats	19.7	310 096	14.6	7.0
Slovenes	7.8	112 391	5.3	6.4
Montenegrins	2.6	114 191	5.4	19.7
Macedonians	6.0	141 479	6.7	10.5
Muslims	8.9	169 984	8.0	8.5
Albanians	7.7	80 070	3.8	4.6
Hungarians	1.9	27 546	1.3	6.5

Sources: for 1971: Statistički Godišnjak 1976 (Belgrade: Savezni Zavod za statistiku, 1976), p. 101; Desa Vlačić, Statisticki podaci o Savezu komunista Jugoslavije. Deseti kongres SKO, (Beograd: Kommunist, 1974), pp. 18-20. For 1981 cf. SGJ 1982, p. 114; Slobodan Stanković, Jugoslawiens Krise des Systems (Köln: Berichte des Bundesinstituts fuer ostwissenschaftliche und internationale Studien, 1984), p. 29.

Table 2-4

Political Activity of Party Members
(in %)

	very active	indifferent	passive
LCY-members			
-1979	28	31	41
-1982	41	26	33
- up to 27 years	16	14	70
- 28 - 55 years	25	25	50
- 56 years and elder	11	24	65
former LCY-members (1982)	18	28	55
non-party-members (1982)	5	19	76

Sources: for 1979: Andjelka Milić, "Ideološka svest i angažovanje članova Saveza komunista", in: Socijalizam Vol. 23, No. 2 (February 1980), pp. 181 for 1982: Vladimir Goati, "Činioci angazovanja članova SKJ," in: Marksistička Misao No. 4 (1983), p. 98 and 102.

confirmed by a survey conducted by sociologist Srdjan Vrcan among students in Split: in earlier years, the students of Split had been a prime source of recruits into the party, but his sample showed that they had become, to a great extent, alienated from the LCY.(70) The economic and political crisis had evidently weakened also the legitimacy of the party.

The evolution of the LCY into a mass party has also changed intra-party life substantially. The theoretically maintained pretension to be a cadres party operating according to democratic centralism is, given the stormy growth in membership, hardly based in fact. There is also the fact that in some wings of the party, political activity is very weak; this phenomenon has been observed, and criticized, for years. At least a third of all party members can be classified as more or less passive. The actual proportion of members who are passive may be even higher, though, as the figures in Table 2-4 show. The level of activity varies widely according to socio-cultural group membership. As a whole, party members have above average incomes, higher education, and more prestigious work than most Yugoslavs;(71) but the politically passive party members are overwhelmingly persons with lower incomes, less education, and lower social status.(72)

It is not only social determinants that restrain many members in their activity, though. The style of policy-making also does little to move members to activity. This seems to have been sharpened, if anything, in the crisis of the last several years. The parrot-like repetitiveness of decisions and the endless resolutions in a language to which the population is scarcely inclined to respond any longer lead ultimately to the retreat of members from the party. The creation of miniscule basic organizations in the party, to parallel the decentralization in the enterprises through the BOALs, has not helped to raise the activity or influence of the rank and file. Today there are about 70,000 basic organizations in the party; 84 per cent of them have fewer than 50 members.(73) Evidence suggests that they have remained relatively inefficient organs, lacking influence. An analysis of basic organizations in Bosnia-Herzegovina revealed that participation in their sessions was irregular and relatively modest, that work reports and initiatives came in large part "from above," and that there was too much "formalism."(74) An analysis in Vojvodina produced similar criticism, noting that the basic organizations did not show any impulses to solve concrete problems.(75) Moreover, the activity of the party base has no tangible influence on the policy adopted in higher party bodies. Political decisions are still largely monopolized by small groups, while, according to Belgrade sociologist Vladimir Goati, "the party membership [is] repeatedly called upon only to ratify decisions."(76) About half of all party members surveyed in Belgrade had never participated either in the discussions at sessions of party basic organizations or in the preparation of these sessions and their decisions.(77)

Even the principles of rotation and collective leadership did little to counter these tendencies toward intra-party oligarchy. While the frequent changes in the leading offices at lower levels not infrequently leads to the problem of finding new qualified persons to take office, rotation at the upper levels has degenerated into a routine horizontal transfer of functionaries from one job to the next.(78)

In the current discussion about the future development of the party, the democratization of cadres policy and the revitalization of intra-party life have quite rightly been named as essential prerequisites for a restoration of the party's capacity to function.(79) It is too soon to judge whether the aforementioned attempt to mobilize the party base in connection with the discussion of the draft resolution of the Thirteenth CC Session can be seen as a way to break out of this torpor. Short-term mobilization actions have generally done little to eliminate structural deficiencies.

CONCLUSION

The League of Communists of Yugoslavia stands in crisis. Even in Yugoslavia itself there are few who dispute this any longer. The crisis shows up both in intra-party life and in the social and political life of the party. The LCY has certainly taken a step toward becoming a mass party; yet as already described, it has remained, to a great extent, a benumbed party dominated by a bureaucratic apparatus, in which there is little room for impulses from the base. The signs of the dearth of authority and legitimacy even among individual members are unmistakable. It is more important to assess the crisis of the party on a global political level. The notably impaired capacity of the central party organs to push through the long-range program of economic stabilization and the disagreements about the reform of the political system show that the LCY is, for the moment, capable only of dilatory compromises in the basic questions. It is true that the differences of opinion are verbally buried in these compromises, but they do not oblige anyone to anything. This is serious enough in times of economic and political calm; in conditions of crisis it is perilous for stability.

The concept of the LCY as an ideologically closed, organizationally federalized, but politically unified party, as developed in the 1970s, has not fared well in the post-Tito era. At the moment when, with Tito's death, the center fell out of the system, the federative dynamic, which had already taken hold in the state structure, began to spread to the party. The idea, that the party could endure as a homogenized and integrative factor in the middle of the federal free-for-all, proved to be a fallacy. The precept of party unity and the federative organizational structure of the party came more and more into conflict with each other. The regular turnover at the upper rungs of party and state have in the process been confirmed as a viable principle of leadership recruitment. Given the reality that in socialist states leaders generally have been changed only when they have died or when they have been overthrown, the performance of the Yugoslav system should not be despised.

There are only two paths whereby the LCY can escape this condition of withering capacity. First, the LCY could openly recognize itself as a confederation of six or eight autonomous parties whose central organs would henceforth serve only for consultation and efforts at consensus among the individual parties. This would entail also a repudiation of democratic centralism. Or, second, the

LCY could retrace its steps through a "de-federalization" of the central party organs, strengthening the party center vis-à-vis the republican parties. Such a solution could, of course, only be reached on the basis of the voluntary acquiescence of the republican parties (which at the present is completely improbable). As a result, the Thirteenth Party Congress, which will take place in 1986, will be confronted with the same task that the Twelfth Party Congress left unresolved.

The development of the party since Tito makes it difficult to fit the LCY into the spectrum of the usual categories of communist rule. Neither the Yugoslav concept of the withering away of the party nor the concept of party monopoly serves to describe the contemporary position of the LCY in the political system. The party has not curtailed its powers of control and taxation even in the past five years, but has actually strengthened them. All political institutions of any weight are almost entirely monopolized by party members. Even at the lower level, they dominate all institutions. Only in the politically less relevant communities or in delegations elected by direct vote of the citizens have non-members been able to fill up to 50 per cent of the posts.(80) Party members account for 75 per cent of deputies in local assemblies,(81) and more than 90 per cent of deputies in republican assemblies.(82) Even at the district level, it is an exception when a non-communist is entrusted with executive functions. Among members of executive organs of Serbian communities, for example, 97 per cent are party members and in the BOALs, party members occupy 85 per cent of the leading posts. The situation is similar in the mass organizations. And though the mass media have recently enjoyed more maneuvering room than even in the 1970s, the party has not abandoned its claims to control the press and has repeatedly reasserted those claims.(83)

If the party's rule over society is unbroken also in the post-Tito era, the label "party monopoly" nonetheless no longer fits the contemporary Yugoslav system. The "federalization" of the LCY in the last few years has given rise to a polycentrism of decision-making centers. While not pluralism, the plurality of more or less autonomous territorial bodies and individual parties has made it possible to take political decisions without regard for partial interests. Even if this has recently produced more negative than positive results, it is, all the same, more than any other socialist systems have been prepared to concede. The current problems of integration notwithstanding, the federal system presents itself, even more than self-management, as the true "pluralizing" element in the Yugoslav political system.

(Translated from German by Pedro Ramet.)

NOTES

1. *Programy i ustavy KPSS* (Moscow: Izdatel'stvo
    politicheskoi literatury, 1969), p. 108.
2. *Program SKJ* (Belgrade: Komunist, 1976), p. 233.
3. *Ustav SFRJ* (Belgrade: Sekretarijat Saveznog
    Izvršnog Vijeća za informacije, 1974), pp. 42-44.
4. Carl J. Friedrich, "Totalitarianism: Recent
    Trends," in *Problems of Communism*, Vol. 17, No. 3
    (May-June 1967), p. 33.
5. M. George Zaninovich, "Yugoslav Party Evolution:
    Moving beyond Institutionalization," in Samuel P.
    Huntington and Clement H. Moore (eds.),
    Authoritarian Politics in Modern Society (New
    York: Basic Books, 1970), p. 484.
6. George Klein, "Yugoslavia--The Process of
    Democratization," in Peter Toma (ed.), *The
    Changing Face of Communism in Eastern Europe*
    (Tucson, Ariz.: University of Arizona Press,
    1970), p. 217.
7. Cf. April Carter, *Democratic Reform in Yugoslavia*
    (London: Francis Pinter, 1982), p. 245.
8. For background, see Dennison I. Rusinow, *The
    Yugoslav Experiment, 1948-1974* (Berkeley and Los
    Angeles: University of California Press, 1977);
    and Othmar Nikola Haberl, *Parteiorganisation und
    nationale Frage* (Berlin: Freie Universitaet
    Berlin, 1976).
9. See Gary K. Bertsch, "Yugoslavia: the Eleventh
    Congress, the Constitution, and the Succession,"
    in *Government and Opposition*, Vol. 14, No. 1
    (Winter 1979); and Willi Erps, Fred Oldenbourg,
    *Innenpolitische Aspekte des XI. Parteitages des
    BdKJ (1978)* (Cologne: Berichte des
    Bundesinstituts fuer ostwissenschaftliche und
    internationale Studien, 3-1979).
10. Pedro Ramet, "Political Struggle and Institutional
    Reorganization in Yugoslavia," in *Political
    Science Quarterly*, Vol. 99, No. 2 (Summer 1984),
    p. 292.
11. Details in the supplement to *Komunist* (January 1,
    1981).
12. M. George Zaninovich, "Yugoslav Succession and
    Leadership Stability," in *Studies in Comparative
    Communism*, Vol. 16, No. 3 (July 1983), p. 179.
13. See Dragoslav Marković's comments at the 14th
    Session of the Central Committee of the Serbian
    party, in *Uzroci i posledice kontrarevolucionarne
    akcije na Kosovu* (Belgrade: Komunist, 1981), p.
    67.
14. *Komunist* (November 20, 1981).

15. Even Stane Dolanc called for an open discussion about democratic centralism in January 1981. See NIN (January 18, 1981), p. 9.
16. Antun Žvan, "Pluralitet interesa i Savez komunista," in NIN (February 23, 1981); and Antun Žvan, "Demokratski centralizam ili demokratsko jedinstvo," in Komunist (August 28, 1981), p. 14.
17. Komunist (August 21, 1981).
18. Nenad Kecmanović, "Demokratizacija ili decentralizacija," in NIN (August 2, 1981), pp. 15-16.
19. NIN (September 12, 1982), pp. 14-15; and Komunist (October 1, 1982).
20. Komunist (September 18, 1981, and March 26, 1982).
21. Ibid. (June 5, 1981).
22. 12. kongres Saveza komunista Jugoslavije (Belgrade: Komunist, 1982), p. 51.
23. See Ramet, "Political Struggle," p. 297.
24. Komunist (June 13, 1980).
25. Ibid. (March 19, 1982).
26. This was probably the Serbian party leader, Dragoslav Marković.
27. Komunist (September 17, 1982).
28. Ibid. (April 15, 1983).
29. Ibid. (July 8, 1983).
30. Ibid. (March 2, 1984).
31. Ibid. (April 13, 1984).
32. Ibid. (June 29, 1984).
33. CK SKJ, Predsedništvo, Ostvarivanje vodeće uloge SKJ u društvu i jačanje njegovog idejnog i akcionog jedinstva (Belgrade: Komunist, 1984), pp. v-vii.
34. Politika (July 13-15, 1984).
35. Ibid. (September 12, 1984).
36. Danas (January 22, 1985), p. 14.
37. Ibid. (October 30, 1984), p. 13.
38. "Pismo Dr. Najdana Pašića Predsedništvu CK SKJ," in Problemi ostvarivanja i razvoja političkog sistema socijalističkog samoupravljanja (Ljubljana: Jugoslovenski Centar za teoriju i praksu samoupravljanja Edvard Kardelj, 1983), pp. 154-164.
39. See, for example, Borba (October 22/23, 1983, and November 16, 1984).
40. Politika (October 18, 1984).
41. See the examples in NIN (October 28, 1984), p. 15.
42. Borba (November 26, 1984).
43. Ibid. (November 14, 1984).
44. Ibid. (November 26, 1984).
45. Komunist (November 30, 1984); NIN (January 20, 1985), p. 15; and Danas (January 22, 1985), p. 18.
46. Danas (January 15, 1985), p. 20.
47. Quoted in Ibid., p. 13.

48. NIN (October 28, 1984), p. 15; and Danas (December 4, 1984), p. 8.
49. Nedeljna Borba (November 24/25, 1984). The accusation of "unitarism" was also officially rejected by the city committee of the Belgrade party organization. See Borba (December 13, 1984).
50. Komunist (October 19, 1984); and Politika (October 18, 1984).
51. NIN (December 30, 1984), pp. 9-10.
52. Politika (November 14, 1984); Danas (November 11, 1984), p. 9; NIN (November 25, 1984), p. 10; and also Komunist (December 12, 1984).
53. Mitja Ribičič, as quoted in NIN (October 28, 1984), p. 16. Aleksander Grličkov spoke in a similar vein in NIN (December 16, 1984), p. 10.
54. NIN (December 9, 1984), p. 11.
55. Borba (December 15/16, 1984); and Danas (January 15, 1985), p. 21.
56. The interim report of the work of the commission on the political system can be found in "Dokle se doslo," in Komunist (November 30, 1984).
57. Vladimir Milić and Djoko Tozi, "Preobražaj i socijalna struktura Saveza komunista Jugoslavije," in Socijalizam, Vol. 14, Nos. 7-8 (July-August 1971), p. 836; and Boris Vusković, "Gibanja u socijalnoj strukturi članstva SKJ," in Socijalizam, Vol. 17, Nos. 7-8 (July-August 1974), p. 682.
58. See, for example, VII. kongres SK Srbije: Izveštaj o aktivnosti SK Srbije i radu Centralnog komiteta (Belgrade: Komunist, 1974), pp. 21f.
59. Komunist (June 26, 1982).
60. Ibid. (February 20, 1981).
61. Vladimir Goati, "Struktura partijskih rukovodstva," in Marksistička Misao, No. 5 (1983), p. 66.
62. Komunist (May 23, 1980).
63. Goati, "Struktura partijskih," p. 74.
64. Komunist (October 7, 1983). The same observation was made in the Rijeka party organization. See Komunist (July 23, 1984).
65. Politika (August 28, 1984).
66. Richard F. Staar, "Checklist of Communist Parties in 1984," in Problems of Communism, Vol. 34, No. 2 (March-April 1985), p. 91.
67. Danas (August 28, 1984), p. 5; Politika (July 10, 1984); and Ostvarivanje vodeće uloge, p. xiii.
68. Danas (January 15, 1985), p. 8; for the Rijeka organization, Komunist (July 13, 1984); and for Serbia, Borba (December 16, 1984).
69. Danas (October 30, 1984), p. 4.
70. NIN (September 4, 1983), p. 12.

71. See _Danas_ (March 13, 1984), p. 25, and (August 28, 1984), p. 8.
72. Andjelka Milić, "Ideološka svest i angažovanost članova Saveza komunista," in _Socijalizam_, Vol. 23, No. 2 (February 1980), p. 185. For more detailed analyses, Vladimir Goati et al., _Svest i angazovanje komunista_ (Belgrade: Mladost, 1981); and Vladimir Goati, "Činioci angažovanja članova SKJ," in _Marksistička Misao_, No. 4 (1983), pp. 96-99.
73. _19. sednica CK SKJ_ (Belgrade: Komunist, 1984), p. 123.
74. _Komunist_ (May 20, 1983); and Mile Lasić, "O nekim aktuelnim pitanjima demokratskog centralizma," in _Pregled_, Vol. 72 (1982), No. 5, p. 671.
75. _Danas_ (March 13, 1984), p. 26.
76. _NIN_ (January 20, 1985), p. 13.
77. Silvano Bolčić, in _Savez komunista i socijalistička revolucija_ (Belgrade: Komunist, 1981), p. 478.
78. Gojko Stančić, "Kreativnost kolektivnog rada," in _Ibid._, p. 413.
79. For example, see _Komunist_ (July 8, 1983, and May 11, 1984).
80. The figures for the local communities are given in _Opštine u SR Srbiji 1980_ (Belgrade: Republički zavod za statistiku, 1981), pp. 26-29; the figures for the delegations and the elections of 1978 and 1982 in Serbia, Croatia, and the city of Belgrade, in _Četvrta sednica CK SK Srbije: Delegatski sistem_ (Belgrade: Komunist, 1979), p. 132; Smiljana Leinert, "Socijalni sastav delegatskih struktura," in _Teorija i praksa delegatskog sistema_ (Zagreb: Fakultet političkih nauka, 1979), p. 62; and _Statistički godišnjak grada Beograda 1982_ (Belgrade: Gradski zavod za statistiku, 1982), p. 19.
81. _Izbori na delegacii i delegatite za sobornite na sobranijata vo SRM 1978_ (Skopje: Statistički pregled, 1979), p. 89; and Vučina Vasović, "Savez komunista u političkom sistemu samoupravljanja," in _SK i socijalistička revolucija_, p. 215.
82. See I. Josifovski and S. Saliu, _Strukturnite belezi na delegacii i delegatite vo SR Makedoniji_ (Skopje: 1979), table 8.
83. See the examples given in Pedro Ramet, "Yugoslavia and the Threat of Internal and External Discontents," in _Orbis_, Vol. 28, No. 1 (Spring 1984), pp. 110-112; and _Politika_ (August 31, 1984).

3
Political-Military Relations in Post-Tito Yugoslavia

Robin Alison Remington

As communist militaries became visible political actors in the 1980s, Western scholars clung, for the most part, to their belief in the leading role of communist parties as tenaciously as policy-makers in Moscow. The concept of the "party in uniform" was put forward to explain martial law in Poland.(1) The prominence of military spokesmen in the succession struggle that followed Leonid Brezhnev's death in November 1982 and continued throughout Yuri Andropov's five-month disappearing act and Konstantin Chernenko's obvious health problems, all appeared to confirm the theory. Yet the dismissal of Marshal Nikolai Ogarkov, the Soviet Chief of Staff, reportedly for "unpartylike tendencies,"(2) raised nagging doubts.

Is it, perhaps, the case, as General Wojciech Jaruzelski warned when he took the job of Polish Prime Minister in February 1981,(3) that communist politicians in uniform are first of all soldiers? And if so, what does that mean for the communist parties that communist armies step in to help?

Such questions take on a particular urgency for post-Tito Yugoslavia, where a rotating collective leadership is struggling for party unity, plagued by perpetual economic crisis, and haunted by the memory of Tito's Godfatherlike image. This analysis does not pretend to have the answers. The evidence is not in. The political drama remains unresolved in the 1980s. In 1985 we are at best at intermission.

Nonetheless, the political actors are on stage. There are various plot lines and emerging relationships. In short, there is more than enough data to begin. Therefore, I shall advance the tentative hypothesis that party-army relations in post-Tito Yugoslavia have moved beyond the constraints determined by the structural characteristics associated with the communist party's effort to make the transition from reliance on charismatic authority to institutional solutions. And as a corollary, the extent to which Yugoslav soldiers in politics have become prominent in the often heated debate on how best to navigate the country's ongoing economic crisis has been less a matter of defending military corporate interests than of defining acceptable limits of political/economic change.

In considering these propositions, it is useful to remember that concern about the political role of the Yugoslav military was being articulated in Yugoslavia a full decade before Poland collapsed into martial law.(4) An army coup was high on the list of gloomy Western speculations for "after-Tito" scenarios. Such fears were undoubtedly on the minds of Yugoslav policy-makers seeking to assure generational adaptability of the League of Communists of Yugoslavia (LCY), when Tito could no longer dominate the political stage. Indeed, they were addressed before he died by a power-sharing arrangement first put in place at the Tenth Party Congress in 1974.

INSTITUTIONAL INTER-PENETRATION: LEGACY OF THE TENTH CONGRESS

The Yugoslav Armed Forces total an estimated 239,700,(5) and, according to Yugoslav sources, more than 98 per cent of all commanding officers are members of the LCY.(6) These officers undoubtedly make up the bulk of the 90,000 communists in the army's party organization. Their political role is directly tied to centrifugal national/ethnic forces manifested in bureaucratic tensions between republican and provincial party organizations, on the one hand, and the federal party, on the other.

This is not the place to retell the story of how ethnic politics reentered Yugoslav political life in the form of a Croatian "mass movement" (euphemism for separatism) in 1970-1971. For our purposes, the impact of rising Croatian nationalism on party-army relations was three-fold. First, some ethnic demands centered on ever-sensitive issues of professional military autonomy. These ranged from the preference that Croatian soldiers serve out their military obligation in their home republic to calls for a territorial army under Croatian control. That came perilously close to pressure for fragmentation of the Yugoslav People's Army (JNA) and at a minimum counterposed the interests of the territorial defense forces to those of the professional army.(7) Second, by June 1971, the officer corps was well on the way to becoming convinced that the main danger to Yugoslavia's security was "nationalism and chauvinism," not external aggression.(8) Third, despite subsequent attempts at backtracking,(9) Tito had bluntly reasserted that the army's job was to defend the Yugoslav revolution from internal enemies as well as those at the borders.(10) When the chips were down, Tito trusted the army above the party and quite explicitly used the army to counter nationalist and decentralizing tendencies of the regional party organizations.

There is evidence indicating that Tito's vision of the domestic mission of the JNA was not shared universally by other high-ranking party leaders. Take, for example, Dr. Vladimir Bakarić's insistence that the function of the army is "not to maintain internal order but only to protect Yugoslavia's frontiers against foreign enemies."(11) Also, despite Tito's optimistic assessment that the army was not "nationalistically minded," the purge of high-ranking Croatian officers along with the Croatian party leadership, in the wake of the Zagreb student strike in December 1971, suggests that as the tension rose, the military leaders divided likewise along national lines.(12) Certainly, hopes and fears centering on the territorial defense forces' role vis-à-vis the professional military was a factor in civilian and military thinking alike.

Given the concern with domestic security, it is not surprising that military men in high party posts increased at the Tenth Party Congress in May 1974.(13) This renaissance of military influence brought 21 generals and other high-ranking officers into positions of political visibility. There was a general on the new 12-member Executive Committee. Defense Minister General Nikola Ljubičić and the head of the JNA party organization, General Džemail Sarac joined the 39-member Presidium of the Central Committee. Fifteen high-ranking officers represented the military on the Central Committee itself, while three generals came onto the Central Committee representing regional party organizations--from Croatia, Bosnia-Herzegovina, and Vojvodina, respectively. Another two rose to key positions in the party statutory and control commissions.

At the same time, the law and order function of the army was strengthened when active-duty General Franjo Herljević took over as the Minister of Internal Affairs, just before the Congress. For the first time since 1946, the civilian security apparatus was run by the military. Another army general became public prosecutor--a warning to those "internal enemies" assailed by Tito during the Croatian crisis.

Ross Johnson lists still other "political generals" who emerged in the 1970s.(14) It is fair to say that by the Tenth Congress, this was to some extent, at least symbolically, a "party in uniform," and this development was sanctioned by constitutional recognition of the army's political role. Nonetheless, even as the points of access to the Yugoslav political process increased, what amounted to a quota system in which the army was assured of representation officially equal to that of an autonomous province limited the military to a clearly defined piece of the political pie. This elaborate power-sharing arrangement was designed to serve as a post-Tito succession mechanism. It both guaranteed military participation in policy-making and established boundaries to the army's potential power vis-à-vis republican and provincial political actors.

Although the Eleventh Party Congress in 1978 did away with the Executive Committee, it reaffirmed the army's access to the new 23-plus-Tito Presidium and the 166-member Central Committee. The new Party statutes kept the same proportional representation on the CC, but in terms of the Party Presidium, the armed forces were represented by Defense Minister Ljubičić, i.e., one representative rather than the two allotted to each of the autonomous provinces. However, the actual number of top-ranking officers again went up because another six generals were elected as representatives of their regional party organizations, an overall increase of 10-14 per cent among Central Committee membership.(15) General Milan Daljevic became one of nine party secretaries.

Nor do these key party posts tell the whole story. For the military also enjoyed input through a number of defense- and security-related advisory bodies such as the National Defense Council (six of whose 11 members were generals in 1978), the Federal Council for Protection of the Constitutional Order (both Generals Ljubičić and Herljević were members), and in 1979 a Council for Civil Defense, headed by General Ivan Mišković. Colonel-General Ivan Dolničar was appointed Secretary-General of the state presidency (also in 1979), while an army colonel had taken over the ideologically sensitive post of editor-in-chief of the party newsorgan, Komunist.

In short, it is fair to say that when Tito died in May 1980, Western speculation about an army coup--by implication, a military alternative to the LCY--substantially missed the mark. The Yugoslav military had no incentive to take power from the party because the communists in the armed forces were the most cohesive element of the party in question. When Tito died, the army had been thoroughly integrated into the orderly running of the country and a succession mechanism was in place, in which the Yugoslav military was assured of continued influence. Even if one would not go as far as I have speculated elsewhere,(16) to conclude that the army was well on the way to becoming the vanguard of the party, one is certainly entitled to say that the civil-military coalition adopted by Yugoslavia at the dusk of the Tito era amounted to a party-army partnership.

THE LEGAL FRAMEWORK: "GENERAL PEOPLE'S DEFENSE"

At the same time, the domestic mission of the Yugoslav military is carried out within the framework of a nationwide defense system that simultaneously supplements and limits the authority of the professional armed forces. For ever since the National Defense Law of 1969, the Yugoslav People's Army has shared its responsibility to defend the nation with territorial defense units organized on a republican/provincial basis.

This return to what may be considered a mixed partisan strategy was a direct response to the threat posed to Yugoslav security by the Soviet-led "allied, socialist" invasion of Czechoslovakia in August 1968. In an atmosphere of heated Soviet-Yugoslav polemics, it was a way of raising the cost and increasing the risk should policy-makers in Moscow decide that now (or later) was the time to eliminate Yugoslavia's independent alternative to the Soviet model along with Alexander Dubček's "socialism with a human face." The concept of "all-people's defense" was rooted in the historical experience of Partisan warfare during World War Two. It could be ideologically justified as the incarnation of Marx's theory of "an armed nation."(17)

Nonetheless, there is reason to suspect that the professional military was not happy with its relegation to a "co-equal" status with the territorial defense units in fulfilling its defense mission.(18) Notwithstanding the use of regular army reserve officers to command the territorial units, tensions between these two branches were openly manifested during the Croatian nationalist euphoria of 1970-1971. Moreover, despite Tito's use of the army to whip the nationalistically inclined regional party organizations back into line, both the revised National Defense Law of 1974 and the 1974 Constitution reaffirmed the right of "the responsible authorities of the republics, autonomous provinces, and districts" to organize territorial defense on their territories.(19)

In these circumstances, it was perhaps to have been expected that one of the first moves to assure military support of the post-Tito political solutions entailed making the professional military the "more equal" of these co-equal defenders. Tito died on May 4, 1980. On May 16, it was reported that a Council for Territorial Defense had been created in the Defense Ministry. This Council was headed by the recently retired Yugoslav Chief-of-Staff, Colonel-General Stane Potočar, with active-duty Colonel-General Rahmia Kadenič, head of the Center of High Military Schools, as his deputy. Its members were described as representatives of the republican/provincial territorial defense headquarters, representatives of the Ministry of Defense and "a number of retired comrades." The function of the Council was to advise the defense minister about all questions of "organization, development, management, and command, military equipment, and training...of territorial defense."(20)

Although the phrase "to advise" is potentially ambiguous, it seems to imply, in this context, that the issues mentioned would be resolved by the Minister of Defense. If so, the authority of the republican/provincial "responsible authorities" mentioned in the 1974 National Defense Law (Article 11), is more symbolic than real. In the current 1982 National Defense Law, Article 11 has become still more obscure. This article, whose main purpose is to make it illegal for the armed forces or any part of it to surrender, goes on to discuss what is to happen if any part of the country should be occupied by the enemy. It asserts that the working people, citizens, army units, self-managing institutions, and other socio-political organizations must continue to fight, observing, all the while, the statutes of the Yugoslav Socialist Federated Republic.(21) The presumption is that the JNA would be in charge of resistance operations against any foreign aggressor; in instances where the JNA would not be present, the territorial defense units would be expected to mobilize resistance on their own.

The 1982 National Defense Law, like the 1969 and 1974 incarnations, is primarily concerned with strengthening the nationwide defense system as a deterrent to possible aggressors. To surrender is high treason. This law spells out the command structure, in case of war, considerably more clearly than did the earlier laws that were passed while Tito was still alive and officially commanding the armed forces.

In wartime, the party would be "at the head of the struggle," charged with directing and coordinating society in the nationwide defense effort (Article 12). According to Articles 106-108, however, command of the armed forces rests with the State Presidency. It may transfer part of this authority to the Minister of Defense (since 1982, Admiral Branko Mamula), who can issue regulations, orders, and instructions, while executing the will of the Presidency. If for any reason the Minister of Defense is not available, the

Chief-of-Staff is to take over (currently Colonel-General Petar Gračanin).

An advisory body has been created within the Ministry of Defense. This Military Council includes the Minister of Defense, the Chief of Staff, the Deputy Minister of Defense, the Chief Inspector of National Defense, all army and territorial defense unit commanders, and other military leaders, at the discretion of the Minister of Defense and the President of the party organization in the JNA. The existence of the advisory council undoubtedly multinationalizes the input into military decision-making, perhaps taking the edge off the implications of the fact that both the Defense Minister and the Chief-of-Staff are ethnic Serbs.(22) Commanders of the territorial defense units are represented, although the relationship to the advisory Council on Territorial Defense (created in 1980) remains to be spelled out.

What is clear, however, is that the line of authority goes from the State Presidency directly to the Minister of Defense. While the degree to which the State Presidency might exercise any direct military authority could be expected to vary according to the military experience of its membership,(23) it is not likely that this body of eight plus an additional five top government and party leaders whom the State Presidency is instructed to invite to participate in its meetings during times of emergency would involve itself in areas of military strategy by going against the wishes of the Minister of Defense charged with running a war. The State Presidency could in principle replace him. But that, too, would be highly unlikely unless the impetus came from within the military itself.

In short, the legal framework within which the Yugoslav military functions in post-Tito Yugoslavia is one that substantially assures the autonomy of the professional military, both in terms of increased control over territorial defense units and in terms of military planning vis-à-vis its defense mission. However, the continued commitment to "All People's Defense" via a mixed partisan strategy incorporates a potential for recurring organizational tensions between amateur and professional soldiers charged to coexist in unified Yugoslav armed forces.

COLLECTIVE LEADERSHIP VS. ONE-MAN COMMAND

In addition to sorting out the institutional relationship between the professional military and the territorial defense units, the extent to which Yugoslavia's armed forces would reflect the same post-Tito organizational principles expected of the party was being openly discussed as early as 1978. It is important to remember that, in contrast to most political leaders, Tito quite successfully orchestrated his own succession. During the last two years of his life, the Godfather of Yugoslav Communism repeatedly stressed the need to extend the principle of "collective work" to all levels of party organization. There would be no more Titos, not at the top of the LCY, nor even "little Titos" used to turning local politics into mini-fiefdoms. Collective responsibility and constant rotation of leadership positions was to be the answer to another long-standing problem for Yugoslav politics as well; the "unhealthy ambitions" of powerful, informal groups, whose members played political "musical chairs" between top party/state/trade union positions, would be remedied.

For the party, the result was to make post-Tito collective leadership into what may be the most elaborate quota system in the world. It is based on a mix of territorial/bureaucratic considerations and staggered rotation schedules, so that each republic and province knows when to expect its turn in top federal positions. Although this has not eliminated what is considered to be a problem of "horizontal rotation" among members of the party Presidium, the State Presidency, and the Federal Executive Council,(24) the rotation schedules have, thus far, been routinely observed.

As of June 1, 1985, Radovan Vlajković (from Vojvodina) was President of the State Presidency, and Ali Šukrija (from Kosovo) was head of the LCY Presidium, with Dimče Belovski (from Macedonia) holding the post of party Secretary.

In some senses, the army representatives are automatically excluded from this political merry-go-round. They are not slated to take a turn at the top of either state or party collective presidencies. However, if former Defense Minister Ljubičić should be elected to a second term in the State Presidency, he would then head that body as the representative from Serbia when the Serbian turn comes up again. If the original rotation schedule simply repeats, that would be in May 1990.(25)

On the other hand, there was a question as to the degree to which the principle of collective work applied to the party organization in the JNA, and indeed to the Yugoslav military itself. This is clearly an issue of military autonomy. If we take the statement of General Dane Petkovski during the third Plenary Session of the Central Committee in Belgrade (April 1979), it seems that the military leadership was willing to accept the idea of collective work in the sense that the officer in charge was to seek opinions from "the majority of officers and also soldiers" before making decisions. Nonetheless, "strict respect for the principle of subordination and a single command" remained a "fundamental factor in relations in the JNA." Therefore, the "spirit and meaning of collective work" that Tito valued so highly was being "realized in the army in various forms and ways, without any weakening of the leadership and command."(26)

Awareness of military sensitivity in this regard was subsequently evinced in a blunt article by the Slovene journalist, Primoz Zagar, who attacked rumors of a post-Tito army coup as the invention of "Western reactionaries and political intriguers, who do not deserve to be taken seriously."(27) Zagar both defended the defense mission of the military and its possible internal role as a "revolutionary instrument of the working class." He handled the implicit paradox of having Yugoslav self-management defended by the one Yugoslav institution that is in no sense self-managing by insisting that the army as an institution could not be self-managing because "relationships within the army have been based on the principle of subordination, one-man command." Of course, decisions are collectively made from the perspective that they reflect the demands of the community as a whole. But "the decision is made by one person, the commander, who is not deprived of his responsibility."

On the face of it, this attempt to present continued one-man command as leadership "in the spirit" of collective work, is not particularly convincing. Nor is it clear to what degree the party organization in the JNA is expected to conform to the standards demanded of the regional party organizations in this regard. If the fact that General Dane Cuić was the only party leader reelected at any sub-federal party conferences prior to the 1982 Twelfth LCY Congress is any indication, military "collective leadership," even at this level, is substantially less collective than that at the republican/provincial levels.

I do not mean to imply that party and army should have the same standards in this regard. The importance of the issue lies rather in the political dynamic involved. When Tito raised the banner of collective leadership, he did not explicitly exempt the armed forces. The military responded by lauding the principle and drawing the line about the degree to which it would change standard military procedure and relationships, i.e., protecting their professional autonomy in terms of the mode of decision-making. Neither Tito nor his civilian successors-to-be pushed the matter further. Indeed, we might say that the Zagar article was a warning or, at least, a recognition of the reality that military coups are linked to the degree of respect accorded armies' institutional and corporate interests in this regard.

Rather than seeing this as a matter of wishy-washy concern for implementing the principle of "collective work" on the side of Yugoslav party leaders,(28) I consider it to have been a wise move on the part of the Yugoslav civilian politicians whose top concern, where the military is concerned, has been to assure itself of solid support once Tito would pass on.

END OF THE ERA: "AFTER TITO, TITO!"

When Tito died, Yugoslav politics lost its charismatic anchor. In the minds of many, Tito was Yugoslavia, and self-management, Titoism.(29) Tito was seen as the linchpin of Yugoslav politics. He walked on a world stage, larger than life. Indeed, for 35 years, Tito's driving personality dwarfed all other Yugoslav political leaders.

Undeniably, Tito was a hard act to follow. Nonetheless, his stubborn struggle against death gave the succession team a full four months to ease into operation before the country actually faced the trauma of his loss. Moreover, the external environment during those months heightened the awareness of the need for party unity and the army's defense mission. For Tito entered the hospital shortly after the Soviet troops invaded Afghanistan in December 1979.

At that time, the Yugoslav army went on a low-level alert. Security measures were stepped up. On January 11, a joint meeting of the State and Party Collective Presidencies discussed a general defense plan. It was then that the Council of the Presidium for the Protection of the Constitutional Order was set up under Dr. Vladimir Bakarić, to advise on matters affecting internal security and territorial defense.(30) Although these measures were officially taken in response to the threat posed by Moscow's move against Afghanistan, they were undoubtedly intended also to counter possible terrorist attacks on the part of anti-Yugoslav emigre organizations which might hope to take advantage of transitional instability when Tito died. In fact, on the day that Tito died, the Yugoslav news agency Tanjug issued a warning against "those who may be contemplating a possible Blitzkrieg against Yugoslavia" that such a move would meet with "the widest total people's resistance."(31)

Subsequently, the then Secretary of the CC Presidium, Dr. Dušan Dragosavac, warned about the external dangers continually posed to independent countries by "imperialistic, and in general hegemonic forces," unwilling to accept the independence of other

countries. His list of the threats to freedom and
independence ranged from "the crudest forms of neo-
colonialist pressure...to armed military interventions"
--a clear slap at the Soviet invasions of both
Czechoslovakia and Afghanistan. In the context of
reiterating Yugoslavia's determination to defend
itself, Dragosavac praised the loyalty of Yugoslavia's
nationalities. He assured those who might be tempted
that the political/security situation of the country
was good, and that "internal enemies" had been
neutralized and had no "scope or opportunity for
organized activities."(32)

This emphasis on external danger, internal
security, and the orderly progression of political life
was combined with the substitution of a Tito myth for
the presence of Tito. When I returned to Yugoslavia in
May 1981 at the time of the annual celebration of
Tito's birthday on May 25, Belgrade was hung with
banners: "We are guarding Tito's way," "After Tito,
Tito!" Young people paraded wearing Tito T-shirts. As
W. H. Auden once wrote in memory of Yeats, Tito "became
his admirers." Party and army were united in their
commitment to his memory.

TRACK RECORD FOR THE 1980s

Despite the unpredicted, remarkably smooth
political transition to collective leadership, the
1980s are undeniably an economic "Time of Troubles" for
Tito's civilian and military successors alike. For all
his political genius, as an economist Tito had feet of
clay. He would not face unpleasant economic reality,
or listen to those pressing for devaluation of the
dinar in 1978. He left it for those who followed to
make the hard choices.

The transition team devalued shortly after the
funeral,(33) and resolutions were passed calling for
the increase of exports, the "rationalization" of
imports, and cutbacks in investment and consumption.
The post-Tito leadership could not afford to economize
where security was concerned, however. On the
contrary, as early as 1978, Yugoslav military leaders
uniformly hammered home the message that the defense
potential needed to be built up so as "to put us in a
position to defeat any potential aggressor, to resist
all pressure, and successfully to wage any war imposed
on us."(34) The question of Tito's responsibility for
the emerging crisis was still more delicate. To move
too drastically, too soon, implicitly undermined the
Tito myth so necessary for the very legitimacy of the
succession process itself. Tito could not
simultaneously function as a unifying symbol of
Yugoslavia and an economic scapegoat, no matter how

justified his successors might have been in calling attention to his flawed economics.

It was a no-win situation. What the new collective leadership needed most was time. But in spring 1981, the province of Kosovo exploded in anti-Yugoslav riots, and the army had to be sent in to restore calm. Despite the presence of the army, intermittent violence continued. The threat posed by the Kosovo riots, which was explained as the work of "subversive activities" directed by Tirana and "others" and perpetrated by enemies of Yugoslavia who would like to see the country fall apart in ethnic violence, underlined the defense mission of the Yugoslav military. Indeed, the army was the key to the maintenance of security in the province.

Army units stayed, while political leaders agonized as to what was to be done. How to get Kosovo back on track without granting republic status that would cut the heart out of Serbia?(35) How to stop the out-migration of Serbs and Montenegrins who, whether or not they were being harassed by their Albanian neighbors, no longer wanted to live there? What to do about the provincial communist party organization and security forces, that many in Belgrade believed were hopelessly infected with "nationalist tendencies"?

This crisis underlined the party's need of the army. It also exacerbated the economic crisis facing Tito's successors. If there was to be any hope of defusing the time bomb of Albanian nationalism, something would have to be done to eliminate the gap between living standards in the province and the more prosperous parts of Yugoslavia. Who would pay the bill for such economic equalization? Who could be trusted to manage the money? Indeed, in the short run, who would bear the cost of rising military budgets directly related to the armed forces' expanded domestic security function? In times of austerity, the increasing resentment of the more developed republics was inevitable.

Under the circumstances, it is perhaps not surprising that the administration elected in May 1982 and headed by the 57-year old Milka Planinc, former president of the Croatian Central Committee, was somewhat cynically described as "a group of sacrificed people."(36) Nor was it surprising that the Twelfth Party Congress in June 1982 was preoccupied with the need for economic stabilization.

This first post-Tito congress ratified continuation of the institutional set-up designed by Tito and preserved the basic contours of party-military relations. In fact, de facto military presence at the top of the party increased to three generals in the 23-member LCY Presidium. General Dane Cuić formally represented the party organization in the JNA, while General Herljević now occupied one of the Bosnian slots, and General Petar Matić took his seat as a representative of Vojvodina. Although not on the Presidium, Defense Minister Branko Mamula undoubtedly works closely with top party leaders through the intrastructure of advisory defense-related councils. At the same time, former Defense Minister Ljubičić took on the job of State President in Serbia--a move calculated to assure the military of a sympathetic ear at the republic level with respect to security problems in Kosovo.

However, there is more to evaluating the importance of the army component of party leadership than counting officers and positions. In the new party Presidium, only seven members returned to that job. Nine of the 23 are ex officio and can be expected to rotate in their capacity as presidents of the republic/province or JNA party organizations. Some 58 per cent of the 165-member Central Committee were elected to that body for the first time. Given the January 1983 death of Dr. Vladimir Bakarić, long considered by many Yugoslav-watchers to be the most important political figure after Tito and Kardelj, the military members at the top of the party are among its most senior members. Subsequently, the election of General Ljubičić to the collective State Presidency in May 1984 guarantees that defense interests will have a powerful voice at the top of the state hierarchy as well.

Whether or not one agrees with Defense Minister Mamula's claim that the army is "the backbone" of the political system,(37) the party-army partnership has incrementally moved beyond the relationship defined in the post-Tito organization scheme. This is so, in part, because in its effort to achieve generational adaptability, the famed "Club of 1941" is being replaced faster in the civilian political sector than within the military leadership.(38) It is a tendency that is reinforced by the fact that the Twelfth Party Congress conspicuously failed to achieve the desired party unity.

THE ARMY AND THE ECONOMY

Although the Yugoslav economy picked up enough during 1984 to ensure continued short-term credits from the International Monetary Fund (IMF) and the prospect of long-term rescheduling of the country's $19.2 billion foreign debt, the fact remains that one million Yugoslavs are unemployed, inflation (now at 67 per cent) continues to rise, and there is no relief in sight for the average Yugoslav household, whose earnings have slipped back to the level of 1968.(39) In short, Yugoslav politicians and citizens alike must live with the politics of scarcity and IMF-imposed austerity programs for the foreseeable future. The party remains deeply divided. Yugoslavia's collective leadership is engaged in a fierce tug-of-war between those who are convinced that market-oriented reform is the answer and those unwilling to make the needed sacrifices of power, privilege, and financial advantage. The party leadership is split between proponents of "mere democratization" and advocates of recentralization, between supporters of the present highly confederal political leadership and those wanting to restore greater authority to the party. In these circumstances, Defense Minister Mamula is understandably worried about his budget, the impact of nationalist infiltration on the armed forces, and the extent of footdragging by "special interests" when it comes to implementing adopted decisions.(40) General Petar Matić had harsh words for the February 1984 session of the Central Committee about "those who negate everything," and at the same time was skeptical about the extent of reliance on "Western financial circles."(41)

In short, there is some reason to think that top military leaders may also reflect the civilian ambivalence as to whether the road to economic salvation lies in close cooperation with the West or in reducing dependence on Western loans with far-reaching implications both for Yugoslav nonalignment and independence from Moscow. Mamula's budgetary complaints notwithstanding, the government has defended absolute military increases against republican critics.(42) Nor is this government's economic record one to be particularly ashamed of under the circumstances. Yugoslavia did increase its exports by 27 per cent in 1983 and showed a healthy balance of payments surplus in 1984.(43) It made the hard decisions and put an unpopular austerity program into place much more quickly than most Western observers thought would be possible.

In any event, it is unlikely that economic collapse would stimulate military intervention, because, having been routinely involved in the struggle for economic "stabilization," the army can scarcely nurture any illusions about easy solutions or a "secret plan" to save the economy. Unless the knife cuts substantially deeper into defense-related spending, the army would probably prefer partial collective responsibility to sole responsibility for radical economic surgery.

With respect to professional autonomy both vis-à-vis the territorial defense units and in terms of the

Table 3-1

Yugoslav Defense Budgets, 1981-1983

1981	101.89 billion dinars	($3.47 billion)
1982	119.00 billion dinars	($2.36 billion)
1983	150.58 billion dinars	($1.62 billion)

Source: The Military Balance, 1981-1982 and 1984-1985
(London: International Institute for
Strategic Studies, 1981 and 1984).

preservation of one-man command, the calls for the
"socialization" of the armed forces in self-management
norms are more of an annoyance than a serious threat at
this time.(44) In the larger context, civilian leaders
in post-Tito Yugoslavia have been consistently
sensitive on such matters, although the nature of the
system means that tension could flare up here, as it
appears to have done over charges that the army favors
"abstract unitarism" (a euphemism for increased
centralism).(45)

This raises what to my mind is the more central
question, viz. whether or not the post-Tito collective
leadership can continue with the federal party serving
essentially as an arena of compromise and negotiation
for republican/provincial actors while the Yugoslav
government makes steady, if frustratingly slow,
progress towards turning the economy around. If so,
then it is likely that Yugoslavia will continue its
civilian-military partnership through the 1980s.
However, if economic nationalism deepens into political
sectarianism and the LCY is unable to complete the
process of functional as opposed to generational
adaptability, then the political dynamics will be
radically altered and all bets are off. It is useful
to remember that Poland collapsed into martial law
under conditions of economic crisis in which the Polish
United Workers' Party suffered political paralysis.
Military rule tends to occur when civilian legitimacy
runs out.

If the bad news is that communist and non-
communist countries alike find it far harder to
implement decisions than to make them, the good news is
that whether or not Yugoslavia slides over into a
military-civilian coalition depends not only on luck
but also on political skill.(46) Here the post-Tito
collective leadership is better than its press, and
Yugoslav civilian politicians are well aware of the
lessons of Poland.

NOTES

1. Amos Perlmutter and William M. LeoGrande, "The Party in Uniform: Toward a Theory of Civil-Military Relations in Communist Political Systems," in _American Political Science Review_, Vol. 76, No. 4 (December 1982), pp. 778-789. In retrospect, the conclusion that Jaruzelski's takeover represented a victory of hardline elements in the Polish United Workers' Party is open to question, given subsequent Soviet unhappiness over his style and pace of rebuilding the party.

2. _New York Times_ (September 13, 1984).

3. _The Statesman_ (Delhi, February 12, 1981).

4. Paul Lendvai quotes an unidentified editor of one of Yugoslavia's most "influential newspapers" as posing two possible scenarios: first, that Tito would not put up with the progressively deteriorating situation and, with the help of the army, would set up a semi-military government to restore law and order; second, that the army would seize power, with Soviet support, when Tito became incapacitated or died. See _Financial Times_ (London, May 25, 1971). Considering that Tito continued to be politically active for another nine years, such suggestions were premature. They do reflect the state of mind in Yugoslavia in the early 1970s. On the other hand, Vladimir Bakarić told a West German newspaper in 1971 that "any attempt by the army to seize power would unleash civil war." _Frankfurter Rundschau_ (December 17, 1971).

5. _The Military Balance, 1984-1985_ (London, International Institute for Strategic Studies, 1984), p. 56.

6. _Review of International Affairs_ (Belgrade, August 5-20, 1977).

7. See Robin Alison Remington, "Balkanization of the Military: Party, Army, and People's Militias in Southeastern Europe," in Kenneth E. Naylor (ed.), _Politics and Modernization in Southeastern Europe_, Supplement to _Balkanistica_, Vol. 5 (1979), pp. 21-41.

8. According to Yugoslav sources, by summer 1971, 54 per cent of army officers polled were more worried about internal than external threats to Yugoslav security. See _NIN_ (June 20, 1971).

9. _Borba_ (January 27, 1972).

10. _Ibid_. (December 23, 1971).

11. _Frankfurter Rundschau_ (December 17, 1971).

12. That the Croatian General Janko Bobetko, who had been stressing the need for the Yugoslav military

to "become part of self-managing society" (<u>Vjesnik</u> (Zagreb), March 18, 1971), was among the most prominent of the Croatian officers purged in the wake of the Croatian nationalist euphoria supports the conclusion that, contrary to Tito's earlier assumption, at least some of the military were "nationalistically minded." Tito's own subsequent reference to those who "little by little wanted to take the army into their own, Croatian hands" (reported in <u>Borba</u>, December 23, 1971) appears to confirm that view.

13. See Slobodan Stanković, "A Brief Preliminary Analysis of the Yugoslav Party Congress," <u>Radio Free Europe Research</u> (May 31, 1974); and Slobodan Stanković, "The Yugoslav Party Congress and the Army," <u>Radio Free Europe Research</u> (June 13, 1974).

14. A. Ross Johnson, "The Role of the Military in Yugoslavia: An Historical Sketch," in Roman Kolkowicz and Andrzej Korbonski (eds.), <u>Soldiers, Peasants, and Bureaucrats: Civil-Military Relations in Communist and Modernizing Societies</u> (London: George Allen & Unwin, 1982), p. 190.

15. Slobodan Stanković, "Changes in the Yugoslav Army Party Organization," <u>Radio Free Europe Research</u> (January 2, 1979).

16. Robin Alison Remington, "Civil-Military Relations in Yugoslavia: The Partisan Vanguard," in <u>Studies in Comparative Communism</u>, Vol. 11, No. 3 (Autumn 1978), pp. 250-264.

17. For Yugoslav discussions, see the collection edited by Olga Mladenović, <u>Opštenarodna odbrana Jugoslavije</u>, translated into English under the title, <u>The Yugoslav Concept of General People's Defense</u> (Belgrade: Medjunarodna Politika, 1970). For Western analyses, see A. Ross Johnson, "Yugoslav Total National Defense," in <u>Survival</u>, Vol. 15, Nos. 3-4 (March-April 1973), pp. 54-58; and Dennison I. Rusinow, "The Yugoslav Concept of 'All National Defense,'" <u>American Universities Field Staff Reports</u>, Southeast Europe Series (November 1971).

18. Rusinow quotes from a long interview with General Viktor Bubanj in <u>NIN</u> (July 25, 1971) in support of his position that reservations did exist among the professional military when it came to sharing their most fundamental mission. See Rusinow, "The Yugoslav Concept," p. 3.

19. Article 11 in <u>Službeni list</u>, No. 22 (May 1974), pp. 647-648.

20. <u>Narodna armija</u> (May 16, 1980).

21. <u>Službeni list</u>, No. 21 (April 23, 1982), pp. 578-579.

22. Although the law recognizes all Yugoslav languages and alphabets as equal in both the JNA and Territorial Defense Units, Serbo-Croatian remains the language of command and military training. However, there is now a provision that in "some units" the language of other nationalities and national minorities may be used. For an analysis, see Slobodan Stankovič, "Yugoslavia's New National Defense Law," Radio Free Europe Research (May 28, 1982).

23. Former Defense Minister Nikola Ljubičić was elected to the State Presidency in May 1984 and in principle is eligible for reelection in 1988.

24. Stane Dolanc, Lazar Mojsov, and Nikola Ljubičić, for example, have all held top posts in the party and governmental apparatus.

25. Ljubičić is 68 years old and would be well into his seventies if he were elected to a second term in the State Presidency.

26. Tanjug (April 5, 1979).

27. Borba (October 22/27, 1979).

28. On the contrary, there is some evidence that the republican and provincial parties themselves were far from uniformly enthusiastic about the deprofessionalization implied by Tito's initiative to ensure constant rotation of party posts. According to the LCY statutes adopted in May 1982, this was left up to the territorial and JNA Party organizations to decide for themselves. See Borba (May 18, 1982).

29. See, for example, Fred Warner Neal, Titoism in Action: The Reforms in Yugoslavia (Berkeley and Los Angeles: University of California Press, 1958).

30. Borba (January 12, 1980).

31. Tanjug (May 4, 1980).

32. Borba (June 13, 1980).

33. Ibid.

34. Borba (Decedmber 27, 1978).

35. Regarding the clash between Albanian and Serbian nationalism in the province, see Peter R. Prifti, "Minority Politics: The Albanians in Yugoslavia," in Balkanistica: Occasional Papers in Southeast European Studies, Vol. 2 (1975); Pedro Ramet, "Problems of Albanian Nationalism in Yugoslavia," in Orbis, Vol. 25, No. 2 (Summer 1981), pp. 369-388; and Mark Baskin, "Crisis in Kosovo," in Problems of Communism, Vol. 32, No. 2 (March-April 1983), pp. 61-74.

36. NIN (May 2, 1982).

37. Narodna armija (April 14, 1983).

38. Note that three of the four new military leaders in 1982 had joined Tito's Partisans in 1941:

Defense Minister Branko Mamula, Chief-of-Staff
Petar Gračanin, and Colonel-General Asim Hodžić,
who has been made undersecterary in the Defense
Ministry. Conversely, members of the Federal
Executive Council are considerably younger and
appear to have been selected to emphasize their
economic and technical expertise. At the same
time, the average age of the LCY CC Presidium was
58.6 years; that of the regional party leaderships
ranges from 51.6 years in Bosnia-Herzegovina to
48.2 years in Macedonia. See Danas (November 23,
1982).

39. See Zdenko Antić, "Yugoslavia to Negotiate Debt
Rescheduling," Radio Free Europe Research (March
28, 1985). This is considerably more optimistic
than Miloš Minić's warning to the February 1984
Central Committee session that by 1990 the
country's foreign debt would reach $40 billion,
with an inflation rate of Latin American
proportions, i.e. well over 100 per cent.

40. Narodna armija (April 14, 1984).

41. Borba (February 29, 1984). Civilian Yugoslav
politicians have also expressed skepticism about
IMF motives as well, such as Dušan Dragosavac, who
charged that the IMF served as an instrument of
"certain capitalist circles" and "interferred" in
Yugoslavia's economic affairs. See Vjesnik
(October 6, 1984), as quoted by Slobodan
Stanković, "'Radical Changes' Suggested by
Yugoslav CC in Discussion of Economic
Difficulties," Radio Free Europe Research (October
31, 1984).

42. Politika (December 15, 1982).

43. Wall Street Journal (January 13, 1984); and Antić,
"Yugoslavia to Negotiate," p. 4.

44. Intervju (Belgrade, March 30, 1984), as discussed
in Slobodan Stanković, "Controversy Surrounding
the Yugoslav Army," Radio Free Europe Research
(April 26, 1984).

45. Speech by Metodija Stefanovski to the Sixteenth
LCY Central Committee Plenum, as reported in
Tanjug (March 5, 1985), translated in Foreign
Broadcast Information Service, Daily Report
(Eastern Europe), March 8, 1985. This issue also
appeared in a sharp exchange between the Slovenian
youth organization's paper, Mladina (Ljubljana,
March 7 and 14, 1985), and the JNA weekly, Narodna
armija (March 14, 1985). For analysis, see
Slobodan Stanković, "A Youth Paper Criticizes the
Army," Radio Free Europe Research (March 28,
1985).

46. This relates to Yugoslavia's place on a continuum
of praetorian involvement that ranges from

military regime to military-civilian coalitions in
which the soldiers in politics dominate their
civilian colleagues, to civilian-military
coalitions in which the military members are
clearly junior partners.

4
Self-Management and Socialization

Sharon Zukin

For nearly all Yugoslavs, the current decade of reexamination began with the need to adjust to two drastically different situations: a perceived absence of effective political leadership and strong inflationary pressures. The crisis that followed during the first half of the 1980s was shaped less by President Josip Broz Tito's death--as many foreigners think--than by the necessity of inflicting austerity measures on a recalcitrant economy. After all, while the Partisan generation aged, Tito's death was anticipated and even planned for. During the last few years of his life, political leaders attempted both veneration and transcendence of the Old Man's exceptional personality. But in the short run, Yugoslavs were woefully unprepared for economic changes. Rapid increases in energy bills, higher costs for raw materials, and continual shortages of hard currency threatened established levels of output, investment, and employment. Cherished gains in economic growth rates and living standards receded into memory.

The effect on people's attitudes was startling. For the first time since the self-management system was introduced in the early 1950s, Yugoslavs felt the lack of a coherent, generally accepted model of social and economic development. They asked what self-management had accomplished for them, and they wondered whether

*The author expresses gratitude to Josip Županov for guidance and encouragement, and to Vladimir Arzensek, Ljiljana Bačević, Veljko Rus, Julie Mostov, and Pedro Ramet for sharing research materials. Research in Yugoslavia was facilited by grants from the German Marshall Fund of the United States and City University of New York. Judgments expressed in this chapter are purely the responsibility of the author.

they were sinking toward the oblivion of an underdeveloped socialist society.

The reassessment of self-management proceeded on three analytic levels. First, social scientists like Josip Županov, Neca Jovanov, Branko Horvat, and Zaga Golubović said that the success or failure of self-management could only be considered in the context of the general crisis that they had described since 1982. Although political leaders were reluctant to follow suit, focusing on the imperfections of self-management represented a half-way position between critics and formulators of official policy. Moreover, the impasse in which a long-awaited economic stabilization program was caught encouraged some politicians to speak openly of social crisis. An escalation of political language was also encouraged by the general sense of malaise that accompanied inflation. Significantly, when Belgrade political theorist Najdan Pašić was given reponsibility for developing a program of political revitalization, he signalled that overall crisis was his point of departure.

A second approach related self-management's problems to the prevalence of counter-productive attitudes and behavior. Causes of particular concern included the failure to integrate young people into the economy and the political system, a lack of hard work and respect for 'social' property, and an inability or unwillingness to mobilize Yugoslav brain power in the new technological revolution. At this time, several of self-management's greatest strengths--encouraging innovation, social integration, and common effort-- began to seem either exhausted or illusory.

On a third level of analysis, Yugoslavs began to take stock of self-management in the 1980s because both the institutions and the idea itself were aging. Sociological articles like "The Fate of Workers' Councils" and "Self-Management--Thirty Years Later" reflected a more philosophical reexamination than either the aura of general crisis or financial deadlines required. Nevertheless, the critical attention that was focused on self-management on all three analytic levels posed questions about its efficiency, its autonomy from political and economic pressures, and its real contribution to the creation of a new society.

Economic crisis added a note of urgency to perennial questions about self-management's effect on Yugoslav society. While socialist theorists still wondered whether self-management could eliminate sources of alienation, economists and politicians asked whether self-management could work the way it was designed. Many ordinary Yugoslavs wondered whether self-management could work at all. But doubts about self-management's effectiveness in the current economic crisis led to an insistence on all sides that the basic principles are legitimate and can work--when given the chance.

Crisis even intensified Yugoslavs' adherence to self-management. For most of them, regardless of their position, self-management still connotes equal rights and social equality. It distinguishes Yugoslavia today from both the troubled Balkans of the not-so-distant past and the repressive regimes in neighboring socialist states. It also suggests that reconciliation is possible between the promises of twentieth-century revolutions in the East and Western revolutions of the eighteenth and nineteenth centuries.

EMERGENT TRENDS

For these reasons, it is important to clarify three trends that have developed in conjunction with the reexamination of self-management. First, there is growing rejection of several key institutions that were adopted or became prominent fairly recently, during the 1970s, and were based on consensual norms. Second, there is increasing desire for reform that would eliminate or reverse some of the unanticipated and dysfunctional consequences of self-management that have evolved over the past few years. Third, there is an emerging effort to retrieve recent periods of collective history that were suppressed or submerged for political reasons. Each of these trends sheds some light on the way Yugoslavs perceive self-management's current crisis.

The most significant institutions under critical review are the BOALs (basic organizations of associated labor), the formally independent, shop-level units into which all business enterprises were divided ten years ago, and the republics and regions (constituting the federal state), which during the 1970s assumed great power in the making of political and economic policy. Increasing the rights of both BOALs and republics had been justified in terms of improving opportunities for self-management. From the beginning, however, some Yugoslavs criticized them for being too small to be autonomous and too self-interested to avoid autarky. The original criticisms had come mainly from economists and business leaders. But by 1983 or 1984, complaints mounted at both the grassroots and elite levels. Specifically, the use or abuse of republican criteria in personnel appointments and parliamentary voting at the federal level led to assertions that the 1974 Constitution had outlived its usefulness. Similarly, the waste and duplication of effort involved in maintaining BOALs as separate business entities led to calls for changes in the 1976 Law on Associated Labor.

In terms of self-management's unanticipated consequences, Yugoslavs have been surprised and disappointed by the realization that people really are not socialized in dramatically different ways. To be a "self-manager" theoretically implies a willingness to take risks and work hard, to initiate and be receptive to new ideas, and to show a social consciousness born of awareness of the multidimensional aspects of individual and collective action. Yet self-management has been accompanied by the persistence of many of the "bad old ways." Yugoslavs show a lack of interest in self-management institutions, a faulty knowledge of the way they work, and a seeming disregard for the consequences of their action. Concern about the resulting duality of attitudes and behavior is voiced almost everywhere. A recent column of television criticism in the labor union newspaper Rad, for example, said, "In the future, instead of [Alfred Hitchcock's] 'Psycho,' they will certainly film 'Socius,' a soul-stirring drama about the causes and consequences of man's divided social being."(1)

An attempt to retrieve slices of the collective past began to animate new plays and novels, especially in Serbia and Slovenia, several years before Tito's death in 1980. Although these efforts were criticized, they generally reached the public and often won acclaim among literary juries. A great deal of attention focused on the Yugoslavs' own period of McCarthyism, during the late 1940s, when the break with Stalin and the Cominform led to domestic purges, including political trials and recriminations that penalized and divided families. Other periods that began to be retrieved for empirical research recalled the brief postwar development of democratic political parties, the entire interwar era, and the circumstances surrounding the creation of the Yugoslav state in 1918.

These three trends—based on a selective rejection of institutions, reversal of consequences, and retrieval of history—shape the immediate future of self-management in Yugoslav society. Though some of their possible implications are certainly excluded, e.g., the establishment of a multi-party political system or the dissolution of the federal state, they suggest the direction of desired change.

In general, public discussions that prepare the groundwork for change focus on three sets of issues: criticism of the values that self-management has inculcated, assessment of self-management institutions, and concern about the patterns of social reproduction that apparently contradict self-management goals.

Perceptions about the current status of self-management
in Yugoslavia show that these issues are interrelated.

CURRENT PERCEPTIONS

In a recent historical survey of "The Fate of
Workers' Councils" following revolutions, Slovenian
sociologist Vladimir Arzenšek summarizes the findings
of all empirical research on Yugoslav self-management
from the 1960s to the 1980s. "There is present in work
organizations," he says,

> an oligarchical power structure that works
> to the advantage of professional management
> and against the workers. Workers' councils
> are under the management's thumb. Therefore,
> both mental and manual workers express a
> feeling of powerlessness concerning the
> possibility of influencing events in the
> work collectives. Workers are alienated from
> their labor. The interests of workers'
> council members and officials of political
> organizations (the party and labor unions)
> coincide more with management's interests
> than with those of the workers. The process
> of bureaucratization of the unions and their
> lack of representativeness are seen in the
> union members' passivity. A majority of
> workers express the attitude that they are
> not even union members. All the socio-
> political groups in the work organization
> have the same feeling of political impotence
> in the sense that the political system does
> not respond to people's wishes and demands.
> Naturally we wonder why, over a thirty-year
> period, the development of self-management
> in Yugoslavia hasn't led to the democratization
> of the decision-making process for the benefit
> of the workers and the workers' councils.(2)

The litany of grievances that Arzenšek recites was
uncovered by the first Yugoslav social scientists who
went to the factories. Led by industrial sociologist
Josip Županov, researchers in the 1960s found hierarchy
instead of equal opportunity to "influence events," and
a stubborn retreat to peasant egalitarianism from the
managerial, motivational, and distributional challenges
that "industrialism" posed.(3) Yet these disturbing
conclusions were submerged by the acute political
problems of the 1970s, including nationalist challenges
in all the republics, fears of a post-Tito coup d'état,
and writing the new constitution and labor and business
laws that gave form to the Yugoslav state. Those
efforts practically consumed a decade.

But with the economic crisis of the 1980s, problems of self-management re-emerged in force. The need to coordinate economic policy, and to allot scarce resources and curtail waste put additional pressure on the ability of self-managing actors to make decisions. In particular, government used blue-ribbon commissions as a pseudo-consensual means of imposing austerity measures. Negotiations with the International Monetary Fund (IMF) also enhanced the role of the state. "Today it is widely known," the Belgrade newsmagazine NIN wrote in 1982, "that the proportion of resources that is invested anywhere in a real self-management fashion is smaller than before, while the proportion of administrative decision-making that is only formally self-management grows."(4)

Fears about how the country would survive inflation were linked to fears about the power of the state. People believed that by enhancing state intervention in the economy, inflation would erode the kernel of self-management that remained. This led to anxious concern about whether self-management would be superseded by a full-fledged command economy. On the one hand, public opinion surveys, even in Slovenia, the richest republic, showed that more than half the country was worried about the economic situation, while a third of the respondents expressed doubts about general social conditions.(5) On the other hand, as the mass-circulation magazine Danas said, "The question that is left hanging in the air [in discussions of inflation] is: How much does our [current] economic policy conform to the system of socialist self-management, whose alpha and omega are the market and [objective] economic laws?"(6)

During the "hot months of 1982," Danas says, self-management was eroded by governmental actions that restricted imports and limited the retention by work organizations of foreign currency earnings. An omnibus bill in the Skupština also froze investments, fringe benefits, and expenditures by the self-managing interest communities that finance public goods and services. A little later, discussion lingered on the possibility that the government would also freeze wages. If the government does these things, Danas asks, does the self-management model belong "only to the so-called golden age?"

Certainly self-management was widely associated with Yugoslavia's highly respectable rate of economic growth during the 1960s. However, recent analysis shows that these results were somewhat worse, on average, than in centrally planned economies. Yugoslavs do not easily acknowledge that their competitive ability has fallen behind that of several East European neighbors whose political leadership has always opposed self-management. Hungary's endorsement by the IMF and Bulgaria's putative success in robotics have damaged the Yugoslavs' pride.(7)

At issue is self-management's failure to provide adequate means and a suitable model for further economic development. As economist Marijan Korosić observed at a conference on worker motivation in 1984, "In Yugoslavia until recently we thought we had found a resolution for the manner and methods of creating wealth. We found that resolution in self-management. But today we find ourselves in a deep, significant, and unexamined socio-economic crisis....Where did we go wrong.?"(8)

Yet Korosić and his colleagues insist that recovering the key to economic development requires greater adherence to rather than abandonment of self-management. They criticize the supersession of self-management by governmental or managerial decrees, and they call for increased worker participation as the most effective means of stimulating work. On several points they seem to agree with the politicians whose intervention they deplore.

First, as Korosić says, "Self-management is not a comprehensive system if it doesn't expand outside the space of productive work organizations...on the levels of the micro-economy, the meso-economy [i.e., the republics], and the global society."(9) Second, as economist Kosta Mihailović warns, "Precisely because [the] system is sluggish, complicated, and ineffective, it is possible for a single competent and enterprising individual with wide authority to take over the whole decision-making process and deliver meaningful results."(10) Third, sociologist Josip Županov argues that, although every Yugoslav survey of workers' attitudes since 1968 attests to the primacy of working for higher wages, the self-management model should restore intrinsic satisfaction as the basic motivation for work.(11)

In other words, according to expert opinion, Yugoslav self-management has tended to be too materialistic, too susceptible to domination by a powerful boss, and, ultimately, too confined to work units that have been cordoned off from the larger political society. Nevertheless, in comparison with West European industrial systems, self-management's great achievement has been to stoke Yugoslav workers' aspirations for greater latitude and greater opportunity as self-managers.(12)

Among the reasons for this continued support is that self-management responds to many needs. On the one hand, as sociologist Veljko Rus notes with approval, self-management makes social conflicts explicit. Thus the system moves toward the

institutionalization of conflict that real democracy
demands.(13)   On the other hand, as Županov critically
observes, the Yugoslav consensus on self-management
often rests on groups' ability to use the system to
their mutual advantage. As in other socialist states,
politicians forge an implicit understanding with blue-
collar workers that tacitly confirms their ideological
roles.   Just as politicians furnish workers with a
certain degree of security by protecting employment and
allowing wage increases, so the workers refuse to
challenge the politicians' overall control.(14)
     Periodic Slovenian public opinion polls indicate
an interesting dynamic in perceptions of self-
management. During the late 1970s and early 1980s, the
2,000 Slovenes interviewed for these surveys
consistently criticized abuses of self-management while
showing equally constant support for the self-
management system. They believe that self-management
facilitates freedom and creativity, and allows greater
participation in the decision-making process. Yet by
1982 they also thought that workers' self-management
did not function as well as before, and that people
showed less respect for both workers and work
itself.(15)   This suggests that the ordinary self-
manager analytically separates the system from its
results. Is this evidence that self-management
encourages an ambidextrous manipulation of the facts
related to the schizophrenic mentality that the
Yugoslav television critic described? Or does it
simply imply the plasticity of self-management's basic
values?

BASIC VALUES

     Although Yugoslav self-management has always been
criticized for serious contradictions between theory
and practice,(16) the plasticity of self-management's
basic values accommodates and legitimizes conflicting
models of behavior. First, these values are not
identified with a specific policy orientation--except
the "official" views at any given time. But because
they are associated with attitudes favoring tolerance
and modernity, the leadership upholds these values as a
negation of "hard-line" and "egalitarian" communism.
More generally, institutionalizing self-management
subsumes values of both "order" and "movement." By
adhering to this ideology, Yugoslav leaders continually
foster the creation of "subversive" values while trying
to control their expression. Not surprisingly, the
tension between self-management and the state
cultivates an air of permanent potential
insurrection.(17)

In a different sense, self-management's values combine idealism and pragmatic strategies. At their most pragmatic, these values are assumed to have a greatly idealistic effect. On the one hand, self-management should motivate work; on the other hand, it should encourage participation and creativity. But the salience of these values has declined for many years. From Bogdan Kavčić's survey of Slovenian workers in 1968 to Djuro Loncar's research in Vojvodina in 1984, Yugoslavs have consistently denied that they work for intrinsic satisfactions rather than for pay.

It follows that the cutbacks in wages and fringe benefits and the dramatic fall in real income since 1979 have sapped worker motivation. Economists estimate that Yugoslavs put in only five-and-a-half hours of work during each eight-hour working day. "The lower our wages, the less we work," runs the ironic refrain. Public opinion has been mobilized to combat this attitude since the end of 1983.(18)

At the same time, surveys of public opinion in Slovenia and Vojvodina show the chance to participate in workers' self-management at the very bottom of the list of what people want to do. Slovenian workers indicate great unwillingness to assume any official position in the self-management organs. As many as 90 per cent of the least educated workers, and half of the highly educated workers and employees, say they are reluctant to be involved. Nor does this attitude represent an abrupt reversal of previous patterns. Research in Slovenian business organizations in the early 1970s suggested, as Arzenšek says, that powerlessness breeds passivity. This was confirmed in later surveys in 1980 and 1981. The Slovenian research also showed that members of workers' self-management organs feel as powerless as non-participants at the skilled worker level. Roughly 60 per cent of blue-collar and clerical workers did not feel like self-managers at all. Significantly, fewer than a quarter of the executives who were interviewed and fewer than a third of the professional and technical staffs had such a low sense of involvement.(19)

Related problems are raised by the issue of whether self-management values stimulate innovation. This question grew acute in 1984 as Yugoslavs asked whether the country would be left behind by the development of advanced technology. Many criticized government policies for inhibiting the intellectual curiosity that self-management was supposed to foster. Especially troublesome were the high tariffs imposed on imported technology, which--in the absence of good domestic products--merely encouraged Yugoslavs to develop their technical skills by smuggling foreign-made personal computers and computer software into the country. Lingering official disapproval and mass distrust of small private-sector entrepreneurs confined the development of competitive data-processing services to semi-clandestine initiatives.(20)

This situation reflects a general dilemma over self-management's rewards for genuinely creative work. Such work is a core value of self-management. However, as Županov describes it, different values give rise to contradictory attitudes. On the one hand, political leaders launch periodic campaigns in support of innovation (including the campaign that began in late 1983); on the other hand, most Yugoslavs regard creativity as 'no-work' because it does not demand physical strain and cannot be measured in terms of pieces of output or hours of time. Self-management permits the expression of these contradictory attitudes on every level of society.

Even more galling for those who would encourage innovative work, self-management decisions about financial rewards have institutionalized "egalitarianism"--the ideological vestige of both early Yugoslav communism and peasant antipathy to the individual who rises above his station. As Županov notes, inventive work in Yugoslavia has never received the financial rewards or social status that it attracts in market economies. Certainly most BOALs are too impoverished to offer glittering prizes. However, self-management encourages them to turn inward, away from the risks and rewards of experimentation and toward mediocrity. Moreover, Županov observes, self-management values have not inhibited Yugoslavs' traditional hostility toward experts amd expertise. Yet in his view, the spirit of enterprise and innovation belongs to a "mature" self-management's deepest values.(21)

Equally inconsistent with self-management's fundamental values are the growing, widely publicized trends of pilfering, moonlighting, and appropriating the "social" property of the BOAL for individual enrichment. According to the public defender of self-management rights in Croatia, stealing from the BOAL takes many forms. These include the failure to repay loans and pay rents as they are due; a legal but irrational use of collective resources by running up the bill on expense accounts and making unnecessary business trips; and failing to make unpleasant changes in the organization of work by, for example, instituting night shifts. Estimated annual losses from all sorts of "foul-dealing" in the BOALs have escalated rapidly since 1975. With the economic crisis that began in 1981, they accelerated sharply.(22)

Between dealienation of labor and respect for social property lies an incomplete corpus of self-management values. At its most extreme, criticism implies that the institutions based on these values work so badly--or so perniciously--that they threaten Yugoslav society.

SELF-MANAGEMENT INSTITUTIONS

In such institutions as the workers' councils of business organizations and the self-managing interest communities of localities and communes, Yugoslavs are supposed to confront the necessity of governing their lives as both producers and consumers. While these institutions should enable ordinary citizens or workers to enjoy effective control over outcomes, the processes by which institutions and participants interact ensure that no single interest takes the lion's share in any sense. Changes in ideology and institutions that were made during the 1970s emphasized the utility of giving expression within each institution to a diversity of interests. Although this emphasis had particular significance for strengthening Yugoslavia's federal system, it was never associated with either the diminution of the League of Communists' (LC) influence or the disappearance of government itself.

The principle of self-management coordinates operations on four different levels of social and economic life. These are the internal organization of business and political units, the organization of product and factor markets, the interaction of macro-economic variables, and the organization of social policy. In view of the constant pressures brought to bear on each level by specific policy choices, it is difficult to distinguish between the functioning of self-managment in general and the peculiarities of Yugoslav institutions.(23)

Nevertheless, institutional and external constraints impinge on the exercise of self-management rights on each level of operation. Most consistent among these constraints are limitations imposed by governmental policy; managerial control and political interference that are expressed, coherently or not, by LC influence on business decisions; and capital accumulation, or the necessity of having a financial surplus--in the form of either profits or subsidies--that can be reinvested in both capital goods and goods for collective consumption. The economic crisis of the 1980s tightened these constraints. Consequently, even more than in the past, the mandates of self-management institutions combine moral imperatives and practical inhibitions.

The emphasis on pragmatism also makes self-management appear as a modus vivendi that has been hammered out among occasionally hostile business organizations or federal republics. Time-consuming consultations between these actors either stitch together a compromise or abandon the issue. In fact, because self-management institutions give the actors an ability to threaten and pursue an individual course of action regardless of consequences to the system as a whole, institutions frequently are caught in a standoff between pressures for association and autarky.

Yet self-management institutions have the virtue of keeping republics and businesses from each other's throats. By permitting participants to "satisfice" their interests, these institutions probably come close to optimizing most of their basic values. But neither satisficing nor optimizing is efficient for re-establishing conditions of economic growth.

The curious dynamic that has ensured the survival of these institutions is that they simultaneously protect the weak and advance the interests of the strong. How they manage this may be interpreted differently. The simplest explanation refers to a functionalist dynamic. Described by Yugoslav economist Rudolf Bićanić during the 1960s and amplified by American political scientist Ellen Comisso in the early 1970s, the fulcrum essentially rests on economic decentralization and political pressure. On the one hand, economically stronger units such as firms or republics always plead for more self-management, i.e., more autonomy to manage their own affairs. On the other hand, weaker units that fear submersion, subordination, or loss of autonomy vis-à-vis competing institutions always plead for state intervention to maintain the status quo. As their relative positions change, individual firms or republics shift their demands. But the strong always press for more self-management, and the weak, for state intervention.(24)

Another way that self-management serves both the weak and the strong refers to the tacit alliance between the socially dominant group of political leaders and the ideologically dominant though relatively poor group of blue-collar workers.(25) As Županov describes it, self-management survives in principle because of the patronage granted by the first group and the legitimacy accorded by the other. The resulting institutional order emphasizes mutual payoffs. But it does not maximize efficiency. Because the alliance implicitly rejects such ultimate sanctions as "internal colonialism" and the loss of employment, it perpetuates irrational management of collective resources by all self-management institutions. Among the republics, however, self-management institutions maintain the political balance between economically developed and underdeveloped areas.(26) In work organizations, "the institutional system of self-management protects the workers from severe Taylorist discipline."(27)

At any rate, the inability of self-management institutions to make a strong response to economic crisis has encouraged an effort to surpass or revise them. At both the grassroots level and in the political elite, dissatisfaction is voiced though not encouraged. Although workers' councils and republics remain inviolate, other self-management institutions are under attack.

Self-management institutions have been criticized on several grounds. First, there is growing public recognition that self-management has been needlessly complicated by overlapping sets of complex laws. A book by political scientist Jovan Mirić stirred an outcry among politicians in 1984 by comparing the Law on Associated Labor with Talmudic hair-splitting. In this book Mirić also associates himself with criticism of state intervention in the economy by Županov and others who disapprove of the "political market" growing "at the expense of the economic market." Mirić generally asserts that the institutions of federal decision-making based on republics and regions have caused more problems than they have solved.(28) Mirić's book was excerpted in <u>Borba</u> in fall 1984 immediately prior to book publication. Many people were perturbed by some of Mirić's criticisms and the presidium of the Vojvodinan Socialist Alliance discussed the matter in October. Some thought the book should not have been published.

Besides Mirić's critique, some politicians have also taken aim at the republics' institutional ability to damage federal interests. The interrepublican committees that some observers have praised for resolving conflict before policies are adopted(29) have come under increasing attack. They are blamed for prolonging the policy-making process and enhancing the role of federal bureaucrats. In their defense, members of the Federal Executive Council blame republican voting blocs in the Skupština for creating bottlenecks. Furthermore, political leader Mitja Ribičič has criticized the exaggerated use of the republican key (or ethnic quotas) because it tends to "put incompetents in office" under the guise of "equal rights."(30)

The other major target of attack is the "BOALization" of the economy that was promoted during the 1970s as the hallmark of self-management. "The more BOALs a factory had, the more modern we thought it was," says one of the oldest workers at a window manufacturer in Škofja Loka (Slovenia). But the BOALs inside the factory subcontracted work outside the plant, and a single product was shipped back and forth between the BOALs until it was completed. "Our BOALization from 1978 on wasn't worth a hill of beans," this worker says in an interview in Rad. "In the collective we're asking now: How much did we pay, first, for BOALization and now, for de-BOALization?"(31)

Indeed, Rad goes to pains to deny the rumor that in Slovenia BOALs have already been abolished. Small units are being merged, after a fashion, often back into the same large firms from which they were created. According to the deputy public defender for self-management rights in Slovenia, there is some reason for confusion about the BOAL's current status. First, because the government's austerity program emphasizes the role of the work organization, workers have interpreted this to mean that BOALs can be abolished in favor of the old enterprise form. Second, because new laws have eliminated the BOAL's zero-account, people have leaped to the conclusion that the BOAL itself has been eliminated. Nevertheless, there is obvious motivation among Slovenes to get rid of the BOAL. "We advised all those who rushed to abolish a BOAL," the Slovenian public defender of self-management rights says, "to introduce new technology first, and then form a BOAL, not to abolish it first and think about technology afterward."

While some Yugoslavs may have acted precipitously in eliminating the BOAL, the party has also expressed criticism. In Belgrade, members of the LC's City Committee related crises at several of the city's leading firms between 1982 and 1984 to BOALization. They asserted that BOALs within the same enterprise show unnecessary disparity in terms of wage scales and projects, and tend to create a fortress mentality. But reformers should proceed with caution. "A new organization [of Yugoslav firms] should be undertaken only if the new resolution will be more economical and more profitable than the preceding [BOALization]."(32)

By all accounts, several of the major institutional innovations in self-management that were made during the 1970s have been judged irrelevant to the economic and social demands of the 1980s. Protecting the weak by symbiosis with the strong did not suggest the long-term synergies that Yugoslavia needed for economic revival. Nor did most Yugoslavs consider that self-management had succeeded in instilling the work ethic that the time demanded. Critics such as Županov suggested greater subtlety and flexibility in norms and institutions. Yet Županov was pilloried in Vjesnik in 1985 for paying inadequate homage to the party. Most officially-connected critics wondered whether--as Mirić writes--"self-management [was] in crisis at the core--in man....Doesn't the crisis of 'mechanisms of mobilization' really refer to self-management's crisis?"(33)

SOCIAL REPRODUCTION

Like the core of any social system, self-management should ensure the survival of Yugoslav society's central values by transmitting the features and patterns that make Yugoslavia nationally, culturally, and politically distinct. Social reproduction in general is not a matter of exact duplication of knowledge or opinions. But it does imply that, across the generations, people in a society tend to act on the basis of similar motivations, define their interests in one way rather than another, and associate these interests with those of some groups but not with those of others. In particular, self-management suggests a more open, or less exclusive, socialization process than in other societies. Self-managers should learn to participate in public events regardless of social class, traditional background, or other socially-imposed divisions, and value this participation above all other rights and responsibilities. If the best of self-management's values are to survive, this is the way that Yugoslav society has to be reproduced. However, there are several problems: notably, with motivating young people, encouraging participation, and eliminating class-biased socialization in the family in favor of socialization by class-blind self management institutions.

It is widely acknowledged that self-management has failed to mobilize young people in a significant way. Certainly no great problem arises from youth's rejection of or resistance to the self-management ideology. But self-management institutions have not integrated young people into positions in proportion to their share of the population. Nor have they induced behavior that is less "alienated"--in relation to current norms--than that of their parents, many of whom lived in rather brutal rural or proletarian conditions until recent years.

In a 1981 survey of young workers in 88 Serbian firms, one out of three respondents reported using up to a month of annual sick leave every year. Nearly twice as many of these "alienated" workers have blue-collar rather than white-collar jobs. In these jobs, according to sociologist Vladimir Obradović, "they confront their own lack of independence more than the simple nature of their work."(34) This age group also contributes to the Yugoslav divorce rate: half of all divorced Yugoslavs are less than 24 years old. But young people often describe life on the job or at school as "an atmosphere of horror," where "good things are packaged as self-management." As they move through young adulthood, they respond to their marginalization by "vulgarizing" life, as a journalist says, "with increasing cynicism and 'spiritual contempt.'"(35)

For the most part, young Yugoslavs don't see any reward in social activism. Although being a full-time youth organization leader does help people into better careers, and offers perquisites like cars and apartments along the way,(36) young people hesitate to get involved. Many fear involvement because of its possible consequences. "You keep quiet," a youth organization representative said at a recent conference, "because getting into a dialogue is like entering a mine field." So young people respond to criticism of their "passivity" by saying they keep quiet in order to survive. According to another young conference speaker, all lessons of socialization converge on the value of silence. "We're systematically taught to keep quiet, in the family, at school, in our youth organization, the LC."(37)

Nor are young people encouraged by the high rate of youth unemployment. Because 80 per cent of all unemployed Yugoslavs are young people under 27, who are often more highly skilled and better educated than the employed, they are said to live in a state of existential despair, waiting for a job.(38) Self-management has not helped them get started in a career. Efforts to encourage the hiring of young people by means of self-managing agreements have not been effective. Business organizations can evade governmental pressure for new hires, especially when workers' councils connive in protecting wages and jobs for current jobholders. Moreover, some business organizations restrict new hires to the children of present employees, often by coaxing these employees to take early retirement and passing their jobs on to their children. Self-management organs have also prevented young workers from getting their rightful share of collective goods. Although it is illegal to exceed 12 per cent of a worker's personal income in compensation derived on the basis of seniority, an examination of the rulebooks in 88 Serbian enterprises showed seniority to be the most important criterion of compensation. In these business organizations, fewer than 3 per cent of the young workers had been assigned enterprise-owned apartments by the workers' council.(39)

The disadvantaged employment situation of young people weighs heavily on the social reproduction of the self-management system. "Whether they go to the countryside or the factories; whether they stay in the cities, with their video-computer ideology, on the one hand, and their lumpenproletariat offensives, on the other, over the next ten years, this army of 1 million [unemployed] young people will decide not only their own future but also the future of socialism in this country."(40)

Despite the number and size of self-management organs, participation in them is not pervasive. In fact, participants come predominantly from the ranks of older people, white-collar workers (including administrators, technicians, and political officials), and political activists from the LC, labor unions, and other organizations. Moreover, people are still socialized about self-management in fairly traditional ways. Conversations with friends and workmates are more important sources of information about affairs at work than meetings of the elected workers' council or open assemblies of working people that everyone attends. Knowledge about politics and society is not always improved by attendance at special political schools. Finally, parental politics are still the surest means of inculcating the general propensity to be politically active as well as specific political orientations.(41)

The tenacity of political socialization in the family is a fascinating topic of research. Not only do children reiterate their parents' party membership and beliefs, but they also tend to reproduce the entire cycle of their parents' activism. Thus children who quit the party often have parents who had quit. Similarly, the longer the father has been a party member, the more family members usually belong. Parental achievements--particularly the father's social position--facilitates the transmission of political attitudes. Parental success encourages activism as much as it fosters the voluntaristic values of self-management and the party.(42)

Surveys carried out between 1969 and 1983 offer striking confirmation of how little self-management has countered traditional factors of social reproduction. Just as attitudes and behavior are influenced most by the family's social status, so self-interest is consistently shaped by occupation, education, and class.(43)

A mid-1970s study of young people in Belgrade found that social activism was expressed primarily by the children of socially active parents: 67 per cent of those whose parents are members of self-management organs, 64 per cent of children of party members, 50 per cent of children whose parents are delegates to various local assemblies and self-managing interest communities, and 49 per cent of those whose parents are politically inactive.(44) In the 1970s and again in

1983, a survey of LC members in Serbia showed that higher education determined attitudes of political tolerance. And a 1982 study identified three distinct clusters of interests in Slovenian business organizations: those of managers, blue-collar, and white-collar workers.(45) In the face of such persistent social patterns, the plasticity of self-management's values may be viewed as a safety valve.

Despite the continuity of social patterns, a shift in attitudes did occur after 1979. Although this reflects a cleft rather than a cleavage, there has been a definite change in the way Yugoslavs experience society. Attitudes recorded in public opinion polls indicate that the institutional reforms of the mid-1970s fostered a rather favorable view of society. Optimism about the economy had probably peaked around 1968, after the market-oriented reforms of 1965. However, during the latter half of the 1970s, this optimism was joined by a reflection of higher living standards that spilled over, in turn, to renewed approval of self-management and the LC. To some degree, in the mid-1970s, the party and self-management were linked in many people's minds. But between 1978 and 1983, this socialization for success was shaken. Most Yugoslavs ceased to identify the LC with either self-management or the general interest.(46)

This shift is documented in Slovenia's annual public opinion polls. Because this republic is often viewed as the harbinger of new orientations, especially toward the economy, the change of attitude there is particularly interesting. The economic crisis has affected Slovenia less than the other republics. However, the Slovenes' perception of an abrupt decline in their standard of living has been accompanied by increased approval for transferring some business activities to the private sector, as well as a call for more work discipline and better business strategy, and a more discriminating attitude toward business investment, especially in modernizing individual plants. Surprisingly, these opinions have been formed in a perennial state of misinformation and a striking absence of participation.

Despite widespread publicity for at least two years, over 46 per cent of the respondents in the Slovenian public opinion poll of 1984 claimed not to be familiar with the government's economic stabilization program. But 46 per cent of those who said they were familiar with it also said they disagreed. Furthermore, when they were asked what socialism meant to them, 31 per cent of respondents mentioned unequivocal social equality, or a classless society, which is not the official view. An even larger group

(33 per cent) replied that they didn't know what socialism meant.

Only a quarter of the respondents were members of workers' self-management organs in 1984, and 15 per cent were members of delegations in their community. Counting former members tripled the number of respondents who had participated in delegations to 44 per cent, and nearly doubled the numbers of respondents who had participated in workers' self-management to 43 per cent.

Nevertheless, the majority of respondents said they had very little or no influence in the major policy areas at work (i.e., distribution of earnings, evaluating work and setting wages, making business decisions, work discipline, new investments, mergers with other work organizations, and organization production). In fact, the perception of having very little influence in workers' self-management grew between 1981 and 1984.

The economic crisis of the 1980s has altered the prism through which self-management and society as a whole are viewed. Comparing this decade with the reconstruction period following World War Two (1946–1952) and the period of relative prosperity between 1965 and 1973, Yugoslavs can look back on two golden ages and the social systems that they produced. On the one hand, after the war, Yugoslavs lived through a golden age of reconstruction when everyone pitched in, sacrificed, and worked for the collective good. On the other hand, the golden age of market-oriented prosperity offered consumer goods to the point of luxury, the expansion of credit to buy them, and the chance to compete in the world economy. Both golden ages left their mark on social values. Just as some values reproduced a self-management of abundance, so others created a self-management of poverty.

CONCLUSION

This analysis does not confirm self-management as a mediator between objective circumstances and subjective values. Nor does it interpret self-management as an unambiguous transition from one developmental stage of socialism to another. The economic crisis of the 1980s has challenged the very idea of transitional stages. Of such uncertainty Yugoslavs are both painfully and ironically aware. A cartoon strip on the inside cover of a recent issue of Danas shows a blue-collar worker discussing Yugoslav society with his tow-headed child. "This is the best, the most progressive, the most forward-looking, the most democratic society," the father declares—as many Yugoslavs do—and the child begins to cry. "But

Daddy," he says in obvious confusion, "at school we learned that this is only a 'transitional society.'" The implications of self-absorption, of self-deception, and finally, of losing one's way have become increasingly apparent.

Yet there are several moderating factors. First is the suggestion in some sociologists' and journalists' interpretations of public opinion polls that Yugoslavs want to assume their historic burden. Not only do the times demand it, but Yugoslavs cannot afford to look the other way. Young non-participants who are otherwise patriotic, unemployed youths who seek volunteer work because they can't pay for vacations, and ordinary party members are said to be willing to perform great tasks. But the LC has not yet devised an assignment or a cogent means of mobilization. A second cause for hope is the recent resurgence of inquiry into Yugoslav history. Third, there has been an attempt to utilize the crisis as an opportunity for expanding self-management. This has been accompanied by a willingness--though always limited by elites--to confront many systemic problems, with the exception of the elite's own role. If self-management has not provided a development model that is adequate to the times, a confrontation between elites and critics is inevitable.

It is conceivable that self-management institutions of the 1970s have outlived their usefulness. It is also possible that self-management in general, as a relatively non-coercive means of mobilizing labor and capital without completely skewing redistribution, has temporarily been stripped of practical value. However, as Deborah Milenkovitch suggests, from the very beginning self-management's pragmatic utility is limited. Realistically, it builds rather than reflects consensus.(47)

The frequent reorganization of Yugoslav self-management institutions suggests that they are crisis-driven rather than crisis-adaptive. Thus reforms that are effective in the short run must constantly be revised. At least until 1990, when political leaders hope the employment crisis will abate, Yugoslavs will try once again to institutionalize self-management. As affirmed by Milan Nikolić, the sociologist who was judged guilty of holding "counterrevolutionary positions" after a political trial in Belgrade in 1984, "Socialism is inseparable from democracy; its heritage comes from bourgeois society, but it is deepened through social ownership and economic and social self-management."(48) Self-management is still at the breaking point between democracy and the socialist state.

NOTES

1. Velimir Ćurguz Kazimir, "Televizija: Pisanje i samoupravljanje," Rad (November 9, 1984).
2. Vladimir Arzenšek, "Sudbina radničkih saveta," Sociologija, Vol. 26, No. 1-2 (1984), p. 13.
3. See the oeuvre of Josip Županov, Samoupravljanje i društvena moć (Zagreb: Naše teme, 1969); Sociologija i samoupravljanje (Zagreb: Školska knjiga, 1977), esp. "Egalitarizam i industrijalizam," pp. 26-75, and ch. 3, 4, 6, and 7 in Marginalije o društvenoj krizi (Zagreb: Globus, 1983).
4. NIN (January 10, 1982), pp. 10-11.
5. Danas (April 2, 1984), pp. 6-7; Niko Toš et al., Slovensko javno mnenje 1984: Pregled in primerjava rezultatov (Ljubljana: Fakulteta za sociologijo, politične vede in novinarstvo, 1984).
6. Danas (August 31, 1982), pp. 6-7.
7. See the speech of veteran politician Mitja Ribičič reported in NIN (October 14, 1984), pp. 17-18.
8. Motivacija radnika za bolji rad u našoj zemlji (Belgrade: Ekonomika, 1984), p. 35.
9. Ibid., p. 9.
10. Ibid., p. 81
11. Ibid., pp. 24-25.
12. IDE Group, Industrial Democracy in Europe (Oxford: Clarendon Press, 1981).
13. Veljko Rus, "Yugoslav Self-Management--Thirty Years Later," In B. Wilpert and A. Sorge (eds.), International Perspectives on Organizational Democracy (New York: John Wiley, 1984), pp. 371-389.
14. See, for example, Motivacija radnika, pp. 60-61.
15. Toš et al., Slovensko javno mnenje 1984; Niko Toš, Vrednotenje načela in prakse samoupravljanja (Ljubljana: FSPN, 1982); Ekonomska politika (December 24, 1984), p. 22; Danas (July 24, 1982), pp. 4-8.
16. See, for example, Sharon Zukin, Beyond Marx and Tito: Theory and Practice in Yugoslav Socialism (Cambridge and New York: Cambridge University Press, 1975).
17. On self-management attitudes as modern and tolerant, see Dragomir Pantić, "Vrednosti i ideološke orijentacije društvenih slojeva," in Društveni slojevi i društvena svest (Belgrade: Centar za sociološka istraživanja, IDN 1977), pp. 269-406. On the Yugoslav state, see Sharon Zukin, "Yugoslavia: Development and Persistence of the State," in Neil Harding (ed.), The State in Socialist Society (London: Macmillan/St. Antony's, 1984), pp. 249-76.

18. Ekonomska politika (December 24, 1984), pp. 22-24, and NIN (September 23, 1984), pp. 10-12.
19. Ekonomska politika (December 24, 1984), pp. 22-24; Vladimir Arzenšek, "Samoupravljanje i struktura moći: Stabilnost sistema dominacije," Revija za sociologiju, Vol. 11, No. 1 (1981), pp. 3-11.
20. See NIN (October 14, 1984), pp. 17-18; and NIN (October 28, 1984), pp. 22-24.
21. See Josip Županov, "Znanje, društveni sistem i 'klasni' interes," in Naše teme, Vol. 27, No. 4 (1983), pp. 1048-54, "Razvoj inventivnog rada: Mobilizacija ili deblokada," Vjesnik industrije nafte (Zagreb: September 15, 1984), p. 10, and "Sociološka ekspertiza i samoupravna demokracija," Scientia Yugoslavica, Vol. 10, No. 1-2 (1984), pp. 29-33.
22. Danas (March 6, 1984), p. 14.
23. Deborah Milenkovitch, "Self-Management and Thirty Years of Yugoslav Experience," ACES Bulletin, Vol. 25, No. 3 (1983), pp. 1-26; for the official Yugoslav justification, see Edvard Kardelj, Pravci razvoja političkog sistema socijalističkog samoupravljanja (Belgrade: Komunist, 1978).
24. Rudolf Bićanić, Economic Policy in Socialist Yugoslavia (Cambridge: Cambridge University Press, 1973); Ellen Comisso, Workers' Control Under Plan and Market: Implications of Yugoslav Self-Management (New Haven: Yale University Press, 1979).
25. See Motivacija radnika, pp. 60-61 and Županov, "Znanje, društveni sistem i 'klasni' interes," pp. 1053-54.
26. On this point, cf. Županov with Kosta Mihailović, Ekonomska stvarnost Jugoslavije, 2nd ed. (Belgrade: Ekonomika, 1982).
27. Županov in Motivacija radnika, p.25.
28. Jovan Mirić, Sistem i kriza: Prilog kritičkoj analizi ustavnog i političkog sistema Jugoslavije (Zagreb: Cekade, 1984).
29. For example, Slaven Letica, "Republički interesi i jugoslavenska zajednica," Naše teme, Vol. 25, No. 12 (1981): 1930-35 and Steven L. Burg, Conflict and Cohesion in Socialist Yugoslavia (Princeton: Princeton University Press, 1983); for a different view, see Pedro Ramet, Nationalism and Federalism in Yugoslavia, 1963-1983 (Bloomington: Indiana University Press, 1984).
30. NIN (October 14, 1984), pp. 17-18.
31. "OOUR ukidaju, zar ne," Rad (March 2, 1984), pp. 10-11.
32. Danas (November 15, 1983), pp. 21-22.

98

33. Mirić, <u>Sistem i kriza</u>, p. 258; see Josip Županov, "Dogovorna ekonomija i politički sistem (teze)" (unpublished manuscript, 1984).
34. Study by Vl. Obradović, in Teodor Andjelić, "Očevi i deca: Naraštaj bez prave odgovornosti," <u>NIN</u> (November 22, 1981), pp. 24-25.
35. Nataša Marković, "Mladi i socijalistički moral: Uče nas da šutimo," <u>Danas</u> (December 6, 1983), p. 21. Although articles in the press describe attitudes and behavior as if they are transrepublican phenomena, the public opinion polls to which they refer are usually conducted within a single republic, generally Serbia, Croatia, or Slovenia.
36. <u>NIN</u> (November 15, 1981), pp. 23-24.
37. Marković, "Mladi i socijalistički moral, " p.21. In a 1977 study of 69 LC members in Zagreb, sociologist Ivan Šiber found that 28 per cent of the respondents believed that party members don't express their views because they have no opinion, while 20 per cent fear the consequences of expressing their opinion. "Konformizam i društveno ponašanje," <u>Naše teme</u>, Vol. 21, No. 2 (1977), p. 370.
38. Andjelić, "Očevi i deca," p. 24.
39. <u>Ibid</u>.
40. <u>NIN</u> (December 2, 1984), p. 20.
41. Andjelka Milić, "Porodica i političko ponašanje," <u>Sociološki pregled</u>, Vol. 18, No. 1 (1984), pp. 67-85; <u>Danas</u> (March 13, 1984), p. 26, and <u>Idejno-političko obrazovanje u Savezu komunista Srbije: Rezultati istraživanja</u> (Belgrade: Dokumenti SK Srbije, 1984).
42. Milić, "Porodica i političko ponašanje" and "Porodica kao činilac društveno-političkog angažovanja, in Vladimir Goati et al., <u>Determinante društveno-političkog angažovanja članova SK</u> (Belgrade: Centar za politikološka istraživanja i javno mnjenje IDN and Marksistički centar organizacije SK u Beogradu, 1983).
43. Conclusion in Goati et al., <u>Determinante društveno-političkog angažovanja</u>; Čuruvija, "Anketa medju vojvodjanskim komunistima."
44. Goati et al., <u>Determinante društveno-političkog angažovanja</u>, p. 21.
45. Jan Makarović, <u>Interesne skupine v organizaciji in družbena neenakost</u> (Ljubljana: FSPN, 1982).
46. For example, the percentage of respondents who said the party's interest coincides with the majority's dropped by more than half between 1978 and 1983 (from 44 to 19 per cent), while the percentage that said the party's interest does not coincide with the majority's rose sixfold (from 2

to an all-time high of 12 per cent). Similarly, when respondents were asked in 1978 to select the LC's role in society from those in a given list, the single top choice, for 30 per cent of the respondents, was "developing self-management and socialist democracy." In 1981, only 24 per cent chose this as the party's major role, and in 1984, 4 per cent. Adding together the three possible responses to the question gives the development of self-management a better "score," but even in that case, it fell from 45 per cent in 1978, to 37 per cent in 1981-82, to 20 per cent in 1984. At the same time, people increasingly perceived the LC's role in terms of creating equal rights for ethnic groups. This choice had been indicated by fewer than 5 per cent of the respondents in 1978; by 1984, it was the top choice of 17 per cent. In terms of all choices, it rose from 24 per cent in 1978 to 39 per cent in 1984. Slovensko javno mnenje 1984, pp. 18-20.

47. Milenkovitch, "Self-Management and Thirty Years of Yugoslav Experience."

48. Vjesnik (February 2, 1985).

5
The Yugoslav Press in Flux

Pedro Ramet

Like Yugoslavia itself, the Yugoslav press is neither of the East nor of the West. Like the communist press elsewhere in Eastern Europe, it is seen as serving political functions determined by the party and as obliged to play a 'progressive' role in society. And like other communist newspapers, the Yugoslav press is dependent on the authorities for subsidies, and subject to confiscation if the limits of official tolerance are transgressed. But unlike the situation elsewhere in communist Eastern Europe, there is no pre-publication censorship in Yugoslavia.

In other respects, the Yugoslav press seems more Western in concept and practice. Reports on train wrecks, drug problems, criminal cases, and hostile emigre meetings—rare in most communist newspapers—are all relatively routine in the Yugoslav press.(1) And whereas the Soviet press, for instance, conceives of its purpose in terms of socializing its readership and mobilizing political support for party policy, and is essentially disinterested in the dissemination of objective information, the Yugoslav press continues to view itself as the conveyor of useful information; and thus, headlines and stories reflect daily news and issues of domestic and world concern, rather than centrally directed quotas in which a fixed percentage of space must be allotted to cheering the progress of the wheat harvest. Yugoslav news articles are interesting, regularly reflect differences of opinion and outright controversy, and are generally written from a balanced point of view. Though the Yugoslav press routinely carries its share of polemical articles (most often when it comes to ethnic intolerance or the

*The research for this chapter was made possible through the assistance of a research grant from the American Council of Learned Societies, financed in part by the National Endowment for the Humanities.

activities of religious organizations)--the general tone of the Yugoslav press is "cool," with a stress on informing or persuading. By contrast, the tone of the communist press elsewhere in Eastern Europe tends to be "hot" and to stress agitation rather than information or persuasion.(2)

It is because of this hybrid character of the Yugoslav press that it has repeatedly resisted or circumvented political controls, and that it has at times endeavored to expand the sphere of its legitimate activity, even to the point of criticizing the government itself. The press has, for example, raised embarrassing questions about the so-called program of economic stabilization on a number of occasions, and gave very balanced coverage in 1981 to the trial of poet Gojko Djogo, whom the authorities had hoped to dispose of quickly for elliptical remarks seen as offensive to the memory of President Tito. The Slovenian daily, Delo, openly attacked the federal law on foreign exchange, and Borba itself, one of the most conservative organs, protested a government proposal to impose a 1,500-dinar exit tax on Yugoslavs making trips abroad.(3) Even self-management, the cornerstone of the Yugoslav system, has, since Tito's death, been subjected to occasional critical reassessment in the public press.(4)

Skeptics are fond of noting that despite the relative openness of the domestic press and general availability of the Western press, the authorities routinely ban specific issues of both domestic and foreign newspapers, recording these prohibitions in the official gazette, Službeni list. But a post-publication ban is rarely as effective as pre-publication censorship, and banned issues of both domestic and foreign newspapers (including of the London-based Nova Hrvatska) manage to circulate anyway. A 1971 report in Borba revealed specifically that

all papers and magazines which judicial authorities have provisionally or permanently banned have been freely sold in Niš streets of late. Thus, the provisionally banned weekly Čik-Ekstra is sold today in all kiosks. It is also sold by street vendors. The same occurred recently with the permanently banned issue of [the] periodical Fles, which was sold in Niš to its last copy in the regular way. In the streets of Niš one can always find the provisionally or permanently banned issues of the Belgrade [weekly] Student or of other publications.

In a blitz-inquiry, Niš newspaper and magazine vendors answered that they are interested in selling what the reading public demands. When something is banned, they say, then the demand is tenfold.(5)

The relative openness of the Yugoslav press is related to the abandonment of state subsidies for unprofitable enterprises in the late 1960s (thus forcing the press to gear itself to the market), and to the federalization of the system generally, which has also resulted in a kind of federalization of the press.(6)

The first factor mentioned, the profit motive, has been an important inducement to innovation and bolder reportage. Many Yugoslav magazines have in fact closed down, because of economic losses, such as the once highly regarded Vjesnik u srijedu (VUS), whose circulation dipped from a high of 400,000 at peak, to about 40,000, just before being terminated in 1977. The Belgrade magazine Duga, which was financially marginal at the outset of the 1980s, took chances in order to build up readership, and began running highly critical articles about the regime's economic policy, about interethnic relations in the province of Kosovo, and on other sensitive areas. Reporter (formerly Zum Reporter) has built up a sizeable readership by combining muckraking with sexually explicit photos and letters. And the prestigious Belgrade weekly, NIN, turned around from being a money-loser (within the multi-organ 'Politika' enterprise) to a money-maker, after pioneering the new surge of investigative reporting in the 1980s.(7)

Forced to compete for readership, Yugoslav periodicals became more willing to enter into the political fray, to publish politically 'marginal' stories, and to engage in polemics with each other. The market, thus, provided an incentive to the championing of press freedom.

The second factor, political federalization, contributed to the openness of the press indirectly. Two issues are at work here. First, the sundry daily papers (all except Borba) see themselves, in part, as advocates of the local interests of their respective federal units or subregions. Second, the republics' party leaders are inclined to view the local press as forums for the views and interpretations of the republican organizations. The result is a kind of natural symbiosis in which the local press becomes the spokesman for local interests, and in which diametrically opposed viewpoints can be found in the daily papers of the different republics on a recurrent basis.(8) This federalization of the press contributes to openness by undermining central direction and by getting people accustomed to seeing different interpretations voiced in the press. Together with the new drive toward investigative reporting, this tends to contribute to the credibility of the press. While certain conservative party leaders have criticized this tendency toward federalization of the press, a Slovenian journalist told me in 1982: "I am a federalist and I want to implement the law in a pragmatic way. Some so-called 'democrats' in this country actually favor recentralization and the diminution of self-management, to include a reorganization of the federation as a whole in order to strengthen the central government. But to a certain extent, federalization is natural, and I don't think this is weakening Yugoslavia as some well-meaning people seem to think."(9)

THE PARTY'S CONCEPT OF THE PRESS

The traditional concept that the League of Communists of Yugoslavia (LCY) has had of the press is that it should be politically engaged, and promote the broad objectives of the party. The party has always insisted that the press function in conformity with the interests of the Yugoslav community and that it does not lie within the province of the press to interpret those interests, or the policies framed to advance them, independently.(10) President Josip Broz Tito put the matter simply, more than 20 years ago: "What purpose should our press--our daily and other newspapers--serve? It should serve to form our socialist man and to develop our socialist relations; and it must be directed to this end."(11)

This traditional concept still has adherents in the LCY, and the Eighth Congress of the Bosnian party organization (May 1982) accordingly called for the press to mobilize the "social action of the working class," to have "an engaged and constructive approach to social reality," and to promote the work of the organs of self-management.(12)

According to the traditional concept, the press is free and supportive of party policy at one and the same time. The logic of this is that the press cannot be free against the people, and that the right of the people to useful information takes precedence over liberal notions of press freedom. An interrepublican party conference held in Novi Sad in January 1975 concluded that,

> our press, radio and television do not exist only
> to satisfy people's mere curiosity. They must
> help people to exchange experiences and to find
> their way in complex social processes; they must
> present to them indispensable facts so that one
> may be a socially engaged and cultured
> personality.(13)

Moreover, as Djoko Stojičić once put it, in a truly democratic society, there is no need for the press to drift into the role of political opposition, because opposition in a self-managed society cannot but reduce itself to opposition to self-management, that is to say, to the very democracy in the name of which it assumes its opposition role.(14) And while Stojičić told an inter-commission session on press policy that the press likewise need not be forced into the role of a mere transmission belt for party policy, his colleague, Vukoje Bulatović, was far more ambiguous on this question.(15)

The crux of the matter is that under traditional Marxism, all information and all interpretation have political dimensions. As longtime party ideologue Edvard Kardelj put it, "every social criticism--even some sort of highly theoretical discussion restricted to professional circles--is at the same time also a political action."(16) It is only with a great deal of agonizing that the Yugoslav party has been able incrementally to shake itself of this conservatism, and even as recently as summer 1975, the Socialist Alliance of Working People of Yugoslavia (SAWPY), headed by the somewhat traditional Todo Kurtović, was talking about a campaign to remove 'foreign ideologies' and bare breasts from the Yugoslav media.(17) Kurtović failed in this.

The Yugoslav press is clearly freer than any other communist press, but there are some very precisely defined limits to that freedom, in the spheres of foreign policy, national mythology, religious policy, and nationalities policy, as well as sundry specific prohibitions.

(1) In the sphere of foreign policy, no criticism or qualification of the policy of nonalignment is allowed and few, if any, transgressions of this rule can be found. Of all the constraints on the press, this is the strictest, most serious of them all.

Perhaps because of the Yugoslav self-image as part of the 'socialist commonwealth', there is far more reportage of the internal politics and economics of the Soviet Union and even China, than of those of the United States, far more on neighbors Albania and Bulgaria than on neighboring Austria, far more on the activities of the communist parties of France and Italy than on other aspects of French and Italian politics. On the other hand, there is far more coverage of Hollywood, the American rock scene, and Western fashions than of their Soviet or bloc counterparts.

Critical comment about Soviet internal affairs is infrequent in the daily press, though Yugoslav newspapers have been, from the beginning, outspokenly critical of the Soviet occupation of Afghanistan. Paul

Lendvai suggests that the Yugoslav press is required to be careful in its reportage of events in the Soviet bloc, and cites the suppression, in 1978, of an issue of the Croatian paper, _Studentski list_, because it reprinted an article from _Le Monde Diplomatique_, which was said to be potentially harmful to Yugoslav-Romanian relations.(18)   Earlier, in 1969, the editor of the prestigious biweekly, _Književne novine_, was fired and put on trial for having published an article comparing the Soviet invasion of Czechoslovakia with the American role in Vietnam; part of the problem was that the article appeared on the eve of a visit by Soviet Foreign Minister Andrei Gromyko, at a time when Tito was trying to patch up his troubled relations with the Kremlin.(19)   The obvious exception to this stricture (regarding coverage of the Soviet bloc) is Bulgaria, because of its not so latent irredentism vis-à-vis Yugoslav Macedonia.

(2)   Under the rubric of 'national mythology' I understand the prestige and dignity of Tito, the official version of the Partisan war, and the portrayal of the wartime Chetniks and _Ustaše_ as purely evil. Also subsumed under this category is any positive reference to Alojzije Cardinal Stepinac, the Catholic Archbishop of Zagreb imprisoned in 1946 on trumped-up charges of collaboration with the fascist _Ustaše_ movement during the war.   Whenever the Catholic biweekly _Glas koncila_ has printed an article which conflicts with the official verdict on Stepinac, the offending issue has been confiscated.(20)

This stricture is occasionally breached.   In 1971, for instance, the editors of the Belgrade university paper, _Student_, produced a special issue, allegedly adorned with pornographic pictures, carrying a "letter from representatives of a Dutch extremist organization, famous for its anarchist and hippie views, addressed to President Tito, in which his reputation and dignity [were] hurt perfidiously and maliciously."(21)   The four members of the editorial board were promptly put on trial for insulting the reputation of the state, and the issue was confiscated.

On the other hand, when, about the same time, the Split journal _Vidik_ ran an article criticizing Tito for having betrayed Croatia and attacking the notion of a unified Yugoslavia, the authorities failed to act and the issue was never suppressed.(22)   Similarly, when, in 1982, the Belgrade daily, _Večernje novosti_, ran an article describing Chetnik leader Draža Mihailović as a "tragic figure" who made "a wrong choice," it came in for no greater punishment than drubbing from other news organs.(23)

(3)   In the sphere of religious affairs, there may be a formal or informal stricture barring the press

from describing religious organizations or activities in positive terms, unless they are activities undertaken in apparent defiance of the leading hierarchs--as in the case of the publishing house Christianity Today--in which case they may be described as 'progressive'.(24)   Religious leaders are never described, in the secular press, as having the interests of the community at heart, and various religious leaders of the major faiths (Serbian Orthodoxy, Roman Catholicism, and Islam) are regularly reviled in the press for reactionary, nationalist, and anti-socialist attitudes, and some have even been accused in the press, without proof, variously of treasonous or criminal behavior.(25)   A sociological study published in 1977 noted that the degree of activity of the local press was an important factor affecting religiosity.(26)   This implied that the press is expected to promote atheization.

(4)   In the realm of nationalities policy, the Yugoslav press is expected to uphold the party line, without the slightest deviation.(27)   Some of the sensationalist reportage of Slav-Albanian relations that followed the Kosovo riots in April 1981 tested the limits of party patience, through its one-sidedly negative focus, but the party limited itself to exhorting journalists to strive for better balance.

(5)   Finally, there is a category of subjects which may not be discussed at all. This category includes military and trade secrets, the exact amount of the foreign debt, and the Belgrade office of the United Nations High Commissioner for Refugees, which handles some 2,000 refugees from the Soviet bloc annually.(28)   In addition, newspapers may not publish any writings by Milovan Djilas, Mihailo Mihailov, or other dissidents, or writings of any figures associated with the Croatian nationalist 'mass movement' (masovni pokret or 'mas-pok') of 1969-1971. Also banned are any articles in defense of Djilas, of Croatian economists Šime Djodan, of one-time Croatian President Savka Dabčević-Kučar or of one-time Croatian Secretary Miko Tripalo, or any defense of the mas-pok.

In a controversial interview with the Yugoslav men's magazine, Start, in 1980, Mitja Ribičič, then president of the Republican Conference of the Slovenian SAWP, urged the party to allow all hostile literature to be available to the Yugoslav public, including material from emigre sources, so that people could judge for themselves.(29)   This suggestion was ignored. However, the political elites and security forces keep track of all available foreign writings about Yugoslavia.   Even today, the Security Service publishes two restricted news service bulletins: Red Bulletin,

Table 5-1

Yugoslav Newspapers with Circulations Larger Than 20,000 in Rank Order (1983)

	Copies printed	Copies sold
Komunist (all editions)	550,000	n/a
Večernje novosti (Belgrade)	379,921	339,859
Večernji list (Zagreb)	342,533	309,839
Politika ekspres (Belgrade)	286,451	249,758
Politika (Belgrade)	278,101	243,826
AS (Sarajevo)	215,159	n/a
Sportske novosti (Zagreb)	169,887	141,247
Sport (Belgrade)	127,712	106,781
Družina (Ljubljana, Catholic)	120,000*	n/a
Glas koncila (Zagreb, Catholic)	110,000##	n/a
Delo (Ljubljana)	105,042	99,840
Vjesnik (Zagreb)	91,116	73,030
Oslobodjenje (Sarajevo)	83,331	71,557
Ognjišće (Koper, Catholic)	80,000*	n/a
Novi list--Glas Istre (Rijeka)	78,976	71,274
Slobodna Dalmacija (Split)	78,242	71,571
Večer (Maribor)	58,477	55,476
Dnevnik (Ljubljana)	53,497	50,723
Mali koncil (Zagreb, Catholic)	50,000	n/a
Rilindja (Priština)	46,252	41,141
Večernje novine	45,670	35,049
Borba (Belgrade, Zagreb)	42,563	30,976
Dnevnik (Novi Sad)	38,697	34,158
Večer (Skopje)	36,771	31,959
Magyar Szo (Novi Sad)	30,279	26,485
Preporod (Sarajevo, Islamic)	30,000	n/a
Nova Makedonija (Skopje)	29,124	25,089
Pobjeda (Titograd)	22,568	20,073
Pravoslavlje (Belgrade, Orthodox)	22,000##	n/a

* = 1973; ## = 1982

Sources: Naša štampa (July-August 1983), pp. 9-10; Naša štampa (Febrary 1984), p. 9; AKSA (May 20, 1983; NIN)(May 22, 1983), trans. in Foreign Broadcast Information Service, Daily Report (Eastern Europe), June 1, 1983; and interviews, Belgrade and Zagreb, July 1982.

in 1,000 copies, which reprints articles from the Croatian emigre press, and Tanjug Foreign, in 5,000 copies, which reprints various articles about Yugoslavia taken from the foreign press.(30)

UNITY IN DIVERSITY

The Yugoslav press shows considerable diversity today, with periodicals geared strictly to entertainment, sports papers, sexually explicit magazines, defiantly rebellious student papers, and an outspoken church press (mainly where the Catholic Church is concerned). Yugoslavia is also the only communist country with a tabloid press and three of the four newspapers with the largest circulations in Yugoslavia--Večernje novosti, Večernji list, and Politika ekspres--are tabloids. In fact, of the ten papers with the largest circulations, four are tabloids, two are sports papers, and two are religious publications; only one prestigious secular paper-- Politika--ranks in the top ten.

Journalists in Yugoslavia have a lot of room for initiative, as is clear from the case of Ranka Čičak, a Vjesnik reporter, who discovered and probed a political scandal in Vojvodina, which was said to have portrayed local functionaries as "stupid."(31) Indeed, most articles which appear in Yugoslav magazines, and a large portion of those in the daily press are written on the initiative of the journalist himself.(32)

One of the most successful Yugoslav magazines is Start, a Croatian magazine which made a false start in 1969 as a recreation magazine oriented toward tourism, automobiles, and vacations. But Vikend had already secured this market and Start looked for a new formula. Photo displays of naked and semi-naked females helped to boost subscriptions, and after the appointment of a new chief editor in 1973, Start began to devote more space to politics and culture, and became a highly respected magazine. With the advent of yet another editor, 35-year old Mladen Peše, in 1980, Start began to aim at the younger generation, with more articles on rock music, young fashions, and modern art, and a regular photo display on sex fads and personalities. Start has also continued a tradition of publishing daring and sometimes highly controversial interviews with well-known Yugoslav personalities, such as Vladimir Dedijer, Bishop Vekoslav Grmič, Professor Fuad Muhič, Mitja Ribičič, economist Berislav Šefer, and Rev. Josip Turčinović. A member of the editorial board of Start told me in 1982: "We are among the most analytical of periodicals in Yugoslavia or in Eastern Europe, for that matter. We have published various articles in Start, which have provoked criticism in political forums, but we are also interested in presenting the good aspects of Yugoslav society. But some of the other newspapers don't like us, because they view us as elitist and being too clever."(33)

The Serbian magazine Zum Reporter devised its own
formula for profit, aiming at a less educated audience
and specializing in scandals, gossip, highly critical
interviews, and strange occurrences, such as miraculous
appearances. Zum Reporter is, according to one
informant, regularly being taken to court over one
story or another, and in March 1984, Vjesnik reported
that the magazine was being sued for the unapproved use
of a series of 15 photos by the subject of those
photos.(34)

The diversity of the press is also suggested by
the differences in the proportion of 'positive' and
'negative' articles. In 1981, the Yugoslav Institute
for Journalism conducted a content analysis of four
daily newspapers (Borba, Politika, Večernje novosti,
Politika ekspres), three weekly periodicals (NIN, Duga,
Student), one biweekly periodical (Omladinske novine)
from Serbia, as well as news broadcasts from Radio-
Television Belgrade. Reviewing some 3,840 articles and
news broadcasts over the period January-June 1981,
concerning developments in Serbia, the study found that
only 16 per cent had a neutral attitude toward the
subject discussed, while 39 per cent were positively
disposed toward the events or phenomena discussed, and
45 per cent were negatively disposed.(35) This finding
clearly would set the Yugoslav media apart from current
practice in the Western press. But breaking this down
by individual news sources reveals the data shown in
Table 5-2:

Table 5-2

Percentage of Articles in Serbian Media with Positive or Negative Orientations toward Content January-June 1981

	% positive	% negative
Radio news	71	14
Television news	65	17
Borba	47	40
Politika	45	42
NIN	37	38
Politika ekspres	36	48
Duga	31	53
Večernje novosti	23	44
Omladinski novine	16	60
Student	16	77

Source: Novak Popović, "Sredstva javnog informisanja
o društveno-političkim zbivanjima u Srbiji,"
in Novinarstvo , Vol. 17 (1981), Nos. 3-4, p.
104.

The considerable diversity and frequent polemics among sundry periodicals are two indications of the relatively favorable climate in which Yugoslav journalists work. But there are limits, and the Yugoslavs themselves not only do not claim to practise absolute freedom of the press, but scorn the idea as socially retrograde. Or, as the LCY puts it, the press

cannot be a mere mirror of everything that is happening and of all trends of thought in various sectors of our society, but must be active socialist forums of self-managers, forums which, with their clear-cut, ideological-political orientation, have a place in the forefront of the struggle for [the] socialist progress of society.(36)

Given that there is no pre-publication censorship in Yugoslavia, how is this to be achieved? Clearly the threat of confiscation of undesirable issues will not suffice to produce "active socialist forums."

To begin with, some 80 per cent of Yugoslavia's 11,000 journalists and more than two-thirds of the 950 journalists employed by the organs of the federation are party members.(37) This exposes them to party discipline for infractions against LCY policy. Second, both the directors and editor-in-chief of any secular paper are appointed jointly by the so-called publisher's council (made up of representatives of the general public) and the publishing house itself, in which the party organization plays an important role. The latter is important in providing a stimulus to the newspaper in question to adhere to the party line, and both the publisher's council and the party organization may be asked by the LCY to review the performance of editorial boards and to replace editors viewed as "unreliable." Communist party members "are in a majority or near majority in most publishing houses"(38)--which provides some internal brake against journalistic deviance. The large number of Croatian editors fired in the wake of the Croation crisis in 1971 is a clear indication of the power of the party to curb the press.(39)

Third, every Yugoslav newspaper is subjected to an annual review by its sponsoring organization, which, in the case of the major dailies, means the respective republican branches of the Socialist Alliance. These reviews have at times resulted in editors being informed that they have been too critical of party policy, and Oslobodjenje, in particular, was warned a few times to watch its step.(40)

Fourth, the media rely in part on government channels to provide them with information. The Federal Committee for Information and the Secretariat of

Information in each of the federal units are the authorized sources for information about governmental matters. Tanjug, the official Yugoslav news agency, is not merely the generator of many stories used (usually verbatim) in the Yugoslav press, but also serves, at times, to set the official line on specific events or news developments, sometimes pointedly correcting alternative versions previously disseminated in the domestic press.

Fifth, the party retains a grasp on the purse strings and can, with ease, suspend a subsidy until a periodical gets in line (as was done with the Slovenian student paper, Tribuna, in 1972), or terminate it altogether, causing the deviant publication to fold (as happened with Praxis, a scholarly journal, in 1975).

And sixth, when these pressures and powers fail to prevent the publication of material considered harmful to the interests of the community or of the party, the offending issues (or parts of them) may be banned or confiscated. Copies of all printed matter must be submitted, upon publication, to the district public prosecutor's office. The public prosecutor may place a temporary ban on any issue, and in this case, the matter is referred to the local court, which decides whether the issue may be distributed or not. Either party (i.e., either the prosecutor or the periodical) may appeal the decision to a higher court, and in practice this quite often happens. In the event that a publishing house fails to submit a given issue, that issue may be placed under provisional ban, as happened in 1981 with the biweekly Kosovar journal, Fjalja.(41)

Despite these impressive levers, party influence remains imperfect. The fact that Vjesnik could mock Komunist for running two articles, in the same issue, with mutually exclusive perspectives on the same problem (42) is indicative of the uncertainty even in the official organ of the LCY. The fact that Yugoslav political organs have to keep reprimanding their own press in a manner unparalleled in either East or West is the surest sign that the press continues to push beyond the limits of official tolerance.

THE YOUTH PRESS

Of all the periodical publications appearing in Yugoslavia, it is the youth press which has proven the most consistently nettling to the authorities. Outspoken to the point of rebelliousness, the young editors of Student (Belgrade), Studentski list (Zagreb), Tribuna (Ljubljana), Vidici (Belgrade), and other papers have repeatedly ignored even the most fundamental taboos. At various times, student-run papers have offended the dignity of Tito,(43)

"slandered the public security service,"(44) published
a distorted version of statements by the Trade Union
president,(45) ridiculed the government's economic
policy,(46) and published a black-framed, front-page
obituary for Yugoslavia, explaining that the death
occurred "primarily because of the demands placed upon
it in accordance with the faithful implementation of
the Long-Range Program of Economic Stabilization, and
not because of the conditions we accepted in attempting
to come to an agreement with the International Monetary
Fund."(47)

The student papers have at various times reprinted
unacceptable articles from foreign sources, have
published anti-religious articles or cartoons (e.g., a
cartoon in a Split paper portraying Christ as a hashish
addict and his mother as a prostitute) considered too
offensive for distribution, and have ridiculed or
disputed the values of the Partisan struggle and the
revolution.(48)

The Belgrade weekly _Student_ has, at least lately,
been one of the boldest. In 1982, it lampooned the
police with the ironic plea, "Don't hit me over the
head, blue comrade," and continued, impishly, "We must
fight the competent people--the incompetent are already
with us!"(49) A subsequent issue, in June 1983,
portrayed the government as refusing to listen to good
advice.

One of the most unusual cases came to light in
early 1982, when Belgrade party organizations charged
that the monthly _Vidici_ and the weekly _Student_, both
student publications at the University of Belgrade, had
displayed "a destructive and unacceptable anarcho-
syndicalist and terrorist ideological orientation" and
were espousing "the overthrow of Yugoslavia's
constitutional order."(50) Subsequent hearings at a
joint session of the Belgrade Municipal Conference and
the Belgrade University Conference of Socialist Youth
took a bizarre turn:

It was reported there that the student literary
monthly _Vidici_ has over the last few years
developed a system of cryptographic writing in
which it has criticized the existing Yugoslav
system in such a way that only the initiated could
understand what was actually being said. This
cryptographic writing allegedly used a number of
key words to analyze the Yugoslav system
critically. Use of the word 'technology', for
example, stood for the existing society; 'boys'
meant top politicians, officials, and
theoreticians; 'mirror' meant the existing system
of self-management. In contrast to these negative
terms, the student monthly used such expressions
as 'personality' to describe individuals who

oppose the system; 'will' to denote any move
against the system; 'apocalypse' to stand for the
definite collapse of the existing system.(51)
A 1981 issue of _Vidici_ published a complete 'Directory
of Technology', giving translations of these code
words, and in later issues is said to have urged the
overthrow of Yugoslavia's political system by "anti-
socialist" forces.(52) _Student_ seemed to have adopted
this code when it ran an article linking the
achievement of 'true communism' to the destruction of
the 'mirror'.(53) Authorities concluded that the
student papers had fallen under the influence of
Friedrich Nietzsche's _Uebermensch_ (superman) theory--an
imputation which also seemed to imply that the students
were intellectual snobs.

If the party continues to be faced with a
rebellious student press, it is because ultimately
there is nothing it can do about it, short of
repressive measures inconsistent with the general tone
of the system. Hence, the party remains content with
replacing offending editors and rebuking papers that go
too far.

SEEDS OF DEBATE (1970-1980)

The 'Croatian Spring' (1967-1971) was a period of
dramatic liberalization for the press. Although
domestic papers continued to be banned and confiscated
for various reasons, the intensity of debate and
freedom of expression in the press was unprecedented in
post-war Yugoslavia. With the bridling of the Croatian
party at the end of 1971 and the subsequent purge of
party liberals in Croatia, Slovenia, Serbia, and
Macedonia, party conservatives set out to 'normalize'
the press. For conservatives this meant that the idea
of an independent press ("the thesis that the means of
information should belong only to the journalists") is
contrary to the principles of self-management, and
that any tendencies toward assuming a critical posture
on the part of the press should be resisted as
equivalent to the formation of political
opposition.(54) Conservatives expressly repudiated the
liberal concept that the party should not "interfere"
in the work of the press, describing this idea as
"anarcho-liberal claptrap."(55) On the contrary, urged
Kurtović, SAWPY should play a greater role in press
policy, and existing agencies should be recognized and
new ones created in order more effectively to supervise
the press.(56)

One of the conservatives' concerns was that the
journalist's natural tendency to play up bad news could
get out of hand. Hence, when a Slovenian journalist
wrote an article, published in the Maribor paper,

Večer, which portrayed Skopje as a center of prostitution and debauchery, the city of Skopje protested and criminal charges were brought against the writer.(57) And in a more dramatic case, Nijaz Selmanović, a _Politika_ correspondent, and Zlatko Stević, a correspondent of _Večernje novosti_, were brought before the Grand Jury of the Priština District for having reported a fight between Serbian and Albanian students at the Law Faculty in the Kosovan capital on December 6, 1971. The Public Prosecutor sought to prove that the journalist had fabricated the story "with the intention of creating discontent and confusion among the people." Unfortunately for conservatives, the evidence presented at the trial made it quite obvious that events had transpired exactly as they had been reported.(58)

But liberals did not give up without a fight, and volubly protested at a joint session of the Commission of the Central Committee of LC Serbia for Ideational Activity and Propaganda Work, the Commission for Social Questions of Public Information of the Republic Conference of SAWP-Serbia, and the Presidency of the Association of Journalists of SR Serbia, held in Belgrade on May 26, 1972. One of those present, Jovanka Brkić, pointedly addressed the issue of 'bad news'. She noted that press coverage of crime is sometimes criticized on the ground that it damages the reputation of the Security Services and causes the public to view them as impotent and incapable; she rejected this criticism and observed that, on the contrary, press coverage helps to defend society against crime.(59) Referring to an earlier discussion of party bodies in which criticism was registered of press reportage of criminality, Brkić argued that "In a civilized society it is quite normal for the press to describe everything that is going on...I repeat: the press must write about everything that happens in society."(60) She warned further that recent social reforms were being eroded--a development she obviously regretted.(61)

Her colleague, Predrag Ajtić, president of SAWP-Serbia and thus technically subordinate to Kurtović, was equally bold in opposing advocates of tighter control. He told the same Belgrade meeting that the "free market of information" was a "precondition of the unity of the self-managing system" and that devolution of powers to the federal units in the sphere of public information was healthy and even necessary.(62)

By 1973, however, party conservatives had succeeded in reimposing stricter controls. This period of stricter control lasted until 1975 or 1976, at which point a slow relaxation of control began to be felt.(63) The late Tito period (1976-1980) could be characterized as 'one-party liberalism'; the party was clearly in control but nonetheless gave the press freer rein. With Tito's death, however, the inter-factional balance of power within the party became uncertain and the resulting indecision opened up possibilities for the press.

DEBATE OVER THE ROLE OF THE PRESS (1980-1982)

Already in the months prior to Tito's death (in May 1980) there had been signs of greater boldness on the part of the press. This tendency received impetus during the latter part of 1980, when various party figures began to call for liberalizing the system.(64) Start magazine began serializing excerpts from Vladimir Dedijer's highly controversial second volume of Novi prilozi za biografiju Josipa Broza Tita, and other media began devoting more attention to labor troubles, corruption in high places, and doubts about offical policy.(65) The breakthrough came in April 1981, however, in the wake of secessionist riots among Yugoslavia's Albanian minority in the province of Kosovo.

Though some 10,000-20,000 Albanians were involved in rioting that engulfed almost the entire province for the first few days of April, the government initially took the position that the riots were without especial consequence. Stane Dolanc, a member of the LCY Central Committee (CC) Presidium, claimed that no more than 2,000 demonstrators were involved and minimized the casualities.(66) The official line, as given by Tanjug, was that "the broad masses of citizens, youth, Albanians, and members of other peoples and nationalities of Kosovo and Yugoslavia, sharply condemned [the rioting], realizing its hostile background."(67) Indeed, between March and April, party conservatives tried to impose a blockade on news coverage of the turbulence and instability in Kosovo.

> Representatives of the media were invited to the
> appropriate political offices where it was
> cordially 'recommended' to them that they divulge
> nothing about the demonstrations in Kosovo except
> what was 'officially' released by Tanjug
> agency.(68)

This blockade was, at first, effective in all the republics as well as in the federal organs. But the political leadership aimed at more, viz., to block not merely information on Kosovo going to the media, but also relevant internal information going to various political bodies throughout the country. This blockade did not last long, however, and soon collapsed amid public criticism in political forums and in the press itself.(69)

By the end of April, <u>Politika</u> editor Slavoljub Djokić, Slovenian party official Jože Smole, and others were sharply upbraiding conservatives for having tried to limit press coverage of events in Kosovo.(70) Now the dam burst: Yugoslav newspapers openly competed to give the most complete and most probing coverage of Kosovo, and this new spirit quickly spread to other topics. Shortly thereafter, the editors of <u>NIN</u> decided to enliven their 'Letters to the editor' section, and planted a couple of controversial letters--one of them, which dealt with the postwar prison, Goli Otok ('Bare Island'), being signed allegedly by a certain Ilog Koto ('Goli Otok' spelled backwards).(71) The public responded, and <u>NIN</u>'s 'Letters to the editor' section soon doubled in size, with numerous frank and probing letters. The effect of this and other post-April changes in the media was electric. The editor-in-chief of a major Yugoslav weekly told me in July 1982: "In the few weeks of April 1981, the press changed tremendously, because we learned that we cannot keep things hushed up. The press is definitely freer and more open since Kosovo than before."(72)

The period between April 1981 and the end of 1982 was one of struggle between advocates of two alternative conceptions of the press. Liberals (including probably most journalists themselves) tried to advance the idea of 'objective' journalism, advocating the unhindered reportage of everything of interest to the society. Conservatives (with strong centers of power in the Croatian and Bosnian party organizations) argued for a 'supportive' role for the press. As Josip Vrhovec, then a Presidium member of the CC LC Croatia, put it in October 1982, "Whoever is not convinced of the real values of our socialism is hardly fit to be engaged in the activity of public information dissemination."(73) In other words, the work of Yugoslav journalists must, for conservatives like Vrhovec, be subjected to specific political criteria.

Both liberals and conservatives agreed that the press should be 'socially responsible,' but they interpreted this formula in different ways. <u>NIN</u> even showed itself willing to defend a fictional story which had been the occasion for the confiscation of the Albanian-language peridical, <u>Fjalja</u>, warning against the dangers of a "totalitarian reading of literature," which becomes overly suspicious of everything," and making the case that

> we do not base our opposition to putting
> literary works on trial on a bourgeois
> untouchability or a 'purity' and 'elevation'
> of the arts, or on the need for some kind
> of compassion toward poets, but rather on

the need to encourage those artistic
aspirations and directions that do not
evade the true problems of the world in
which we live, to direct the artistic
inspirations toward the very essence of
our common survival on this earth.(74)

But the press was not content to defend its domain
abstractly, but proceeded to put these ideas into
practice. Though at least some Yugoslav newspapers
enjoy access to all party sessions,(75) Večernji list
lodged protests in May 1982 against the secretiveness
with which matters proceeded in Slovenia. In
particular, Večernji list was disconcerted that the
Croatian party declined to announce its elected leaders
ahead of the Congress.(76)

A more recent article in Zagreb's Start magazine
even dared to call into question the rectitude of the
behavior of party members. According to Start,

although there are no precise figures on
how many members of the LC are among those
who have committed crimes, economic offenses,
serious misdemeanors, and breaches of work
duties, it is reliably known that the number
is not negligible. It is estimated, for
example, that members of the LC were a
majority in committing about 5,000 economic
offenses in SR Croatia in 1981: [enterprise]
directors, commercial directors, chief
bookkeepers, warehouse managers, sales
clerks, cashiers, etc. All of this confirms
that there are truly good reasons for
debating the moral image and differentiation
in the LC. And something else. The removal
of opština officials and [enterprise]
directors (which in recent days we have
been reading about often in daily newspapers)
is evidence that the supervisor and the
worker are equally responsible for poor
work and abuses.(77)

It is one thing to point to abuses and corruption. It
is quite another matter to charge that party members
are responsible for a majority of economic crimes, as
Start did. Clearly, some sectors of the press were
attempting to take some journalistic ethic for their
guide, rather than considerations of party prestige and
party policy.

One of the earliest salvoes in the conservative
counterattack came in September 1982, when Dragoslav
Marković, a member of the CC Presidium, bemoaned that
"[Yugoslav] journalists behave like inspectors of
social self-management, above the entire mechanism of
our society."(78) Another Presidium member, Kosta
Krajinčanić, echoed these sentiments, telling the same

meeting that the effect of media "radicality" was "to
divert attention from proper vital questions to
subordinate matters."(79)

A two-day conference of Vojvodina journalists
opened in Kikinda on October 7, 1982 to take up the
same subject. Party Secretary Nikola Stojanović
described the danger of a clash between rival centers
of power—press and party—and declared he could no
longer tolerate the groundswell of criticism in the
press.(80) And for Ivan Stambolić, president of the
Belgrade party organization,

the information media are trying more and more
often to prove that what is taking place is not
a crisis but a breakdown of the system. Instead
of seeing the League of Communists in the throes
of creative activity, they see it as being in an
agony from which it does not know the way out.
At times, it is impossible to escape the
impression that the press wishes, aspires,
and struggles to assume the role of Tito and
of the vanguard itself....The spreading of
anti-communist ideas is also apparent. How
far all this has come is evident from the fact
that the view that Lenin's nationalization was
nothing but plunder is already being publicly
printed. If this situation continues, we can
justly ask ourselves whether we should really
be surprised if, within a few months, we will
be able to read that our nationalization, too,
was plunder.(81)

Journalists had been outraged already in March-
April 1982, when local Kosovar authorities prevented
domestic television crews and photographers from NIN,
Ilustrovana politika, Večernje novosti, and other
Yugoslav periodicals from filming or photographing
renewed unrest in the province. Instead, the photo-
journalists had been hauled off to the police
station.(82) Now, the 'Vjesnik' publishing house was
criticized for the reportage of its sundry
publications, with its magazine Danas singled out for
special criticism. At the party's order, the editorial
board of freethinking NIN had to reshuffle the
positions of some of its members. The well known
writer, Duško Radović, was expelled from Radio Belgrade
because his highly popular satirical program irritated
the authorities.(83) Other periodicals—such as Duga,
Ilustrovana politika, Zum Reporter, Intervju, Auto
svet, Osmica, the Slovak-language youth paper Vzlet,
and even some specialized women's magazines—which had
been criticized for 'negative' reportage earlier in the
year (84) were put on guard.

A TAMER PRESS? (1983-1984)

By the end of 1982, editors and prominent journalists were being summoned before various party organizations and subjected to hour-long recriminations.(85) Dragoljub Trailović, editor-in-chief of Politika, and his two subordinates were forced to resign, allegedly for failing to criticize a play expressing Greater Serbian views, but actually for a variety of transgressions, including remonstrating against the federal government's decision to proclaim the exact amount of the foreign debt a state secret. Joza Vlahović, editor-in-chief of Danas, was also forced out, after Croatian official Jure Bilić assailed the Zagreb weekly for seeking to change the role of the party in society (an allusion to a series of provocative articles on that subject). In April 1983, most of the editorial board of Karlovački tjednik was fired. In June 1983, the entire editorial board of Književne novine resigned because of "various mistakes," and the magazine ceased publication. Two leading editors of the Hungarian-language youth periodical, Uj Symposion, were also fired, for "ideological-political deviations," and the editorial office of Duga was warned that it "has long gone politically astray" on the subject of interethnic relations.(86)

But instead of buckling under, the press continued to resist. In a series of articles headlined "Against a directed press," Vjesnik urged that journalists have a responsibility to think for themselves, spoke out against "a return to some kind of censorship," and argued that freedom of information contributes to political democracy and social responsibility. Vjesnik writer Marko Lolić concluded with a strong defense of "complete freedom of information."(87) Serbian journalists followed suit in April 1983, at the annual conference of the Association of Journalists of Serbia, held in Sokobanja. Most of the 120 delegates present spoke against recent party policy on the press. Politika's popular journalist, Miroslav Radojčić, probably spoke for most of those present when he told them:

A desire is imputed to us that we wish to become
partners [of the party]. I do not want to be a
partner at all. I would like to be a
journalist....The best journalists can never
be the most obedient journalists. People who
would like to have this type of journalist
have no right to complain [about] dull,
bulletin-like newspapers.(88)

This retort may have struck a sensitive chord, for about the same time, the party was reviewing, with disappointment, the findings of a recent poll, showing that 44 per cent of subscribers to <u>Komunist</u> (ridiculed in some circles for its uninspired subservience to party policy) could not recall a single article which had attracted their interest in that newspaper, while 32 per cent admitted that they did not read <u>Komunist</u> at all.(89)   <u>Komunist</u> is automatically distributed to party members without cost.

Lately, party spokesmen are claiming that the role of the media must be radically changed.(90)   Draft legislation has been introduced to give Yugoslavia its first federal press law since 1972.   A hotly debated measure, the proposed law would strengthen the role of the publishing council in appointing editorial staffs and would set up a new administrative organ, the Social Council for Information, which would be responsible for reviewing everything published and assessing its political content.   The establishment of this Social Council would, thus, unmistakably tighten post-publication censorship and weaken the position of the press vis-à-vis the party.(91)   The Slovenian SAWP organization has already gone on record as believing that federal press regulations should be limited to "regulating only the key questions" and that "the most important thing is to assure and stimulate the further socialization of public information, [and] to assure complete publicity of the work of all who participate in social decision-making."(92)

Differences of opinion within the party remain, reflecting differences in priorities.   For some, priority must be given to social "responsibility" and to avoidance of the multiple pitfalls of "sensationalism, popularization of bad taste, imitation of foreign models of the [bourgeois] way of life, foreign values and entertainment, praising and cherishing a petit-bourgeois mentality, looking down on work and creativity, cherishing the star cult, and a deviant glorification of the consumer society."(93) For others, however, stress is placed rather on "objective and honest reporting and writing," with less fretting about the risks entailed.   And while the former group tends to become dismayed when the media deviate from the party line, or from the policy in the particular republic, party secretary Dimče Belovski, representing the latter current, urged in 1984 that

public statements made [in the media] are not and need not always be a reflection of the position of the government and state. Our foreign partners should understand and accept this situation in our socio-political system. We must get them used to the fact that positions stated publicly by newsmen, socio-political organizations, the Socialist

Alliance, the Trade Unions, the youth
organization, the League for Peace, and even
the League of Communists of Yugoslavia need
not always and in every way coincide with [the]
position of the government and that every public
statement cannot and should not be interpreted
as the stance of the state....[Indeed,] there
is no need for or even any possibility of trying
for uniformity.(94)

CONCLUSION

The Great Political Experiment in which the LCY
has been engaged since the institution of self-
management in the early 1950s has been to create an
entirely new political formula, synthesizing strands of
anarchism, communist collectivism, and even classical
liberalism into a new political tradition. The
difficulty in smelting these rival traditions, together
with the alternative views of the smelting held by
different political currents in the country, account,
at least in part, for the girations and fluctuations in
the political evolution of postwar Yugoslavia.

The same predicament is reflected in the debates
and struggles over press policy. What the party would
like, ideally, is to create a 'self-managing' synthesis
of anarchism and communist collectivism in the sphere
of the media, to create a "socially responsible" press
intuitively responsive to party preferences broadly
conceived. But despite all the clamor about 'anarch-
liberal' and 'technocratic' ideas, at least some party
officials and many journalists are sensitve to the
strengths and advantages of an independent or
autonomous press. The problem is how to square the
circle.

Stevan Nikšić, a Yugoslav writer, addressed this
issue recently. "None of the existing models of the
press," he wrote,
created within the frameworks of the system of
bourgeois pluralist democracy or the one-party
system of state socialism is in the position to
respond to the specific demands of self-managing
society and of its social and political
organization.

A new, original, Yugoslav 'model' of the
press, of a self-managing press, has, up to now,
not been devised in Yugoslavia. The truth is it
is being created, formed incrementally, already
more than three decades. But that process does
not flow smoothly, [or] without problems...(95)
According to Nikšić, Yugoslavia has failed thus far to
work out a clear concept of the press, and there have
been serious abuses both in the direction of

manipulating the press as a transmission belt of party policy and in the direction of antagonistic rivalry with the authorities. Hence, in his view, "the press...[is] today probably one of the weakest links in the Yugoslav political system."(96)

But if the weaknesses and internal contradictions of the Yugoslav press, like its strengths and unique perspectives, are but the reflection of the weaknesses, internal contradictions, strengths, and unique perspectives of the Yugoslav political system, then it is folly to expect a final resolution of differences over the press, as long as the internal contradictions and conflicts of the system itself continue.

123

NOTES

1. See, for example, a report on the escape and
   recapture of serious criminals in Croatia, in
   Politika (March 26, 1984), and reports of other
   criminal cases in _Vjesnik_ (December 2 and 12,
   1984, and March 8, 1985).
2. Paul Lendvai, _The Bureaucracy of Truth: How
   Communist Governments Manage the News_ (Boulder,
   Colo.: Westview Press, 1981), p. 52; and Gertrude
   Joch Robinson, _Tito's Maverick Media: the Politics
   of Mass Communications in Yugoslavia_ (Urbana,
   Ill.: University of Illinois Press, 1977), pp.
   130-153. I have also discussed the press briefly
   in Pedro Ramet, "Yugoslavia 1982: Political
   Ritual, Political Drift, and the Fetishization of
   the Past," in _South Slav Journal_, Vol. 5, No. 3
   (Autumn 1982), pp. 15-17.
3. Interview conducted by the author, Ljubljana, July
   1982; and _Frankfurter Allgemeine_ (July 30, 1981).
4. For details, see Pedro Ramet, "Jugoslawien nach
   Tito--zerbrechliches Gleichgewicht und Drang nach
   Legitimation," in _Osteuropa_, Vol. 32, No. 4 (April
   1982), p. 293.
5. _Borba_ (May 20, 1971), trans. in _Joint Translation
   Service_ (JTS), No. 5940, p. 45.
6. Interviews with newspaper editors, Ljubljana and
   Zagreb, July 1982.
7. Interviews with magazine editors, Belgrade and
   Zagreb, July 1982.
8. Interviews with journalist, Belgrade, and
   newspaper editor, Ljubljana, July 1982.
9. Interview, Ljubljana, July 1982.
10. Carter R. Bryan, "The Press System of Yugoslavia:
    Communism with a Difference," in _Journalism
    Quarterly_, Vol. 43, No. 2 (Summer 1966), p. 294;
    and _Vjesnik_ (November 3, 1982), summarized in
    Foreign Broadcast Information Service (FBIS),
    Daily Report (Eastern Europe), November 19, 1982,
    pp. I4-I6.
11. Quoted in Antony Buzek, _How the Communist Press
    Works_ (New York: Frederick A. Praeger, 1964), p.
    112.
12. _Osmi kongres Saveza komunista Bosne i Hercegovine,
    18 maja 1982_. (Sarajevo: Oslobodjenje, 1982),
    pp. 104-105.
13. Radio Belgrade (January 5, 1975), trans. in FBIS,
    Daily Report (Eastern Europe), January 10, 1975,
    p. I14.
14. _Informisanja i sredstva informisanja u
    samoupravnom socijalističkom drustvu_ (Belgrade:
    Kosmos, June 1972), p. 89.
15. _Ibid._, p. 25.

16. Edvard Kardelj, <u>Beleške o našoj društvenoj kritici</u> (Belgrade: Kultura, 1966), p. 45, as quoted in Todo Kurtović, <u>Komunisti i aktuelna pitanja informisanja</u> (Belgrade: Komunist, April 1974), p. 37.

17. <u>International Herald Tribune</u> (Paris, June 24, 1975).

18. Lendvai, <u>The Bureaucracy of Truth</u>, pp. 126-127. This may be changing now, judging from an article by Dimče Belovski, Secretary of the Presidium of the CC LCY, which bemoaned the fact that "for many years we placed ourselves in a position of not saying a single critical word about countries we were friendly with, of skirting problems and failing to inform the public of existing difficulties. Great vacuums were thus created in the perception of the Yugoslav public and Yugoslav citizens and this led to difficulty in understanding later events that showed up the uncritical nature of such reporting." Dimče Belovski, "Yugoslavia and the World," in <u>Review of International Affairs</u> (September 20, 1984), p. 2.

19. <u>The Times</u> (London), October 9, 1969, and October 23, 1969.

20. Interview, Zagreb, July 1982.

21. <u>Politika</u> (December 18, 1971), trans. in JTS, No. 6118, p. 22.

22. The article in question is Vlado Gotovac, "Mogućnost izdaje," in <u>Vidik</u>, Vol. 18, Nos. 32/33 (July-August 1971), pp. 21-23.

23. See <u>Vjesnik</u> (February 28, 1982).

24. See Pedro Ramet, "Factionalism in Church-State Interaction: the Croatian Catholic Church in the 1980s," in <u>Slavic Review</u> (in press).

25. This is discussed in <u>Glas koncila</u> (August 7 and 28, 1983).

26. Sergej Flere, "Dekompozicija religiozne svesti kao oblik procesa ateizacije," in <u>Sociologija</u>, Vol. 19, No. 4 (1977), pp. 600-602.

27. <u>Politika</u> , (May 31, 1981), trans. in FBIS, <u>Daily Report</u>, (Eastern Europe), June 15, 1981, p. I5.

28. <u>Seattle Times</u>, (April 3, 1984).

29. Mitja Ribičič, in interview with Jelena Lovrić, in <u>Start</u> (December 10, 1980), trans. in Joint Publications Research Service (JPRS), <u>East Europe Report</u> No. 77484 (March 2, 1981), p. 64.

30. <u>Nova Hrvatska</u> (December 19, 1982), p. 8.

31. These functionaries took revenge by tricking her into making some disparaging remarks about the coffee shortage and the program of economic stabilization and obtaining a small jail sentence for her on charges of slandering the state. See <u>Neue Zuercher Zeitung</u> (February 6, 1983, and May

9, 1984); <u>Vjesnik</u> (December 24, 1982), trans. in
FBIS, <u>Daily Report</u> (Eastern Europe), January 3,
1983, p. I7; and <u>Omladinske novine</u> (January 29,
1983), trans. in JPRS, <u>East Europe Report</u> No.
83282 (April 18, 1983), pp. 176-177; and <u>Los
Angeles Times</u> (April 3, 1983).

32. Interview with magazine deputy editor, Zagreb,
   July 1982.

33. Interview, Zagreb, July 1982.

34. <u>Vjesnik</u> (March 17, 1984).

35. Novak Popović, "Sredstva javnog informisanja o
   društveno-političkim zbivanjima u Srbiji," in
   <u>Novinarstvo</u>, Vol. 17 (1981), Nos. 3-4, p. 103.

36. Quoted in Paul Underwood, "Yugoslavia," in George
   Thomas Kurian (ed.), <u>World Press Encyclopedia</u>,
   Vol. 2 (New York: Facts on File, 1982), p. 1045.

37. Tanjug (December 7, 1982), and <u>Borba</u> (October 13,
   1982), trans. respectively in FBIS, <u>Daily Report</u>
   (Eastern Europe), December 8, 1982, p. I13, and
   October 21, 1982, p. I9.

38. Underwood, "Yugoslavia," p. 1045.

39. For details, see Pedro Ramet, <u>Nationalism and
   Federalism in Yugoslavia, 1963-1983</u> (Bloomington,
   Ind.: Indiana University Press, 1984), chapter 7.

40. Interview with newspaper editor, Sarajevo, July
   1982.

41. Tanjug (June 3, 1981), trans. in FBIS, <u>Daily
   Report</u> (Eastern Europe), June 4, 1981, p. I4.

42. <u>Vjesnik</u> (October 19, 1982).

43. <u>Omladinski tjednik</u> (1970) no. 87, as reported in
   <u>Politika</u> (April 17, 1970).

44. <u>Student</u> (January 15, 1971), as reported in
   <u>Politika ekspres</u> (February 25, 1971), trans. in
   JTS, No. 5871, p. 18.

45. <u>Tribuna</u> (1982), nos. 10-11, as reported in <u>Borba</u>
   (January 29, 1983), trans. in FBIS, <u>Daily Report</u>
   (Eastern Europe), February 4, 1983, p. I8.

46. <u>Omladinske novine</u> (February 5, 1984), trans. in
   JPRS, <u>East Europe Report</u> No. EPS-84-033 (March 7,
   1984), pp. 94-95.

47. <u>Tribuna</u>, as quoted in <u>Oslobodjenje</u> (March 30,
   1984), trans. in JPRS, <u>East Europe Report</u> No.
   EPS-84-060 (May 9, 1984), p. 88.

48. <u>Omladinska iskra</u> (Split), banned in March 1981, as
   reported in Zdenko Antić, "Some Yugoslav Party
   Quarters Concerned about the Student Press", <u>Radio
   Free Europe Research</u> (February 8, 1982), p. 4;
   and Tanjug (March 15, 1982), trans. in FBIS, <u>Daily
   Report</u> (Eastern Europe), March 17, 1982, p. I8.

49. <u>Student</u>, as reported in <u>Die Welt</u> (June 15, 1982),
   trans. in JPRS, <u>East Europe Report</u> No. 81391 (July
   29, 1982), pp. 57-58.

126

50. Večernje novosti (January 22, 1982), as quoted in Antić, "Some Yugoslav Party," p. 3.
51. Antić, "Some Yugoslav Party," p. 2.
52. Oslobodjenje (January 21, 1982).
53. Student (1981), nos. 20 and 21, as reported in Antić, "Some Yugoslav Party," p. 3.
54. Kurtović, Komunisti i aktuelna pitanja, pp. 73, 67-68.
55. Tanjug (June 2, 1973).
56. Kurtović, Komunisti i aktuelna pitanja, p. 55.
57. Politika (March 21, 1972).
58. Politika (February 12, 1972); Politika (February 15, 1972); Politika (February 25, 1972), trans. in JTS, No. 6175, p. 27.
59. Jovanka Brkić, in Informisianja i sredstva informisanja , p. 40.
60. Ibid. pp. 39, 40.
61. Ibid. p. 37.
62. Predrag Ajtić, "Uvodno izlaganje," in Informisanja i sredstva informisanja, pp. 12-13.
63. Interview with a magazine editor, Belgrade, July 1982.
64. See Pedro Ramet, "Yugoslavia's Debate over Democratization," in Survey, Vol. 25, No. 3 (Summer 1980).
65. Los Angeles Times (December 17, 1980).
66. Vjesnik (April 7, 1981), trans. in FBIS, Daily Report (Eastern Europe), April 13, 1981, p. I2.
67. Tanjug (April 2, 1981), trans. in FBIS, Daily Report (Eastern Europe), April 3, 1981, p. I3.
68. Stevan Nikšić, Oslobodjenje štampe (Belgrade: Mladost, 1982), p. 232.
69. Ibid., pp. 232-233.
70. Zdenko Antić, "Kosovo Riots stir Sharp Polemics over Information Policy," Radio Free Europe Research (April 23, 1981), pp. 1-3.
71. Interview with magazine editor, Belgrade, July 1982.
72. Ibid.
73. Quoted in Vjesnik (November 3, 1982).
74. NIN, (September 20, 1981), trans. in FBIS, Daily Report (Eastern Europe), October 1, 1981, p. I27.
75. Interview with newspaper editor, Ljubljana, July 1982.
76. Večernji list (May 8-9, 1982).
77. Start (March 26, 1983), trans. in JPRS, East Europe Report No. 83734 (June 22, 1983), p. 54.
78. Borba (September 11, 1982), trans. in JPRS, East Europe Report No. 82028 (October 20, 1982), p. 85.
79. Radio Belgrade (September 11, 1982), trans. in FBIS, Daily Report (Eastern Europe), September 13, 1982, p. I4.

80. Radio Belgrade (October 7, 1982), trans. in FBIS, *Daily Report* (Eastern Europe), October 8, 1982, p. I6.
81. *Borba* (November 12, 1982), trans. in FBIS, *Daily Report* (Eastern Europe), December 1, 1982, p. I5.
82. Tanjug (April 1, 1982), and Radio Belgrade (April 1, 1981), trans. in FBIS, *Daily Report* (Eastern Europe), April 2, 1982, pp. I19-I20.
83. *Vjesnik* (October 18, 1982); and *The Guardian* (January 4, 1983), trans. into Croatian in *Nova Hrvatska* (January 16, 1983, p. 17.
84. Tanjug (February 12, 1982), trans. in FBIS, *Daily Report* (Eastern Europe), February 18, 1982, p. I11; and Tanjug (March 24, 1982), trans. in FBIS, *Daily Report* (Eastern Europe), March 25, 1982, p. I9.
85. *Neue Zuercher Zeitung* (December 23, 1982).
86. *Le Monde* (May 11, 1983), trans. in FBIS, *Daily Report* (Eastern Europe), May 11, 1983, p. I9; Slobodan Stanković, "Yugoslavia: the Party and Press Freedom," *Radio Free Europe Research* (May 19, 1983), p. 3; Zdenko Antić, "Controversy over the Role of the Press in Yugoslavia," *Radio Free Europe Research* (February 25, 1983), p. 3; Slobodan Stanković, "New Efforts in Belgrade to 'Discipline' the Press," *Radio Free Europe Research* (July 13, 1983), p. 3; Slobodan Stanković, "Top Zagreb Journalist Forced to Resign," *Radio Free Europe Research* (May 19, 1983), p. 1; and Tanjug (February 7, 1983), trans. in FBIS, *Daily Report* (Eastern Europe), February 8, 1983, p. I16.
87. *Vjesnik* (February 17, 1983).
88. *Danas* (May 24, 1983), quoted in Stanković, "New Efforts," p. 3.
89. Slobodan Stanković, "Yugoslav Party Weekly Criticized; Press to be 'Disciplined,'" *Radio Free Europe Research* (July 10, 1983), p. 3.
90. *Politika* (September 1, 1984).
91. Zdenko Antić, "New Yugoslav Draft Law on Information Policy Discussed," *Radio Free Europe Research* (August 9, 1983), p. 3: and Slobodan Stanković, "Yugoslavia's First Private Newspaper Proposed," *Radio Free Europe Research* (March 22, 1984), p. 2.
92. *Borba* (January 6, 1984)
93. *Politika* (July 12, 1984), trans. in FBIS, *Daily Report* (Eastern Europe), July 20, 1984, p. I5.
94. Belovski, "Yugoslavia and the World," p. 3.
95. Nikšić, *Oslobodjenje štampe*, p. 120.
96. Ibid., p. 124. See also p. 123.

Part 2

Domestic Issue Areas

6
Nationalities Policy and the "National Question"

Dennison Rusinow

Once upon a time, in the 1950s and early 1960s, few Western observers of the Yugoslav scene disagreed with the regime's claim that the Yugoslav "national question" was at least on its way to a peaceful and happy solution, if indeed it had not already been solved. They were wrong, as they soon learned and everyone now knows. Vladimir Bakarić's 1965 warning, that the national question was still "at least" the country's "question number two" which could again become its "question number one,"(1) proved to be accurate in its first part and prophetic in its second. For better or for worse (more accurately for better **and** for worse, as will be argued later), ethnic nationalisms, new as well as old, were and are still alive, well, and extremely active factors in all aspects of Yugoslav life.

Today, half a decade into a troubled post-Tito era, foreign observers and Yugoslavs within and outside the regime all agree that overtly nationalistic behavior and public disputes involving conflicting national and regional interests and perspectives are once again increasing in frequency and intensity. They also agree that these things and the deepening economic troubles, the paralysis of the political system and its divided leaderships, and the ideological and general malaise that are described elsewhere in this book are intimately related, in chicken and egg fashion, as mutual irritants locked in a historically familiar vicious circle of reciprocal escalation and intractability. There is less agreement, however, about what the current status of interethnic relations and attitudes portends and how seriously it should therefore be taken. Here the views of the observers, reflecting a similar spread in the Yugoslav press and political utterances, range from apocalyptic to almost but not quite complacent.

Judging from many speeches made at a series of meetings of regional and federal central committees and presidencies of the League of Communists devoted to this subject in 1983, for example,(2) nationalist prejudices and suspicions and the number of ominous "nationalist excesses" are at their highest levels since 1970-1971, when they were at the heart of Yugoslavia's most severe postwar political crisis to date. Evidence cited in these debates and in the press has included recent attitude surveys taken among youth across the country and purporting to show that nationalist values and prejudices are widespread and deeply rooted in another new generation supposedly indoctrinated with the "brotherhood and unity" of the Yugoslav nations.(3) At the apocalyptic end of the spectrum, some qualified observers have seen the nationalist rioting and violent outburst of anti-Serb sentiments that convulsed the Albanian population of Kosovo in the spring of 1981 as an omen of similar chauvinistic and separatist manifestations elsewhere and the beginning of the disintegration of the multinational state. Others speculate that this last has in effect already taken place, so far peacefully and piecemeal. As one of the ablest Yugoslavia-watchers puts it, "There is much to uphold the contention that the degree of power now vested in the country's six republics and two provinces...is so substantial that Yugoslavia can no longer be regarded as one country."(4)

Still others--some of them, including the present writer, with firsthand experience of the 1970-1971 atmosphere as a basis for comparison--have been unable to collect sufficient evidence to justify the contention that the current situation is already analogous and that a similar crisis (but without a Tito to resolve it) is therefore likely to ensue. Those taking this relatively optimistic line have noted, for example, that many of the recent "nationalist excesses" cited by the domestic and foreign press and Yugoslav officials turn out on closer examination to have been extraordinarily trivial or to have a doubtful or no "nationalist" content.(5) (This argument may be less persuasive when it is recalled that the escalation of ethnic nationalism that led to the 1970-1971 crisis also began with banal incidents that were similarly discounted and therefore tolerated, encouraging escalation.) Some also cite the large and unexpected increase in the number of Yugoslavs who recorded themselves as "Yugoslavs" rather than Serbs, Croats, Muslims, et al., in the 1981 census; while subject to various interpretations (discussed below), at least many of these surely represent a kind of vote, in impressively growing numbers, _against_ divisive nationalisms. Observers of this persuasion also tend to see the trouble in Kosovo as announcing a Yugoslav Northern Ireland, a festering irredentist sore that will not go away, and will erupt in periodic violence but will continue to be containable and only mildly contagious.

The important question is not whether the glass of intoxicating nationalist juices is at the moment half full or half empty--which is what much of the argument seems to be about--but whether or not it will fill up and overflow, washing away many or all of the complex institutional and political arrangements that currently define the Yugoslav "system" and perhaps even Yugoslavia as a united and defiantly independent state. Here a calculus of controversial evidence, purporting to measure the current volume and heat of various nationalist passions and prejudices, is probably a less useful indicator--unless overflow is already imminent, as some contend--than a different angle of analysis. In the longer run, if such is granted, the stability of Yugoslavia will depend primarily on the extent to which institutions and elites, themselves largely shaped by successive attempts to answer the national question, prove capable of reconciling recurring conflicts between particularistic-national and pan-Yugoslav interests and demands in a changing and currently more difficult economic and political environment at home and in the world. Looked at this way there are two interlocking dimensions, comprising a circle that may or may not be vicious: the impact of the national question on institutional arrangements and their functioning, and the impact of the latter on the national question.

SHAPING THE 1980s: THE NATIONAL QUESTION IN THE TITO ERA

During Tito's reign, the "Titoist" solution to the national question, subjected to repeated strains arising from its own weaknesses as well as from the complexity and intransigence of the question, passed through four phases. Each has left visible marks on present arrangements and on elite and popular attitudes and perceptions and is therefore an active as well as explanatory factor in the current equation that merits brief review.(6)

The first phase, like other aspects of the early postwar system a virtual carbon copy of the Soviet "solution," brought full recognition of five separate Yugoslav nations (something the <u>ancien régime</u> had latterly sought to deny even to Serbs, Croats, and Slovenes by redefining them as "tribes" of a single "Yugoslav nation") and the institutionalization of this recognition in a federation of six republics (with a constitutional right to secede) and two autonomous regions that acknowledged the even greater ethnic and historic complexity of the situation. These symbolic and formal arrangements and a considerable degree of genuine cultural autonomy and recognition of cultural differences (for example in folklore and languages) were counterbalanced by a highly centralized but carefully multinational one-party dictatorship, police apparatus, and centrally planned "command" economy. For a time this combination was not without virtues. The fact and psychological impact of even the formal creation of the republics and acknowledgement of multiple nationhood and of multi-ethnic rather than Serb-ruling apparatuses, added to popular revulsion against ethnic nationalism after the horrors of civil war, acted to pacify ethnic tensions at least temporarily. Where this was not enough, the regime and its police ruthlessly suppressed any display of what it chose to define as "nationalist" rather than acceptable "national" sentiment. In the ensuing quiet on the national front, it was momentarily possible to imagine that the national question really had been solved.

The second phase began after Yugoslavia's break with Stalin in 1948 and with Stalinism after 1950, when the regime's first modest steps in the direction of political and economic decentralization reopened the question in a new form: competition among regions and localities, and therefore among national communities, over the means of economic development. The power and incentives to take economic initiatives like the building or expansion of factories and to support and protect local economic interests and clienteles devolved to the republics and districts (opštine/općine) and their "self-managed" enterprises. At the same time, however, most investment funds, fiscal instruments, and control over foreign currency and trade remained centralized at the federal level. In this contradictory situation, interregional competition over the allocation of scarce, important, and centrally allocated resources, although argued in terms of Marxist or market economic principles, inevitably came to be regarded as competition among the nationalities. Questions like priority for basic or processing industries (concentrated in different regions), or which resource, seaport, railroad, or highway should be developed first, were again and by 1963 openly interpreted as national questions by those involved and by the public at large. Political leaders defending local and economic interests were regarded (and increasingly saw themselves) as national leaders defending vital national interests.

The first reaction to new evidence that divisive and potentially disintegrative nationalisms were alive and incarnate in communist officials as well as "reactionaries" was a short-lived campaign for "Yugoslavism," defined as a pan-Yugoslav patriotism, culture, and economy that would function as a supranational and unifying umbrella over the country's diverse national identities, cultures, and economies. The campaign coincided with efforts by conservative elements in the party and police to halt or reverse a new wave of economic liberalization and political decentralization that was drawing its principal support from Slovenia and Croatia, economically more developed and demonstrably the losers in competition for central funds and favors. For a number of reasons only partly connected with national prejudices and preferences, the most visible protagonists of the conservative and recentralizing camp happened to be Serbs and Montenegrins (widely viewed as merely taller, fiercer Serbs) in federal party and state apparatuses, including the state security service, where these two nations were in any case disproportionately and in some views dangerously overrepresented. Linked in the perceptions of most non-Serbs, "Yugoslavism" and the centralizers were seen as an ominous attempt to repeat King Alexander's efforts to decree a "Yugoslav nation" that turned out to be the self-image of the Serb nation and nolens volens a device for Serb domination and Serbianization. In the face of these reactions, the campaign for "Yugoslavism" was abandoned. Then the combined opposition of non-Serb regional leaders and proponents of economic and/or political liberalization, finally enlisting Tito's vital support, brought the downfall of the centralizers. A purge of the latter and the security service in 1966 ended the second phase.

If nationalism and national disputes were not to be suppressed by a centralized and ultimately Serb-dominated dictatorship, killing divisive nationalisms with kindness might provide an alternative solution. The third phase brought, in effect, such an effort. It was done in the name of "self-management" and by the political coalition forged in the struggle against centralism by ideological and economic liberals (only later a pejorative term in the Yugoslav political vocabulary) and regional party barons whose motivations were sometimes liberal, sometimes localist and nationalist, and sometimes all of these. The beneficiaries of the resulting expansion of political participation, liberty, and autonomy in general included individuals and a broad range of social and interest groups as well as national communities per se. It is the primacy of regional barons in the power equation that made these changes possible, and the importance of regional and national interests and prejudices in their reasons for playing this role, that justify the contention that Yugoslavia's multinationality and multiple nationalisms, hitherto and subsequently more often blamed than praised, were the principal and essential driving force behind this broad-ranging liberalization and its benefits.

A major reform of the economic system proclaimed in 1965 was supposed to introduce a genuine (socialist) market economy and enhance the power of "self-managed" enterprises--and hence, in theory, that of the working class--through a withering away of the state's role in the economy, then commonly called "de-etatization" (<u>de-etatizacija</u>), at all levels. The reforms eliminated almost all central planning and control over investment funds, which were turned over to banks and enterprises, and virtually completed the liquidation of federal economic powers, which were not largely limited to partial funding of development in underdeveloped regions and the foreign currency regime. It is now recognized, however, that <u>de-etatizacija</u> stopped with the destruction of the federal citadel, leaving other "etatisms" intact and correspondingly strengthened. With most enterprises and banks limiting their activities to the territory of a single federal or smaller unit and most enterprises too inefficient and financially weak to forswear turning to the state and party for help, tendencies to regional autarky persisted and "politicization" of the economy was in fact enhanced at the regional and local level. But for 20 years the commitment to a market economy and further <u>de-etatizacija</u> was to be as firm a part of the establishment credo, legitimizing efforts to attain them, as self-management itself.

In the political sector per se, a series of constitutional amendments and then a new constitution (in 1974) were meanwhile turning Yugoslavia into a <u>de facto</u> confederation. The powers of the federal center were reduced to foreign policy, defense, and a minimum of economic instruments, with decision-making even in these spheres to be the product of consensus among representatives of the federal units. The number of these units was also effectively enlarged from six to eight as Vojvodina and Kosovo, although still formally autonomous provinces within the Serbian Socialist Republic, acquired most of the attributes of separate republics.

Of equally lasting importance, appointments to federal as well as lower-level administrative and elective bodies, including party ones, passed into the hands of republican and provincial party and state leaderships. Rigid application of so-called "republican and ethnic keys" in apportioning and rotating senior and many middle-rank jobs (for example, ambassadorships) in all federal departments, frequently on the basis of equal numbers from each republic regardless of population, provided smaller republics and nationalities with further guarantees that their interests and cadres would be well represented--but has also complicated staffing and often had a negative effect on the quality of federal personnel, not to mention sentiments of "brotherhood and unity" in otherwise qualified individuals passed over because it was some other republic's turn for a desirable post.(7) Meanwhile, "federalization" of cadre selection now also means that those with political ambitions, knowing that their careers are dependent on the approval of the republican and provincial apparatuses who send them to Belgrade and to whose ranks they will return, are often reluctant to accept a federal post and always responsive to their home constituencies when they do. This has further increased the power and attractiveness of local offices while reducing the power and quality of central ones.

While these arrangements were evolving in the later 1960s and early 1970s, they were subjected to a severe test that produced the most serious political crisis of the Tito era. The growing autonomy of the republics and debates about how much further the process should go generated a surge of nationalist feeling almost everywhere. It was particularly intense in Kosovo, where a series of Albanian nationalist demonstrations and an exodus of frightened or bitter Serbs were a mild foretaste of 1981, and in Croatia, where young, popular, and self-confident leaders (themselves more liberal than nationalist) accepted the political help and growing influence of non-communist and nationalist elements to push demands for even fuller autonomy, with symbols of sovereignty. Federal lawmaking and administration were virtually paralyzed by mutual vetoes that constitutional amendments had made possible and that were now invoked with increasing frequency. As passions and tensions mounted, the tendency to subsume all other questions and conflicts in the national one and to interpret and simplify every issue in national terms, reminiscent of old Yugoslavia and the Habsburg Monarchy and always an important subtheme in the new Yugoslavia, again became nearly universal.

In the autumn of 1971, these trends alarmed Tito into taking drastic action. Threatening to use the army if necessary, he summarily brought about the removal of the Croatian leadership in an expanding purge of "nationalists" and "liberals" later extended to Serbia, Vojvodina, Slovenia, and Macedonia. He further denounced any "federalization" of the League of Communists of Yugoslavia (LCY), moved to reassert central party discipline and authority (as always in the sacred name of democratic centralism), and referred to key liberalizing meetings and events in party history since 1952 in ominously negative terms. The dynamics of the national question, described above as the major factor in the process of general political and economic liberalization in the 1960s, had now become the major cause of a retreat from political liberalization, again proving that Yugoslavia's multiple nationalisms are a two-edged sword.

Tito's coups of 1971-1972 ushered in a fourth phase in the "Titoist" solution. It did not change as much as many were fearing or hoping at the end of 1972. The _de facto_ confederal structure of the state was maintained and indeed reconfirmed in the 1974 Constitution; the only significant changes were in providing additional and potentially more efficient modalities for reaching agreement on disputed issues. The autonomy of enterprises and of similarly "de-etatized" social services like education and health was also maintained and formally enhanced by the mammoth Law on Associated Labor, adopted in 1976, although elevation of the Basic Organizations of Associated Labor (BOALs) to sovereign actors on the economic scene and the creation of the Self-Managing Interest Communities for social services have not worked as intended.

This fourth phase, which Tito's successors were to inherit, nevertheless differed from the third in several respects. Although "cadre selection" (the Yugoslav equivalent of the Soviet _nomenklatura_) was not really recentralized, the party in Tito's last years was again--if in lesser measure than Tito had apparently intended--a somewhat more centralized, disciplined, and authoritarian agency than in the third phase. In part, this merely reflected Tito's reassertion of _his_ unchallengeable authority. In part, it was because new regional party leaderships, although in the Yugoslav context potentially as localist and therefore nationalist as their deposed predecessors, were usually lackluster people without the inherent or accumulated personal stature, the right moment, and the local political base and following to assert or expose themselves in this way. This was particularly true of the new Croatian leadership, living under and apparently internalizing the lessons of 1971 so well that this once notoriously "liberal" regional party has become one of the most "conservative," especially in suppressing dissent.

More generally, the open expression of nationalist sentiments and intransigent defense or promotion of national-regional interests were temporarily inhibited by the freshness of the two cardinal "lessons" of the crisis that ended the third phase. The first was that Tito would not tolerate them, and that he still possessed and would use the means to intervene. The second was the meaning of the sigh of relief with which many or most Yugoslavs, including many Croats, greeted Tito's initial moves to resolve the crisis: a new awareness that nationalist sentiments and quarrels could get out of hand and threaten other equal or superordinate values. Besides, the 1970s were again economically and socially good years for most Yugoslavs of all nationalities, which made it easier to overlook or suppress the feeling that some others were getting a larger share of the growing pie than one's own nation.

Eight years of relative quiet on the national front after 1971--marred portentously, in retrospect, by more small-scale demonstrations and waves of arrests in Kosovo in the mid-1970s--must have seemed to Tito, at the end of his reign, a vindication of his action. But the embers of national and nationalist fires were not extinguished and the institutions and modalities that were used to paralyze central governments and fragment the economy along national-regional lines at the end of the 1960s were still in place, as noted above. Moreover, all of the distinguishing features of the fourth phase that made the 1970s a generally calm and stable period were or could prove to be singularly temporary. To begin with the most obvious, only Tito could have dealt with the crisis of 1971 as he did, and Tito is no longer there.

AFTER TITO: PORTENTS AND PROSPECTS

If this resumé of the national question in the Tito era presents a reasonably accurate picture, the reciprocal relationship between multiple nationalisms and changing political and economic structures and their performance--in which the national question appears, so to speak, as both an independent and a dependent variable--has not been a straightforward story leading to simple conclusions.

We have seen, for example, how the political dynamics of national diversity were arguably the most important factor in bringing about the significant expansion of group and individual autonomy and "pluralization" of participation in making public choices that characterized the later 1960s, only to play an opposite role in the early 1970s. We have also seen how the affirmation of separate nations in a federation, after the ancien régime's denial of their existence and a fratricidal civil war among them, served temporarily to assuage their nationalisms but in the longer run legitimized their assertiveness and generated new forms of dispute and means of disputing. And we have seen later how the elimination of most central powers and purses, designed to eliminate the quarrels over their distribution that had aggravated the national question in "phase two," encouraged a fragmentation of the economy along national-regional lines that is now rekindling the national question in another new-old way, as discussed below. One need not be a Marxist to see an ugly dialectic at work, or to put it more simply: a case of damned if you do and damned if you don't at each stage.

Three generalizations about the net product of this history meanwhile seem to be justified:

-- The legacy of the Tito era's first phase ("Stalinist" on the national question and in general) and of many aspects of the second phase, loaded on top of earlier experience, is a deep aversion on the part of most members of non-Serb nationalities, and of many Serbs who fear "Stalinism" more than they desire a Serb-dominated Yugoslavia, to any measures that they fear could lead back toward a centralized party autocracy or Serb domination. There is here an enduring echo, throughout Yugoslavia, of something a subsequently purged Serbian party leader said to the present writer in 1969, when the defects of laissez faire in a highly imperfect market were increasingly apparent and criticized: "We are not economic illiterates, as some economists charge. We know the economic costs of our policies. What they fail to realize is the political cost [of deviating from those policies], because there is still much Stalinism in our system and mentality; we could still go backward." Antipathy to "Stalinism" and to Serb domination are mutually reinforcing reasons for anti-clericalism, although they may affect different people. This is why, however strongly and logically they may be urged by Western creditors, the International Monetary Fund, and despairing domestic economists, any steps that smell of recentralization are and will be strongly resisted on nationalist and/or "anti-Stalinist" grounds.

-- The pivotal role in the national question historically played by Croatia and the Croats and by Serb-Croat relations has been significantly if temporarily diminished by the psychological as well as political consequences of the 1971 crisis and its denouement. The impact of these was greatest, both in intensity and in the number of individuals and social groups involved, for the Croats: the bitterness of euphoria disappointed, extensive purges of Croatian nationalists and "nationalists," the inglorious collapse of the Croatian "mass movement," the character of the new republican leadership, surprise at the survival and even extension of decentralizing reforms, and the "lessons" implicit in all of these. Initially ubiquitous bitterness has generally and variously given way to resignation, accommodation, a feeling that republican and national autonomy has gone as far as is desirable (perhaps even further), or all of the above in the same or successive moments--such is at least this observer's impression of the "mood" of most Croats, among whom the fall-out of 1971-1972 is still stronger than elsewhere. In these circumstances, the Croatian front of the national question has been unusually (and perhaps deceptively) quiet for 13 years, which is why the Croatian factor is conspicuous by its absence from the discussion of current national-question issues that follows.

-- The legacy of successive decentralizing reforms in phases two and three is two-fold and contradictory. On the one hand, much of this legacy tends to undermine the appeal of divisive nationalisms. There is very little left at the center by way of power, funds, and favors to be redistributed or other spoils to quarrel over. Most of the other "nationalist" demands that gave expression to legitimate Croatian, Slovenian, Macedonian, and other national grievances have also been met, even while those who originally made them were being purged from public life. The individual republics now have nearly as much control over their economic fortunes and cultural identities as the sovereign states in the European Economic Community (i.e., not quite sovereign control). Their local political leaderships, while actually less freely and competitively elected than in the late 1960s, are at least their own, internally imposed by co-nations rather than externally imposed by a central and nationally alien authority; and those who represent the republics in federal institutions are genuinely delegated by and responsible to these local and native leaderships. On the other hand, many of the consequences of this same process of extreme decentralization, including disintegration of the Yugoslav market into eight mercantilist and protectionist regional fiefdoms and an enhanced tendency to regard the republics as separate political and national communities (i.e., confederated nation-states), are now having an opposite and counter-balancing effect. In other words, they are undermining the undermining of divisive nationalisms that was supposed to be the happy result of regional autonomy.

The current predominance of this second aspect is a consequence and concurrently a cause of the multiple miseries that coincided with the beginning of the post-Tito era and have sorely tested his institutional and collective successors. The apparent inability of the latter to find and implement appropriate and timely responses to deepening economic crisis and unrest in Kosovo launched an expanding but so far inconclusive reappraisal of manifestly deficient economic and political arrangements. Initially inhibited by reluctance to tamper with the Titoist legacy (who could say what might come out once that Pandora's box was open?), the collective leadership is now questioning core aspects of both sets of arrangements as laid down in the 1974 Constitution and the 1976 Law on Associated Labor. As the debate expands in scope and in sound and fury, but with few and flawed conclusions and woefully limited improvement in the economimc situation, regional nationalisms have played their historic dual role as both dependent and independent variables: progressively aggravated by the course of events in the economy, Kosovo, and the debate itself, and at each stage both shaping and frustrating efforts to make existing systems work or to change them so that they will. In the process, however, some significant departures from familiar patterns may be overlooked when the plot is oversimplified into a struggle between "recentralizers" and "decentralizers," or "conservatives" and "liberals," and especially when these are typecast by nationality and on the basis of past performance.

The role of the national question in this ongoing inter-elite and public debate and as a determinant of its currently still uncertain outcome is particularly clear and important with regard to four basic issues. These are: triumphant and apparently ineluctable economic regionalism founded on ethnic jealousies, the status of Serbia's two autonomous provinces in the aftermath of the Kosovo riots of 1981, a new "Bosnian Question," and interregional consensus as a prerequisite of most decisions made by federal state and party organs. The remainder of this chapter will briefly survey the national dimension of these issues and some grounds for perverse optimism.

THE FRAGMENTED ECONOMY

In the country as a whole, the initial and until recently primary locus of the drama has been the beleaguered economy. Here everyone has been declaring <u>ad nauseam</u> that a major source of current woes and the principal barrier to "stabilization" and recovery is the disintegration of the Yugoslav market into regional-national fiefdoms. The diagnosis is not in dispute, but the disease is pervasive and resistant.

The origins and strength of these now notorious "eight closed and autarkic republican and provincial

economies" derive from a compound, with regional
nationalism as its binding element, of one original and
two subsequent aspects of Yugoslav federalism described
earlier in this chapter: the national base and
rationale of most of the federal units, devolution of
control over political appointments and careers to the
regional level, and a "de-etatization" of the economy
that stopped with the dismantling of most federal
economic powers, leaving it highly politicized at
regional and local levels and only marginally subject
to "market forces" and "self-management."

In combination, these three characteristics have
created a symbiosis of regional political leaderships
and regional economic interests perhaps best described
as classic mercantilism aggravated by modern
nationalism. Regional leaders are primarily the
protectors and promoters of their regional economies,
which are regarded as national and not merely regional
in nature. They are supported and obeyed--and
recognized as national leaders of their respective
nations, which is a potent substitute for free election
or "charisma" in establishing authority--in accordance
with how well they are seen to do it. In a world in
which the defense of "national interests" has a
superordinate and emotive value that mere regional ones
do not, the national element in this formula is its
strength (and theirs) as well as its cement. It is
also a formula that will resist changes that would
weaken any of its three elements.

In the 1970s, the worst economic and political
consequences of these petty autarkies and of zero-sum
interregional competition for inadequate and wastefully
deployed domestic resources were evaded by mortgaging
the future with the help of foreign credits, translated
into temporarily "free" supplementary resources, that
mitigated conflict (and the costs of economic
inefficiency) by subsidizing everyone's "megalomanic"
schemes. This strategy collapsed under its own growing
weight and the impact of exogenous factors (the second
"oil shock," recession in the West, etc.) just as the
post-Tito era began. The foreign credits have now come
back to haunt, and evasion is no longer possible.
Furthermore, as Steven Burg points out, the interregional compromises that facilitated decision-making
and lowered the temperature of inter-ethnic relations
in the 1970s were generally based on "trade-offs" and
"package deals" involving reciprocity, which is easier
when decisions are made incrementally. Now, however,
the more complex and interrelated economic problems of
the 1980s seem to require comprehensive responses and
have long-term and uncertainly distributed costs,
making reciprocity an elusive calculation. "In these
circumstances," Burg concludes, "it is difficult for

any regional leadership to endorse an entire 'program'. Moreover, each objects to a different part thereof, making it impossible to formulate a 'package deal' that preserves the substance of the program."(8) Rightly concerned that their respective constituencies will each scream that it is their nation that has been robbed of resources for development by any form of centralized redistribution or pan-Yugoslav economic strategy (as each did, with selective proofs, after the Reform of 1965), regional leaderships therefore find it difficult to agree on anything more than urgent stop-gap measures, often dictated by international and foreign banks as a condition for rescheduled or new credits, and hard to insist on the enforcement even of these when local interests are threatened.

The "official" and global solution, reiterated from a multitude of party and other podiums and in the general section of the Krajgher commission's program for economic stabilization (adopted in July 1983 and discussed in chapter 8) is again a "genuine" market economy and "self-management decision-making" which would complete the interrupted process of de-etatization. Whether anybody really believes that either of these sine qua non for the destruction of republic economic "etatism" is possible--the first in present and the second in any circumstances--is questionable. Meanwhile, however, an increasingly acerbic discussion of specific parts of the stabilization program and reasons for the slow implementation of ostensible agreements has included the unusual charge that leading advocates of "a so-called free market," who are sometimes accused of "Thatcherism" or "Reaganomics," are in reality "conservative neo-liberal forces...with technocratic-bureaucratic tendencies"; their goal, although perhaps nolens volens, is said to be the restoration of a crypto-capitalist system, which almost happened under the tutorship of these same "forces" in the 1960s.(9)

More remarkably, such charges now tend to emanate from Croatia, among the principal advocates of a genuine market economy in the 1960s, while the strongest defenders of a market orientation are now often found in Serbia, traditionally a stronghold of "etatist" preferences. The line of demarcation on this and more specific economic issues still tends to coincide with republican and national boundaries, but some suggestive changes of position seem to have occurred.(10) Although Slovenes and Croatians, who earn the lion's share of Yugoslavia's foreign currency, still adamantly oppose the establishment of a centralized foreign currency market, they are less certain than formerly about the virtues of genuine "marketization" and openness to world markets and prices. The reasons are partly changed perceptions of how these may affect their economic interests but also their old political fear of any recentralization, which elimination of interregional economic barriers along with marketization now seems likely to entail. Economic and "national" interests no longer seem to coincide as tidily as they once did, which opens a whole new dimension in the politics of a "pluralism of (self-management) interests."

SERBIA AND ITS PROVINCES

The dramatic Albanian nationalist disturbances in Kosovo in the spring of 1981 were the most serious and widespread breach of the peace in Yugoslavia since the 1940s. They and the Serbian nationalist backlash they provoked have temporarily overshadowed Serb-Croat relations as Yugoslavia's most acute national problem.

Kosovo is a classic case of competing irredentist claims, one historic and the other primarily demographic in nature.(11) For the Serbs, the province is the historic heartland of their nation and state, justly "redeemed" from Ottoman rule and the threat of Albanian pretensions in 1912-1913, lost and redeemed again during World War Two, and now on its way to being lost once more. For the Albanians, since the eighteenth century most and now more than 79 per cent of Kosovo's population, this demographic fact makes it an undeniably Albanian land in which the majority nation has repeatedly been denied the right to "national self-determination," i.e., to a state of its own choosing. In this situation, the national grievance subsumes all others, including the greatest poverty and highest unemployment in the country as well as the scars of ethnic discrimination and Serbian domination. Those Albanians who are irredentists in the literal sense consider Kosovo a terra irredenta of their sovereign motherland next door; for them, "Kosovo--Republic," the slogan of the demonstrations, is only a stage on the road to secession and annexation. Others, usually regarded as a minority (12) but arguably including even many putative irredentists among the demonstrators, would consider their aspirations for statehood adequately or better fulfilled in a full-fledged republic, with national symbols identifying it as a (second) Albanian state within the (con-)federal Yugoslav community of nations.

"Kosovo--Republic" is rejected as a solution on several grounds. That Albanian nationalists are said to be demanding republican status only because it includes a constitutional right to secede, which will be exercised forthwith, is the least serious because the right to secede is not credible. That formal elevation to the status of a republic is believed to be totally unacceptable to the Serbs, who have had enough trouble stomaching the <u>de facto</u> republican status achieved by their autonomous provinces in the 1970s and other blows to their national pride, is more persuasive: the prospect of eight million violently angry Serbs can be more daunting--especially for Serb leaders contemplating their political fate in the wake of such a concession--than suppressing perennial rebelliousness among 1.7 million Albanians. Finally, there is the problem of precedent: to make Kosovo a republic would legitimize questioning the status and boundaries of other federal units, a can of worms that almost no one wants to open.

Rejecting an upgrading of Kosovo's constitutional status, the regime has found nothing better than a familiar combination of repression, "differentiation" (the current euphemism for political find-and-purge), and a supposedly new program of accelerated economic development to quell the unrest. The development program is not new. Former Kosovo party boss Mahmut Bakalli, ousted in the aftermath of the 1981 riots, outlined an almost identical program in an interview with the present writer in November 1979, saying it had Tito's approval. Repression including the intimidating presence of army units in the early months and continuing arrests--official sources speak of "658 persons convicted and about 2,000 persons fined for taking part in various aspects of irredentist activity" between April 1981 and December 1983, when another serious outburst led to more arrests in the following months (13)--has been only partly effective. Largely driven underground, Albanian nationalist sentiments continue to surface in sporadic outbursts and symbolic acts like the desecration of Serbian tombstones, graffiti that appear overnight, arson, and bombings. The exodus of Kosovo's remaining Serbs and Montenegrins, already reduced to 15 per cent of the provincial population at the time of the 1981 census, also continues and is further evidence that "the security situation in the province is still complicated" (a euphemism that became a cliche in 1981).(14)

Nevertheless and as the relative optimists predicted, the Kosovo problem per se has so far proved to be a Yugoslav "Northern Ireland," festering on and doomed to periodic violence but basically containable, rather than a contagious separatism to which Croats and others would also prove susceptible. With one exception, even the predictable Serbian nationalist backlash has been inchoate and largely confined to grumbling ("Kosovo is lost"), graffiti (e.g. a self-ironic "Serbia--Republic" as a counter to "Kosovo--

Republic"), and the style and bias of most Serbian press reports about Kosovo and its beleaguered Serbs. A tidal wave of <u>Serbian</u> separatism, which would be a departure from Serbian nationalism's traditional pan-Yugoslav "hegemonism" that some observers are anticipating, is apparently still inhibited, as it always has been, by concern for the fate of diaspora Serbs in non-contiguous regions.

The exception noted above is an aggravated reopening of a discussion of the relationship between Serbia and its autonomous provinces—the multi-ethnic province of Vojvodina, with a bare Serbian majority (54.4 per cent) and large Hungarian, Slovak, and other minorities, as well as Kosovo—that was adjourned for lack of consensus in 1977.(15) The immediate issues on both occasions concern the prerogatives of the all-Serbian Central Committee and its organs vis-à-vis those of the provinces and the proper interpretation and use of two articles in the Serbian constitution that specify when and how agreement (<u>dogovaranje</u>, a term that includes the process as well as the product) must or may be obtained from the provincial assemblies, for legislation to be passed by the republican one. The underlying issue is much broader, pitting Serbian concern that partly <u>de jure</u> and partly <u>de facto</u> extensions of provincial autonomy to republic-like status is a quiet secession that has reduced their republic to "narrower Serbia," otherwise known as "Serbia without the provinces," against stubborn provincial defense of that status.

The renewal of this debate in the aftermath of Kosovo, with high tides of intensity and acrimony in the spring and fall of 1981 and again in the winter of 1984-1985, differs from the 1976-1977 round in three respects: because of Kosovo, emotions and a sense of urgency are stronger; this time the dispute is noisily public (the 1970s round, now described as also "stormy," took place largely behind closed doors); and Kosovo's political leaderships, humbled and doing penance for their province's misbehavior (except for clannish protection of compromised comrades), are not publicly playing a very active role. This means that the current phase is in effect a confrontation between Serbia and Vojvodina and therefore between Serbians (the Serbs of "narrower" Serbia) and the <u>prečani</u> ("over-the-river") Serbs who set policy in Novi Sad. The thesis that ethnic solidarity always wins out is thereby and suggestively confounded on at least one important interregional issue.

MUSLIM NATIONALISM AND THE BOSNIAN QUESTION

Five of Yugoslavia's republics are officially defined, in subtly different constitutional phrasings, as the <u>national</u> states of their respective titular nations. The sixth, Bosnia-Herzegovina, is not so defined. It is merely "the socialist democratic state and socialist democratic community of...the Muslims, Serbs, and Croats, and of members of other nations and nationalities living in it." The "Muslims" that now head this list, historically claimed by both Serbs and Croats as Islamicized members of their respective communities and thereby reinforcements for their rival territorial claims to Bosnia and Herzegovina, have been fully and unequivocally recognized as a separate South Slav nation only since 1968 and after 25 years of regime hesitation and ambivalence.(16) Today self-identifying members of this nation are a clear plurality (but not a majority) of the republic's four million inhabitants, who were 39.5 per cent Muslim, 32.0 per cent Serb, and 18.4 per cent Croat in the 1981 census. They are also the third most numerous nation in the country as a whole, where the same census recorded two million Muslims-by-nationality,(17) 81.5 per cent of them living in Bosnia-Herzegovina. Recognized (some would say invented) as a separate nation at least partly in order to end a perennially dangerous Serb-Croat territorial dispute by justifying the anomaly of a trinational republic in which no nation can claim a majority, an increasingly numerous and assertive Muslim nation has in fact reopened "the Bosnian question," which once started a world war.

Bosnian Muslim historiography, like that of all "new nations" but with better evidence than some, is busily pushing the origins of their self-awareness as a distinct cultural community and its development into a modern secular "national consciousness" back in time. However this may be--i.e., whether the regime "invented" a Muslim nation or merely "affirmed" and encouraged an existing one--its existence today, defined in terms of widespread national consciousness and variously militant and defensive nationalist behavior, is manifest to any observant visitor. Although such a thesis is unprovable, many observers would agree that the success of the 1984 Sarajevo Winter Olympics, in determined defiance of underdevelopment, financial problems, and other Yugoslavs' expectations and jokes about the alleged stupidity and primitivism of Bosnians (read Muslims),(18) is ultimately explainable only in terms of the "mobilizing" power of the national consciousness and pride of all concerned and of the Muslims in particular.

Bosnia-Herzegovina is not, however, the national state of the Slavic Muslims in the way Serbia is for the Serbs, Croatia is for the Croats, etc. Nor are those who consider themselves Muslims by nationality unanimous about the nature and implications of their particularity as a nation, which is officially defined as the composite product of autochthonous Bosnian Slav and Islamic elements and a national identity as distinct from (and close to) Serbian and Croatian national identities as these are distinct from (and close to) one another. These two problems, although essentially symbolic and a projection of "real" problems like poverty and perceptions of relative deprivation (never mind that isolated Bosnian valleys like that of Bugojno, where Tito was wont to hunt, have been desecrated by forests of factory chimneys and modern if shabby highrise housing), constitute the core of the new Bosnian question.

The idea that each South Slav (Yugo-slav) nation should have a republic of its own, endorsed for the five then official nations in the federal formula proclaimed by the new regime at its birth in Jajce in 1943 and explicit in later constitutional definitions of the five republics that bear their names, inspires many Muslims to assert their later official nationhood and its political implications by demanding that Bosnia-Herzegovina should now similarly be "theirs." But what would then be the status of those Serbs and Croats, together still more numerous than the Muslim plurality in their republic, who are also named as "co-owners" of Bosnia-Herzegovina in the current constitution? The answer, based on precedents set by other republican constitutions, is in principle clear: renouncing national pretensions to a land each of their nations has claimed as its own with great passion and periodic bloodshed for more than a century, and doing it in favor of a generally despised but once dominant group whose claim to separate nationhood most of them still do not accept, they would merely be "members of other nations and nationalities who live there," i.e., the status of diaspora minorities currently recognized in the constitutions of Croatia, Serbia, Macedonia, and Montenegro. The explosive potential of this proposal, in a region where a particularly brutal and bloody trinational civil war raged only 40 years ago, hardly needs elaboration.

The challenge of Muslim nationalism is complicated and aggravated particularly for the regime, by ambiguities in the definition of the Muslim nation and the rank-order of its characteristics: in what measure is it Islamic and in what measure "secular" or "socialist" (whatever that means) in origin and essence? In a plethora of definitions and polemics on such at first glance abstruse questions,(19) three schools are identifiable, reflecting the divergent values and interests of three rival claimants to leadership and representation of this nation in search of identity. These are the party and regime together with establishment intellectuals, the Muslim clergy and its lay supporters ("clericalists" in party parlance), and those whom the party calls "traditional bourgeois-nationalist intellectuals"--although, as a further and typical Yugoslav complication, sub rosa representatives of each group can also be found in the ranks of the others.

The "party school" no longer attempts, as it once did, to reduce Islam to a minor factor in the shaping and essence of Muslim nationhood. The "clericalists," however, insist that Islam is the determining and constitutive element. Islam and the nation are identical, and the nation is Islam. In one sense a consistent development of traditional Islamic concepts of the relationship of Islam to society and the state (Islam din wa dawla) tainted by European concepts of nationhood, this thesis is also a political claim with serious implications. If it is true, who has a better right to speak for this people and represent them in dealings with other social and political agencies, especially the (incidentally communist and so formally atheistic) state, than their clergy? And does such a nation not naturally have closer and more meaningful links with other Muslim societies and with pan-Islamic ideals than with the other and secular nations of the Yugoslav "socialist commonwealth"?

The authorities are convinced that this is what the "clericalists" are aiming at (20) and may also be apprehensive, despite public denials, that the shiver of excitement and pride with which Yugoslavia's Muslim communities are reacting to worldwide Islamic revival may presage a more active and undesirable reaction-- although foreign journalists seeking Middle Eastern echoes have beaten the backwoods for a "Yugoslav Khomeini" and evidence of fanatic Muslim fundamentalism in vain.(21) The regime is therefore hypersensitive to minor straws-in-the-wind like articles in the Muslim religious press that seem to be extolling the exclusive and superior virtues of Islam or a statement by a Muslim cleric (at a quasi-public meeting in Bugojno in 1979) that "those who eat pig come to resemble the animal they eat." Rebuttals and sanctions--e.g., the arrest of the Bugojno hodža and severe sentences for 13 Muslim "counter-revolutionaries" convicted in 1983 for reiterating (in an "Islamic Declaration") the ancient thesis that Muslims must live in an Islamic state--are immediate, harsh, and widely publicized. For the same reasons, the large number of young Bosnian Muslims studying at Al Azhar in Cairo and other Muslim universities in the Middle East, formerly proudly touted as an example of Yugoslav communism's liberal attitude to religion and to Islam in particular, have been subject to critical reexamination, resulting (inter alia and ironically) in communist regime sponsorship of the establishment of a Muslim theological faculty superimposed on the ancient medresa in Sarajevo. This is also why wartime collaboration with the occupiers and the Ustaše by many Muslim clergy is being dredged up again after being strictly banned from public discussion for many years, leading to polemics between the party-controlled press and Preporod, the fortnightly organ of the Association of the Islamic Community in Bosnia-Herzegovina, and abrupt changes in Preporod's editorship in 1979.(22) As one party official told the present writer during a discussion of this affair: "They are not going to get away with the myth that they, and not the principled position of the party on the national question, saved the Muslim community at that time."

The third or "bourgeois-nationalist" school, which actually seems to have as many advocates in the party as outside it, poses a different sort of challenge to the establishment's view and purposes. Their thesis, called Bosnjaštvo (Bosnianism), accepts the establishment view that the Muslim nation, which they prefer to call a Bosnian nation, is a modern "secular" nation in which Islam has been a vital but basically cultural formative ingredient. As such it deserves a republic "of its own," which makes members of this school vociferous proponents of Bosnia-Herzegovina's redefinition as the national state of the Muslim (or Bosnian) nation. Because this view is in principle consistent with the logic of Yugoslav federalism, its advocacy is harder to censor or punish, when it is discreetly expressed, than "clericalist" views. Advocacy of backlash counter-proposals that challenge more basic existing arrangements are, however, more readily punishable: a lecturer at the University of Sarajevo, Vojislav Šeselj, has been sentenced, in a widely publicized trial, to eight years in prison (subsequently reduced to four years), for publishing a proposal, in fact not new, that Yugoslavia be reorganized into only four republics, incorporating Montenegro into Serbia (because Montenegrins are "really Serbs") and partitioning Bosnia-Herzegovina between Serbia and Croatia (the homelands of their two true nations).

Caught between these fires, those who "affirmed" a Muslim nation are attempting to control the national and nationalist sentiments that they encouraged, if they did not invent them, to solve old problems and not

to create new ones. Their current slogan is
"differentiation and togetherness" (<u>diferencijacija i
zajedni</u>š<u>tvo</u>), which may be like trying to square the
circle. The "clericalists" are right about at least
one thing: all parties are trapped by "Europocentric"
definitions of nation and nation-state.

INTERREPUBLICAN CONSENSUS REVISITED

Frustration with stalemated federal decision-
making, non-implementation of whatever is finally
decided, with divided or indecisive leaderships, and
with the strength of protectionist regional economic
"etatism" has led an increasing number of people,
unevenly distributed by region and nation, to conclude
that a reform of the political system and not merely a
reform of political "behavior" is now an unavoidable
precondition for the changes in economic systems and
behavior that all ostensibly agree are necessary to
cope with the current economic crisis. The ensuing
debate (23) is questioning the foundation stones of the
current phase of the "Titoist solution" to the national
question. These are interrepublican consensus as a
prerequisite for federal decision-making on almost all
subjects, the "federalization" of the LCY into nine
parties (republican, provincial, and army) that has had
an analogous effect in the sphere of party policy and
its implementation, and "republican and ethnic keys"
rather than competence as the first criterion for most
federal state and party jobs. The confrontation
between Serbia and its autonomous provinces over the
parallel "federalization" of Serbia and the Serbian
League of Communists (LC) has become a subtheme in this
broader debate, which has become an apparently unending
process preoccupying and dividing party and government
forums, the press, and now a hierarchy of provincial,
republican, and federal commissions for constitutional
affairs.
    The position of the Serbian leadership, further
developed and reiterated in a set of 33 theses on "the
development of the political system of socialist self-
management" adopted by the Serbian party's Central
Committee in November 1984, is to date the least
ambivalent and apparently solid republican commitment
to a package position on these questions. It includes
the following items that directly impinge on inter-
nationality relations: specific measures to strengthen
the prerogatives of the Republic of Serbia vis-a-vis
those of the autonomous provinces; more scope for
making decisions on countrywide issues by majority vote
when interrepublican consensus cannot be achieved;
strengthening the role of the Federal Executive
Council; changes in both parliamentary and party

electoral systems to provide for multiple candidacies in both (including genuine election of federal party bodies at LCY congresses instead of merely formal "confirmation" of candidates forwarded from regional and army party congresses and conferences); enforcement of "democratic centralism" at the federal level to accompany "democratization" of the party through contested elections and other measures at all levels; and strengthening the prerogatives of enterprises at the expense of their now sovereign sub-units, the Basic Organizations of Associated Labor (BOALs), in order to make the former into stronger (and putatively market-oriented) competitors of both "polycentric" and federal "etatism."

These proposals merit two comments. First, the package as a whole defies easy labelling as "liberal" or "conservative" as these terms are usually applied, particularly by outsiders, in the Yugoslav communist context. If strengthening central authority is "centralism" and symptomatic of residual Stalinism, the two traditional defining criteria of Yugoslav communist conservatism, this is a conservative platform, which is what conventional wisdom expects from the Serbian party. If advocacy of contested elections, practical measures to strengthen enterprise autonomy and "market forces," and consistent support of the economic stabilization program's liberalizing reforms are "liberal" positions that also happen to strengthen central authority, it is harder to define and may represent predominantly liberal predilections. That this is in fact probable is also suggested by recent (but not unblemished) Serbian liberality toward open debate, disputable literature and art, and unorthodox ideas in and even outside the party ranks. Conclusion: the blurring of traditional lines and anticipated national-regional alignments already noted in considering "the fragmented economy" extends to other questions as well. Second, the usual reaction in most other parts of the country (implicit when published and explicit in conversation) has been the knee-jerk kind: if a proposal is Serbian in origin, and especially if certain supporters were previously viewed as conservative or tainted with Serbian nationalism, it must be part of a Serbian nationalist and thereby "unitarist," "hegemonistic," and possibly crypto-Stalinist plot.

Whether or not it is justified, this reaction to Serbian advocacy has tended to muzzle those in Croatia and Slovenia, for example, who are otherwise prone to favor many of these same reforms because they too despair of alternative remedies for the dysfunctional aspects of politics by consensus and polycentric etatism. Although positions on some issues are ambivalent or ambiguous here and elsewhere, those who purport to speak for these two republics and Vojvodina have become increasingly outspoken about "behavior" rather than "systems" as the principal root of current evil, which is a convenient way of denying the necessity of serious political reforms that are likely to have "undesirable" (re-centralizing) consequences. Some have been led to ask whether such defense of the status quo is not in fact the "conservative" position in present circumstances. Be that as it may, all such labelling (etiketiranje) and "a priori (pausalni) attitudes about the political acceptability or nonacceptability of specific solutions"(24) help to ensure that both advocacy and opposition are usually based more on nationality than on a calculus of "objective" group and regional or ideological interests.

The deadlock continues, further aggravating intra-elite and inter-communal relations at the federal level and in several republics, which makes the deadlock progressively harder to break. Deep divisions within the present Central Committee of the LCY have been evident since its First Session, on the day it was installed at the June 1982 party congress, when Serbia's most prominent politician, Dragoslav Marković, initially failed to obtain the two-thirds majority required for election (now by secret ballot) to the Central Committee's Presidency--an unprecedented occurrence and snub.(25) They again assumed dramatic proportions at the Tenth Session in October 1983, described in the Yugoslav press as a "stormy" meeting, during which draft "conclusions" submitted by the Presidency were rejected, rewritten into noncommittal generalities by an ad hoc committee, and then accepted in that form after a heated debate. At the Thirteenth Session in June 1984, eight months later, acceptance or rejection of draft conclusions again submitted by the party Presidency was simply adjourned, ostensibly in order to hear the views of all party members, who were bidden to an unprecedented countrywide "discussion" of the draft with an end-of-year deadline that was not met.

A new version and the purported views of "the party base" (several newspapers rudely wondered, usually with reference to other republics, whether they had been asked or told what to say by their leaderships) were finally presented to a delayed Sixteenth Session in March 1985. This time the discussion was reportedly calm and civilized, but basic differences were still manifest. They usually appeared in choices of themes (who spoke of the need for changes in the foreign currency system and who did not?) and the use of "code phrases" (which meetings and documents from as far back as 1965 were mentioned, and how often and in what context was "democratic centralism" pronounced?), which subtly differentiated primarily Serbian protagonists of liberalizing and/or centralizing reforms from defenders of the constitutional and institutional status quo, most of them from Croatia, Slovenia, and Vojvodina. The revised resolution, duly adopted after further amendments, was again inconclusive. Speakers from all regions now spoke of the Thirteenth Congress of the LCY, currently being prepared and scheduled for 1986, as a (new) deadline for decision.

Meanwhile, all agreed in a chorus of _nostra culpa_ about one thing other than obligatory recommitment to self-management and other "basic principles of the Yugoslav revolution": the party base, summoned to pass judgment in eight months of discussion, had been right in accusing regional leaderships and the Central Committee of the LCY of being more seriously and dangerously divided along national lines than the party and the populace as a whole. If true, this is also significant. Veteran foreign observers of the Yugoslav scene may be reminded of the popular view, just before the crisis of 1970-1971, that regional-national political leaderships were in fact promoting and exaggerating regional-national differences to save themselves, whether "unitarist" or "nationalist," from political and social redundancy.(26)

Sometimes referring to 1970-1971 and always to the allegedly imminent risk of serious social unrest and inter-communal turmoil if party disunity and no clear policy choices continue, some frustrated speakers at the Sixteenth Session reiterated that "time is not working for us" in urging that the nettle be grasped sooner rather than later. As one Macedonian member put it, "the inertia of [the] status quo is making the situation still worse, and it comes to a point where retroactive readiness to change something will no longer have a practical effect."(27) Such warnings also appear to presume that continued deadlock at the center will lead to one of three outcomes, each of which some people might view with enthusiasm: an inertial tendency toward an even looser confederation; disintegration of the state, either in installments as the "end game" of confederation or suddenly and violently if national antagonisms continue to escalate; or some kind of coup d'etat to forestall or reverse either of the above. The logic of the triad is impressive, but another intermediate outcome that could forestall all three--a new supranational political alliance, similar in effect to the "reform coalition" of 1964-1969--is also possible and merits consideration.

156

Surveying these same recent developments up to the June 1984 Central Committee meeting, Steven Burg divides the Yugoslav leadership into three "tendency groupings" that he tentatively labels "confederationalists," "ideological conservatives," and "liberal reformers," each for the moment blocking effective action by the others.(28) The first will by definition comprise regional (but perforce not always national) leaderships seeking to defend or expand their political autonomy and economic power at the expense of the center. It presently appears to include all except a few mavericks in the leaderships of Slovenia, Croatia (including its Serb members?), and multinational but predominantly Serb Vojvodina. The second, a regionally and nationally more heterogeneous group whose adherents Burg finds primarily "among the military and veterans, members of the revolutionary generation, and leaders of the underdeveloped regions,"(29) include all "who are generally sympathetic to a more centralistic, primitively egalitarian, and 'closed' model of society...and hostile to the establishment of a market economy and its integration into the world economy." The third "are found primarily among the Serbian party leadership, and especially the Belgrade party organization," but also among economists (to whom I would add banking and business circles), establishment as well as dissident social scientists and other intellectuals, and individual politicians in other regions, where their impact is less significant because they lack support from their respective party organizations.

I have quoted and paraphrased this classification at length because it is persuasive and a marked improvement over my own latest attempt to do the same thing,(30) and also because the conclusions which Burg derives from it correspond to my own impressions of the current situation and possible futures. Even if the mutual blocking power of these groupings or "tendencies" continues to frustrate substantive reforms of inefficient political and economic institutions and agreement on long-term global strategies, ways of muddling through more effectively than to date—of restoring an effective and responsive central governance sufficient unto the day and its problems—can be found in existing constitutional and statutory arrangements. These permit decisions to be made at the federal level by majority vote, or in other ways that also evade the need for interrepublican consensus, in prescribed subject areas and circumstances (which are open to broader construction than has so far been the case) by several federal institutions acting singly or in combination. These are the collective State Presidency (which also has other deadlock-breaking

powers previously exercised by Tito), the Federal
Chamber of the Federal Assembly, and in the party
realm, the collective Presidium of its Central
Committee.(31) What has been missing--except on rare
"emergency" issues like annual "provisional" interrepublican allocations of foreign currency--has been
the will to use these modalities. As Burg argues,

>to do so would require a majority coalition
>in all of the above institutions, and enough
>broad-based support to ensure compliance.
>Ideological conservatives, although the most
>powerful tendency at present and seemingly
>in the majority in the recently-elected
>Presidency, could not do this alone. They
>do not appear to offer any program that
>would be broadly acceptable either at home
>or among the country's international
>creditors. Liberal reformers, on the other
>hand, while the least powerful tendency,
>have formulated an acceptable and compre-
>hensive program. Moreover, that program
>contains centralizing elements attractive
>to ideological conservatives. While the
>difficulty of establishing a stable majority
>of any kind at this time, in support of any
>policy, should not be underestimated, a
>coalition between ideological conservatives
>and liberal reformers, based on a shared
>belief that "something must be done," might
>establish the requisite conditions for a
>strategy of "governance by temporary
>measures."(32)

Burg believes (and I agree) that current events
"give the strong impression that such an alliance may,
in fact, be emerging," which would be a curious
permutation of the coalition between regional-national
political barons (Burg's "confederationalists") and
liberal reformers that gave rise to the "liberal
ascendancy" and reforms of 1965-1971. This one, if it
happens, would obviously require a different and
peculiar label. More importantly, such a further
incremental adaptation of institutions and elites to
the dual and often contradictory exigencies of the
national question and economic problems would buy badly
needed time for longer-term improvements in both the
structure of the economy and inter-nationality
relations. On the second score, moreover, time present
and future may be working together with the lessons of
time past to generate a renewed and enhanced awareness
that a Yugoslav community of vital interests and values
exists and can provide an adequate functional
substitute for a (non-existent) national community in
building and maintaining a viable, prosperous, and

independent modern state. One argument in favor of this possibility concludes this chapter.

THE "YUGOSLAV IDEA" REVISITED

A serious flaw in the concept of federalism as the basic solution for Yugoslavia's national question is also a potentially two-edged sword that can unite as well as divide. The republics, except for Bosnia-Herzegovina, are in theory the national states of their respective nations, bound together in a federation. However and with the exception of Slovenia and "narrower" Serbia without its autonomous provinces, all of them contain numerous and often large national minorities and are in actuality multinational states, a series of "Yugoslavias" writ small. Even Slovenia, which is adding a growing army of Yugoslav <u>Gastarbeiter</u> (immigrant laborers) from other, less developed republics to its small historic Italian and Magyar minorities, is becoming multinational.

The potential for trouble arising from this flaw in a theory that mistook historical for ethnic frontiers--not out of ignorance but <u>faute de mieux</u> because ethnic state frontiers cannot be drawn in an ethnic patchwork--is most obvious in three cases. The first is Croatia, with its many minorities and in particular its large Serb community (15 per cent of the total population) with lively memories of the attempted genocide by Croatian <u>Ustaše</u> during World War Two. The others, already discussed, are the national definition of trinational Bosnia-Herzegovina and the problem of Kosovo, along with adjacent Albanian-inhabited parts of Macedonia and Montenegro.

Paradoxically, however, the multinationality of the republics and provinces can also be a force promoting at least a reluctant and again <u>faute de mieux</u> reconciliation. Again to cite an obvious and important case, concern for the fate of fellow-Serbs living as sizeable minorities in Croatia, Bosnia-Herzegovina, Kosovo, and elsewhere can and often does not make Serbs the most genuinely "Yugoslav" of Yugoslavs. They might prefer a Yugoslavia again dominated by Serbs as its most numerous and allegedly "state-making" nation (<u>državotvorni narod</u>), but if this is not possible, then Yugoslavia as it now exists is clearly preferable to a disintegration that would deliver up so many of their kinsmen to alien and potentially unfriendly rule. The ethnic map reveals many other cases of this kind.

The conclusion is that a Yugoslavia dissolved into small and only supposedly national sovereign states would be condemned to a plethora of ill-treated minorities and a plague of mutual irredentisms, increasing their susceptibility to external domination and exploitation as well as the certainty of permanent strife and risk of war among them. This is as true today as it was in 1915, when Professor R. W. Seton-Watson, the great Scottish patron of Slav and Romanian national aspirations in Central Europe, wrote to Serbian Crown Prince Alexander (later King of Yugoslavia) to beg him not to deviate from the goal of a Kingdom of the South Slavs as an Allied war aim in favor of the lesser one of a Greater Serbia:

> ...For it would certainly be unnecessary to point out to your Royal Highness that if Croatia became an independent state alongside Serbia, the situation of the latter would be still less favourable than before the war; for in that case the two sister nations would be enemies; in place of the idea of the national unity of all the Serbs, Croats, and Slovenes in a single state, we would have an acute conflict between two opposing Slav programmes; and in view of the impossibility of drawing any territorial line of separation between Serbs and Croats, each of the two states--the new Serbia as well as the new Croatia--would be torn apart from one end to the other by two rival irredentisms--the Catholics and Muslims of enlarged Serbia looking to Zagreb, and the Orthodox of Dalmatia and Croatia to Belgrade. I do not need to emphasize the extreme danger of such a situation, from a political, economic, military, and above all dynastic point of view.(33)

The same argument applies, _ceteris paribus_ and in varying degrees of intensity, to all of the nationalities of today's federation under Tito's institutionalized communist dynasty. In this sense, the impossibility of drawing ethnic frontiers in the Balkan ethnic patchwork, a primary reason for the invention of the original "Yugoslav idea" as historic competitor to Greater Serbian, Greater Croatian, and other unitary or separatist concepts, continues to be a compelling reason for a united Yugoslavia. There is considerable evidence, both impressionistic and from some survey research (which contradicts other surveys, as is usual in that business), that most Yugoslavs share this view and draw appropriate conclusions.

Perhaps this is also one reason for the remarkable growth, which took everyone by surprise, in the number of Yugoslavs who recorded themselves as ethnic "Yugoslavs" in the 1981 census. Despite what seems to have been an official desire to discourage the choice of this non-national self-designation,(34) the number who did so rose from a nadir of 273,077 in the 1971

160

census, 1.3 per cent of the population at the time, to
1,219,024 or 5.4 per cent of the 1981 total (with 36.3
per cent Serbs, 19.8 per cent Croats, 8.9 percent
Muslims, 7.8 per cent Slovenes, 7.7 per cent Albanians,
6.0 per cent Macedonians, and 2.6 per cent
Montenegrins). Almost all (94.2 per cent) of these
1981 "Yugoslavs" were found in three republics: in
Serbia with 36.3 per cent of them (22.3 per cent in
"narrower Serbia" and 13.7 per cent in Vojvodina), in
Croatia with 31.1 per cent, and in Bosnia-Herzegovina
with 26.8 per cent. This distribution suggests that
most of the approximately one million "new" Yugoslavs
since 1971 are "former" Serbs, Croats, and possibly
Muslims or offspring of same being recorded for the
first time. This logical conclusion is in turn
supported by an analysis of changes in the sizes of
these nations as recorded in the same censuses, also
taking into account differential birth and death rates
(compiled from other sources) to calculate their
anticipated "natural increment" in the intervening 10
years.(35) The 1981 census recorded about 99,000 fewer
Croats and 3,000 fewer Serbs than in 1971, but
factoring in birth and death rates during that decade
to determine how many adherents these nations "should"
have had in 1981 indicates a far larger number of
apparent defections: approximately 361,000 "lost"
Croats and 543,000 "lost" Serbs. Even the Muslim
nation, whose high birthrate accounts for most of its
growth by 267,000 (11.6 per cent) between 1971 and
1981, appears in this way to have lost 49,000 of its
natural increment in the same period. Despite minor
deficiencies in the calculations on which these
conclusions are based, it is suggestive that the sum of
these three figures almost precisely equals the
increase in the number of Yugoslavs recorded in 1981.

A number of explanations, some of them polemical,
have been advanced to account for part or all of the
quantity and distribution of this Yugoslav phenomenon.
A growing number of ethnically mixed marriages and
therefore multinational offspring, particularly Croato-
Serb and Croato-Slovene but also other and now
sometimes trinational combinations, clearly accounts
for some of it (and is itself a significant
development). It has also been suggested--more
ominously in the light of the history of the national
question--that many Serbs and some others have declared
themselves Yugoslavs in defiant reaffirmation of
"integral Yugoslavism," which is always widely regarded
as a disguise for the sins of "Serbian hegemonism" and
"Croatian unitarism," or in order to claim that
"Yugoslav" is, after all, also a nation or "supra-
nation," which is officially denied on theoretical
grounds but primarily because the concept of a Yugoslav

nation has historically been associated with Serbianization. Yet another hypothesis holds that fear of retribution from an imminent new wave of nationalist passions and hopes of evading it by denying their ethnicity explain the adoption of a Yugoslav identity by members of local minorities like Serbs in some parts of Croatia and others in Vojvodina (who will not become Serbs).(36) But even if all of these and others are valid explanations of many cases, there would appear to be a large residual group whose motivation is a symbolic rejection of the divisive ethnic nationalisms that have wrought such havoc in Yugoslav history and appear to be poised to do so again.

If the first and last of these hypothetical explanations together account for most of the sudden boom in the number of Yugoslav "Yugoslavs" (as a supra-national and supervenient identity and not a supra-nation), and if these represent a trend that is continuing under the surface of contemporary national and nationalist turbulence—two large "ifs"—then a race against time between the putative trend and the demonstrable turbulence may well prove to be the determining factor in the outcome and even the survival of the Yugoslav experiment. This in turn depends, however, on a gift of time that other developments described in this book may not grant. In any case, the national question—for better as the principal guarantor of some form of political pluralism and against recidivist centralized autocracy, and for worse as the primary challenge to stability and the survival of a multinational anachronism in a world of nation-states—is still question number one.

NOTES

1. In an interview in <u>Borba</u> (March 6, 1966).
2. As reported in the Yugoslav press at the time. To avoid a clutter of footnotes, specific references to leading dailies and weeklies like <u>Politika</u>, <u>Vjesnik</u>, <u>Borba</u>, <u>NIN</u>, and <u>Danas</u>, which are major sources for this chapter, will generally be omitted when the information, such as reports of meetings and events can be found--albeit selectively and with different interpretations--in most or all of them on or around the date in question.
3. As noted by George Schöpflin, "The Yugoslav Crisis," in <u>Soviet Analyst</u>, Vol. 12, No. 2 (January 26, 1983).
4. George Schöpflin, "Yugoslavia's Growing Crisis" (an update of the article cited in the previous footnote), in <u>Soviet Analyst</u>, Vol. 13, No. 25 (December 19, 1984).
5. An illustrative and notorious "excess" in the trivial category, extensively discussed in press and party for months and ending in prison sentences for two of those involved (of four years, and two and a half years), consisted of the singing of the pre-war lyrics (i.e., with the names of two Croatian national heroes in place of "forward Partisans!"), now considered nationalistic in some circles, of a traditional Croatian song at an alcoholic birthday party in a Zagreb student dormitory in October 1982 and the beating of a Serb student who complained (author's inquiries in Zagreb, December 1982; and <u>Danas</u> (April 19, 1983): other published reports apparently exaggerated what actually happened).
6. Adapted and abridged from Dennison I. Rusinow, "Unfinished Business: the Yugoslav National Question in the Tito Era and After," <u>American Universities Field Staff Reports</u> (1981), No. 35.
7. Personal observation and conversations with Yugoslav officials, various dates.
8. Steven L. Burg, "Yugoslavia in Crisis" (unpublished paper, September 1984, based in part on interviews conducted in Yugoslavia in November 1983 and May/June 1984), pp. 17ff.
9. E.g., <u>Danas</u> (September 4, 1984), pp. 4ff. But see also <u>Danas</u> (November 13, 1984), pp. 4-7, for reversion to the more traditional thesis that the "centralist" threat can be evaded by a genuine market economy that would destroy "polycentric etatism" and thereby the argument for its centralist alternative.

10. Albeit with significant inconsistency: cf. other
    leading regional press attitudes (e.g., in
    Politika, NIN, and Delo for the period in
    question) with the Danas articles cited in the
    previous note.
11. For background and details, see Dennison I.
    Rusinow, "The Other Albania: Kosovo 1979,"
    American Universities Field Staff Reports (1980),
    Nos. 5-6, which is a firsthand report on the
    situation 18 months before the explosion; Jens
    Reuter, Die Albaner in Jugoslawien (Munich: R.
    Oldenbourg Verlag, 1982); and Pedro Ramet,
    Nationalism and Federalism in Yugoslavia, 1963-
    1983 (Bloomington, Ind.: Indiana University
    Press, 1984), pp. 156-171.
12. E.g., Jens Reuter's view (Die Albaner, p. 10):
    "There is no doubt that the majority of
    Yugoslavia's 1.7 million Albanians desire
    secession from the SFRY and unification with the
    mother country, Albania."
13. "Situation and Problems in Yugoslavia's Domestic
    and Foreign Policy," in Yugoslav Survey, Vol. 25,
    No. 1 (February 1984), p. 26; Politika (May 24,
    1984); and Patrick F. R. Artesien and R. A.
    Howells, "Yugoslavia, Albania and the Kosovo
    Riots," in The World Today, Vol. 37, No. 11
    (November 1981).
14. For an official view of the situation to the end
    of 1983, as presented to the CC LCY that December,
    see Socialist Thought and Practice, Vol. 28, No. 1
    (January 1984), pp. 3-41. The text of the party's
    mammoth "Political Plan of Action" to deal with
    the Kosovo crisis is translated in Ibid.
    (November-December 1981), and in Yugoslav Survey,
    Vol. 23, No. 1 (February 1982), pp. 31-70.
15. NIN (May 17, 1981, January 3, 1982, and November
    11, 1984), and Danas (November 20, and December 4,
    1984) contain useful overviews of the 1981 and
    1984 phases with "flashbacks" to 1977.
16. The ethnogenesis of the Yugoslav Muslim nation and
    related issues are summarized in Dennison I.
    Rusinow, "Yugoslavia's Muslim Nation,"
    Universities Field Staff International Reports
    (1982), No. 8; and described in greater detail in:
    Steven L. Burg, The Political Integration of
    Yugoslavia's Muslims: Determinants of Success and
    Failure (Pittsburgh: Carl Beck Papers on Russian
    and East European Studies No. 203, 1983); Zachary
    T. Irwin, "The Islamic Revival and the Muslims of
    Bosnia-Hercegovina," in East European Quarterly,
    Vol. 17, No. 4 (January 1984); Atif Purivatra,
    "The Phenomenon of the Moslems of Bosnia-
    Herzegovina," in Socialist Thought and Practice,

Vol. 18, No. 12 (December 1974); and Pedro Ramet, "Primordial Ethnicity or Modern Nationalism? The Case of Yugoslavia's Muslims," in Nationalities Papers (in press), as well as Nationalism and Federalism in Yugoslavia, chapter 8.

17. Not to be confused with Muslims as a religious category, in Yugoslavia also nominally including Turks, most Albanians, some Macedonians, etc., but not atheist Muslims-by-nationality.

18. E.g.: "Question: What happens when a bear migrates from Lika [one of the most backward Croatian regions on the Bosnian frontier] to Bosnia? Answer: Lika has lost a leading citizen, but Bosnia has gained an intellectual."

19. Numerous examples are cited in Ramet, "Primordial Ethnicity."

20. Interviews with officials in Sarajevo and Belgrade, January 1981.

21. Basically a silly game: Yugoslav Muslims are not Shiites and Islam in the Balkans, like most "frontier" Islam (cf. Indonesia), tends to be liberal if not heterodox.

22. The focus of this polemic was a book by Dervis Sušić, a Muslim writer and ex-Partisan, which strongly criticized the behavior of Muslim clergy and politicians before and during the war, and which was serialized in the quasi-official Sarajevo daily, Oslobodjenje.

23. The following is again largely based on the Yugoslav press and conversations with what journalists call "well-informed Yugoslav sources." Other contentious issues in this broad-ranging and crucial debate, including de-federalization and cadres policy, are discussed in chapter 2.

24. Milan Potrč (Slovenia), speaking at the Sixteenth Session of the CC LCY and quoted in Borba (March 7, 1985).

25. First publicly revealed only three months later by then CC Presidium Chairman Mitja Ribičič. For details, see Dennison I. Rusinow, "Yugoslavia 1983: Between 'Continuity' and 'Crisis,'" University Field Staff International Reports (1983), No. 3.

26. As noted in Dennison I. Rusinow, "The Price of Pluralism," American Universities Field Staff Reports, Southeast Europe Series, Vol. 18, No. 1, 1971).

27. Milan Džajkovski, as quoted in Borba (March 7, 1985). The instant conclusion that "nothing happened" at a session previously touted as a moment of decision, although justified by its public and published proceedings, is subject to one caveat: almost all foreign observers of the

Eighth Congress of the LCY in 1964 came to the
same conclusion about that gathering, which later
proved to be highly inaccurate.

28. Burg, "Yugoslavia in Crisis," pp. 30ff.
29. But far from all, particularly in the
"revolutionary generation" category. The myth
that all or most old Partisans in former or
current leaderships are instinctive
"conservatives" if not quasi-Stalinists was never
true, as observers well acquainted with some of
them have always known. The strikingly "liberal"
public position recently assumed by a number of
these is therefore not really a surprise.
30. See Rusinow, "Yugoslavia 1983."
31. The circumstances and modalities are stipulated in
the party statutes and in the 1974 Constitution,
Part 4, chapters I, II, and IV (see especially
Articles 286, 294, 302, 319, and 356.
32. Burg, "Yugoslavia in Crisis," pp. 37ff.
33. Hugh Seton-Watson, Ljubo Boban, et al. (eds.), R.
W. Seton-Watson and the Yugoslavs--Correspondence
1906-1941 (London and Zagreb: Yugoslav edition by
Grafički zavod Hrvatske, 1976), I, p. 238: letter
of September 17, 1915 (in French).
34. For example, the 1981 instructions for census-
takers (copy in author's files) implicitly
disparaged and disapproved this answer: "Question
9. Adherence to nation, nationality, or ethnic
group....If a citizen wishes to record Yugoslav as
an answer to this question, the census-taker is
obligated to record even that answer, although the
citizen does not thereby declare himself
concerning adherence to a nation or nationality"
(emphasis added).
35. Ruža Petrović, "The National Composition of the
Population," in Yugoslav Survey, Vol. 24, No. 3
(August 1983), pp. 21-34, which contains the
calculations cited below, and Nacionalni sastav
stanovništva po opštinama konačni rezultati
(Belgrade: Savezni zavod za statistiku,
Statistički bilten No. 1295, May 1982), passim.
36. Found, for example, in an interview with Dušan
Bilandžić, published in Vjesnik's "Sedam dana"
supplement (April 16, 1983): this particular
interview, reportedly done in haste, was widely
misunderstood and precipitated an extended polemic
in subsequent issues of the same and other
journals.

7
The Dynamics of Yugoslav Religious Policy: Some Insights from Organization Theory

Pedro Ramet

In approaching the subject of religious policy, there are several questions with which one is confronted. First, should religious policy be treated as an autonomous issue area in isolation from other issue areas, or should it be interpreted with attention to a purported organic relationship with other issue areas, such as nationalities policy, educational policy, foreign policy, and so forth? Second, should policy in general, and religious policy in specific, be seen as the result of a factionalized environment or as the product of a system in which internal conflicts are of no policy importance? Third, should policy be seen as the product of clear objectives or as a complex outcome of sundry variables? Fourth, does the policy of a given organization, in this case the League of Communists of Yugoslavia (LCY), tend toward consistency or inconsistency over time and space? And fifth, is religious policy (in Yugoslavia) best viewed as an output of the system as a whole or in terms of the separate policy-making of the system's federal sub-units? In the following pages, I shall argue that Yugoslav religious policy is better understood in terms of the complex side of these alternatives and that, in this regard, it is a typical Yugoslav policy sphere. I shall also argue that organization theory can be useful to highlight some structural and behavioral facets of Yugoslav religious policy.

Organization theory is concerned, among other things, with elaborating the environment in which decisions are made and policies carried out. It assumes the necessity of some principle of hierarchy and of a division of labor, and a purposiveness in

*I am grateful to Zachary Irwin and Robin Remington for their helpful comments on an earlier draft of this chapter.

organizational behavior.(1)   Some of the insights
gained from organization theory are, I believe, helpful
in understanding the dynamics of Yugoslav religious
policy-making. At the same time, the evidence from the
Yugoslav case is germane to an assessment of the
relative applicability of alternate theories of
organization.

Fred Luthans outlines four distinct approaches in
organization theory.(2)   <u>Classical bureaucratic theory</u>,
which may be associated with Max Weber, Peter M. Blau,
and Robert Michels, presents a mechanical model of
bureaucracy, in which the tendency to oligarchy is
sometimes seen as irresistible.(3)   <u>Behavioral theory</u>,
which may be associated with James G. March, Herbert A.
Simon, and Philip Selznick, stresses the role of
people, their perceptions and motivations, in
organizational behavior and policy-making.(4)
Behavioral theory stresses organizational structure in
both its formal and informal aspects.   <u>Systems theory</u>
stresses the input-output aspect of organizational
behavior, as well as the interrelatedness and
inderdependence of elements in the whole.   Systems
theory is concerned, then, with identifying the
"strategic" points in the system, the "nature of their
mutual dependency," the processes which link the system
together, and the goals of the system as a whole.(5)
And finally, <u>contingency theory</u>, which may be
associated with Joan Woodward, William L. Zwerman, Paul
L. Lawrence, and Jay W. Lorsch, urges that
environmental factors such as, specifically,
technology, may be more important than organizational
structure and processes for organizational output. The
findings of Lawrence and Lorsch may be summarized as
follows:
        1. If the environment is uncertain and
        heterogeneous,   then the organization should be
        relatively unstructured...
        2. If the environment is stable and homogeneous,
        then a rigid organization structure is
        appropriate.
        3. If the external environment is very diverse
        and the internal environment is highly
        differentiated, then there must be very elaborate
        integrating mechanisms in that organization
        structure.(6)
While all of these theories have something to offer,
the <u>behavioral</u> variant seems especially well suited to
the Yugoslav case, and most of the citations from
organization theory, in what follows, come from
behavioralists.

THE INSTITUTIONAL SETTING

The regime's relations with religious bodies are conducted through two parallel structures. On the one hand, there are the republican Offices for Relations with Religious Communities, which are nominally subordinate to the Federal Office for Relations with Religious Communities, but which are, like almost everything in Yugoslavia, actually run by the respective republic governments. Alongside these offices are similar ones established under the rubric of the Socialist Alliance of Working People of Yugoslavia (SAWPY) and its republic branches. These are separately staffed, but judging from their activity and from the frequency of mention in the press, it seems clear that the governmental offices play a more important role in the day-to-day management of Church-state relations.

In form, this has the appearance of hierarchical subordination. In practice, each republic has its own separate legislation regarding religion, which differs in particulars from republic to republic,(7) and hence the guidelines, under which each republican Office for Relations with Religious Communities operates, differ.

While the party itself has, technically speaking, no formal apparatus for coordinating its religious policy, it exerts its influence indirectly through the aforementioned agencies and also through the press, which has often served as the vehicle for expressing party views on the subject of religion. And finally, the Marxist intellectual community, most especially sociologists concerned with religion, contribute to the understanding of religion in Yugoslavia and thus to defining the contours of religious policy in that country.

Add to this federalization the confessional heterogeneity in the country and one arrives at a strong expectation that religious policy will have distinct differences from one republic to the next. This expectation seems to be borne out by the evidence.

In Macedonia and Slovenia, Church-state relations are cordial, and in Macedonia one may even speak of a certain warmth in the relationship. Indeed, the regime was strongly supportive of the creation of an autocephalous Macedonian Orthodox Church in 1967, seeing in this ecclesiastical structure an instrument in its polemic with Bulgaria over the ethnicity of the Macedonians. In the Slovenian instance, although Catholic clergy there have occasionally spoken out on human rights issues and on the subject of "atheization" in the schools, on the whole Church-state relations are relatively uncomplicated.

The situations in these two republics are comparable in another respect, viz., the relative absence of factionalization on either side of the equation. The Macedonian political elite has every reason to support the Macedonian Orthodox Church, since both are wary of Bulgarian pretensions (Bulgaria asserts that Macedonians are merely Bulgarians), and there is no evidence of any division within the Macedonian political elite on the subject of religious policy. Similarly, the Macedonian Orthodox Church, finding its autocephaly repudiated by the Serbian Orthodox Church,(8) looks to the republican government for support; none of the Macedonian clergy have been involved, thus, in politically controversial activities.

Factionalization is also absent, as mentioned, in Slovenia. The Slovenian party organization is dominated by "liberals" and it has been years since there have been reports of any anti-Church directives in that republic. And while the same cannot be said of the Catholic Church--the only religious organization that counts for anything in Slovenia--its "progressive" wing, represented in Slovenia largely by Bishop Vekoslav Grmič,(9) is of no particular significance. In Slovenia, as in Macedonia, thus, there are strong sources of impetus toward cooperation, and Church-state relations in these republics are organizationally simpler.

The Macedonian Orthodox Church is not the only religious organization in whose prosperity the LCY has had a vested interest. A flourishing Islamic community is important to the regime both because the regime has wanted to stimulate a Muslim ethnic consciousness among Bosnian Muslims and because of the importance which Yugoslavia places on its ties with the Arab world. In recent years, however, there have been repeated symptoms of rising Muslim assertiveness, including calls for a Muslim cultural society (which the regime will not allow), and demands for the redesignation of Bosnia as a "Muslim Republic," which is likewise unacceptable, since Muslims account for only roughly 40 per cent of Bosnia's population. As a result of this new Muslim assertiveness, however, the Bosnian party's policy vis-à-vis the Islamic community has become tinged with ambivalence.(10)

In fact, Church-state relations are generally more complex in Bosnia, as they are also in Croatia and Serbia. This is a result of the greater complexity of issues, the Serb-Croat rivalry in the former two republics (producing a generally higher level of tension in interethnic and thus in interconfessional relations), and the greater degree of factionalization both within the political elites and within the

respective religious bodies. The first two issues are
interrelated, for it is the greater ethnic and
confessional heterogeneity which, in part, accounts for
the greater complexity of issues. The political elites
here, unlike those in Slovenia and Macedonia,
repeatedly return to the theme of "clerico-
nationalism," warning the Churches to steer clear of
nationalist causes.(11) There are also specific
features that distinguish one republic from the other:
in Croatia, there is the traditional rivalry between
the archbishops of Zagreb and Split, as well as the
presence of theologically liberal clergy in the
Christianity Today organization. In Bosnia, the
Franciscan presence adds a complicating variable to the
equation; and in Serbia, the institutional weakness of
the Serbian Orthodox Church has meant that it has been
less capable than the Catholic Church of mounting
effective challenges to regime policies. And where
factionalization is concerned, there have been
tensions, in these republics, between theological
liberals and theological conservatives in the Catholic
Church, between Franciscans and diocesans again in the
Catholic Church, between lower clergy and hierarchy in
the Serbian Orthodox Church, and between "liberals" (in
different senses) and "conservatives" where the
political elites are concerned.(12)

In the other federal units, finally, Church-state
issues are less salient, even though the press has
occasionally accused both Muslims and Orthodox in
Kosovo of "meddling" in nationalism. Vojvodina is
distinct in being the only federal unit with a large
number of active Protestant churches. In Vojvodina, as
in Montenegro, Church-state relations are distinctly
low key.

Overall, thus, institutional decentralization and
the federalization of policy-making have resulted in
the emergence of discrete policy arenas. The distinct
concerns and differences in factionalizaation assure
that religious policy will vary from republic to
republic.

Behavioral-organization theory tells us that
decentralization, such as that found in Yugoslavia,
    results in departmentalization and an
    increase in the bifurcation of interests
    among the sub-units in the organization.
    The maintenance needs of the subunits
    dictate a commitment to the subunit goals
    over and above their contribution to the
    total organizational program.(13)
Bifurcation of interests is also reinforced by
differences in the training and experience of
administrators in different republics. Given local
environmental differences, March and Simon inform us,

FIGURE 7-1(15)

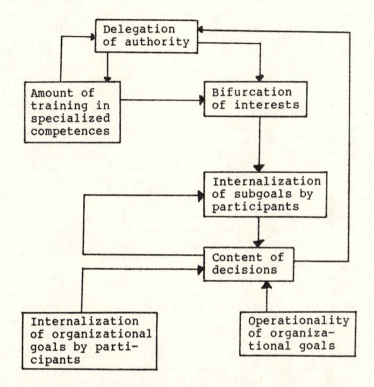

the struggle for internal control not only affects directly the content of decisions, but also causes greater elaboration of sub-unit ideologies. Each sub-unit seeks success by fitting its policy into the official doctrine of the large organization to legitimize its demands. Such a tactic increases the internalization of subgoals by participants within sub-units.(14)

This tactic also obscures the differences between policies of the federal sub-units, since each sub-unit presents its own policy, of necessity, as consistent with the overall policy of the organization, in this case the LCY. The resulting pattern is reflected in Figure 7-1, which is a modified version of a model originally devised by Selznick (see above).

RELIGIOUS DEVELOPMENTS IN CROATIA AND BOSNIA

The recent Church-state frictions in Yugoslavia are a case in point and bear out the relevance of organization theory. For within the federalized Yugoslav context, these frictions have been localized rather than a feature of nationwide developments. In fact, it is chiefly in Bosnia and Croatia that there have been prolonged polemics over religious conditions and religious activity. Where Croatia is concerned, the party's nervousness in the early months following Tito's death was quickened by Archbishop Kuharić's outspoken demands for an expansion of ecclesiastical prerogatives (e.g., in terms of access to army recruits and to prisoners), and by 1981, the atmosphere in the regime's relationship with the Catholic Church was soured by mutual distrust, reciprocal polemics, and periodic "corrections" which served, inter alia, to sustain the polemics. When the theologically liberal Christianity Today publishing house ran afoul of certain bishops in 1981, the regime quickly endorsed the Christianity Today clergy--in a move that was interpreted on the Church's side as unwarranted interference and that probably was, if anything, embarrassing to the clergy of Christianity Today.

Yet despite repeated reports of petty harassments of Catholic clergy in Croatia,(16) LCC policy in the sphere of religion remains the outcome of factional politics. In a striking example of this, Nenad Ivanković, longtime specialist on religious affairs for the Zagreb newspaper, Vjesnik, and spokesman for more moderate elements in the establishment, defended Popes Pius XII and John Paul II, in 1982, after their public disparagement by former Croatian Assembly President Jakov Blažević.(17)

The regime press sometimes charges individual priests with having Ustaše sympathies and with singing old Ustaše songs. It appears that these accusations are not always accurate. What they accomplish,however, is to foster the idea that ecclesiastical involvement in nationalism is apt to be fascistic. The liberal Croatian theologian, Fr. Tomislav Šagi-Bunić, recently replied to such equations in an extended discourse on The Catholic Church and the Croatian People. Rejecting any notion that the Church is entitled to identify itself with the Croatian nation, Šagi-Bunić proceeded to distinguish between "healthy nationalism" (or "patriotism") and "unhealthy nationalism," and defended the Catholic Church's "care" for the language, culture, history, and welfare of the Croatian community.(18) While the book was well received in the regime press, Croatian nationalism remains a delicate subtheme in relations between the party and the Catholic Church.

While the religious scene in Slovenia, Macedonia, and arguably Croatia too, has been unshaken by any dramatic new developments in the 1980s, the same cannot be said for Bosnia-Herzegovina, where two distinct be said for Bosnia-Herzegovina, where two distinct events have dramatically heightened the religious self-awareness of Catholics and Muslims.

The first of these was the alleged appearance of the Madonna, on June 24, 1981, to six Herzegovinan children (for the first time) in the village of Medjugorje in the district of Čitluk. The regime initially blamed Franciscan Father Jozo Zovko for concocting the miracle and put him in prison on a three-and-a-half year sentence, charging him with manipulating the believers in the interest of fomenting Croatian secessionism and anticommunism.(19)   The LC Bosnia-Herzegovina was worried that the steady stream of pilgrims to Medjugorje, which soon began to flow (at the rate of 6,000-10,000 per day), would stimulate Croatian nationalism and complicate interconfessional relations in the republic.   Yet while the party was trying to debunk the alleged miracle, the Church itself remained cautious, appointing an investigatory commission to study the miracle and pass judgment on it.

Meanwhile, the children continue to report almost daily visitations by the Madonna, who, they say, has confided various "secrets" to them.(20)   Pilgrims and tourists continue to come to Medjugorje, including many from abroad, and some 25,000-26,000 people took part in third-anniversary masses in Medjugorje in June 1984. By then the authorities were starting to see the phenomenon in a new light and began to talk of developing hotels and other touristic facilities in the area in order to attract hard currency from foreign visitors.   As of mid-1985, the chief frictions produced by the miracle seem to be intra-Church (between the diocesan Bishop of Mostar, who disputes the authenticity of the miracle, and the Franciscans, who benefit from it and endorse it), rather than between Church and regime.(21)

In the case of the Muslims, on the other hand, it has been much harder to draw the line between what is religious and what is nationalist, and correspondingly harder to persuade the Muslim clergy to restrict themselves to "purely religious" functions.   It is this complication, above all, that accounts for the sharp ambivalence in religious policy in Bosnia, where the Muslims are able to build mosques without any problem-- there were 2,037 in Yugoslavia as a whole in 1976,(22) and many more have been constructed since then--opened a new theological faculty in 1977, and launched a new theological journal, Islamska misao, in 1979.   The regime has even allowed theological students to study in the Middle East.   In essence, thus, the party has been broadly tolerant of Islam.

At the same time, the regime has shuddered at any hint of pan-Islam or Muslim nationalism. As Zagreb Professor Milan Kangrga put it in 1982,

> the danger of Islam lies not in itself, as such, but rather in the tendencies contained within it, which do not shrink from openly and militantly advocating that Marx's science (which is European par excellence) be replaced by the Islamic religion and the Koranic way of life.(23)

And this was, in fact, the charge later levelled against a group of 13 "Muslim nationalists" tried in Sarajevo in summer 1983. The leading defendants--Omer Mustafa Behmens and Alia Mustafa Izetbegović--were given jail sentences of 15 and 14 years respectively, while most of the others received sentences of between five and 10 years in duration. They were said to have made a visit "of an exclusively inimical character" to an unnamed Islamic country, to have propagated an 'Islamic Declaration' which called for the "purification" of Bosnia, and to have begun organizing for the establishment of an "Islamistan" in Bosnia.(24) The trial attracted a great deal of foreign attention, including in the Middle East, but did not have any particular consequences for the practice of Islam in Yugoslavia, except to stimulate Muslim self-awareness, at least temporarily.

BASIC VS. ROUTINE DECISIONS

Within the federalized, factionalized context of Yugoslav policy-making, religious policy must be attuned to diverse factors, including the need to maintain a good image in the West (the source of tourists and credits), the desirability of avoiding offense to Middle Eastern countries,(25) the importance of maintaining the loyalty of Orthodox Macedonians in the face of Bulgarian claims, the fear that religious organizations may adopt the role of spokesmen of national communities, and so forth. At the same time, as I have indicated in the foregoing pages, the "rational actor model"(26) is largely irrelevant to understanding religious policy in Yugoslavia. On the contrary, religious policy can be better interpreted as the variegated outcome of pre-established procedures and routines, conflicting interests and views, accidents of policy sequence, and strategies of "satisficing".(27) Herbert A. Simon once put it this way:

> Discussions of administrative centralization and decentralization often bog down on the question: "Who really makes the decisions [in an organization]?" Such a question is meaningless--a complex [policy] is like a

great river, drawing from its many tributaries
the innumerable component premises of which it
is constituted.(28)
The formulation of religious policy in Yugoslavia is
thus fully consonant with the expectations engendered
by organization theory.

Yet it is clear also that the LCY (or Tito
personally) has intervened at different junctures,
especially prior to 1980, to set forth certain
fundamental principles. A recent instance involved the
case of a Marija Car of Duga Resa who was expelled from
the party in July 1983 because she allowed her newborn
child to be baptized in church. Although not a
believer herself, she consented to the baptism at the
insistence of her husband. She appealed her expulsion
to the Commission for Statutory Problems of the LCY,
thus bringing the central party apparatus into the
dispute.(29) The Statutory Commission upheld her
expulsion, however, and took the occasion to reaffirm
party policy of excluding all believers from
membership.

Other similar interventions could be cited. One
way to understand the relationship between these
interventions on the part of the LCY and the more usual
federalized policy-making context is in terms of the
distinction between basic decisions and routine
decisions. Basic decisions involve long-range
commitments, broad questions of fundamental direction,
and, in the Yugoslav context, any questions of cadres
policy. Such decisions are broad in scope, infrequent,
and taken at the highest level; they are apt to be
taken under duress or pressure. Routine decisions, by
contrast, have little impact of consequence on the
organization but contribute to the formation of the
policy environment.(30) They are generally taken at
lower levels of the organization, affect narrowly
defined issues of a specific nature, and are apt to be
reversible. Routine decisions lie exclusively within
the domain of the federal units.

THE SERBIAN ORTHODOX CHURCH AS LOYAL OPPOSITION

While the Catholic Church and the Islamic
community are in many ways as strong as ever, the
Serbian Orthodox Church seems to be experiencing a
gradual decline. There are several tell-tale signs.
First, secularization, as a natural process weaning
believers from their faith, has hit the Serbian Church
the hardest. A 1982 opinion poll, reported in
Ilustrovana politika, found that while a third of youth
in traditionally Catholic regions are religious, the
proportion in traditionally Serbian Orthodox regions is
about 3 per cent, while a 1984 survey in the Niš area

(in Serbia) found few real believers.(31)   Second, the
Serbian Orthodox Church has the least favorable
clergy/believer ratio of the three major denominations.
For while there is one imam for every 1,250 Yugoslav
Muslims and one Catholic priest for every 2,239
Catholics, there is only one Serbian Orthodox priest
for every 5,714 believers.(32)   Third, the Serbian
Orthodox Church is the least organized of the three
major religious bodies when it comes to religious
instruction.(33)   Fourth, the Serbian Orthodox Church
has been by and large less successful than the other
religious organizations in obtaining permits to build
new churches.(34)   And finally, the authorities keep a
tighter rein on Serbian Church publications, requiring
that every religious publication in Serbia be submitted
for approval 15 days before it is to appear in
public.(35)   This, of course, means that a daily or
even a weekly publication--possible for the Catholic
Church in Slovenia and in Croatia, where prior approval
is not required--would make little sense for the
Serbian Orthodox Church.
        Seen in this light, it is not surprising that
Pravoslavlje, the organ of the Belgrade Patriarchate,
unlike its Catholic counterpart, Glas koncila, is a
generally uncontroversial publication, content with
commemorating the saints and discussing theological
matters.   Nor is it surprising, perhaps, that the
current Serbian Patriarch, German, has taken pains to
underline his loyalty to socialist Yugoslavia,
observing at one point, "All of those who are opposed
to a socialist Yugoslavia are also the opponents of the
Serbian Church and are our enemies."(36)
        Still, Pravoslavlje does occasionally speak out
critically--usually in defense of Serbian national
interests in the face of perceived threats in the
"borderlands".   When the Croatian nationalist euphoria
reached a crescendo in 1970-1971, the Serbian Orthodox
Church was on hand to "defend" the Serbs from Croatian
nationalism.   When Kosovo, the ancient homeland of the
Serbian people, exploded in Albanian-nationalist riots
in 1981, Pravoslavlje issued an "Appeal for the
Protection of the Serbian Inhabitants and their Shrines
in Kosovo."(37)   And throughout the period since the
secession of the Macedonian Orthodox Church in 1967,
the Serbian hierarchy has interpreted its repudiation
of Macedonian ecclesiastical autocephaly as a Serbian
nationalist cause.
        In the late 1950s and early 1960s, the Serbian
Orthodox Church felt it had a protector in Aleksandar
Ranković, Yugoslavia's Vice President and head of the
security police.(38)   When he fell from power in 1966,
the Serbian Church felt it had lost its protector--a
fear that seemed confirmed when the Macedonian clergy

began to press for autocephaly four months later. Since that time, the Serbian hierarchy has found it difficult to escape the feeling that the Serbian Orthodox Church has been singled out by the authorities for discriminatory treatment.(39) The Church continues to complain of interminable delays in the granting of permission to build new church edifices in Belgrade and Split, of the failure of authorities to honor an agreement to return sacred artifacts from the Zagreb historical museum, and of "conduct of certain governmental organs toward the Church [which] is not always in accord with the constitution."(40) In spring 1984, a Serbian priest even complained that "in other republics religious people can be members of the party and send their children to religious instruction while here it is not allowed."(41) In other words, some Serbian clergy at any rate believe that the federalization of religious policy works against the Serbian Church.

Yet Serbian Church difficulties should not be exaggerated. The Church has been able to open new churches both in Serbia and in other republics, for example at Tutnjevac in August 1981, at Nova Gradiška (in Croatia) in October 1982, and at Jasenovac (Croatia) in September 1984, and local authorites at Celje (Slovenia) granted permission in 1982 for the construction of a Serbian Orthodox church to cater to the roughly 1,000 local Orthodox believers.(42) In addition, the Serbian Orthodox Church laid the foundation stone for a new four-storey theological faculty in Belgrade, in May 1984, which, when completed, will accommodate 200 students. The ceremonies were officiated by Patriach German and attended, _inter alios_, by various representatives of the Serbian government, the Serbian Academy of Sciences, and the University of Belgrade.(43) Finally, the Serbian Orthodox Church has maintained a lively publishing activity, of which it is justifiably proud, capping this recently with the publication of the first official Orthodox Church translation of the New Testament into Serbo-Croatian.(44) Hence, when the secular press reports that relations between the Serbian Orthodox Church and the state are "generally good,"(45) this is, in fact, generally accurate. At the same time, there is much lingering distrust on both sides.

THE PROTESTANT CHALLENGE

The authorities have become accustomed to the three traditional religions of Yugoslavia (Orthodoxy, Catholicism, Islam), and vice versa. But the presence and proselytization of newer Protestant sects present a challenge to both--a challenge with which both the authorities and the traditional religious organizations find it difficult to deal.

The chief Protestant Churches in Yugoslavia are: the Reformist Christian Church, which caters largely to Hungarians in Vojvodina, with about 60,000 members; the Evangelical-Lutheran Churches, with 72,385 members (in 1976), many of them Vojvodinan Slovaks; the Pentecostal Church, with 5,000 members; the Seventh-Day Adventists, with 10,600 members; the Baptist Church, with 3,500 members; the Methodist Church, with 3,700 members; the Jehovah's Witnesses, with 10,000 adherents; and the Church of the Brethren, with adherents in Serbia, Croatia, and Slovenia.(46)

Of these, the Pentecostals, the Baptists, the Seventh-Day Adventists, and the Jehovah's Witnesses have been the most active in proselytizing. In fact, the Jehovah's Witnesses publish their <u>Kula stražara</u> (<u>Watchtower</u>) publication in more than 32,000 copies: 14,000 copies in (Latinic) Croatian, 8,000 in (Cyrillic) Serbian, 10,000 in Slovenian, and an unspecified number in Macedonian. The Jehovah's Witnesses and the Adventists have been active in Serbia since at least the early 1970s, when they started to try to win converts from the Orthodox Church. Mija Milačić, a district party official, reported at the time that these Churches were

insolently selling their publications
through the mails. Baptist magazines are
reaching some addresses on a COD basis.
The Jehovah's Witnesses are distributing
their literature in the villages of the
Morava valley. The Seventh Day Adventists
sell their publications to Serbian Orthodox
folk at the church in the monastery of
Ravanica. Unpleasant scenes between the
two groups frequently occur.(47)

Similar reports emerge periodically, and "smaller Protestant communities" have been accused, in particular, of disrupting Catholic and Orthodox church services and of proselytizing on the grounds of Catholic and Orthodox churches.(48)

On the whole, the authorities seem to prefer to ignore the Protestants. Intermittently, one may read passages, in the secular press, such as the following:

The Adventist sect is active in many of our
cities. [Adventists] are very isolated and very
dangerous. They are recognizable by the fact that
they refuse to work or go to school on Saturdays
or to carry weapons in the service. They pay
money when they join the sect, and it is difficult
to leave. They are dangerous because their
children must also be members of the sect. They

do not agree to any compromises, and they condemn
every outside authority. They are exclusively
against self-management and self-managing
democracy.(49)
Because of their energetic proselytization, the
Adventists and Jehovah's Witnesses will probably remain
anathema to the authorities in any of the federal
units. Yet there have also been Protestant clergy who
have achieved reputations for cooperativeness with the
authorities, such as Dr. Juraj Struharik, Bishop of the
Slovak Lutheran Church in Yugoslavia.(50)

CONCLUSION

The argument has come full circle. I began by
stressing the limits to the commonality of religious
policy in Yugoslavia, highlighting different religious
conditions and legislation in the republics, and the
very substantial autonomy enjoyed by the latter. Now
it seems that there are also limits to heterogeneity.
These limits can be seen in the Marija Car case, and
likewise in the general distrust with which authorities
in any republic view certain neo-Protestant groups
especially.
There are other limits. Organization theory
teaches that policy-making in an organizational setting
is conditioned by individual motivations, associational
group loyalties (e.g., to Serbia, or Catholicism, or
peasant farmers), and organizational structure,(51) and
that decision-making should be viewed as the process of
"drawing conclusions from premises."(52) The latter
equation traces decisions to processes of information-
processing in which premises derived from party
affiliation, regional concerns, group loyalties, and
personal development affect the way in which
information is received, manipulated, and acted upon.
Moreover, information-processing cannot be
disassociated from organizational structure, and one is
entitled to posit that structural commonalities will
produce common policy proclivities and common decision-
making dilemmas. Both organizational structure (which
is very much the same from republic to republic) and
basic premises set limits, therefore, on policy
heterogeneity.
The chapter began with five questions about
religious policy in Yugoslavia. On every score, the
question has been answered on the side of complexity.
Religious policy in Yugoslavia is susceptible to the
influence of considerations of policy in other realms,
is worked out in a factionalized, federalized
environment in which formally proclaimed "clear
objectives" are often lost in a complex shuffle of
intervening variables, and in part for these reasons is

moderately heterogeneous across republics and across confessions. In approaching the subject matter, organization theory made sense of this complexity by differentiating between basic decisions and routine decisions, by linking decentralization to the reinforcement of the bifurcation of interests, and by stressing the importance of organizational structure, group loyalties, and operational premises in policy-making.

At the same time, this chapter has provided a more particular vindication of the approach of James March and Herbert Simon, an approach referred to as <u>behavioral organization theory</u>. The importance of perception and group affiliation, which is borne out by the evidence, is nowhere stressed as much as in <u>behavioral-organization</u> theory, which, in general, seems better attuned, than other variants of organization theory, to the complexities of the Church-state dynamic in Yugoslavia.

NOTES

1. Wendell L. French and Cecil H. Bell, Jr.,
   Organization Development, 2nd ed. (Englewood
   Cliffs, N.J.: Prentice-Hall, 1978), pp. 30-34;
   and Herbert A. Simon, Administrative Behavior, 3rd
   ed. (New York: Free Press, 1976), pp. 5-6.
2. Fred Luthans, Organizational Behavior, 2nd ed.
   (New York: McGraw-Hill, 1977), pp. 117-175.
3. For a discussion and critique of classical
   organization theory, see Nicos P. Mouzelis,
   Organization and Bureaucracy: An Analysis of
   Modern Theories (Chicago: Aldine, 1967), pp. 7-
   37.
4. See James G. March and Herbert A. Simon,
   Organizations (New York: John Wiley & Sons,
   1958).
5. William G. Scott, "Organization Theory: An
   Overview and an Appraisal," Academy of Management
   Journal (April 1961), p. 16, as given in Luthans,
   Organizational Behavior, p. 156.
6. Paul L. Lawrence and Jay W. Lorsch, Organization
   and Environment (Cambridge, Mass.: Harvard
   University Press, 1967), as summarized in Luthans,
   Organizational Behavior, pp. 161-162.
7. See Stella Alexander, "Yugoslavia: New
   Legislation on the Legal Status of Religious
   Communities," in Religion in Communist Lands, Vol.
   8, No. 2 (Summer 1980).
8. Nova Makedonija, Sabota supplement (October 10,
   1981), trans. in Joint Publications Research
   Service (JPRS), East Europe Report, No. 79748
   (December 29, 1981), pp. 37-41.
9. See Start (April 25, 1981), pp. 7-8, and (July 18,
   1981), p. 8.
10. See Zachary T. Irwin, "The Islamic Revival and the
    Muslims of Bosnia-Hercegovina," in East European
    Quarterly, Vol. 17, No. 4 (January 1984); and
    Dennison I. Rusinow, "Yugoslavia's Muslim Nation,"
    Universities Field Staff International Reports
    (1982), no. 8.
11. For details, see Pedro Ramet, "Religion and
    Nationalism in Yugoslavia," in Pedro Ramet (ed.),
    Religion and Nationalism in Soviet and East
    European Politics (Durham, N.C.: Duke University
    Press, 1984).
12. Regarding factionalization, see Pedro Ramet,
    "Factionalism in Church-State Interaction: the
    Croatian Catholic Church in the 1980s," in Slavic
    Review (in press).
13. March and Simon, Organizations, p. 41.
14. Ibid., p. 42.
15. Derived from Ibid., p. 43.

182

16. See, for instance, <u>Frankfurter Allgemeine</u>
     (February 5, 1985).
17   <u>Danas</u> (July 13, 1982), pp. 9-10, and (July 20,
     1982), pp. 13-14, 42.
18. Tomislav J. Šagi-Bunić, <u>Katolička Crkva i hrvatski
     narod</u> (Zagreb: Kršćanska sadašnjost, 1983), esp.
     pp. 8-18.
19. <u>Večernji list</u> (August 18, 1981), as cited in <u>Glas
     koncila</u> (September 13, 1981).
20. See Fr. Tomislav Vlasić, OFM, <u>Our Lady Queen of
     Peace, Queen of Apostles is Teaching us the Way to
     the Truth and Life at Medjugorje, Yugoslavia</u>
     (Enfield, U.K.: Pika Print, 1984).
21. See <u>The Economist</u> (London, January 26, 1985), p.
     46.
22. Erich Weingartner (ed.), <u>Church Within Socialism:
     Church and State in East European Socialist
     Republics</u> (Rome: IDOC, 1976), p. 222.
23. <u>Filozofska istraživanja</u> (Zagreb), Nos. 4-5 (April-
     May 1982), trans. in Slobodan Stankovic, "Tito's
     Successors fear 'Moslem Nationalism,'" <u>Radio Free
     Europe</u> (April 18, 1983), p. 4.
24. <u>Komunist</u> (August 5, 1983).
25. The Iranian news agency IRNA condemned the
     Sarajevo trial of "Muslim nationalists" in June
     1983 and claimed that Yugoslavia's Muslims were
     the objects of unfair discrimination.
26. See Graham T. Allison, "Conceptual Models and the
     Cuban Missile Crisis," in Wolfram F. Hanrieder
     (ed.), <u>Comparative Foreign Policy</u> (New York:
     David McKay Co., 1971), pp. 324, 327-336.
27. See <u>Ibid.</u>, pp. 343-348.
28. Simon, <u>Administrative Behavior</u>, p. xii.
29. Sandra Oestreich, "Yugoslav Papers Report on the
     Case of Marija Car," in <u>Keston News Service</u>, No.
     184 (October 6, 1983), p. 14.
30. Dalton E. McFarland, <u>Management Principles and
     Practices</u>, 4th ed. (New York: Macmillan, 1974),
     p. 268, as cited in Luthans, <u>Organizational
     Behavior</u>, p. 181.
31. <u>Ilustrovana politika</u> (February 23, 1982), cited in
     <u>Aktuelnosti Kršćanske Sadašnjosti</u>, Informativni
     bilten (AKSA), March 5, 1982; and <u>Duga</u> (August 25,
     1984), cited in AKSA (August 31, 1984).
32. Calculations from figures given in Trevor Beeson,
     <u>Discretion and Valour: Religious Conditions in
     Russia and Eastern Europe</u>, Revised ed.
     (Philadelphia: Fortress Press, 1982), pp. 291-
     294.
33. <u>Jedinstvo</u> (Priština, January 18, 1973).
34. Interviews conducted by the author, Belgrade, July
     1982. But see below for counterexamples.

35. Chris Cviić, "Die Katholische Kirche in
    Jugoslawien," in Paul Lendvai (ed.),
    Religionsfreiheit und Menschenrechte (Graz:
    Verlag Styria, 1983), p. 220.
36. Quoted in Vjesnik (July 15, 1978), trans. in JPRS,
    East Europe Report No. 72058 (October 17, 1978),
    p. 49.
37. Pravoslavlje (May 15, 1982). This appeal was also
    printed, by the patriarchate, as a separate
    pamphlet in 10,000 copies.
38. Stella Alexander, Church and State in Yugoslavia
    since 1945 (Cambridge: Cambridge University
    Press, 1979), p. 282.
39. See, for example, Pravoslavlje (April 1, 1977),
    trans. in JPRS, East Europe Report No. 69153 (May
    25, 1977).
40. Ibid. (June 15, 1983), trans. in JPRS, East Europe
    Report No. 83897 (June 15, 1983), p. 61.
41. Ibid. (April 1984), excerpted in AKSA (March 30,
    1984).
42. AKSA (September 18, 1981, August 27, 1982, and
    September 3, 1982); and Vjesnik (September 3,
    1984).
43. AKSA (May 18, 1984); and Keston News Service, No.
    202 (June 21, 1984), p. 8.
44. Keston News Service, No. 2155 (December 20, 1984),
    p. 8.
45. Politika (October 24, 1984).
46. Weingartner, Church Within Socialism, p. 222;
    Beeson, Discretion and Valour, p. 293; and Rudolf
    Grulich, "The Small Religious Communities of
    Yugoslavia," in Occasional Papers on Religion in
    Eastern Europe, Vol. 3, No. 6 (September 1983),
    pp. 3-7.
47. Večernje novosti (November 4, 1971), trans. in
    JPRS, Translations on Eastern Europe No. 54499
    (November 16, 1971).
48. Ibid. (October 1, 1983), cited in AKSA (October 7,
    1983).
49. Omladinske novine (January 28, 1978), trans. in
    JPRS, East Europe Report No. 71042 (May 1, 1978),
    p. 78.
50. Vjesnik--Sedam dana (November 12, 1983), as cited
    in AKSA (November 15, 1983).
51. Simon, Administrative Behavior, pp. xiii-xxv, 198-
    199, 205-208.
52. Ibid., p. xii.

8
Can Titoism Survive Tito? Economic Problems and Policy Choices Confronting Tito's Successors

Chris Martin and Laura D'Andrea Tyson

Since 1980 Yugoslavia has been caught in the throes of a major economic crisis. Although of unprecedented severity, this crisis is not essentially different from other economic crises that have recurred in Yugoslavia during the postwar period. Since the early 1960s, Yugoslav economic growth has been characterized by repeated stop-go cycles. Periods of rapid growth have been followed by periods of restrictive policies and economic and social strain. Despite its similarities with events in the past, the current crisis differs from previous stop phases in two important ways: first, the world economic situation is worse than it has been since the foundation of Yugoslavia; and second, for the first time, Yugoslavia is confronting its serious economic and social problems without the charismatic and often politically astute leadership of Tito.

In a typical Yugoslav cycle the economy first enjoys a period of sustained, rapid expansion. Growth rates are high and standards of living improve. At the same time foreign borrowing and inflation increase rapidly and soon become uncontrollable by ordinary policy tools. The authorities are forced to introduce extraordinary restrictive policies, mainly controls on investment and worker incomes, to bring the economy back under control. The restrictions usually have the desired results: cuts in investment and consumption, declines in imports and improvements in the current account.

The economic crisis that began in 1980 followed the pattern of the typical Yugoslav cycle. Between 1976 and 1979, Yugoslavia embarked upon an ambitious growth and investment strategy that pushed the economy into a boom period. The predictable consequences of this strategy were accelerating inflation, growing balance-of-payments deficits, and rapid increases in borrowing from Western financial markets. The new set of economic institutions put into place by a series of reforms between 1972 and 1976 both resulted in this strategy and hindered effective policy responses to the problems it created. Thus there were important internal causes of the economic difficulties that engulfed Yugoslavia in 1980.

On the other hand, the external causes of these difficulties were also significant. Like most other newly industrializing countries, Yugoslavia was adversely affected by the external shocks of the 1970s. In 1973-1975 and 1978-1979, large increases in the price of oil caused sharp deteriorations in Yugoslavia's terms of trade. The ensuing world recessions in 1974-1975 and 1980-1983 reduced demand for Yugoslav exports. In addition, the situation in the later period was aggravated by an increase in real interest rates and a tightening of lending conditions which worsened Yugoslavia's already difficult debt-servicing problems. Recent estimates by Balassa and Tyson indicate that the balance-of-payments effects caused by these external shocks amounted to 7 per cent of Yugoslavia's GNP in 1974-1976 and 8 per cent in 1979-1981.[1]

These estimates show that although the effects of external shocks were substantial they were similar in magnitude to those realized in many other oil-importing newly industrializing countries. Like Yugoslavia, these other countries now confront major balance-of-payments crises and have been forced to introduce serious austerity measures to meet their debt obligations.

In this chapter, we focus on the internal causes of Yugoslavia's economic crisis, and we examine both actual and potential policy responses that are currently at the heart of the political debate among Tito's successors. The chapter is divided into three parts. The first part summarizes the reforms of the 1970s and analyzes their economic and political implications and their contributions to the economic crisis. The second part describes the actual policy measures adopted during the 1980-1984 period and provides the main features of Yugoslav economic performance. Finally, in the third part, we consider the proposals for economic reform that are currently being debated in Yugoslavia and the political controversy surrounding them.

REFORMS OF THE SEVENTIES, PROBLEMS OF THE EIGHTIES

Theoretical studies of self-management have usually assumed the existence of a market economy and have then gone on to deal with the behavior of self-managed enterprises in such an economy. Special consideration of the complexities of Yugoslav economic institutions is needed, however, for an adequate understanding of Yugoslav economic performance. The history of self-management in Yugoslavia has been marked by two major institutional reforms. The first wave of reforms occurred in the mid-sixties and introduced a kind of imperfect market socialism. These reforms were followed by the economic and political crisis of the late sixties and the nationalist and leftist discontent of 1968. After a period of informal experimentation, these disturbances resulted in a second wave of reforms between 1972 and 1976. These reforms were embodied in a new constitution, a new law on economic activity and a new law on planning.

The reforms of the sixties were important both in what they provided and what they neglected. The system of the sixties was an explicitly market or, in Yugoslav terminology, commodity economy. Groups of workers were organized into "enterprises" and were expected to behave as "collective entrepreneurs." Their incomes were to be earned by their sales on the market, their savings, their investments and their assumption of risks. These reforms, however, neglected a number of important markets. In particular, both capital and foreign exchange continued to be allocated administratively, and their prices remained arbitrarily low. Because the incomes of workers depend on the net incomes earned by their enterprises, these distortions in the prices of capital and foreign exchange spilled over into distortions in personal incomes. On an aggregate level, personal incomes were artificially high because artificially low prices of capital and foreign exchange translated into artificially high levels of enterprise net income. On a disaggregated level, this system meant that inter-enterprise and inter-sectoral differences in personal incomes depended not just on the quality of labor or entrepreneurial ability but on inter-enterprise and inter-sectoral differences in access to capital and foreign exchange. Overall, the distorted system of input pricing undermined both efficiency in resource allocation and the notion that workers were to be rewarded according to their labor and entrepreneurial efforts.

The institutional reforms of the 1970s were designed to address the economic and political problems that confronted Yugoslavia in a consistent and ideologically sound manner. The fundamental <u>political</u> problem was how to achieve unity and order in a federal system composed of divergent and often conflicting regions and interest groups, while maintaining the dominance of the League of Communists of Yugoslavia (LCY). The fundamental <u>economic</u> problem was how to achieve greater macroeconomic control and more efficient microeconomic decisions without violating the principles of market socialism and workers' self-management. The same basic strategy was adopted to deal with both of these problems. In both the economy and the political structure, decentralized units were required to negotiate with one another to reach consensual agreements before action could be taken by any individual unit. At the apex of the complicated bargaining arrangements stood the LCY, whose task it was to promote negotiation and help formulate compromise solutions.

The reforms of the seventies have been described in detail elsewhere(2) and will not be reviewed here. Instead, we wish to focus on a few features of the reforms that played a critical role in the deterioration of economic performance in the 1976-1980 period and that continue to hamper policy efforts to improve economic conditions. In our view, the new allocation systems for investment funds and foreign exchange created by the reforms of the seventies deserve pride of place because of their particularly injurious consequences.

As a result of changes in the investment system, banks and most enterprises lost control over decisions to regional authorities and managers of some of the larger enterprises. These decision-makers gave preference to local objectives rather than to the efficiency and profitability of the economy as a whole in their investment choices. As a result, existing tendencies to import-substitution and the duplication of production capacity were strengthened. In addition, the new system failed to eliminate excess demand for investment because it did nothing to establish effective enterprise budget constraints or to place investment decision-makers at financial risk. Consequently, the investment drive of the 1976-1980 social plan led to growing macroeconomic disequilibria, inflationary credit creation, and growing dependence on foreign sources for financing investment projects.

The foreign exchange system established by the reforms relied on a similar combination of distorted pricing and complex non-price allocation schemes and produced several deleterious effects. First, because the effective exchange rate varied across importers and exporters, it was impossible to compare the efficiency of various sectors and enterprises as earners and users of foreign currency. Second, as a result of the overvaluation of the dinar, a bias of incentives against exports to hard currency economies led to worsening trade performance. Third, as prices failed to allocate increasingly scarce supplies of important imports, rationing schemes caused increased uncertainties and interruptions in the flow of materials needed for domestic production. Finally, the existence of substantial unsatisfied demand for foreign exchange resulted in a proliferation of "rent-seeking" activities. These activities included lobbying for allocation of foreign exchange, generation of impossible plans for export promotion, and attempts to restrict flows of exchange across republican boundaries.(3)

The reforms of the seventies also changed the character of economic and political decision-making. Formally, they increased self-management by basing the economic and political structure of free associations of workers and citizens in small local bodies which were then to associate in larger interest groups and communities. In fact, they resulted in increasing administrative intervention in investment, foreign and internal trade, and other important aspects of economic life. Selection of the "representatives" of the producers and citizens in the more important positions remained under the control of informal groups within the party so that democracy at this level did not increase. Instead, the diffuse and ill-defined accountability of the associationist model made statist intervention easier and assignment of responsibility for mistakes more difficult.

Finally, the reforms of the seventies dismantled the federation's powers in a wide variety of economic decisions and made consensus and bargaining among republics and provinces the linchpin of economic policy formulation and execution. This new system, although understandable given Yugoslavia's long-term commitment to reducing "statism" in the economy and its long-standing sensitivity to multinational concerns, was detrimental to the objective of rational, timely policy at the economy-wide level. Ironically, it also turned out to be detrimental to the very objectives it was designed to achieve. Statism in the Yugoslav economy was not on the decline during the 1971-1980 period. On the contrary, the economic system was riddled with growing government intervention in economic life--intervention that was ad hoc, local and uncoordinated in character, and that increasingly distorted the market forces guiding enterprise decision-making. In addition, the new framework of multi-regional bargaining, did not alleviate regional concerns about unfair treatment, but apparently aggravated them. With growing emphasis on regional costs and benefits as the first step in policy formation, regional participants were increasingly concerned with the regional implications of policy measures that might be clearly desirable from a national point of view.

Altogether, the institutions for economic policy and decision-making established by the reforms of the seventies aggravated the distortions in the Yugoslav economy, thereby contributing to the continued decline in the efficiency of resource use and to the loss of effective macroeconomic control. In this sense, then, the reforms were important internal causes of the serious economic difficulties confronting Yugoslavia by the end of the decade.

SHORT-TERM POLICY RESPONSES TO THE ECONOMIC CRISIS, 1980-1984

Response to worsening inflation and growing balance-of-payments deficits in 1979-1980 was slow, both because of the policy paralysis that accompanied Tito's illness and death, and because of the cumbersome nature of the new decision-making apparatus. By the spring of 1980, however, the critical nature of the situation, especially in the balance of payments, mobilized the post-Tito leadership into introducing a serious stabilization program. This was the first in a series of stabilization programs initiated during the 1980-1984 period. The basic objective of these programs was a sustained reduction in domestic demand both to reduce the demand for imports and to redirect output from domestic use to exports.

Despite its stabilization efforts, Yugoslavia faced severe balance-of-payments and debt repayment problems, and was forced to rely on a series of stand-by agreements with the International Monetary Fund during the 1980-1984 period. This gave the IMF considerable leverage in influencing both the extent and the form of stabilization policies actually introduced, and IMF influence increasingly became an issue of heated political controversy within Yugoslavia. Continued IMF pressure for large devaluations of the dinar as a component of stabilization was particularly controversial within Yugoslavia.(4) Internally, exchange rate adjustments were a major source of friction among Yugoslavia's ruling elites at the republic level. The continued devaluation of the dinar was strongly opposed by leaders in regions, such as Bosnia-Herzegovina, which were disproportionately dependent on imported intermediate inputs from convertible currency areas and which were relatively less dependent on exports to these areas. Since under the consensual decision-making rules of the Yugoslav system, devaluations had to be approved by all republics, negotiations over them were often extremely time-consuming, bitter and divisive.

There was also resistance to devaluations in Yugoslavia on the grounds that they tended to aggravate inflationary pressures, at least in the short run. In this regard, the Yugoslav decision-makers could point to convincing empirical evidence that increases in the dinar price of imports, either as a result of an increase in world prices or as a result of a depreciation of the dinar, are passed on through increases in producer and retail prices. Moreover, existing empirical and theoretical evidence on the impact of devaluations in other semi-industrial countries supports the view that devaluation can be inflationary. Given the severe inflationary problem which Yugoslavs were confronting in the 1980-1982 period, it is not surprising that they were extremely concerned about the potential inflationary consequences of the IMF's recommendations for repeated devaluations.

Yugoslavia's scope for policy discretion, however, was severely constrained by its critical need for IMF support to put together the financing required to cover its international obligations. The IMF's role was especially important in 1982 when private capital market flows to Yugoslavia fell sharply. In response to tightening capital market restraints, Yugoslavia was forced to cut imports sharply for the second year in a row and nonetheless found itself with only $1.7 billion in convertible currency reserves, less than one month's imports from the convertible currency area. In response to Yugoslavia's alarming reserve position, the IMF organized a series of meetings of Yugoslavia's major creditor banks during the first half of 1983. At the same time, the Swiss government organized a group of OECD countries to help assemble an aid package of credits from public sources.

The result of these two sets of meetings was an emergency rescue package which, for all intents and purposes, was the equivalent of a rescheduling agreement for Yugoslavia. The package amounted to about $6.5 billion in loans financed by approximately 500 Western commercial banks, 15 Western governments, the IMF, the Bank of International Settlements (BIS) and the World Bank. It was understood that the package was to provide financial support to underwrite the 1983 adjustment program whose targets and policy measures were laid out in Yugoslavia's standby agreement with the IMF. The critical role of the IMF's initiative and seal of approval in pushing forward the aid package undoubtedly strengthened the Fund's negotiating power vis-a-vis the Yugoslav authorities.

The combination of a series of real devaluations and a variety of policies to reduce domestic demand had predictable effects on Yugoslav economic performance during the 1980-1984 period. These effects show up clearly in the economic performance indicators from the period contained in Table 8-1. First, total domestic demand slowed dramatically in 1980 and 1981 and then

Table 8-1

<u>Domestic Macroeconomic Indicators of Economic Adjustment, 1979-1983</u>
(percent rate of growth)

	1979	1980	1981	1982	1983
Output Indicators					
Gross material product (produced)(a)	7.0	2.2	1.4	0.9	-1.3
Gross material product (utilized)	9.7	1.3	-0.8	-4.8	-3.6
Personal consumption	5.2	0.7	-1.0	-0.1	-1.7
Social consumption	7.9	2.7	-4.8	-1.7	-5.0
Fixed investment	6.4	-1.7	-9.8	-6.2	-13.0
Final domestic demand(b)	5.8	-1.8	-4.4	-2.2	-5.5
Prices and Incomes					
Retail prices	21.9	30.4	46.0	30.0	39.0
Cost of living	20.0	30.2	41.0	32.0	41.0
Producer prices	13.1	27.3	45.0	25.0	32.0
Real personal income per worker(c) (social sector)	0.0	-7.5	-5.7	-4.2	-10.3
Financial Indicators					
M1	19.0	23.0	26.6	26.6	20.1
Domestic credit(d)	26.3	28.3	22.9	22.9	31.5
Interenterprise trade credit(e)	-	-	36.7	51.3	250.0

(a)GMP corresponds to the western measure of GNP minus the output of most services (education, health, housing, government services, etc.).

(b)Final domestic demand is GMP utilized minus the change in inventories.

(c)Nominal personal income per worker in the social sector deflated by the cost of living index.

(d)Includes credits to domestic clients, securities and small amounts of pooled resources.

(e)Based on figures of the total stock of outstanding interenterprise claims, whether voluntarily or involuntarily extended, at the end of the period. 1983 figure shows the growth between the end of the first quarter and the end of the fourth quarter.

Sources: 1979-1982: <u>OECD Economic Surveys, 1982-1983: Yugoslavia,</u> (Paris: OECD, May 1983).

1983: WEFA <u>CPE Current Analysis,</u> May 21, 1984 and official government reports released to western banking community.

fell sharply in 1982 and 1983. By 1983, real final domestic demand (total domestic demand minus the change in inventories) had fallen by about 12 per cent relative to its 1980 level. Second, despite the decline in demand, inflation rates remained high and even accelerated toward the end of the period. Inflation persisted despite sharp contractions in the real money supply and real credit availabilty and despite periodic price freezes. Third, within total domestic demand, a disproportionately large share of the cutbacks was borne by real fixed investment which fell every year between 1980 and 1984 and by 1983 was only about 69 per cent of its 1979 level. This performance conformed to the objectives of the Yugoslav authorities and was similar both to adjustment patterns in Yugoslavia during earlier periods of stablization in the 1970s and to adjustment patterns throughout Eastern Europe during the 1980-1984 period. It also reflected the fact that the credit controls most immediately available for demand management in Yugoslavia had their biggest impact on investment spending rather than on consumption spending. Fourth, according to gross material product accounts, personal consumption levels declined each year between 1980 and 1983 with an estimated 3 per cent total decline between 1980 and 1983.(5) Collective or social consumption levels also fell between 1981 and 1984, after decelerating sharply in 1980. All of these declines in the components of domestic demand were quite dramatic when compared to the buoyant conditions of 1978-1979, when domestic demand increased at an average rate of about 7 per cent, with fixed investment growing at an average rate of nearly 10 per cent, personal consumption at an average rate of 6.1 per cent and social consumption at an average rate of 6.5 per cent. Clearly, by 1982-1983, the sustained adjustment measures finally produced the declines in domestic demand that were a necessary condition to improving external performances.

As was the case in other countries, cutbacks in domestic demand were accompanied by a slowdown in the rate of growth of output. Real gross material product growth declined sharply from an average of about 7.5 per cent in 1978-1979 to 2.2 per cent in 1980, 1.4 per cent in 1981, 0.9 per cent in 1982 and turned negative in 1983. At least some of the decline in real growth can be interpreted as the necessary result of bringing the inflationary gap conditions of the late 1970s under control. However, the major reasons for the adverse supply performance lay in the effectiveness and inflexibilities of resource allocation mechanisms, especially the mechanisms for allocating capital resources and foreign exchange.

Table 8-2

External Indicators of Economic Adjustment, 1979-1983
(billions of $)a

	1979b	1980	1981	1982	1983
Exports (fob)--					
convertible currency	4800	5749	5720	5854	6271
Exports--total	6800	8977	10205	10241	9913
Imports (cif)--					
convertible currency	11400	11550	10600	9635	8069
Imports--total	14000	15064	14532	13334	12154
Trade balance--					
convertible currency	-6600	-5801	-4880	-3781	-1798
Trade balance--total	-7255	-6086	-4327	-3093	-2241
Current account balance--					
convertible currency	-3300	-2203	-1821	-1420	299

(a) Official Yugoslav figures reported in a variety of sources.
According to official Yugoslav practice, foreign trade
transactions denominated in different Western currencies are
aggregated using statistical exchange rates that are changed
infrequently rather than using prevailing world market exchange
rates. Frequently, especially during the 1980-1983 period of
large exchange rate changes in world markets, there have been
divergences between the statistical cross rates used by the
Yugoslavs and actual exchange rates, as a result of which the
official indicators of external performance have been distorted.
Recent attempts by the analysts of WEFA to provide adjusted
estimates that correct for these distortions suggest that the
overall patterns and magnitudes of change in official numbers
reported here are reasonably accurate.

(b) OECD estimates rounded to the nearest hundred million.

Sources: 1979: OECD, Economic Surveys 1982-1983: Yugoslavia (Paris:
OECS, May 1983).

1980-1983: official Yugoslav statistics reported in a variety
of published and unpublished statistical sources.

As far as the foreign exchange allocation mechanism is concerned, it is important to emphasize that throughout the 1980-1984 period both the level and the distribution of imports were controlled by an elaborate set of formal and informal rationing systems that had a number of undesirable features.(6)   As a result of the reforms of the seventies, administrative intervention in the distribution of foreign exchange among enterprises increased at the regional level and interregional flows of foreign exchange were substantially restricted. The rationing of foreign exchange along regional lines produced unnecessary output losses because available foreign exchange in one region could not be easily mobilized for use to purchase critical inputs in another region. Furthermore, because the rules for allocation both within and across regions were always changing in unknown ways, the incentives to earn exchange were correspondingly diminished because of the uncertainties surrounding its final disposition.   In addition, enterprises that did earn foreign exchange were reluctant to repatriate their earnings because of uncertainties about how much they would be able to keep for their own use and about the price and conditions at which they would be compelled to turn over the remainder. Clearly, the persistent devaluations of the dinar also contributed to this reluctance. As a result of these distortions and inflexibilities, the output losses associated with a given dose of aggregate import restraint were greater than they would have been in a more unified rationing scheme, and the exchange rate that would have been required to restore equilibrium between the demand and supply of foreign exchange was correspondingly higher.

The combination of cutbacks in domestic demand, import rationing and improved incentives in the second half of 1982 and 1983, as a result of the real devaluation of the dinar, produced dramatic improvements in the convertible currency trade deficit and current account deficit (See Table 8-2). The convertible currency trade deficit declined from $6.6 billion in 1979 to $1.7 billion by 1983, and the current account deficit which reached $3.3 billion in 1979 was transformed into a small surplus of $300 million by 1983.(7) In each of the years between 1980 and 1983, import cutbacks from the convertible currency area were substantial and were not totally offset by a diversion to Eastern sources of supply, as a result of which total imports fell year by year in value and volume terms.   Export gains in convertible currency areas were initially modest between 1980 and 1982, but then improved dramatically in 1983. The evidence shows that the $745 million increase in convertible currency exports in 1983--representing an increase of about 13.5 per cent in nominal terms--coincided with an almost equal decrease in exports to Eastern markets, especially the Soviet Union, suggesting some diversion of export supplies from Eastern to Western markets. Preliminary evidence for 1984 showed a further improvement in Yugoslavia's convertible currency trade and current account position. Convertible currency exports increased an estimated 16 per cent between May 1983 and May 1984 and convertible currency imports increased over the same period by an estimated 3 percent--the first increase registered since 1979.

FUTURE ECONOMIC DIFFICULTIES AND THE PROSPECTS FOR ECONOMIC REFORM IN THE LONG-RUN

The current account and trade account performance of 1983 and the projected performance of 1984 are indicators of the short-run success of the adjustment measures adopted by the Yugoslav government. These indicators, however, tend to obscure the significance of future difficulties stemming from the capital account constraints which Yugoslavia will face throughout the remainder of the decade.

At the end of 1983, Yugoslav officials placed Yugoslavia's gross covertible currency debt at about $19.0 billion. The servicing requirement of this debt will remain substantial at least through 1990. The magnitude of the difficulties imposed by these requirements is suggested by the 1983-1984 experience. Yugoslavia's amortization obligations on medium- and long-term debt amounted to about $2.5 billion in 1983 and were projected at about $3.0 billion for 1984. In the absence of a substantial current account surplus, the Yugoslavs have to rely primarily on foreign credits from both official and commercial sources to cover these obligations and other convertible currency requirements (increases in foreign exchange reserves, reductions in short-term borrowing, etc.) In 1983, official medium-and long-term credit amounted to about $1.7 billion--of which the IMF provided abut 34 per cent and the World Bank about 16 per cent--and commercial bank medium- and long-term credit amounted to about $1.6 billion--of which $600 million represented new money and the remainder the refinancing of existing credit. The corresponding figures for official and commercial credit projected for 1984 are about $2.2 billion in official credit--of which the IMF accounts for about 21 per cent and the World Bank about 13 per cent--and $1.3 billion in commercial bank credit, all in the form of refinancing. Since annual debt servicing requirements are unlikely to decline from their 1983-1984 levels through the end of the decade, capital market constraints on Yugoslavia's room for maneuverability will remain extremely tight.

Essentially, the Yugoslavs can meet these requirements in only one of two ways: they can either generate larger current account surpluses to cover maturing debt obligations, thereby reducing their outstanding debt level; or they can rely on the refinancing of old credits or the provision of new credits to rollover their existing debt level. The second course of action, however, depends critically on the willingness of both commercial and noncommercial lenders to continue to make funds available to Yugoslavia and this, in turn, depends critically on Yugoslavia's ability to generate larger current account surpluses which are considered a sign of a credible, sustained adjustment program in the international financial community.

All of this suggests that Yugoslavia will have to continue to adopt measures that produce a growing excess of domestic production over domestic demand throughout the rest of the decade. During the 1980-1984 period such an excess was generated mainly by restrictions on domestic demand rather than by measures that promoted domestic supply. Indeed, as the earlier discussion indicated, demand restrictions actually resulted in a deceleration of domestic production. The result was an adjustment process that placed a heavy burden on the domestic population, a burden that has generated widespread public dissatisfaction and heated controversy about the future course of economic and political decision-making in Yugoslavia.

Over the longer run, the burden of adjustment on the domestic population can be reduced only if the Yugoslavs undertake a series of economic reforms that improve the output and productivity performance of the economy. Reforms in the allocation of capital and foreign exchange and reforms to break down the regional barriers to the movement of goods and resources are especially critical. The Krajgher Commission Report, adopted by the Yugoslav government in July 1983, gave formal recognition to the need for such reforms as part of Yugoslavia's long-term stabilization and development program. The report came down firmly on the side of economic reform and on the need for a reduction in ad hoc political intervention in economic decision-making.

The Commission report was greeted with a fair amount of optimism. By mid-1983 there seemed some chance for changes which would provide for long-term stability and economic growth. Those favoring reforms to strengthen market forces, "radicals" in the current Yugoslav terminology, won the public debate easily. They had support of the press from the beginning and the severity of the economic crisis quickly convinced the public of the need for changes. Reformers' attacks on a number of extremely unpopular institutions, and their appeals to Yugoslav patriotism were quite popular. As reflected in the media, the public seemed to believe that, although reforms would mean the sacrifice of many amenities and privileges, the proposed changes would bring long-term gains.

After mid-1983, however, the reform proposals began to encounter serious overt and covert opposition. The nature and methods of this opposition are best described using the example of currency and foreign exchange reform. Here, given the foreign debt and balance-of-payments problems, the current crisis is most pressing. Convertibility has been suggested as a solution by both specialists and non-specialists, and there is no lack of administrators with experience in the technical aspect of the solution. Despite all of these circumstances and universally professed good will, the reform has floundered and is now largely aground.

The reform of the seventies eliminated mandatory sales of hard currency to banks and transferred ownership to the organizations which "earned" the currencies by direct sales to tourists or by exports. These organizations were then free to dispose of the "earnings" by self-management agreements with other organizations or in accord with social compacts which formed the republican and federation plans.

The results were not too astonishing. The relatively small number of exporting and tourist organizations, their concentration in the more developed regions and republics, and the provisions for local and republican intervention in their decisions all were fertile ground for monopoly and other market distortions. Those who supplied direct exporters with raw materials, the proverbial farmer or coal miner in Macedonia, Serbia proper, or Kosovo, saw little or none of the incentives offered to their customers who enjoyed a sort of monopoly on foreign exchange. Meanwhile the republics and autonomous regions, particularly the less developed parts of the federation, sought to retain and acquire as much foreign exchange as possible by forcing export industries and duplicating import-substitution projects already underway in more developed regions.

The nature of the problem is not unknown to Yugoslavs. The popular press discusses it in general terms. A more theoretical treatment can be found in scholarly journals or heard in public forums at the universities. Talking with managers in private one can hear detailed descriptions of particular economic scandals arising from the currency laws, and everyone instinctively knows the approximate magnitude of the dinar overvaluation. Judging by the press there is even a strong consensus for reform.

Of course numerous groups profit from the laws as they are now written: for example direct exporters, and republican and regional officials who are able to control and allocate some fund of hard currency; and less efficient organizations which are able to prevent competition from other republics on the grounds that "imported" goods require some hard currency payment and therefore drain the foreign reserves of the "home" republic. These groups, which include people from all levels of society, from workers to high government officials, have taken up the opposition. The popularity of reform seems to have prevented any open opposition to change; hence those who profit by the status quo have taken to supporting only the most cosmetic of reforms. For this they have come to be called "cosmeticians" in the press. Their overt opposition to substantial change has taken the form of attacks, mostly from official platforms, on the press and other critics for "opposition to self-management," "accusing the party of incompetence" and other subversive activities. They have also made occasional attempts to enter the ideological debate with various "new-left" arguments against markets in general and against "exploitation" of republics through centralized control of foreign currencies.

Covert opposition has proven even more important. The recently deposed finance minister(8) was able to delay and gut proposed changes in the laws governing foreign currency by making expert use of the endless process of consensual decision-making which is the norm for Yugoslavia. As a result, the call for centralized sales and purchases of hard currencies at uniform prices has become a proposed law that requires organizations to sell that part of their hard currency earnings "which are not needed for their operations and investment program." Thus the Krajgher Commission's clear program for action now proceeds through the legislative bodies at a glacial pace accumulating modifications and qualifications as it goes.

Nor is the opposition of officials and politicians dictated solely by a desire for profit. The Yugoslav party and government have retained and expanded their control over society for the past decade without either massive repression or mass support. Instead they have exploited their ability to distribute economic benefits to buy the compliance of key groups in Yugoslav society. Economic pricing of foreign exchange, capital and other goods which they now administer would remove a great part of their base support. Only a portion of the party and government could hope to gain legitimacy through a reform. The best prospect open to a greater portion of those now in power would be a quiet retirement from public life at a decent pension.

In fact, the reform of the laws on foreign exchange and other economic reforms face another major obstacle in the organization of the political system. As a result of the reforms of the seventies, the political system is designed for consensus and compromise among established interest groups, but economic problems now demand quick and decisive action which goes against the interests of many of these established groups. Tito, and perhaps a few of his contemporaries, had the personal legitimacy to effect such radical changes. None of the current leaders seem to be able to take his place.

At the moment the prospects for "radical" change in Yugoslavia are quite bleak. The desire of the population as a whole for such change tends to break down as practical proposals touch the special interests of each group within the nation. Political leaders might save themselves by decisive action, but such action would harm many of their contemporaries and subordinates. The risks of a leap into a more market-oriented system have inspired a sort of nostalgia for a more controlled economy and society, but the taste which Yugoslavs have acquired for economic and political freedom make a return to Stalinism virtually impossible. In the short run the best course for the Yugoslav establishment seems to be continued small changes and partial compromises. Emergency measures can keep the economy from disaster. They even have the short-term advantage of increasing the role of politicians in the allocation of resources. Unfortunately, a course of cosmetic change will continue to erode the already weak legitimacy of the party and government and encourage destructive national disputes over the distribution of scarce resources. Under this scenario, Yugoslavia will continue to adjust to changed international economic circumstances but at a greater than necessary cost to its population.

NOTES

1. Bela Balassa and Laura D'Andrea Tyson, "Policy Responses to External Shocks in Hungary and Yugoslavia, 1974-76 and 1979-81," in US Congress, Joint Economic Committee Report on Eastern Europe (Washington DC: US Government Printing Office, forthcoming in 1985).

2. See, for example, Laura D'Andrea Tyson, The Yugoslav Economic System and its Performance in the 1970s (Berkeley, California: Institute of International Studies, 1980); and Martin Schrenk, Cyrus Ardalan, and Nawal A. El Tatawy, Yugoslavia: Self-Management Socialism and the Challenges of Development (Baltimore and London: Johns Hopkins University Press, 1979).

3. For further discussion of the costs of the new foreign exchange system, see Sherman Robinson, Laura D'Andrea Tyson, and Mathias Dewatripont, "Yugoslav Economic Performance in the 1980s: Alternative Scenarios," in US, Congress, Joint Economic Committee.

4. For more detail on IMF-Yugoslav relations 1980-1984, see Sherman Robinson, Laura D'Andrea Tyson, and Leyla Woods, "Conditionality and Adjustment in Socialist Economics: Hungary and Yugoslavia," Paper prepared for a conference on the Soviet Union and Eastern Europe in the World Economy, Kennan Institute, Washington DC (October 1984).

5. The decline in real personal income per worker was much sharper than the decline in personal consumption, both because non-wage sources of income did not decline as fast as wage income and because households reduced savings rates in order to limit declines in consumption. Real personal income per worker in 1983 was about 18 per cent below the 1980 level and 26 per cent below the peak 1979 level.

6. See Sherman Robinson and Laura Tyson, "Foreign Trade, Resource Allocation, and Structual Adjustment in Yugoslavia," in Journal of Comparative Economics, Vol. 9, No. 1 (March 1985).

7. It should be noted that there has been considerable skepticism in the West about the reported 1983 surplus. The reason is that the official balance of payments showed negative errors and omissions amounting to nearly $1.1 billion, largely attributed to the fact that the official statistics counted as 1983 export receipts earnings that would not be realized until 1984.

8. Joze Florijančić from Slovenia. See NIN (December 13, 1983).

9
The New Feminism in Yugoslavia

Barbara Jancar

The "woman question" is a perennial subject of discussion in the advanced industrialized countries of Western Europe and the United States. In the communist countries, the official position ever since the Russian Revolution is that the question has been "solved." By definition, the inauguration of a "socialist" regime brings with it the ultimate emancipation of women. In all of the countries where a communist party has triumphed, the regimes have single-mindedly and with scarcely any deviation from the norm, put into law the principles embodied in the Bolshevik declaration of policy on women made at the First International Conference of Working Women, in Moscow in 1920. The essential features of the statement were: to bring women out of the home into the working world; to end the traditional household organization which kept women in subservience; to provide equal educational opportunities for women; to mobilize women into political work; and to provide adequate working conditions "to satisfy the particular needs of the female organism and...the...needs of the woman as mother."(1)

Official statements to the contrary notwithstanding, the impressive corpus of legislation on women and the family in the communist countries has not been able to prevent the "woman question" from resurfacing in those societies. The problem has assumed various forms. Primary among these has been the phenomenon of the "second shift," an issue first publicly identified by Polish sociologist Magdalena Sokolowska in the 1950s.(2) Since that time, the Soviet Union and every East European country have amassed impressive data on the added hours worked by women in the home and the fewer hours she has for leisure time activities than men. In the 1970s, Hungary and East Germany in particular saw the emergence of women writers of world stature who addressed themselves to specific problems of women, such as female poverty (Hungary) and the continued male dominance at home and at work (East Germany).(3)

In the 1980s, the most exciting and significant reexamination of the "woman question" in the communist countries is taking place in Yugoslavia. A generational gap has appeared between the young generation of women who have no experience of the war years, and the older generation of women who occupy the bureaucratic positions in the women's and veterans' organizations, the seats in the federal and republican assemblies, and other prominent posts in the Yugoslav party and government. Both generations are impatient with one another. The older generation believes that contemporary Yugoslav youth may not have the determination, the courage, or the stamina to defend their country with gun in hand. The younger generation thinks that 40 years of venerating wartime heroism is enough and that the time has come to put that experience behind and to face the problems of the present.

This chapter looks at this widening generation gap along two dimensions. The first examines Yugoslav women's gains in the post-World War Two years, and the perspective of women who were instrumental in making those gains possible. The second examines recent writings of the "neo-feminists," as they are called, in an attempt to evaluate the significance and permanence of their contribution to modifying the position of women in Yugoslav society.

WOMEN'S GAINS AND THE OLDER GENERATION

Women's gains in Yugoslavia since the Second World War are typical of the political and economic advances made by women in the postwar communist industrializing societies,(4) and indeed in all industrializing societies.

In 1923, women represented around 20 per cent of the industrial work force.(5) Most women were employed in agriculture, since 80 per cent of the total population of the country lived in the countryside at that time.(6) In 1954, women represented 24.8 per cent of the total work force, including those employed in the socialized agricultural sector. During the 1970s, their share in the total work force increased to around 35 per cent, where it has remained. In 1979, employed women represented approximately 53.7 per cent of all women in the economically active ages between 20 and 55, 46 per cent of whom were unskilled.(7)

Like elsewhere in the industrializing world, woman's mass entrance into the industrial job market brought the feminization of job categories. Today,

Yugoslav women are employed primarily in three areas: Women represent 56.3 per cent of those employed in cultural and social welfare activities, 42 per cent of those employed in public services and public administration, and 41.8 per cent of those employed in trade and catering.(8)   If the data is looked at from the standpoint of women employed, 37 per cent of all working women work in manufacturing; 18 per cent in trade, catering, and tourism; 11 per cent in education and culture, where elementary school teachers are virtually all women; and 11 per cent in public health and social welfare.(9)

The percentage of women employed as a function of the total work force varies from republic to republic. The largest percentage of women in the work force (43.9 per cent) is in Slovenia, where over 70 per cent of the employees in social welfare, educational and cultural activities are women, and the lowest in Muslim Kosovo, where women represent only 20 per cent of the employed population and 32.1 per cent of those employed in "non-economic activities."   In terms of education, women represent on the average 23.4 per cent of all employed university graduates, again with a concentration of women in the education, culture, health, and social welfare fields.   Primary school women graduates predominate in the same categories and also in catering and tourism, and retail and wholesale trade.(10)

Since the Second World War, illiteracy has virtually disappeared among women, and women represent almost 40 per cent of university students. In higher education as in the work world, women tend to concentrate in particular disciplines: pharmacology (84.9 per cent of all students are women); social work (87.1 per cent); and two-year medical studies (83.4 per cent). In 1978, women represented 18.5 per cent of all Ph.D.s.(11)

The acquisition of full political rights resulted in a pattern of women's participation in the self-managing institutions similar to the participation of women in political bodies in all the industrialized countries. Women tend to be well represented at the lower levels, and decrease in number as the government body becomes politically more important.   Thus, approximately 34 per cent of all delegates in the basic organizations of associated labor (BOALs) or enterprises are women. Women, however, represent only 7.2 per cent of all the members of the local community organs.   This last figure constitutes a drop in participation from a high of around 15 per cent in 1971.(12)   As might be expected, women are better represented in urban councils (16.7 per cent), and in the more developed republics such as Slovenia (15.3 per cent).(13)

Approximately 16 per cent of party members are women. As of January 1985, there was not a single woman in the party's Central Committee Presidium, and only one woman in the Federal Executive Council, Milka Planinc, the Council president.(14)

Since the Second World War, then, Yugoslav women have gained full civil and political rights, and access to education, jobs, social welfare, health care, and political posts. However, the evidence suggests that they have a considerable distance to go to reach equal status with men as far as jobs, and social and political position are concerned. There is wide recognition in Yugoslavia of a general apathy among women to participate in public life.(15) A typical woman will work her required hours, and leave to come back and prepare dinner for her family in the late afternoon. Most seem to prefer a life centered around children and family activities, and the woman's work world for the most part intrudes minimally in the family routine.(16)

The apathy may be considered a reflection of the profound impact Yugoslavia's transformation from a traditional-agrarian society to a modern-industrial one has had on women's lifestyle. Since World War Two ended, the country has undergone one of the most rapid processes of urbanization in history, moving from a situation in which 80 per cent of the population was rural in interwar Yugoslavia to one in which more than 70 per cent of the population lived in urban environments as of 1978.(17) In the process, families have become uprooted, and the traditional way of life and thought has come under assault. Women have found themselves at the same time freed from parental or marital tutelage, and cast into a sea of social and economic uncertainty with family protection gone. Vera St. Erlich has sensitively documented the problems encountered by Yugoslav women as the patriarchal style of family life was wrecked on the shoals of industrialization to be replaced by a more democratic form. And she suggests that women's lack of appreciation of their low status in the patriarchal family could very well be the product of the closeness and protection with which many women were surrounded in the traditional zadruga.(18) Part of the explanation for women's failure to move aggressively, in the early postwar years, into the areas of public life opened to them may be that many Yugoslav women felt confused by social change.(19) Indeed, it could be argued that the rising postwar divorce and abortion rates are more indicative of women's political reaction to their changed circumstances than is their participation in the formal organs of power.(20)

An equally important source of Yugoslav women's failure to develop a more aggressive role in Yugoslavia's economic and political arena must be sought in women's personal experience of the Second World War, or, as it is called in Yugoslavia, the National Liberation Struggle, and the legacy of attitudes toward women which has been handed down from the wartime experience.

In December 1984, I was privileged to be able to interview women who had been major participants in that war. Some of them are now National Heroes, decorated for their wartime bravery. All of them held high administrative and political positions after the war. Some went into retirement early. Some are still active workers. The recollections of these women point up the invaluable contribution women made to the war effort, both in the front lines and in the rear. They also confirm a pattern of shared attitudes and convictions that may not necessarily have been part of the official party line, but which nevertheless appeared to inform women's actions during the war, and to shape the views of those who survived in the postwar world.(21)

The Yugoslav National Liberation Struggle was both a civil war among contending Yugoslav political factions, and a war of resistance against fascism. It was one of the bloodiest and most brutal theaters of the Second World War. One hundred thousand women fought in the Partisan forces, 25,000 of whom died and 40,000 of whom were seriously wounded. Some 2,000,000 were involved in the Anti-Fascist Front of Women, officially established in 1942 to mobilize women in the rear. Six hundred thousand were carried off to German, Italian, Hungarian, Bulgarian, and Ustaše concentration camps where around 282,000 women perished. The large majority of those who fought and died were under 25 years of age.(22) In the course of the fighting, about 2,000 women attained an officer's rank, and many were elected members of the Communist-organized local and regional governments under the Anti-Fascist Council of National Liberation of Yugoslavia. In the postwar period, 91 women were accorded the honor of National Hero, the large majority of whom again were young teenagers who gave their lives in incredible feats of bravery and self-sacrifice on the battlefield.

The legacy of women's participation is one commanding the highest honor and respect, and a height of achievement which many of the younger generation of women see as a one-time event which is too out of the ordinary for contemporary Yugoslav women to use as a role-model.

The most salient element of the legacy is the women's own record of self-sacrifice and heroism. Women had different reasons for joining the Partisans.

Whole villages were wiped out in the ceaseless conquest, fall, and reconquest of Partisan territory. Women fought because their homes were gone, their children fatherless, or they themselves orphaned. Women fought because the war brought change along with destruction and pain, and women born into centuries of tradition welcomed the winds of change. Women fought because they believed that the end of fascism would bring real freedom to their country. Macedonian and Montenegrin women had a long history of fighting alien conquerors, while Slovenian women wedded the age-old will for national survival with new-found skills. Working women and intellectuals fought because they believed that the end of fascism would bring in a new society of equality and justice to replace the injustices they had experienced in Yugoslavia's pre-war capitalist society. This belief was buttressed by an image of the Soviet Union as a workers' paradise and unyielding bastion against fascism. Few women who had been associated with leftist movements or the pre-war Yugoslav Communist Party had visited the Soviet Union, and information was virtually nonexistent. For these women, the Soviet Union seemed, by comparison with the evils of the present reality, to symbolize utopian aspirations and achievements.

The heroism with which women gave their lives for these diverse and often incompatible goals has been celebrated in countless books, memoirs, scientific studies, and compilations of documents which were published during the war. To a far greater extent than may be realized, woman's wartime self-sacrifice was almost automatically carried over as the norm for her participation in postwar Yugoslav society. Women who fought in the war speak with nostalgia of the high moral values which existed during the war: the spirit of comradeship, the sense of dedication to a noble cause, the exhiliration which came from doing their duty, and above all the unselfishness in giving of themselves. These women see the modern Yugoslav woman as insufficiently imbued with these qualities. Acting mainly out of self-interest, the younger women are unable to understand a time which many of the older generation look back upon as the best and proudest moment of their lives. The modern woman questions military service, and, in the view of the wartime generation, has been so coddled that it is doubtful whether she could fire a gun if she had to. Most problematic of all, the older generation is not convinced that a modern woman would be capable of sacrificing her life for another, as they had done during the war.

A second aspect of the legacy is the fact that many women did indeed find liberation in the war.

Their aspirations of equal participation were realized. While all the women interviewed were emphatic that feminism was never an issue in the wartime struggle, they all unequivocally stated that there never was a time during the war when they were not treated as equals with men. For some, the sign of equality was the gun. At the beginning, the Partisan command believed that woman's place was in the cities or in the rear. But women pressed forward to join the Partisans. The high command changed its view and women were called to active fighting. One of the interviewees spoke of her first missions, and the kindness of the male commandant in showing her how to aim and fire a gun. For others, equality meant the comaraderie of hard fighting and shared living, where "immoral" relationships were strictly taboo. The war years gave many women their first experience of being treated as human beings rather than as sex objects or household property.

To women in the villages, the war gave a social and political significance to tasks which women had traditionally performed in the home as mere "woman's work." Knitting, sewing, cooking, planting, harvesting, education, taking care of children and the wounded, giving aid to those in the concentration camps: women's traditional home economic and nurturing functions suddenly became of supreme importance to national survival. Women realized that in a very fundamental sense, women's work <u>was</u> the wartime economy. And woman's traditional acts of caring were the social welfare and medical arm of the Partisan state.

For those women who joined the Anti-Fascist Front of Women or became politically involved, the war provided the opportunity to step into new roles. Many villages were completely empty of men: many had gone off to join the Partisan army, others had died. The women who stayed behind began to take over tasks hitherto performed only by men, such as the administration of local government and the organization of supplies for the army. Urban and rural women who joined the Communist Youth Movement or became members of the party were sent to organize educational and propaganda programs, to mobilize the rear, and to recruit new people into the movement. Some found themselves overnight acting as doctors in Partisan hospitals. In pre-war Yugoslavia, such activities were open to women only as exceptions. The war gave some women the chance to discover that they could do these tasks as well as men.

For all the women who became involved in the Partisan struggle, the war brought the official proclamation of equal rights, including the right to vote which had been one of the principal political objectives of women in pre-war Yugoslavia, and which had been consistently denied them. One of the first acts of the Anti-Fascist Council was to extend the suffrage to women, and women's vote and political participation were actively solicited in the liberated and even the unliberated areas.

Last but not least, the women who had shown the most dedication to the Partisan cause, were given honor and status as members of the ruling elite in the new Yugoslavia. Female and male veterans obtained privileges. Women received high administrative posts. Indeed, the generation of war veterans still dominates the women's conference and occupies the honorary positions in the federal and republican governments. Many went on to get doctoral degrees and became respected professionals. Some, like Vida Tomšić, became the country's leading authorities on women and are regularly consulted on women's issues.

Given the outcome of the war for the women who fought and survived, it is not surprising that women of that generation are of the opinion that the war liberated women once and for all. There is no need to reopen the question again. In effect, their wartime experience _was_ liberation. How much more liberated can a woman be than to risk her life, fighting side by side with a man? Women interviewed admitted that many of the wartime goals had been achieved on paper but not in practice. But the failure was temporary and not a function of Yugoslavia's postwar social structure. What was needed was money. When Yugoslavia became as rich and prosperous as the United States, there would be sufficient money to build the day-care centers, cafeterias, and other public services that would usher in the final stage of woman's emancipaton.

The older generation admits that patriarchal customs still survive in Yugoslavia and that these have hampered the realization of the wartime objectives. According to Ana Tankosava-Simić, the Chair of the Women's Conference of Yugoslavia and herself a distinguished wartime veteran, the only way for women to overcome these old prejudices is to adopt the same fighting spirit women had shown in the war. Women have to be shaken from their inactivity. They have to mobilize in the factories and workplaces to insist that their elected delegates vote for the factory kindergartens or social services women need rather than giving priority to other programs. Women have to come forward as candidates in factory and community elections, as they did during the war. Always, the war years are the reference point.

The wartime legacy, then, is a reference point which is seen by those who participated in it as an idyllic period, where men and women were truly equal, each motivated by the spirit of self-sacrifice, where every male job was open to women and where women's work assumed a national significance it had never before achieved and which it has not retained since. During the war and in the immediate postwar period, the Communist Party passed into legislation every part of the emancipation policy it had promoted during the war. Liberation had been achieved. For the women veterans, the "woman question" exists no longer. Those who would reopen the issue are staining the revolutionary banner.

Thus, to the wartime generation of women and men, feminism is a dirty word, virtually synonymous with disloyalty to Yugoslavia. It is seen as an import from the West and a product of capitalist decadence. As R. Iveković cumbersomely expressed it in the official woman's journal, Žena [Woman], "It seems to me that it is very dangerous when some pseudo-theoretical or current political-ideological discourse of ready formulas...serves as theory or in place of theory, where it is assumed that everyone knows what is what and initial concepts are never defined."(23) According to Marija Šoljan-Bakarić, wartime veteran and internationally recognized researcher on woman's role in the war, "There is no new approach" to the woman's question.(24)

THE NEW FEMINISM

In the late 1970s and early years of the 1980s, a new generation of intellectuals began to challenge this official and widely accepted view of the status of women in Yugoslavia. The new feminism is a movement without official recognition. Originating in Zagreb (still its main base), it is looked upon with some suspicion by women intellectuals in other parts of the country. Women scholars in Belgrade would joke that "feminism" had not yet corrupted Serbian women, while researchers in Skopje indicated that the issues raised did not seem to relate to Macedonian women's problems.

The movement first broke into the Yugoslav national consciousness with the staging in Belgrade of an international conference on women's emancipation in the fall of 1978. The conference was without official backing and invited feminists from France, West Germany, Hungary, Poland, the United Kingdom, and Italy. Among the findings of the conference was the assessment that Yugoslavs generally do not see that there is a woman's problem in their country and that self-management had failed to liberate women. The official press response to the conference was similar to what feminists have experienced elsewhere:

ridicule, attempts to trivialize the meeting, and accusations of female intellectual aggressiveness.(25)

Perhaps because of their maverick status, only a few feminists have published substantially. Primary among these one should mention Slavenka Drakulić-Ilić, a sociologist who has contributed articles to mass media and professional journals. A collection of her journal articles, entitled Smrtni grijeŝi feminizma: Ogledi o mudologiji [The Deadly Sins of Feminism: Essays on "Testicology"] was published in Zagreb in 1984. A second individual to write substantially about the new feminism, although he may not consider himself a feminist, is Vjeran Katunarić, whose provocative study, Ženski eros i civilizacija smrti [Female Eros and the Civilization of Death] also came out in Zagreb in 1984. The book covers a whole range of ideological, sociological, and psychological issues associated with the "woman question." These two works will form the basis for the discussion which follows, supplemented by information derived from interviews with various Yugoslav feminists.

The new feminism in Yugoslavia is a movement whose philosophy is in the process of formation. At the present time, five propositions may be distinguished as central to the feminist position. First, the history of the woman's movement is separate from the struggle of the working class and is autonomous in its own right. Second, while women's contribution to the Partisan struggle was remarkable and essential, it was dogmatically organized. Partisan dogmatism eventually led to the total subordination of the women's movement in Yugoslavia to the bureaucratic interests of postwar Yugoslavia. Third, there is a universality or communality to women's experience in all industrializing and industrialized societies. Fourth, far from uprooting traditional patriarchalism, industrialization has produced a new and perhaps more virulent form, dubbed "testicology" by Drakulić-Ilić. And fifth, the use of the mass media to market products has contributed to the reification of human relationships. The treatment of every human exchange as a commodity to be bought and sold has played a significant role in keeping women in their place. We shall examine each of these propositions in turn.

Lydia Sklevicky is one of the younger generation of university-educated women who has attempted a systematic reexamination of the history of the Yugoslav women's movement based on Western sociological analytic models. She has summarized her study of the interwar period in two concise articles which appeared in 1984 in Polja, a progressive journal for cultural, artistic, and social questions, published in Novi Sad. Her analysis of the movement during the war was also

published in late 1984 as a special publication of
Povijesni prilozi, the journal of the Croatian
Institute for the History of the Workers' Movement.(26)
Through careful documentation, Sklevicky develops the
thesis that the Yugoslav women's movement between the
wars was not unidimensional but was a very complex
phenomenon composed of religious, bourgeois, and
leftist currents, in which the Communist Party was not
the only organization to strive "consistently" for the
political and social equality of women, as the official
view would state it.(27) Sklevicky's data show that
the bourgeois women's organizations, such as the
original Yugoslav Women's Union and the later Alliance
of Women's Movements, founded in 1926, were equally
persistent in their demands for political and economic
equality.   Indeed, the Alliance was the principal
organizer behind the massive action for the right of
women to vote in 1939.   Moreover, these movements
attracted a greater following of women.   In 1921, the
Union had 205 affiliated societies with a membership of
50,000, while women's participation in the Communist
Party of Yugoslavia (CPY) did not exceed one per cent
of the total membership up to 1940.
     What distinguished these bourgeois organizations
from the leftist women's groups was not their platforms
but their insistence on autonomy, which they tried to
secure through political neutrality--whence the
official negative label of "feminist."   However,
Sklevicky points out that although working class women
participated massively in strikes and ad hoc
demonstrations for equal pay and improved working
conditions, this type of activity cannot be considered
an adequate measure of political commitment.   The
activists who joined the CPY were in the definite
minority.   And many of these were young women
intellectuals, who, under party guidance, organized the
Youth Section of the Women's Movement Alliance in 1935,
with a view to bringing the organization under direct
party control.
     According to Sklevicky, the increase in women's
membership in the party came after the Fifth National
Conference of the CPY in 1940, when the leadership
incorporated a women's policy into the party platform
which contained essentially the economic and political
demands that had constituted the main thrust of the
Alliance's program.   The conclusion that Sklevicky
draws from her data is that "even though the position
of women...was not promoted at that time by a single
social class, the organized activity of women achieved
its historic objectives: the entry of women onto the
stage of history, her recognition of her personal
position, and the attainment of that level of general

and political education which would enable her to take part in subsequent historic events."

Needless to say, this interpretation challenges the official Yugoslav view of the history of women in Yugoslavia.(28) Nevertheless, echoes of it may be heard in descriptions of the communist effort to exploit and "piggy-back" on the backs of the autonomous women's movement.

In an interview with the author, Mitra Mitrović, a leading organizer of communist infiltration into the "bourgeois" feminist organizations, stressed the diversity of the interwar women's movement. She described it as composed of numerous relatively small circles, many of which were affiliated with the Alliance. Primary among the Alliance's aims were equal rights, equal pay, the end of legal discrimination, and the right to vote. After joining the Communist Youth Organization (CYO) in 1932, Mitrović was sent to the official women's movement to negotiate the formation of a youth section within the Alliance. She successfully persuaded the leaders that they only represented the older generation (the thirties) and that she and her colleagues represented youth. The organization needed young people. The "older" women, as she called them, agreed. In her words, "They gave us a lot of freedom. We very quickly became a hefty organization," with meetings, classes, lectures and discussions every week. She stressed that communists were infiltrating all the organizations. However, within the host organization, she did not talk about revolution but about women's rights. From 1935 to 1940, CYO and the Youth Section of the Alliance had "excellent cooperation" with the "older" women of the official movement. The cooperation broke down with the Youth Section's failure to come out against the Molotov-Ribbentrop Pact, and the Section left the Alliance.

Sklevicky's interpretation also runs counter to the traditional Marxist position regarding the necessity of subordinating the women's movement to the working class revolution as the one and only way to achieve their real emancipation. Independent leftist feminism died with Clara Zetkin in communist-dominated regimes. It may be in the process of rebirth in modern Yugoslavia.

Confirmation of the rebirth of an independent Marxist variant of feminism in Yugoslavia may be found in the work of Vjeran Katunarić. While most of Ženski eros concentrates on an analysis of the woman's experience in the West, he does discuss briefly the "social and ideological variables" of the woman's question in Yugoslavia. Referring to the development of "feminism" in the 1970s, he states that it is "too early to make a determination about the prospects of alternative activities as a contribution to the woman question, but it is possible to say that the large interest and activation within the silent majority of urban women has the potential to clash with the still strong obstacles of fear and cultural inertia, leading to still larger amounts of self-repression and repression."(29)

For the new generation of feminists, everything must be carefully investigated and no subject is a closed book. The National Liberation War might have provided opportunities for women, but an objective consideration of the documents suggests that for the large majority of women participants, these opportunities were in women's traditional domain: housework, sewing, planting, and in fact, offered them little change from the traditional lifestyle. Moreover, very few women actually fought in the Partisan forces. Those that did were very young, ill-trained, and could thus be considered more sacrificial cannon-fodder than heroes. However one views women's mobilization during the war, there is no doubt that they responded so enthusiastically to the call that there was a danger of the Anti-Fascist Front of Women becoming a "feminist," i.e., autonomous, organization independent of party control. The last years of the war thus saw the implementation of measures to bring the Front completely under CPY supervision. The result was that when the war was over, women were deprived of an organizational base from which to make claims on the new regime.

The above picture of the new feminist view of the war may be a little harsh. Many would modify its contours, while keeping the essential argument. Admittedly, these views are not novel outside Yugoslavia,(30) but it is significant that they are being increasingly openly expressed by Yugoslav feminist scholars on the basis of detailed study of wartime documents. Over and over again, the author was urged to "go to the Archives," if she really wanted to know about women's participation, and not to be satisfied with published materials.

The above interpretation of women's role in the Partisan struggle is in sharp contrast with the official view of the mass mobilization of women under the Partisan banner, as set forth by the Women's Conference and the Veterans' Organization. The official heroic view constituted the basis for the selection for publication of documents relating to women's participation in the war. Given the huge number of documents, stringent editing was necessary. Nevertheless, the uniform light cast on all aspects of women's wartime role in every republic raises doubts and questions. From the author's own research, the feminist perspective would seem to offer a more realistic, if less romantic, wartime picture of what was surely a kaleidoscope of women's motives, experiences, and achievements during the war.

The third proposition of the new feminism concerns the universality of women's experience in the industrialized world. The new feminists take as their point of departure a critique of traditional Marxist feminism, based primarily on American sources: publications by leading American feminists, including Kate Millett and Betty Friedan, material from the American feminist movement of the sixties, and American sociological data. European sources, such as Simone de Beauvoir's Le Deuxieme Sexe and European statistical material are also used. The international context underscores the communality of Yugoslav women's experience with that in other industrialized societies. At issue is the demonstration that the woman question has not been solved in Yugoslavia or in any other country, East or West. As Yugoslavia reaches levels of economic and social development similar to those in the West, the difference between women's problems there and in Yugoslavia decreases. The Yugoslav "woman question" equally makes contact with the situation of women elsewhere in Eastern Europe and in the other "socialist" states at the point where bureaucratic authoritarianism impedes women's further development.

A well reasoned critique of Marxism may be found in Katunarić's work. He points out that while Marxism identified women's interests automatically with the working class, in fact women's status is more the product of intra-class than of inter-class stratification. It is also a product of different time periods. The strategies and techniques needed to bring women out of patriarchal society are different from those needed to emancipate women in industrial society, but at no time can the woman question be subsumed under the interest of a particular class.

The tendency in Yugoslavia to what Katunarić calls "false universalism" is an example of the imposition by the elite of irrational authority and runs counter to Marx's view of political emancipation as set forth in The Jewish Question. By what logic, asks Katunarić, must the woman, like the Jew, renounce her special interests in order to achieve equality? The adoption of such a position leads to an instrumentalist approach to women's problems (emancipation or demography), conservatism, and silence on the issues.

Citing Kate Millett's and Carol Pateman's work in the United States, he agrees that emancipation of a social class may not be enough. The concept of worker participation is essentially male. He agrees with Carol Pateman that there is a rationale for women to seek their own forms of participation on a broader democratic foundation. While definitely not writing for the same purpose or on the same subject matter, Katunarić and Sklevicky would seem to be of the same opinion that it may be unliberating to fit women into some predetermined mode of action. History demonstrates that women can develop organizational forms of participation suited to the time and place which will help them reach their current set of objectives.

The commonality of woman's experience in all modern societies, including Yugoslavia, is best substantiated by a comparison of women's situation in Yugoslavia with that of women in the West. Slavenka Drakulić-Ilić's book, <u>The Deadly Sins of Feminism</u>, mentioned earlier, comments in an ironic and frequently amusing fashion on the changing relations between the sexes and the sexual revolution in the West, the stilted counsel given to parents on how to tell their children about sex, and the tension created by the unreasonable demands put on mother love, again in the West. The book documents the pressure experienced by all women in adjusting to the demands of the marketplace and the demands of a yet unrestructured situation between the sexes at home. Although Drakulić-Ilić is careful to aim her commentary at conditions in the West, her provocative choice of subject matter is revealing as an indication of the nature of the issues with which Yugoslav women are concerned.

Drakulić-Ilić's method is best illustrated by one of her articles published at the end of 1984 in the weekly magazine, <u>NIN</u>. Entitled "Men for the Home," the article focuses on American and international studies documenting the problems faced by women between the ages of 25 and 34, who are intelligent, successful, ambitious--and live alone. The problem, as she sees it, is a generational one, as these women are the product of the sexual revolution of the fifties and sixties. She presents statistics to show that men in their 30s and 40s prefer less intelligent "marriageable" women. Only two types of men will marry the woman in her mid-thirties, according to her findings: the "Real Man," who is rich enough and self-confident enough to be able to handle an intelligent woman, or a man seven to 10 years her junior, who does not feel threatened by an intelligent woman. Although virtually all the data in the article are from the United States, Drakulić-Ilić presents the problem as universal, existing in "Zagreb and Belgrade," as well as Milan and New York.(31)

Within this universal paradigm of women's experience, the neo-feminists see the situation of women in Yugoslavia as exhibiting special characteristics. According to Katunarić, what distinguished Yugoslav society at the end of World War Two from the West European countries was that it was still largely patriarchal. The subsequent mass migration to the cities inevitably resulted in family conflict. The old patriarchal family was broken up into nuclear families. Women began to work outside the home and to find a separate identity. Family relationships splintered as divorce and abortion initiated by women increased. "The atomized family became the point of conjuncture between the industrial economy and women's emancipation."(32)

The "logic of women's emancipation" thus led directly to a crisis of collective institutions. The majority of the populations of the expanded cities were scarcely one generation removed from the old patriarchal traditions. Women with lower educational skills moved into the lower paying jobs, earning as much as 20 per cent less than men. None of the various campaigns to establish women's quotas in the delegate system succeeded in eliciting long-term interest among women or in changing their low political status, while socially and culturally the patriarchal tradition prevailed. Indeed, all the officially sanctioned educational, economic, and political efforts in effect changed women's position very little. The crisis of collective institutions has yet to be given permanent solution.(33)

For Katunarić, the situation of women in Eastern Europe and the Soviet Union became if anything worse, because patriarchalism was incorporated into the form of government. "In the authoritarian conscience, the woman is located in the family as in her vital center. She is in the first place mother and everything is done to conserve and maintain this model of women from destruction."(34) The new feminists have moved a considerable distance from the adulation of the status of women in the Soviet Union characteristic of the communist and leftist women activists of Yugoslavia in the 1930s.

The fourth proposition of the new feminism is derived from the first and third. The persistence of the woman question is a function of the persistence of patriarchal values. What industrialization has brought is the reformulation of patriarchal values based on men's dominance in the economy.

Drakulić-Ilić argues half jokingly and half seriously that patriarchalism has surfaced in a new form, which she irreverently calls "testicology." Testicology is found on three principles: sexism, traditionalism, and totalitarianism. Sexism, she says, is rooted in the phallic worship of the ancient world.

However, since the social differences between the sexes have diminished in modern society, phallocracy hides itself in sexual discrimination, putting women down. Traditionalism seeks to convince women that the domination of men and the subordination of women is the natural division of work and tries through legislative/economic means to regulate the power relations between the sexes. Finally, totalitarianism posits that civilized society must be established upon some order. Women must be placed in society according to their abilities in such a way as to give men free scope for their abilities. With this definition, Drakulić-Ilić goes on to find evidence of testicology in contemporary Yugoslav writers. Once again she uses the ridiculous to make a point about the woman question in Yugoslavia--in this case, the prevalence of male chauvinism in Yugoslav society.(35)

The perception that patriarchalism may not be dying out but may be reviving in a new and even stronger form is one shared by other women intellectuals interviewed by the author. The perception is present in comments about the need to change "the bureaucrats" in power, to develop real self-management, to do away with "dogmatic tendencies." As noted earlier, even the women of the wartime generation admit that the survivals of patriarchalism among both men and women constitute one of the severest impediments to women's further progress in Yugoslavia. Indeed, it is perhaps not reading too much in their comments on the younger generation to detect a degree of disillusionment. The war called forth the highest ideals and the most idealistic expectations. Comments such as "Everything seemed so easy then," "We never doubted we could do it, but it would be difficult to do it now," indicate the tenor of their thought. So much seemed realizable during the war. Yet how fundamentally little women's situation has changed since then!

The fifth proposition is one which relates directly to the impact of industrialization and technology on society, the reification of human relationships. Economic development brought the break-up of the protective family. Women were cast adrift. In an article entitled "Why Women Like Stories," Drakulić-Ilić argues that modern women's attraction to the cheap novels, the sensational literature, and television serials betrays their desire to find their own aims and their own niche in modern society.(36) While reading and television-watching do not solve the problem, they give women a sense of contact with their reality and the illusion that their difficulties can be solved.

The fact is, however, that the cheap novels and television serials only imitate the television commercials in their depiction of women as stereotypes. In commercials for cars, cosmetics, and a host of other products, every woman is beautiful, sensuous, and full of life, computerized, and programmed for the game of sexual relations with men.(37)   Woman's beauty is portrayed exclusively as there for the satisfaction of men.   In commercial after commercial, woman's body is glorified, not for itself, but to sell commodities. The mother sells dishwashing detergents, and smiling two-children families sell toothpaste, vacations, cereal.   Human relationships become reduced to what they can sell or buy.

As in her other critiques of women's condition in modern society, Drakulić-Ilić takes most of her data from the United States, this time from ads published in Playboy.   But her descriptions apply equally to the glamorous beauties and happy families who fill the ads and make the announcements on Yugoslav TV.   If anything, the Yugoslav commercial models reflect the "come hither" glamor and implicit sex of the 1930s in the United States.   The use of the soft, round, submissive females rather than the angular and jerky features of the more aggressive Western woman model lends substance to Drakulić-Ilić's thesis that old fashioned patriarchalism has found a secure anchor in the cardboard relationships depicted on the TV screen.

The new feminists' condemnation of the reification of human relationships in modern society shares the view of Western feminists that the mass media's exploitation of women as sex objects is a major step on the road to the dehumanization of all human contacts. Barbara Ehrenreich and Deirdre English, for example, in For Her Own Good, masterfully trace the history of modern medical, sociological, and psychological attempts to give scientific definition to "women's place," only to see that effort collapse before the mass media's successful harnessing of the liberated woman to its commercialization of human behavior as a cost/benefit exchange.(38)   Whereas in traditional patriarchal society, women's submission could be argued on umimpeachable moral grounds, such as love, loyalty, and self-sacrifice, the disintegration of traditional authority and the mass media's marketing of human relationships as commodities leave nothing sacred. Emotion and morals are banished from the center of human activity.

Antigone's choice in Sophocles' ancient drama of whether to conform to the values of the state or to follow her sense of personal duty and bury her brother has long ceased to be a moral issue.   Her agony in today's object-oriented world signifies nothing.   In submitting to play the role of the acquiescent Ismene, in Katunarić's view, modern women perpetuate the Oedipal male power struggle and male dominance.(39) Czech author Milan Kundera beautifully dramatizes the consequences of the reification and "betrayal" of human relationships in his book, <u>The Unbearable Lightness of Being</u>.(40) His characters act out the new feminists' message that a life without the weight and the permanence of personal commitment is not fully human. But the new feminists carry the logic of that position to its ultimate conclusion. There can be no rehumanization of human relationships under industrial conditions without a fundamental change in social institutions to bring women to centerstage, and to reinstate emotion as a central value in personal intercourse.

CONCLUSION

The lives of Yugoslav women have been more rapidly transformed in the space of forty years than have those of their counterparts in the more industrialized countries of the Western world. The war opened the way for women to move out from under patriarchal authority, yet failed to provide a wide enough opening for patriarchalism to lose its hold over the official party line. In a single generation, Yugoslav women have moved from their place in traditional agrarian communities, capable of defending their household and land with gun in hand, to finding themselves independent wage earners in a society where the mass media exploit their new and still uneasy status to sell any and every product for mass consumption.

The new feminism in Yugoslavia has taken stock of the change, and has brought the skeleton out of the closet. In so doing, the movement has not only run against the official ideology, but has offended the deepest sensibilities of the wartime generation of women.

There is a rough logic in the Yugoslav authorities' condemnation of the "feministiki" for their honesty in calling sisterhood global. No leadership wants to hear that forty years of officially directed women's liberation has in effect contributed little to the real emancipation of the "second sex," nor can it readily accept the idea that women were quite possibly "used" to win the battles which brought them to power, and that the real struggle for a more equitable society has yet to begin.

Only time will tell whether the nascent feminist ideology in Yugoslavia will spread or remain contained among the universities, a largely intellectual protest. Drakulić-Ilić would argue that all revolutions are

started by intellectuals, and the possibility always
exists that feminism will gain momentum. But the
probability seems small, for the message is so far
clothed in too much sophistication to attract a mass
audience. But the message has been heard by the
authorities. Whether the movement expands or not, the
feminists have injected into the national debate over
the future of Yugoslavia an issue which is more
fundamental than the republican quarrel over political
chairs: Any reform which is worthy of the name must be
directed toward genuinely egalitarian and democratic
institutions.

NOTES

1. The Conference was held concurrently with the
   Second Comintern Congress. It is significant that
   at the time, the "woman question" was not
   considered of sufficient urgency to merit
   discussion on the Congress floor. For the
   Conference's policy statement on women, see
   "Statement of Position on the Organization of
   Working Women to the Second Comintern Congress,"
   in Pravda (March 6, 1920). See also my discussion
   of that policy in Barbara Jancar, Women under
   Communism (Baltimore, Md.: Johns Hopkins
   University Press, 1978), pp. 84-86.
2. Magdalena Sokolowska, Kobieta pracujaca [The
   Working Woman] (Warsaw: Wiedza Powszechna, 1963).
3. See Sharon Wolchik (ed.), Women, State, and Party
   in Eastern Europe (Durham, N.C.: Duke University
   Press, in press).
4. For a discussion of these gains, see Jancar, Women
   under Communism, chapter 2.
5. This is Dušanka Kovačević's statistic. See
   Dušanka Kovačević, Women of Yugoslavia in the
   National Liberation War (Belgrade: Jugoslovenski
   pregled, 1977), p. 10. Lydia Sklevicky sets the
   figure a little higher, at 23 per cent. See Lydia
   Sklevicky, "Karakteristike organiziranog
   djelovanja zena u Jugoslaviji u razdoblju do
   drugog svjetskog rata (I)," in Polja, No. 308
   (October 1984), p. 415.
6. Kovačević, Women of Yugoslavia, p. 10.
7. Figures from Statistical Pocket Book of Yugoslavia
   1980 (Belgrade: Federal Statistical Office,
   1980), pp. 32-33; Vida Tomšić, Women in the
   Development of Self-Managing Yugoslavia (Belgrade:
   Jugoslovenska stvarnost, 1980), pp. 194-196;
   Jancar, Women under Communism, p. 15.
8. Tomšić, Women in the Development, p. 194.
9. Statistical Yearbook, p. 41.
10. Tomšić, Women in the Development, pp. 194-195.
11. Ibid., pp. 196-198.
12. Jancar, Women under Communism, p. 95. For
    additional data on women in the self-managing
    institutions, see Pedro Ramet, "Women, Work, and
    Self-Management in Yugoslavia," in East European
    Quarterly , Vol. 17, No. 4 (January 1984), pp.
    459-468.
13. Ibid., p. 201.
14. East European Leadership List, Radio Free Europe
    Research (February 1, 1985), pp. 31-35.
15. The Chair of the Women's Conference of Yugoslavia,
    Ana Tankosava-Simić, asserted that women failed to

222

understand the self-management system and how to
utilize it to their benefit.
16. Author's observations.
17. Statistical Yearbook, p. 35.
18. Vera St. Erlich, Family in Transition: A Study of
300 Yugoslav Villages (Princeton, N.J.: Princeton
University Press, 1966).
19. For a penetrating study of the patriarchal
lifestyle in Yugoslavia, see Dunja Rihtman-
Augustin, Struktura tradicijskog mišljenja
(Zagreb: Školska knjiga, 1984).
20. Vjeran Katunarić, for example, sees divorce and
abortion as women's acts of revolt against
patriarchal authority. See Vjeran Katuranić,
Ženski eros i civilizacija smrti (Zagreb:
Biblioteka Naprijed, 1984), pp. 231-233.
21. Unless indicated, the women will not be mentioned
by name. For a more in depth analysis of these
interviews, the reader is referred to the author's
forthcoming book, Women in the Yugoslav
Revolution. The author wishes to express her
thanks to the Federal Institute for International
Scientific, Technical, and Cultural Cooperation,
the Women's Conference, and the Yugoslav Veterans'
Association for arranging the interviews. The
opinions expressed are the author's alone.
22. Statistics from Leksikon Narodnooslobodilački rat
i revolucija u Jugoslaviji 1941-1945 (Belgrade:
Narodna knjiga, 1980), Vol. 1, p. 17, and Vol. 2,
p. 1251.
23. Rada Iveković, "Da li klasno pitanje iscrpljuje
žensko pitanje," in Žena, Vol. 40, Nos. 2-3
(March-July 1982), as quoted in Slavenka Drakulić-
Ilić, Smrtni grijeŝi feminizma: Ogledi o
mudologiji (Zagreb: Znanje, 1984), p. 104.
24. Drakulić-Ilić, Smrtni grijeŝi, p. 105.
25. For a good review of the conference, see Pedro
Ramet, "Gleichberechtigung der Geschlechter,
Parteipolitik und Feminismus in Jugoslawien,"
Osteuropa, Vol. 33, No. 7 (July 1983).
26. Sklevicky, "Karakeristike organiziranog...(I),"
and Lydia Sklevicky, "Karakteristike organiziranog
djelovanja žena u Jugoslaviji u razdoblju do
drugog svetskog rata (II)," in Polja, No. 309
(November 1984), pp. 454-456; and Lydia Sklevicky,
"Organizirana djelatnost žena hrvatske za vrijeme
Narodnooslobodilačke borbe 1941-1945," in
Povijesni prilozi (1984), o. 3, pp. 85-127.
27. Kovačević, Women of Yugoslavia, p. 11.
28. For a presentation of documents on the history of
the women's movement, based on the official line,
see Marija Šoljan (ed.), Žene Hrvatske u radničkom
pokretu do aprila 1941 (Zagreb: Izdanje

Konferencije za društvenu aktivnost žena Hrvatske, 1967); and Jovanka Kecman, Žene Jugoslavije u radničkom pokretu i ženskim organizacijama 1918-1941 (Belgrade: Narodna knjiga-Institut za savremenu istoriju, 1978).

29. Katunarić, Ženski eros, pp. 242-243.
30. The author came to the conclusion regarding the Anti-Fascist Women's Front independently of her field research in Yugoslavia by a reading of the published documents. See Barbara Jancar, "Women in the Yugoslav National Liberation Movement: An Overview," in Studies in Comparative Communism, Vol. 14, Nos. 2-3 (Summer/Autumn 1981), especially pp. 155-158 and 162-164.
31. Slavenka Drakulić-Ilić, "Muškarac za po kuci," in NIN (December 30, 1984), pp. 26-27.
32. Katunarić, Ženski eros, pp. 232-233.
33. Ibid., pp. 233-238.
34. Ibid., p. 225.
35. Drakulić-Ilić, Smrtni griješi, pp. 59-77.
36. Ibid., pp. 44-45.
37. Ibid., p. 55.
38. Barbara Ehrenreich and Deirdre English, For Her Own Good: 150 Years of the Experts' Advice to Women (London: Pluto Press, 1979), pp. 282-292.
39. Katunarić, Ženski eros, pp. 243-251.
40. Milan Kundera, The Unbearable Lightness of Being, translated by Michael Heim (London and Boston: Faber and Faber, 1984).

10
Environmental Protection: "The Tragedy of the Republics"

Barbara Jancar

Environmental protection in Yugoslavia is of recent venue. Before the Second World War, Yugoslavia was primarily an underdeveloped agricultural country. The war devastated both population and land, and brought industrial development to a standstill. Thus, virtually all of the country's industrial and urban growth has been forced into the 40-year timespan since the war. Both industrialization and urbanization have occurred at a very rapid pace and with little thought given to their impact on the environment. Yugoslavia today is faced with increasingly serious environmental problems which only yesterday seemed inconsequential. The solution to these problems is rendered more difficult not only by the technological and financial measures required but perhaps more important by the self-management system given constitutional form in 1974, which sets up an essentially confederal arrangement between Yugoslavia's six national republics and two autonomous provinces.(1)

In 1948, Yugoslavia had a total population of 15,901,000. In 1979, it had grown to 22,160,000, a 39 per cent increase over the immediate post war figure.(2) During that time, interrepublican migration was heavy, with thousands of peasants leaving the land in search of jobs in the industrializing cities. According to the 1971 census, more than one million people had changed their place of residence since the previous census 10 years earlier. Of these, 460,000 had migrated <u>from</u> Bosnia and Herzegovina (BiH) and 568,500 had migrated <u>to</u> Serbia, primarily to Belgrade. The unidirectional thrust of the migration is illustrated by urbanization figures. In 1948, there were 83 urban centers with populations above 10,000. In 1971, there were 148. From 1931 to 1971, Belgrade grew 3.1 times; Zagreb, 3.5 times; Ljubljana, 2.9 times; Skopje, 4.6 times; Niš, 14.6 times; and Split,

16.5 times. In 1946, approximately 20 per cent of the population lived in cities; in 1978, 70 per cent.(3) As Yugoslavs do not hesitate to point out, the process of urbanization in Yugoslavia has been one of the most accelerated in the history of urban development, generating a set of pollution problems which by and large were non-existent even a decade ago.

Industrialization has also been rapid. Between 1947 and 1975, the average annual rate of economic growth was 6.2 per cent, and between 1953 and 1964, an impressive 8.6 per cent. In 1947, industry accounted for approximately 19 per cent of the work force. In 1977, industry accounted for 40 per cent while the number of workers in agriculture had decreased accordingly. In 1951, there were 6,825 automobiles and 1,150 buses. In 1976, there were over 17.3 million cars and 21 thousand buses.

These developments have upset traditional land use practices and wrought havoc with the environment. The production of energy has increased over 18 times. The number of paved roads has grown from one paved road out of Belgrade before the Second World War to a network of highways criss-crossing the country covering over 20,000 kilometers.(4) The amount of agricultural land fell 3 per cent from 15 million hectares in 1961 to 14.6 million in 1976. About 20,000 hectares of agricultural land are lost to production yearly and the situation has reached crisis proportions.(5) Forested land decreased a substantial 12 per cent from 10.3 million hectares in 1961 to 9.1 million in 1976. The loss of forests has been a primary factor in the rampant erosion which has now become critical. In 1976 agricultural land represented 56 per cent of the total land area of Yugoslavia, forests 35.7 per cent, water, 1.5 per cent, human settlements, 2.6 per cent, transportation networks, 1.2 per cent, and remaining areas, 3.1 per cent.

The quality of water has steadily deteriorated so that virtually every river has fallen from a higher water classification to a lower, sometimes by as much as two grades. In Kosovo, where rivers were relatively unpolluted 10 years ago, analyses have shown that not a single river in the province was of a water quality which could be designated first class.(6) The Adriatic Sea has fallen victim to increasing pollution despite the signing of international and regional agreements. The water quality of the two rivers of Yugoslavia, protected by regional compacts, the Neretva and the Sava, have become national scandals. The Sava is Yugoslavia's main water artery. Along its shores stretches the bulk of the country's industry and its water is used for both industrial and household consumption by Belgrade. Pollution caused by oil seepage into the river has earned the Sava a name evoking memories of Lake Erie, "river without life."(7) In urban locations throughout Yugoslavia, water quality monitoring has revealed significant pollution everywhere. Almost 50 per cent of the population is now supplied by public water systems, and 11 per cent of the water designated for urban settlements comes from surface water threatened by contamination. In 1976, one-third of the urban water systems lacked adequate treatment facilities, and many local water systems required substantial reconstruction, having been built by laymen rather than experts. According to the Federal Council for the Environmental Protection and Territorial Planning, only 25 per cent of all urban water systems had water treatment components. By 1984, sewerage disposal had also become a major problem, increasing pollution at the outlets of rivers, in lakes and the sea.(8)

Air pollution is highly visible, particularly in the larger cities. Newspapers in the republican capitals and major urban centers publish data daily on air quality. Almost without exception during the winter months, the ambient air quality in one of Yugoslavia's larger cities exceeds the permissible legal level for the major pollutants.(9) The main culprit is SO_2. In Belgrade, particles of coal dust descend from the sky in the wintertime, covering buildings and streets with black film, while the air is saturated with the acrid smell of coal fires. According to newspaper reports, daily measurements in Skopje have shown that in some parts of the city, pollution is so high that it impedes "normal breathing."(10)

Fortunately for Yugoslavia, air pollution remains primarily an isolated urban problem. Although the country is a signer of the European Trans-boundary Air Pollution Agreement, the long-range transport of air pollution is so far not a significant domestic issue. The official environmental study prepared in 1976 for the Federal Executive Council and the executive councils of the republics and provinces identified 68 areas where permanent or critical air pollution had been monitored. Of these, 25 were in Serbia, with severe contamination registered in the industrial centers of Belgrade, Kraljevo, and Niš. On the territory of Serbia alone, experts have cited as many as 2,500 industrial installations with inadmissible levels of emissions.(11) Happily, Yugoslavia benefits from Košava, a strong westerly wind, which periodically blows across the central plain, sweeping away the coalspecks, dust particles and other pollutants which blacken the Belgrade skies, leaving the city's air cold and clear. Health officials count on this wind to prevent the development of killer smogs or similar phenomena dangerous to human health.(12)

The growth of heavy industry has brought a rapid increase in solid waste. The Adriatic port city of Rijeka has been cited as "probably the most threatened area in the North Adriatic" as a result of the continued discharging of all industrial and municipal waste water directly into the sea.(13) The Neretva River contaminated by waste water discharged along its length, pours its polluted contents into the Adriatic.(14) Waste disposal has reached a point where ways are now being discussed for managing it either through recycling, or using the secondary by-products in the production of new goods.

Perhaps the most salient environmental degradation (ED) feature of the postwar period has been the chaotic growth of towns at the expense of the countryside. Far exceeding the planned forecasts, the expansion of the cities has demanded the creation of totally new infrastructures or the enlargement of existing facilities of limited capacity to handle the environmental problems generated by the influx of migrants to the urban areas. The newcomers to the cities have left their farms to be cared for, more often than not, by their aging parents, or have abandoned them all together. No longer able to undertake the physical work necessary to make the small five-hectare parcel yield its modest livelihood, those who have remained on the land have preferred to sell their plots to the newly prosperous in the towns for summer vacation homes. Erosion, soil deterioration, and the permanent loss of once arable land have been the result.

On their part, the cities have grown higgledy-piggledy with either very little planning, or with the unanticipated rapid growth outstripping planning capabilities.(15) Although the investment in housing and utilities represents around 10 per cent of realized investment by the social sector,(16) 80 per cent of all Yugoslav housing today is built privately. Much of it is built according to regulations in designated areas as an urban home or as the much desired "vacation home." But construction costs are extremely high for most Yugoslavs and the purchase of a ready-built house beyond their pocketbook. The housing shortage in the city is chronic. The result is that the immigrants to the cities stop at the city limits and put up small shacks, because they cannot find an apartment and have no money to buy. City inspectors are reluctant to evict or convict the inhabitants of these dwellings because of possible public outcry and the appearance of discrimination against the poor. The unplanned sprawl expands around the city's edge, upsetting the orderly development of urban sewer, water and transportation systems. In the words of one reporter, "we have the phenomenon of the growth of large polluted cities and the abandonment of smaller villages and agricultural land, resulting in harmful consequences for the country's economy, for life and for defense."(17)

Finally, there is the problem of the preservation of the country's green areas, natural landmarks and unspoiled regions. Here the record is slightly better. In the immediate postwar period, the country voted to set aside restricted areas for nature reservations and natural landmarks. In 1951, there were three national parks. Currently, there are 15 with a total area of 301,704 hectares.(18) Yugoslavia boasts eight biosphere reserves under the protection of the United Nations' Man and the Biosphere Program (MAB), among these the world renowned Plitvice Lakes in northern Bosnia, Durmitor National Park in Montenegro, and the Tara River Canyon. But industrial and tourist inroads, particularly along the Adriatic, are despoiling the country's natural beauty. People had to fight to prevent the building of a nuclear power plant on Vir Island in the Adriatic. And increasingly, economic development needs are making demands on some of Yugoslavia's most beautiful scenery. The most recent example was the attempt to build a dam on the Tara River in Montenegro, where it would flood the dramatic Tara River Canyon.

The need to finance one's own budget created by the inauguration of the self-management system has posed the additional problem of maintenance and preservation of the protected areas. As of 1976, 12 of the 15 national parks had secure incomes. The three which did not all lay in Montenegro and unfortunately, included Durmitor. The record for regional parks is less impressive with only two of the 17 having assured financial means.(19)

Since Yugoslav economic and urban growth are largely phenomena of the last three decades when the consequences of pollution were already known, the question may justifiably be raised why the builders of the new industries and the urban planners did not take better environmental precautions. The answer divides into three main parts: perception of the problem, economics and politics. The first two admit of relatively easy solutions: education and money. The last requires major rethinking of the relationship between Yugoslavia's republics and in the absence of reform, may result in a tragedy for Yugoslavia's environment. Only a brief discussion will be made of the first two problems. The rest of the chapter will concentrate on the republican issue, using the Sava River and Tara Canyon controversies as examples.

There is a prevailing perception in Yugoslavia
that pollution has not reached a crisis point and that
there is time to do something about it. As one
Yugoslav official explained it to the author, the
United States did not realize its pollution problems
until after it had become the most highly
industrialized nation on earth. Although it is only a
developing nation, Yugoslavia has taken legal
precautions, some of them dating back to the period
immediately after the Second World War. Where an
environmental crisis has been imminent, as in the loss
of agricultural land in Slovenia, the republic has
intervened to solve the problem. Where no immediate
crisis is apparent, the various governments of
Yugoslavia have moved slowly but purposefully toward
improving environmental management.(20)

There is some justice to this position. Almost
every republic has passed a set of environmental laws.
The federal government has also passed legislation
within its sphere of competence, namely interrepublican and international environmental concerns.
There are over 130 Yugoslav statutes now on the books,
with amendments to existing laws modifying that number
every year. The most recent have been modifications of
the laws on waste disposal, the forest laws, changes in
the federal water law, and proposals for study of a
federal agricultural land law.(21) Serbia, Croatia and
Slovenia have the most comprehensive legislation, but
all the republics have laws covering the major
pollution areas. In addition, the current five-year
plan for the first time has incorporated environmental
procedures into the planning system, requiring
enterprises to report environmental conditions and
making the granting of construction loans contingent
upon the inclusion of appropriate pollution controls in
plant plans for all new industrial development.(22)

The problem is that as in many countries, the
legislation is not observed. One reporter charged
enterprise managers with "ignorance" in the deliberate
importing of cheap but "dirty" foreign machinery.(23)
There is little doubt that managerial perceptions have
not yet been sufficiently sensitized to ED, as managers
continue to prefer to put short-term gains over long-
term benefits. A second Yugoslav explanation of the
prevailing attitude is that environmental controls are
a "luxury" that only rich countries can afford.(24)
But perhaps the most characteristic answer for
environmental indifference told the author was that
Yugoslavs have not yet adopted a caretaker attitude
toward their land, because of their experience of 400
years of Turkish rule and the resultant concentration
on obtaining national independence.

Perhaps the strongest objective explanation that might be offered for the prevailing Yugoslav attitude toward pollution is that most Yugoslavs are only one generation removed from their rural heritage where environmental protection was not an issue. People tilled the soil, sewed and reaped as they had done for generations. The large majority of city dwellers are unaware that the environment can be a problem. Many throw trash on the streets or in the parks without thinking of the consequences. The realization that human actions can cause ED is increasingly taking hold of the Yugoslav mind, particularly in the more northern republics, but it has required a revolutionary change in thinking in a very short period of time. The Yugoslav official was right in insisting that the people should be credited for having embarked upon an environmental protection program before development went too far.

A second answer to the apparent failure of Yugoslavia to take better environmental precautions is economics. Many Yugoslav officials insist that money is the primary obstacle to improved environmental protection. Pollution control equipment is expensive and must be purchased from abroad, while enterprises must face pressing demands in other areas. At the present time, the Yugoslav economy is in a serious situation with a foreign indebtedness of some $20 billion(25) and a massive internal indebtedness.(26) National priorities clearly must go toward putting the economy on its feet.

In current Yugoslav thinking, therefore, there can be no question that energy has a higher priority than pollution. The country has only limited options regarding choice of fuel, and its reduced financial situation has not improved them.

In the 1960s, Yugoslavia contracted to build a pipeline from the Hungarian border to Belgrade in order to heat the city with oil rather than polluting coal. Construction was halted when the government ran out of funds. Polish coal was an alternative until its import was stopped, once again from lack of money. Until money can be found, there is no choice but to burn the cheap local high-sulphur coal. Environmental experts are aware of the pollution dangers. In its periodic pollution control campaigns, the press has published articles, for example, showing Belgrade homeowners how to operate a coal fire in order to minimize pollution.(27) But the fact is the city has no alternative to burning the calorically inferior and more polluting domestic product.

Energy has become a critical factor in Yugoslav industrial development. Those who have shivered in underheated buildings in Yugoslavia's cities or have turned on a light, to find the power supply temporarily cut off, are acutely aware of the country's energy problems. Of all the republics, Macedonia, Bosnia-Herzegovina, and Montenegro probably face the most serious energy shortages, especially in the area of electric power. Macedonia has in fact been criticized for its failure to build energy installations.(28) A main problem is the country's reliance on oil imports. To reduce this dependence, the federal energy plan up to the year 2000 mandates the accelerated development of domestic energy sources, particularly coal and hydropower, as well as conservation measures.(29)

Replacement of imported oil with domestically produced fuel is a costly business. It is estimated that an investment of 22 billion dinars would be necessary to replace by a domestic fuel a million tons of imported oil valued at 11 billion dinars. Since oil was responsible for 47 per cent of fuel consumption in 1980, one way to raise the money, in official opinion, is through a higher tax on all oil, particularly heating oil.(30) But the government must be careful not to create a situation where people cannot afford to heat their homes.

Clearly, the forced choice of unpalatable alternatives represents the optimum solution neither for energy production nor for the environment. A factory outside of Belgrade is coal-fired. Citizens, who are also employees of the factory, have complained of the smoke and foul-smelling air emanating from the plant. There is no choice but to burn coal. If the environmental authorities were to uphold the law, they would have to close or demand the relocation of the plant, risking the jobs of the factory's employees. If they are less strict, they will let the factory pay the mandated fine and keep the plant open.(31) In Kragujevac, the Serbian "Detroit," residents have complained about paint fumes coming from the paint shop of the Zastava automobile plant. However, the company's chief environmental engineer says the plant can do nothing about the fumes. The paint is imported and apparently, the paint supplier will not reveal its chemical composition arguing that the formula is protected by international patent.(32) Again, rigid legal enforcement would demand closing the paint shop. The compromise with legality is to let the company continue to pay its fine and to keep the shop open.

Attitudes and economics are serious impediments in themselves to the successful implementation of an environmental protection program, but neither challenges the fundamental organization of Yugoslavia's social and political system. Already, environmental education is being introduced in the schools, and an experimental inter-disciplinary post-graduate program of environmental study at Belgrade University is exploring ways to promote professional cooperation in the solution of environmental problems.(33)

Moreover, if the attitude is willing, the financial and material resources can be found to control pollution. Perhaps the most dramatic example in Yugoslavia of "where there is an environmental will, there is a way," was the draining and cleaning of Lake Palić near the town of Subotica on the Yugoslav/Hungarian border. In the nineteenth century, the aristocracy and new bourgeoisie of the Austro-Hungarian Empire spent their summer vacations on the lakeshore. The construction of industry and the growth of nearby Subotica after World War Two resulted in the lake becoming the dumping ground for both industrial and municipal sewerage. By the 1950s, the fish were gone and the water was too polluted for swimming. The vacationers were ceasing to come. Palić had become a dead lake. An enterprising headmaster of a local school together with concerned area scientists headed a movement to clean up the lake. The scientists volunteered time and designed the clean-up. The town residents voted by public referendum to give a certain percentage of their wages for the next 10 years to fund the project. The lake was drained and a sewerage system put in. Palić has become again a prime vacation spot for both Yugoslavs and Hungarians across the border.(34) Lake Palić is one of the environmental successes of the self-management system and an example to all local communities, that when a community becomes sufficiently concerned, ED can be stopped.

A problem which is harder to solve because it goes to the heart of the Yugoslav socio-political system is the administration of environmental protection. The core of Yugoslavia's environmental legislation and the basic elements of self-management were written into law in the 1970s. The two evolved separately from one another with virtually no attention given to the impact of a decentralized system of government on the development of adequate pollution control and ED prevention mechanisms. Two recent environmental issues have brought the relationship between the self-management principle and environmental protection to the fore: the pollution of the Sava River and the Tara River Canyon. These two cases will serve as illustrations of the problems posed by self-management to the formulation of a workable environmental protection policy.

Yugoslavia's confederal self-management system arose from the twin necessities to demonstrate a specific Yugoslav path to communism upon Tito's break with Stalin,(35) and to find an accommodation between the republic's constituent nationalities which would survive Tito's death.(36) The 1974 Constitution attempts to resolve the problems of national diversity and the decentralization of state power by applying confederation at the republican level and the self-management principle throughout Yugoslav society. The unifying element is the League of Yugoslav Communists (LCY) whose primacy is constitutionally guaranteed.(37)

Self-management in essence enables the republics to decide their own internal affairs, assigning the federal govenment a very limited set of powers when compared with the American system.(38) In the environmental area, the federal government has competence only in matters concerning two or more republics and in international transboundary pollution. So far under the new constitution, three federal environmental laws have been passed, all of them having to do with water: the 1974 Law on Seacoasts, the 1974 Law on Interrepublican and International Water, and the 1977 Law on Sea and Internal Shipping.(39) While the Federal Assembly decides basic economic questions, the details and day-to-day economic issues are left to the republics.

The Assembly is composed of two chambers, one representing the lower self-managing industrial and other organizations, and the local communities (the Federal Chamber) and the other elected by the republican and autonomous provinces assemblies, representing the federal principle (the Chamber of Republics and Provinces). This latter body does not reach a decision by accepting the majority of individual votes. Rather, each republican and provincial delegation acts as a bloc. Every decision they make must have the approval of their corresponding republican or provincial legislature. The republican and provincial assemblies in agreement with the Chamber of Republics and Provinces decide the most crucial policy questions: the national social plan, the size of the budget, economic issues, such as monetary regulations, foreign trade, price control, credits for the underdeveloped areas, and taxation. In addition, the second chamber decides independently of the Federal Chamber questions relating to the contraction of credits for national defense, the supervision of federal administrative agencies, and the formulation of enforcement policies for the implementation of federal statutes. These last two provisions give the republics jurisdiction over both federal and republican environmental enforcement organs (Article 286). Limited federal jurisdiction is thus juxtaposed against substantial republican power.

Self-management further gives considerable latitude to the districts (opštine) to protect the local environment through the passing of regulations, the planning and implementation of pollution control measures, and the organization of their own environmental inspection systems. Self-management, in effect, means that in theory, every enterprise, social or scientific organization and every local government unit is self-supporting. This means that local government has to raise the money to fund local social welfare programs (pensions, medical care, education, public transport, water systems) from the revenues of local industry. However, the localities have little say as to the projects they are to fund. The required social welfare programs and the share of money to be given to the corresponding social welfare organizations (called "self-managing interest communities") formed to administer them, are determined by the Federal Assembly. Environmental protection is not a required public service. Environmental programs thus cannot benefit from an assurance of permanent funding but each program must seek its own financing. Since local government and local industry have substantial portions of their budget already allocated to mandated fields, there is little incentive to undertake costly environmental improvements, especially in the economically less advantaged communities. The pay-your-own-way system has resulted in the richer republics and districts being able to provide better services and environmental protection than the poorer. Richer localities can also hire the specialists and environmental inspectors which the poorer districts cannot afford.

Secondly, the system has resulted in a parcelization of environmental programs. If a project is to be undertaken that extends beyond the boundaries of one enterprise or locality, a self-managing "compact" must be signed between the project partners. This agreement must specify the contracting parties, the work to be done, and what each party is to contribute materially and financially to the project. Such negotiations are understandably sensitive, and organizations are not going to sign a compact on an environmental project unless there is some ecological disaster pending or economic benefit to be derived. The signed agreement in principle binds the contracting parties to their obligations. Compacts need not always be so specific. The two major interrepublican environmental agreements, the 1980 Neretva and the Sava River compacts,(40) have largely remained on paper, partially, in the author's opinion, because the wording is so vague as to commit the contracting parties in principle only.

Self-management has thus encouraged local interest at the expense of the common interest. Agreements do not become operative, first, because of conflict between contracting districts over environmentally irrelevant issues, such as the location of a national park's headquarters,(41) second, fear of economic disadvantage-ment, such as the delay in signing the Una River "Forever Wild" Compact, and third, procrastination in fulfilling the contract after signature, as in the case of the Sava and Neretva River compacts.

Success stories, however, do happen. Primary among these is the elaborate sewerage disposal system designed to preserve the pristine character of Lake Ohrid on the border between Yugoslavia and Albania. The lake has a world reputation for its unique ecology, and the wealth of architectural and cultural monuments along the Yugoslav shoreline. It is one of the oldest lakes in the world, sharing the distinction with Lake Baikal in the Soviet Union of being one of the two bodies of water which have preserved marine life from prehistoric ages. In Roman times, the Via Appia crossed its waters as the main trade route between Byzantium and Rome. In the eleventh century AD, Ohrid was the seat of an independent Christian archbishopric, and a world renowned center of learning. After World War Two, tourism was encouraged with little thought to environmental impact until 1970. Hotels, campsites, and summer homes mushroomed along the lakeshore. As is the case with many old settlements, sewerage from the lakefront villages was being discharged into the lake, threatening its delicate ecological balance.

Evidently, Lake Baikal was the catalyst for rethinking the consequences of uncontrolled building. Three Yugoslav districts decided to develop a sewerage disposal system. Forty-four studies were prepared with the help of the OECD, UNESCO, and Macedonian and other Yugoslav universities and institutes. A three-stage plan was devised. Only the first stage of the plan has been realized. But the agreement on that laid out the cost of the system, identified the organizations which would contribute the necessary monies and set forth the bases of the contributions by the different districts. A referendum was held in each of the districts to vote the money. Reportedly, experts went from village to village informing the public of the need to preserve the lake and the value of its preservation to their future. Four designs for the system were presented, ranging from five separate systems to one single system with a single treatment plant. The last option was selected at an estimated cost of $3.5 million at the time. Twenty per cent of the money was to come from the communes, 40 per cent from the International Bank and 40 per cent from federal sources inside Yugoslavia. Of the 20 per cent to be raised locally, Ohrid, as the largest district, was to contribute 58 percent. The

money was to come from local taxes, water levies and
other tax sources, plus a 5 per cent surcharge of
incomes for a specified period of time.(42)

Even more than in the cleaning up of Lake Palić,
the Lake Ohrid pollution control project unequivocally
demonstrates that under self-management, environmental
protection measures impose sizeable burdens upon local
communities, even when they act in concert. A 5 per
cent surcharge on one's income is considerable in any
country, and residents everywhere are likely to vote
down a project demanding such sacrifices. Fortunately,
the referendum was positive, opening the way for the
completion of the project's first stage. The last two
have yet to be undertaken.

The evidence thus suggests that self-management
has worked to the disadvantage of environmental
protection. It provides neither a central coercive or
deliberative organ with sufficient authority to
coordinate a national environmental program, nor a
certain source for financing necessary local projects
in the absence of local funding.

These difficulties have been recognized and
attempts have been made to deal with them. Two
examples are appropriate here. The first concerns
water management. From 1945 to 1963, water management
was under central governmental control, with some shift
in 1953 from the central to the republican level. With
the introduction of self-management in 1965, water
management organizations responsible for water
conservation and consumption became self-funding, while
those involved in water construction projects continued
to be funded from republican and provincial sources.
In 1974, all water management organizations became
self-managing.(43) In 1975, the first "self-managing
associations of interest" (SIZ) for water were formed,
and these spread over all the republics. Like other
SIZ, the water SIZ are financed out of local revenues
by a tax levied on water consumption. In the larger
republics of Croatia and Serbia, water administrative
regions were formed. The regional administrations
formed a republican water management association and in
1979, the republican SIZ joined together in a Union of
Water SIZ (Savez SIZova za vodoprivredu).(44)

The second example involves the formation of
special environmental councils attached to the organs
of government administration. In principle, there
should be an environmental committee, department, or
council at every level of government. Each work and
SIZ (social welfare) organization should have a
council. There should be an environmental council
attached to the district executive, and corresponding
councils at the republican level. In practice,
enterprises tend to assign the environmental function

to a section already in operation, while many districts are too insufficiently developed to have a separate environmental section, and simply give the responsibilty to another existing unit, most often, the urban affairs committee. Environmental councils do exist at the republican and provincial levels. Their chief purpose is to collect information on environmental conditions within their area, and to recommend action to improve those conditions to the appropriate governmental organ. In 1974, a Federal Council on the Environment and Territorial Planning was formed, again with the task of collecting information and to articulate environmental concerns at the federal level. The council also facilitates interrepublican environmental exchange both through the republics and through the exchange of opinions in the working groups in the various environmental areas attached to the council. Finally, the Council serves as a center for public education on environmental issues.(45)

The development of an interrepublican water SIZ association is encouraging, but it still leaves the control of water management in republican hands, hampering the formation of a coherent national water management policy. The main problem with the councils is that they are advisory only. Thus, although they may serve as a forum for the exchange of inter-republican environmental concerns, they are in no better position to impose environmental obligations upon unwilling republics than any other federal or republican organ.

Two recent environmental controversies illustrate the potential environmental consequences of the absence of a solution to the centripetal tendencies of republican power brought about by the current organization of self-management.

The first concerns the Tara River Canyon. The Tara River rises in the mountains of Montenegro and flows northwest to join the Drina River near Foča. The Drina River empties into the Sava about 50 miles west of Belgrade. The two rivers together form a water system which spans three of the Yugoslav republics, Serbia, Bosnia-Herzegovina, and Montenegro. The Tara rises in some of the wildest scenery in Yugoslavia. As it cuts its way north, it passes through a fantastically beautiful canyon which is adjacent to Durmitor National Park. The canyon walls rise steeply above the river in rugged formations. The valley road twists and turns as the river turns, and at each new bend, there is an ever changing kaleidoscope of rock, water, and sky. The canyon is beginning to be known by Western tourists, but the easy accessibility of the Adriatic has, perhaps fortunately, kept the number of visitors relatively low. The Canyon has been a

nationally protected area since 1973 and in 1977, it
came under international protection and was
incorporated into the United Nations' Man and the
Biosphere (MAB) worldwide system.

To understand the political context of the
controversy, it must be repeated that all of Yugoslavia
suffers from an energy shortage. As noted earlier,
Bosnia and Montenegro are in particularly difficult
situations. During the winter of 1983, a cold snap
made such a draw on available energy supplies that both
republics were forced to cut off electricity for
consumers during certain specified periods of the day.
The development of coal resources is a poor strategy
for republics which have little coal reserves. Studies
showed that the production of hydroelectricity had not
yet been exploited to capacity on the Drina River
system and on the Morača, a smaller river flowing west
down the Montenegrin mountains into the Adriatic. The
two republics together with Serbia determined to
explore the possibility of the construction of a
hydropower system spanning the Morača and Drina River
systems. A large-scale construction project envisaging
the building of multiple dams on the two systems was
drawn up.

Because the project was interrepublican, requiring
funding agreement among three republics, it had to be
approved by the Chamber of Republics and Provinces.
Energy consumption was not at a critical level in
Serbia, but the Serbian electric power company
reportedly cut off electricity to Serbian consumers to
show solidarity with the Bosnian and Montenegrin
companies. The mass media, particularly the TV, made
much of the problem. A political climate was generated
in favor of the project. On May 29, 1984, the
Agreement for the Exploitation of the Hydroenergetic
Potential of the Drina and Morača Rivers became law.

The only section of the project at issue was the
proposal to build a dam across the Tara River at a
location near the high bridge at the boundary of the
Durmitor National Park. The construction of the dam
would flood 52 kilometers of the most beautiful section
of the Tara Canyon. The agreement was attractive to
Montenegro because the republic would have to invest a
non-returnable sum which was considerably less than its
partners would have to contribute, and would be
increasing its hydropower sources with substantial
assistance from its more affluent neighbors.(46)

While the project was before the Federal Chamber,
there apparently was little public discussion of it.
Nevertheless, those informed were making their views
known regarding the preservation of the canyon.
Primary among the critics of the dam site were the
Yugoslav Committee for the Protection of the Tara River

and its Canyon, the President of the Assembly of Durmitor National Park, Mihajl Brajović Beba, the Federal Council for the Protection and Improvement of the Environment, the Federal Society for Clean Air, the Interacademy Council, the Association of University Professors and Teachers, and last but certainly not least, the Federal Conference of the Socialist Alliance of the Working People of Yugoslavia (SAWPY), the umbrella socio-political organization which encompasses all permitted political and interest activity in the country, including the LCY.

At the beginning of April 1984, the draft agreement was published in the press. A few days later, the press published a letter by Dr. Beba which created allegedly a "storm" at SAWPY and among scientists hired by the Alliance as consultants. The SAWPY Presidency adopted a unamimous resolution that the canyon had to be preserved at any price, and requested a public discussion on the issue. The resolution was never made public, although two newsmen from the Yugoslav news agency Tanjug were reportedly present at the meeting.(47)

After the bill was passed, the organizations which had expressed their opposition to the dam earlier began to generate greater pressure. The pressure was coordinated by and large by the Federal Council for the Protection and Improvement of the Human Environment, the official environmental socio-political organization, whose then Secretary-General, Dr. Milovoje Todorović, was a very energetic and dedicated environmentalist. The May-June issue of the council's Man and the Environment published a letter signed by the Chairman of the Presidency and Chairman of the Conference of SAWPY to the effect that the Conference urged the government to change its legislation, pointing to international as well as national opposition to the dam. In August, the influential Belgrade paper, Politika, pleaded that it was "not too late to save the Tara."(48) In September, Politika published a statement by Dr. Todorović representing the Federal Council for the Protection and Improvement of the Environment, asking the government to reconsider,(49) and at the end of September, a congress of Yugoslav environmentalists meeting at Ohrid, came out strongly against the dam.(50)

The pressure had its effect. The government did reconsider. A compromise was reached whereby the dam would not be built at the high bridge but up river where it would flood an area that did not form part of the park and was outside the MAB reserve.

The Tara River Canyon controversy is instructive of Yugoslav environmental politics for two reasons. First, it is the first time that an environmental issue in Yugoslavia became the object of national concern by a significant portion of interested organizations across the entire country. The issue clearly went beyond local interest. The local people lived in small traditional communities with little appreciation of what kinds of changes the dam would bring. Local residents of the canyon apparently felt strongly neither one way or the other. A few would be displaced by the flood waters. More felt their life style threatened. Others felt the dam would bring progress. But the local districts did not stand in the way of construction.(51) The protest came from scientists, university academics, and professionals across the breadth of Yugoslavia. Their success in changing federal legislation came from their organized efforts within the framework of the permitted interest organizations at the federal level. As such, it is a stunning example of the relative independence of these organizations from republican influence and of their ability to mobilize for an environmental cause.

Second, the controversy indicates the strength of republican power, when the republics act together. By limiting pre-law public discussion and consenting to the Serbian "sympathy brown-outs," the republics were able to influence the federal chamber responsible for republican affairs to approve the hydroelectric project without modifying the location of the Tara River dam. Public discussion was and could be limited because of republican control over censorship, while the temporary cut-offs of Serbian electric power reflected republican support of the power companies in the three republics. It should be noted that the opponents of the dam on the Tara River initially wanted no dam built. Once the legislation was passed, the question of no dam became a dead issue. Subsequent pressure on the government revolved around relocation of the site. In short, a "compromise" was reached whereby Montenegro obtained its dam on the Tara, and the environmentalists preserved the most scenic section of the Canyon. For an environmentalist, that decision cannot be the best one. Given the strength of republican power, the decision was the best that could be obtained in that particular circumstance.

The Sava River presents a different set of problems. By 1980, pollution of the Sava River had aroused sufficient concern to bring about an inter-district agreement to clean up the river among the communities located in the four republics through whose territory the river flowed. The agreement was signed in February of 1980.(52) The agreement is very non-specific, calling for information exchange, and the coordination of water management planning. In essence, it imposes obligations on the districts and towns along the river rather than on the republics, and the districts are the signatories. In the summer of 1984, oil seepage from upstream became noticeable in Belgrade. The public health authorities were alerted, but said that the seepage did not threaten Belgrade's water supply. As the level of oil concentration in the river increased, <u>Politika</u> rather ruefully noted that more than 800 normative acts, laws, and ordinances had been passed regulating the water quality of the river and still no one knew what "needed to be done" to clean it up.(53)

One of the main difficulties in protecting the Sava's water quality is the absence of an independent monitoring and inspection system. The federal water act passed in 1974 provides that federal agencies monitor water quality in agreement with the corresponding republican organs and that reporting of data and warning on water quality levels be also undertaken only in cooperation with republican agencies. The provisions leave control of water inspection in republican hands. Reportedly, the republics would only assent to the law under these conditions. The result is that each republic is reponsible for the monitoring of water quality within its boundaries but has no jurisdiction over the monitoring of water quality in sections of the river outside its territory. Slovenia, Croatia, and Bosnia-Herzegovina all lie up river of Serbia. Yet Serbia has no means of independently checking on how these republics are living up to their obligations as set forth in the numerous agreements and compacts, and the others have no means of checking on Serbia, although what Serbia does is of much less importance to them.

The environmental problem is rendered more complex by the political rivalries between the republics which have surfaced in the public discussion over reform of the constitutional system. The Serbians have pressed for "integration" and condemned the increasing independence of the country's republics and autonomous provinces, while Slovenia and Croatia have spoken out loudly in favor of autonomy versus what they perceive is a new effort by Serbia to dominate Yugoslav politics.(54) Under these circumstances, there is little impetus to compromise.

The Belgrade newspapers have indicated that the oil seepage is coming from Croatia. Croatia stands on its prerogative of controlling water-monitoring within its territory. In the meantime, jokes are being made in Belgrade about drinking oil with one's coffee, as Serbian-Croatian relations deteriorate. The problem of the Sava has become so publicized that a bill has been introduced to change the federal water law, which is anticipated to be passed within 1985.(55)

The Sava River controversy illustrates the strength of republican power under the present self-management system, when republics are divided and set one against the other. Yugoslavia can ill afford to let its water resources deteriorate much further. There are only a few rivers in the country left which can qualify as Class I or "unpolluted" waterways. The Neretva River suffers from similar problems as the Sava. If a federal water inspectorate is created, it will be the first environmental organ at the federal level with some authority over interrepublican environmental data collection and control of pollution. It would be a tragedy if false republican pride and a past history of unhappy relations result in the Sava's actually becoming a "river without life."

Environmental degradation in Yugoslavia has not yet reached a crisis stage except in a few instances, as with the Sava. The self-management system established in 1974 is still in its infancy. It is significant that some steps have been taken towards guaranteeing the protection of the environment and at the same time, leaving the republics sufficient autonomy to direct their own development. But it is well recognized by now that the republics have acquired too much independence. Canada and Australia provide examples of basically confederal systems which have come to terms with the realities of environmental management. It is hoped that Yugoslavia will be able to develop its own means of managing pollution control between proud and independent republics while there is still time.

NOTES

1. The six republics are Slovenia, Croatia, Serbia, Bosnia-Herzegovina, Monetenegro, and Macedonia. The two autonomous provinces are Kosovo and Vojvodina.

2. Federal Statistical Office, *Statistical Pocket Book of Yugoslavia, 1980* (Belgrade: Federal Statistical Office, 1980), p. 31.

3. Except where indicated, these and the figures which follow have been taken from the excellent official summary study of environmental conditions in Yugoslavia, *Čovekova sredina i prostorno uredjenje u Jugoslaviji* prepared for the Federal Executive Committee and Executive Committees of the Republics and Provinces of Yugoslavia (Belgrade: Publishing Graphics Bureau, 1976), passim.

4. *Statistical Pocketbook*, p. 95.

5. Figure from *Politika* (June 20, 1984).

6. *Privredni pregled* (Belgrade, March 29, 1979), p. 3. Water quality in Yugoslavia is measured by a four-class classification system passed into law in 1968 and amended in 1978.

7. *Politika* (December 25, 1984).

8. *Vjesnik* (Zagreb, June 5, 1982).

9. Author's sampling of Belgrade, Ljubljana and Zagreb environmental data published in the daily newspapers over a three month period in the winter of 1981.

10. *Vjesnik-Sedam dana* (December 8, 1979), p. 15.

11. *Ibid.* (November 8, 1980).

12. Author interview with Dr. Hasara, Chief of Department of General Hygiene, Belgrade Municipal Institute of Public health, March 27, 1981.

13. *Vjesnik* (December 8, 1979).

14. *Oslobodjenje* (Sarajevo, April 8, 1981).

15. See *Politika*'s comment on the uncontrolled growth of towns in its June 10, 1984 issue, p. 7.

16. *Statistical Pocketbook, 1980*, p. 63.

17. *Privredni pregled* (July 23-25, 1983).

18. *Covekova sredina*, p. 74.

19. *Ibid.*, p. 76.

20. Author interview with Dr. Srećan Mitrović, Section on the Protection of the Human Environment, Federal Planning Board of Yugoslavia, May 1981.

21. Author interview with Dr. Milovoje Todorović, former Secretary General of the Yugoslav Council for the Protection and Improvement of the Environment, which made the proposals to the Federal Skupstina, December 1984.

22. Author interview with Dr. Srećan Mitrović.

23. *Vjesnik* (November 9, 1980), p. 5.

244

24. <u>Vjesnik-Sedam dana</u> (November 8, 1980).
25. For a recent commentary by Flora Lewis, see
    <u>International Herald Tribune</u> (November 26, 1984).
26. Pedro Ramet, "Yugoslavia and the Threat of
    Internal and External Discontents," in <u>Orbis</u>, Vol.
    28, No. 1 (Spring 1984), pp. 106-108, 118-119.
27. Author interview with Dr. Milica Kacarović,
    Director, Department for Environmental Protection,
    Institute for Technology of Nuclear and Other Raw
    Materials, March 24, 1981.
28. <u>Nova Makedonija</u> (Skopje, February 16, 1982).
29. Oil consumption in 1980 decreased 16 percent from
    it 1979 level. <u>Ekonomska politika</u> (January 25,
    1982), p. 21.
30. <u>Ekonomska politika</u> (January 25, 1982), pp. 19-20.
    Some Yugoslavs told the author privately that the
    purchase of oil abroad might not explain the drain
    on Yugoslav dollar reserves and the huge foreign
    debt, that in fact most of the oil imports are
    paid for by reciprocal purchases of goods and
    services, and that less than 20 per cent of the
    imports required payments in dollars. The author
    was unable to verify this information.
31. Author interview with Dr. Milica Kacarović.
32. Author interview with Jelena Vuković, Chief
    Engineer of Zastava Automobile Plant, Kragujevac,
    April 14, 1981.
33. One of the main tasks of the Yugoslav Federal
    Council for the Protection and Improvement of the
    Environment is to promote a comprehensive program
    of environmental education from the lowest level
    to the highest. An environmental course of study
    is now integrated into the school system. At the
    post-graduate level, Serbia has been experimenting
    with training in the multi-disciplinary approach
    for professionals already employed in
    environmental occupations. The pilot course of
    study is a four-year program at Belgrade
    University's Multi-disciplinary Center, and
    combines pure science, applied science and social
    science in a two-year graduate program. (Author
    interview with Dr. Radoslav Radosavljević, Docent,
    Chair, Department of Economic Studies, Center for
    Multi-disciplinary Studies, Belgrade University,
    March 11, 1981).
34. The story has been told in an excellent film,
    "Palić Lives Again," and in a book, Djula Selesi,
    <u>Jezero Palić, odumiranje i sanacija</u> (Lake Palic:
    Death and Restoration) (Subotica: Fond za
    Sanaciju Jezera Palić, 1973).
35. In 1953, Milovan Djilas published his attack on
    the Stalinist model in <u>The New Class</u>. The 1958
    Program of the League of Yugoslav Communists (LCY)

outlined the principles of self-management as the
Yugoslav path to communism.

36. During the 1960s, experimentation with
decentralization affected all aspects of social
life, and most importantly, the government and
party organizations. The result was a resurgence
of national feeling on the part of the country's
constituent republics, which culminated in the
Croatian events of 1971. (Barbara Jancar,
"Dissent and Constitutionalism in Yugoslavia,"
Annual Meeting of the Midwest Slavic Conference,
Ann Arbor, Michigan, May 5-7, 1977.)

37. Article VIII of Basic Principles, The Constitution
of the Socialist Federal Republic of Yugoslavia
(Ljubljana: "Delo," 1974), p. 73.

38. Articles 283 and 285, Constitution, pp. 235-236,
238-240.

39. Čovekova sredina, p. 123, and Službeni list SFRJ
[Official Register SFRJ], Vol. 30, No. 2 (January
10 1974).

40. Vjesnik (June 5, 1982).

41. Vjesnik (January, 26, 1983).

42. Author interview with Vasilka Zarova, Architect
and Planner, Institute for Territorial Planning,
Ohrid, May 16, 1981.

43. The discussion on changes in water resource
administration has been summarized from M.
Miloradov, "Water Management in the SFR
Yugoslavia," Transactions of the "Jaroslav Cerni"
Institute for the Development of Water Resources,
Nos. 60-63, 1977, pp. 44-45.

44. See Pedro Ramet's informative paper, "Federal
Relations in Socialist Yugoslavia: Inter-
republican Cooperation in Control of Water
Pollution," unpublished (1981), pp. 9-10.

45. For a history of the formation of the councils,
see Conseil de l'environnement et l'amenagement du
territoire, "L'Environnement en Yougoslavie,"
(Rapport national), unpublished paper, Belgrade,
June 1978.

46. Politika, May 30, 1984.

47. Marjan Rožić, President of Federal Conference
SSRNJ, "Sačuvajmo kanjon Tare," Čovek i životna
sredina (Man and the Environment), Number 3, 1984,
pp. 4-5.

48. Politika (August 26, 1984).

49. Ibid. (September 24, 1984).

50. Ibid. (September 26, 1984).

51. Author interview with Dr. Milovoje Todorović,
December 1984.

52. For the text of the agreement, see Službeni list
SFRJ, No. 5, 1980 (February 1, 1980), pp. 183-184.

53. Politika (December 25, 1984).

54. For an airing of the republican dispute over integration or autonomy, see _Politika_ (January 10, 1985).
55. _Politika_ (January 9, 1985).

Part 3

Foreign Policy

11
Yugoslav Nonalignment in the 1980s

Zachary T. Irwin

Yugoslav spokesmen describe nonalignment as the basis of the country's overall foreign policy orientation and maintain the relevance of nonaligned principles to relations with all states. Ultimately these principles must bear close resemblance to those enunciated by the nonaligned movement. Other states, however, have considered the movement's principles as distinct from policy toward specific states. For example, India and Egypt do not view their respective security arrangements with the Soviet Union and the United States as inconsistent with their nonaligned status. Like some other nonaligned states they remain part of the nonaligned movement in a declaratory sense. Yugoslav nonalignment represents a policy stance in a constituent sense; that is, Yugoslav communists have insisted on the mutual dependence of socialism and nonaligned principles.(1) And in the Yugoslav constitution, foreign policy goals are featured prominently alongside self-management.(2)

As its ability to shape the nonaligned movement declined in the 1980s, however, Belgrade confronted a widening gap between its own policy requirements and the goals and rhetoric of the movement. I wish to consider several aspects of nonalignment that developed as a consequence of Yugoslavia's situation: first, the impact on internal consensus about foreign policy goals; second, specific Yugoslav objectives for the program of the nonaligned, and third, efforts to adapt nonaligned purposes to Yugoslav goals outside the movement. Initially, it is appropriate to examine Yugoslavia's general goals and status as a nonaligned socialist state.

YUGOSLAV FOREIGN POLICY GOALS

The global scope of nonalignment lends legitimacy to the universalist assertions made on behalf of self-managing socialism. Yugoslav communists have long insisted on the broader significance of self-management and on the relevance of Yugoslav experience to developing and socialist countries alike.(3)   Of course, different conditions permit wide variation in socialist practice, but the nonaligned principles of noninterference and active peaceful coexistence remain basic conditions for the practice of socialism and socialist foreign policy. According to former Foreign Minister Josip Vrhovec, the most essential principle of nonalignment is its opposition to hegemony and imperialism, that is, to "all forms of foreign interference" implicitly associated with the Soviet Union and the United States.(4)   Belgrade's efforts to gain recognition as a socialist state are matched by similar efforts to win recognition for nonalignment from European neutrals, other nonruling communist parties, and members of the Warsaw Pact. Belgrade's opposition to Cuba's recognition of the Soviet Union as a "natural ally" of the nonaligned represented a defense of the movement's universalism and the integrity of nonaligned independence. As one Yugoslav writer explained, "the proponents of a 'natural alliance' of all progressive forces are striving, in fact, to narrow the movement of nonalignment and to 'purge' it of 'conservative countries'."(5)

According to Raymond Aron, a small state generally seeks to develop "defensive power" for the purpose of "safeguarding autonomy, maintaining its own manner of life [and] not accepting the subordination of its internal laws or its external action to the desires or decrees of others."(6) Aron contrasts this course with the "offensive" capability of alliance, initiative, and leadership enjoyed by great powers.   Aron's classification may be qualified by the case of small states that limit such goals within the framework of alliance and by a category of middle powers which project power beyond their boundaries.(7)   Yugoslav foreign policy certainly includes the goals ascribed to small states, but Belgrade's objectives are pursued within the Balkans and in the global arena of nonalignment. Rouhollah Ramazani's characterization of the foreign policy of a "medium power" (Iran) are suggestive of Yugoslavia. Medium powers "act to create and maintain a favorable regional environment while aspiring to global political stature."(8)   While Yugoslavia lacks the resource base of other middle or medium powers,(9) its leadership role in the nonaligned movement and in the Balkans is unmistakable. This role permits Yugoslavia to act as an aspiring medium power whose intentions and stated goals conform to those of other such powers regardless of how their capabilities are measured.

An aspiring medium power enjoys regional status and limited prospects to assert interests beyond its region. Israel, Cuba, and South Africa represent states whose regional interests have been reinforced by global involvement. Unlike other powers whose capabilities and goals are congruent, an aspiring medium power relies on third parties or on some particular attribute to enhance its status. Cuba has depended on Soviet support to assert its interest in Africa; Israel depends on the World Jewish community in pursuit of a variety of external goals, and South Africa's regional role has been buttressed by circumstances following the collapse of Portuguese colonialism and the sudden increase in the price of gold. Yugoslavia, for its part, has projected a modest global presence through nonaligned leadership. For the aspiring medium power, sharp distinctions may vanish between regional security concerns and more distant objectives, especially where third parties are involved. Hence, the major setback to nonaligned objectives presented by the Soviet invasion of Afghanistan in 1979 was perceived in Belgrade as a threat to Yugoslav regional security.(10) A focus on the objectives of Yugoslav nonalignment as an extension of regional influence, may address the uncertainty about the contribution of nonalignment to immediate security.(11)

Yugoslav efforts to create a secure regional environment predate the adoption of nonalignment. Stalin aborted Tito's project for a postwar Balkan Federation with Albania and Bulgaria. Following its dispute with the Cominform, Yugoslavia organized the Balkan Pact, a 1954 military alliance with Greece and Turkey.(12) At the time, the pact's provisions for military cooperation and political consultations appeared to link Yugoslavia with NATO. Yet, within two months of the agreement, Tito banned participation in any "anti-socialist" bloc and later affirmed an interest in "collaboration [with socialist states] based on parity of rights."(13) By the autumn of 1954, Tito's espousal of "peaceful coexistence" during visits to India and Burma marked a new phase in Yugoslav foreign policy. Although the Balkan Pact's provisions became inoperative owing to the rise of nonalignment and Greco-Turkish conflict over Cyprus, Belgrade did not abrogate the treaty in 1974, as it might have chosen to do. Instead, there is evidence of Yugoslav efforts to organize military contacts with Greece and Turkey. In 1981, for instance, the chief of staff of the Yugoslav Peoples' Army, Admiral Branko Mamula, met with his Greek and Turkish counterparts to promote military cooperation.(14) And in July, President Nicolae Ceauşescu received General Nikola Ljubičić, and the two recognized "the importance for strengthening links between the armies of the two countries as a component part of the general development of Romanian-Yugoslav relations."(15) From Yugoslavia's viewpoint, the absence of Soviet troops in Romania permits Belgrade to narrow its defense against a possible Soviet invasion to the Danubian Plain bordering Hungary.

Within the context of increased political and economic agreements between Yugoslavia and other Balkan states, nonalignment has become a frequent theme of accord. As early as 1975 Yugoslavia supported Romania's request for "observer" status at the 1976 Nonaligned Conference in Sri Lanka. Bucharest has subsequently been accorded "guest" status at conferences, a distinction reserved for European rather than developing countries. While Romania's vocal association with other nonaligned states has diminished recently, Yugoslav-Romanian communiques have recognized the "role and significance" of nonalignment as an "independent extra-bloc factor in international relations."(16) The Greek socialist government of Andreas Papandreou has added impetus to improved relations with Yugoslavia and Romania through a vigorous endorsement of nonalignment and multilateral cooperation among Balkan states. Cyprus and Yugoslavia have likewise been close, nonaligned allies.

Attempts to adapt nonaligned principles to Yugoslav interests on a multilateral basis in the Balkans have been less promising than bilateral contacts with neighboring states. Belgrade's idea of a "code of good neighborly relations" among Balkan states would require that Albania and Bulgaria accept Yugoslavia's multinational political order.(17) Albanian criticism of Yugoslavia's "great Serbian" policy regarding the Albanian minority and endorsement of republican status for Kosovo are taken in Belgrade to express "territorial pretensions" on the part of Tirana, while Bulgaria's refusal to recognize a Macedonian nationality has also been assumed to represent a claim against Yugoslavia, despite Bulgaria's formal declarations to the contrary. Yugoslav preferences that the Balkans become a "zone of peace," if realized, would amount to a multilateral endorsement of most nonaligned principles, including that of a "nuclear free zone" in the area. However, there is no precedent among the nonaligned requiring recognition of an ethnic minority by a foreign state. Lacking such recognition from Bulgaria, Belgrade remains unenthusiastic about the idea of a Balkan summit on behalf of a nuclear free zone.(18)

The second major dimension of Yugoslavia's "medium power" status concerns its "global aspirations" expressed through nonaligned association. Nonalignment may be approached as a specific global "issue area" with respect to the distribution of its membership and the scope of its interests. Yugoslavia has been highly active in organizing the movement as a global "issue area" in several ways: First, through prominent leadership in summit conferences and ministerial meetings; second, in efforts to create a permanent "coordinating bureau" on nonaligned states, and third, by efforts to organize and articulate issues and positions among a coalition of states within the movement. Yugoslavia's role has become more defined with the emergence of challenges to its leadership within the movement. Conflict concerning goals remains a distinguishing feature of an "issue area," and although the concept has been defined variously, the earliest, offered by James Rosenau, applies to the Yugoslav position on the nonaligned movement. "An issue area," according to Rosenau,

is conceived to consist of (1) a cluster
of values, the allocation or potential
allocation of which (2) leads the affected
or potentially affected actors to differ so
greatly over (a) the way in which the values
should be allocated or (b) the horizontal
levels [state entities] at which the allocation should be authorized that (3) they engage
in distinctive behavior designed to mobilize
support for the attainment of their particular
values. (19)

The "allocation of values" within the nonaligned issue area has fluctuated among general East-West issues, North-South economic and colonial issues, as well as functional and specific issues among the nonaligned. Recent polarization of nonaligned members between "progressives" and "moderates" has concerned the movement's overall orientation and, for Yugoslavia, the applicability of that orientation to foreign policy goals outside the movements. For example, by the early 1980s, Bulgaria had successfully enlisted "progressive" nonaligned states to support Bulgaria's "peace policy" in the Balkans.

Nonalignment emerged in the 1950s in what Carsten Holbraad has called a "dualistic" international system. (20) He finds similarities between the nineteenth century system of German states and the current dualistic system, in that both avoid total polarization as well as diplomatic concert. Dualistic systems are also alike in their tendency to spawn "some sort of composite third party" to the central antagonistic relationship, permitting middle powers within it relative freedom "to pursue regional interests and local concerns of their own."(21) Systemically, this freedom would be jeopardized if the "composite third party" were to become a coherent third force, as it could have during the early 1960s under Chinese leadership or, as the "progressives" envisioned during the late 1970s through a "natural alliance" with the Soviet Union. The promotion of détente on East-West issues, the extension of nonaligned membership, and the creation of permanent nonaligned institutions have remained central objectives of Yugoslav foreign policy. All serve to support Yugoslav leadership among a group of states with sufficiently diverse interests to accommodate an aspiring middle power in a specific geopolitical setting.

DOMESTIC CONSENSUS AND NONALIGNMENT

Traditionally, Yugoslav foreign policy goals associated with nonalignment have enjoyed an apparently high level of internal support. Within Yugoslavia, maintenance of nonalignment is seen as tantamount to the maintenance of autonomy within the international system. Evidence for this perception was demonstrated by the 1975 campaign against an allegedly pro-Soviet "Cominformist" faction within the League of Communists. According to Vice-president Vladimic Bakarić, members of this "illegal organization" within the LCY had become "instruments of alien influences whose political line amounts to compelling Yugoslavia to join the Warsaw Pact."(22) The emphasis on a Cominformist threat to nonalignment throughout the campaign became a means of dramatizing the danger posed to self-management and a means of mobilizing support against pro-Soviet tendencies. By stressing the theme of "alien" influence Bakarić hoped to deal with past "neglect" of the problem. The Cominformists "were not regarded as representing a serious danger; we did not pay enough attention to them, and some party members failed to draw a clear ideological line between us and the [Cominformists]. . ."(23) Outright repudiation of nonalignment would be unacceptable to broad sections of Yugoslav society. Charges of "alien influence," however accurate, represent a tactic of struggle against political opposition intended to isolate opponents as enemies of nonaligned independence.

Tito's role as a spokesman for the nonaligned, coupled with his ability to win endorsement of Yugoslavia's independence in Moscow and Washington, is an important consideration explaining foreign policy consensus. As long as Tito enjoyed unqualified internal support for a foreign policy agenda, "self-managing" political actors could engage in relatively unhindered political activity without risk of censure. Nonalignment set acceptable limits on the affinities felt by individual republics toward specific areas outside the Federation, e.g., on the putative orientation of Croatia and Slovenia toward the West, of the Southern and Eastern republics toward socialist East Europe, and of Islamic Bosnia-Herzegovina toward the Middle East.(24) Patterns of cultural and economic activity with foreign states by the federal units are in fact constitutionally sanctioned. This activity is relevant to nonalignment consensus in two ways. First, a credible nonalignment is desirable because it permits Yugoslavia financial advantages with the West and commercial benefit from the East. In 1984, some 1,267 foreign trade enterprises were officially credited.(25) Yugoslavia's extensive diplomatic establishment at the federal level is complemented by an equally extensive foreign trade of firms at the local level.

Yugoslavia's republics and provinces participate in the shaping of foreign policy in several ways. They may serve as a point of contact between the Federation and kindred nationalities in foreign states. The units may send and receive delegations from either unitary or federal states for the purpose of economic, cultural or border cooperation; spokesmen from local league or republic institutions take part in receiving or negotiating with foreign partners at the federal level, and finally, all federal members are guaranteed representation in institutions responsible for making foreign policy.(26)

The direct impact of the federal units on nonalignment depends on their interests. Local party spokesmen have used local institutions to link nonalignment and domestic political objectives. Aleksandar Grlickov, a LCY Presidium Member, told the Serbian league Congress in 1982, that the maintenance of a "tolerant political culture of dialogue" within Yugoslavia and the "foreign political strategy" of nonalignment are linked.(27) Speaking to the Slovenian Congress in the same year, Mitja Ribičič, Chairman of the Presidium of the Central Committee LCY, broadly criticized lagging Soviet economic performance and scientific innovation as a negative example for Yugoslav self-management. He called Moscow's view of the nonaligned as 'natural allies' of the Warsaw Pact a particular Soviet perversion: "This is the old Cominform theory about former colonial countries serving as a sort of 'antichamber of socialism' and as a reserve for socialist revolutions."(28)

National interests have had a less desirable impact on nonalignment. For example, during his 1982 visit to Belgrade, Greek President Andreas Papandreou spoke of nonalignment's "immense importance for all countries struggling for national independence."(29) The President of the Yugoslav State Presidency, Petar

Stambolić, held up Greek-Yugoslav "understanding and cooperation" as a model of inter Balkan relations. But not much came of these bilateral talks, and the President of the Macedonian Foreign Relations Committee later spoke of the "negative effect" of Greece's continued nonrecognition of the Macedonian nationality and Athens' refusal to send delegates to the Vardar River Commission held in Skopje. It is unlikely that Belgrade can ignore Macedonian concerns regardless of any favorable disposition Athens might show toward nonalignment.

Muslim nationalism in Yugoslavia represents a more delicate and uncertain problem.(30) Since the mid-1950s, nonaligned heads of state and delegations have been the guests of Muslim religious officials in an apparent attempt to contrast Yugoslav and Soviet treatment of Islamic minorities. Furthermore, since the late 1970s, Yugoslav Islamic delegations have traveled to Mecca on the hadž. In 1956, Presidents Nasser and Sukarno were welcomed in Sarajevo. During the Nasser visit "thousands" of citizens turned out in a "strong manifestation of Yugoslav-Egyptian friendship," in the words of the Islamic religious community executive, the Reis-ul-Ulema.(31) Doubtlessly nonalignment enjoyed great popularity among Yugoslav Muslims, but by 1973 the popularity of the Arab cause against Israel exceeded acceptable limits. Following the Middle East War, demonstrations of solidarity with the Arabs were judged hostile to international relations and to nonalignment. Moreover, the Muslim religious community itself had become too outspoken. Both the community's publication Preporod and the demonstrations were condemned. Preporod had put forward its own "theory" of Jewish-Islamic relations and had "failed to understand the significance of nonaligned and socialist Yugoslavia whose people. . . wholeheartedly supported and are still supporting the struggle of the Arabs."(32) Since 1979, indeed, authorities have taken measures to repress what has been called "Khomeini style socialism" as unacceptable Pan-Islamic political expression.(33)

Yugoslavia's relations with Islamic states have not been affected by this. Yugoslav communists have avoided direct accusations of interference in the country's affairs. Typically reference has been made to "attempts to manipulate the religious communities from abroad for certain political purposes"; reference to such "interference" has usually been left to Islamic officials who refute specific information in Islamic periodicals. Evidently neither Yugoslavia nor any of its Islamic partners wishes to risk an open breach. At present, Libya and Yugoslavia have established commercial and military relations, although Belgrade disassociated itself from the Libyan intervention in Chad.(34)   Between 1979 and 1983, Irani-Yugoslav commercial turnover increased from $20 million to $400 million, although Yugoslavia has not agreed to enter into cultural and inter-university relations as sought by the Iranians.   Iran has also entered into direct economic relations with the Republic of Croatia, exchanging delegations in 1983 and 1984. During a 1983 meeting between the Yugoslav Foreign Minister and his Iranian counterpart both sides criticized "interference by non-African elements" in Africa, but the Iranians avoided describing their policy as "nonaligned," possibly owing to Iraq's vocal activity as a member of the movement.(35)

The incipient pro-Soviet drift of the nonaligned movement at the end of the 1970s was disquieting for Belgrade.   In August 1981, prior to the preliminary New Delhi Conference, LCY Presidium member Vladimir Bakarić spoke pessimistically about the future of nonalignment; he maintained that the movement had become "polarized," not simply because of "bloc pressures," but because individual members had sought "military security" over "independence"--an admission they were no longer nonaligned.(36)   He was equally skeptical about the socialist potential of "state capitalism" present in nonaligned countries. Bakarić further objected to new forms of nonaligned cooperation, especially to those that were costly.   A common investment fund was impossible because "even the CMEA (Comecon) countries cannot do this."   He concluded that Yugoslavia's greatest contribution to the cause of nonalignment might instead be in a successful adaption of the Yugoslav economy to "world market conditions.... [because] if we fail to achieve that, all our crying for cooperation with the nonaligned and developing countries will have been in vain because then our system will not suit them."   The implication of this position amounted to a disassociation from more radical nonaligned demands for new international economic order and to maintaining a less costly diplomatic profile. In fact, 10 of Yugoslavia's diplomatic and consular legations were closed about that time for financial reasons.(37)   Bakarić's prestige as a close associate of Tito's allows one to speculate that his position represented a deeper current of thought within the League, especially among Yugoslavia's more developed regions, but it was not shared unanimously.

Former Foreign Minister and Serbian LCY Presdium member Miloš Minić, for example, disagreed.   Minić attached "exceptionally great significance" to the possibilities of nonaligned cooperation and the "constantly increasing consciousness" among them. Yugoslavia would do all it could do to maintain its

prestige. All of this depended on Yugoslavia's ability
to "take initiatives."(38)

The "new initiatives" of the nonaligned probably
referred to the "Economic Action Program" adopted at
the 1976 Colombo Summit and reaffirmed in Havana.
Yugoslavia had joined eight of the 17 functional
committees created to implement the Program's plans for
nonaligned cooperation. These committees included such
areas as financial and monetary cooperation, scientific
and technological development, nuclear energy and
cooperation, food and agriculture, health and
fisheries. Yugoslav membership on these committees
could promote its political influence, but by the 1980s
the certainty of economic burden had arguably exceeded
the promise of political benefit. The country's
overall debt approached $19 billion and a debt service
of approximately $3.6 billion annually. Trade with
COMECON countries reached 49 per cent of all commercial
exchange. New "initiatives" with the nonaligned would
not address Yugoslavia's debt and balance of payments
crises. The logic of Minić's position was to join with
other developing countries in demanding cancellation or
rescheduling of debt repayment. Some Yugoslav
republican leaderships (e.g., the Croatian) had already
taken this position without adding the arguments of
Third World countries in support of a New International
Economic Order. The most controversial "initiative" of
the Havana Conference for Yugoslavia was included in
the Economic Declaration. The nonaligned rejected
"unacceptable tendencies of some developed countries
and international institutions under their control to
make the provision of development resources conditional
on the imposition of externally fixed priorities in the
national plans and programs of the recipient
countries."(39) Before 1983, acceptance of such
"priorities" sought by the IMF and Western banks as a
condition for further loans had become a subject of
divisive debate in Yugoslavia.

Bakarić and other federal officials spoke the
language of "world market conditions," that is, of
austerity and of efforts to reorient Yugoslav trade
towards the convertible currency area. Closer
identification with new "initiatives" and the
"constantly increasing consciousness" of the
nonaligned, cited by Minić, would only complicate
Belgrade's delicate negotiations with Western financial
institutions. Besides, the arguments on behalf of
accepting greater austerity in spending and other
conditions sought by Yugoslavia's creditors were
relevant to nonalignment as well. Nijaz Dizdarević, a
leading federal spokesman from Bosnia-Herzegovina,
spoke on behalf of emergency legislation to control the
economy. He warned that "economic relations with

foreign countries may grievously damage Yugoslavia's overall international situation and its resistance to various forms of pressure that could be exerted against our country."(40)

YUGOSLAV OBJECTIVES AMONG THE NONALIGNED

Despite disagreement within Yugoslavia over the desirability of close identification with the nonaligned movement, federal spokesmen have remained unanimous in their praise of the "authentic" or "original" principles of the movement. Between 1978 and 1983 the character of these "original principles" emerged through an acrimonious debate between Belgrade and other "progressives" in the movement. Typically, more was written about dangers surrounding the abandonment of the "original principles" than about their specific contents. LCY Presidium member, Miloš Minić, referred to a "stirring up of a kind of campaign...aimed at redefining the policy of nonalignment and 'reorienting' the nonaligned movement." This campaign, Minić charged, wanted to scuttle

> some of the basic principles, including
> abandonment of the position on the non-bloc
> character of the nonaligned movement; rejec-
> tion of the jockeying and rivalry of the big
> powers and blocs as the principal source of
> international tension...confining the policy
> of nonalignment to anti-imperialism, anti-
> colonialism and anti-racism, and rejecting
> the opposition to hegemony and all other forms
> of domination; producing 'natural alliances'
> between the nonaligned countries and the East
> European socialist countries...division of the
> nonaligned countries into 'progressives' and
> 'conservatives'.(41)

Yugoslavia's approach to nonalignment required that the movement become neither a coherent third force that could discipline its members, nor a coopted ally of either bloc. With the decline of "Afro-Asian Solidarity" as a concept of Third World organization and the growing size and variety of nonaligned membership, there was little danger that the movement would become a "third force." For the first decade of nonaligned summit meetings, the threat of bloc cooptation seemed equally remote. Between the first Belgrade Summit in 1961 and the third in 1970 at Lusaka, nonaligned documents had preserved a relative balance between East-West questions of peace and North-South questions of anticolonialism. Condemnation of "blocs" as a threat to peace allowed Yugoslavia relative impunity from Western sanctions to take up

anticolonial issues. In fact, Yugoslavia could argue
its anticolonialism had been more consistent than the
Soviet Union's. For example, Belgrade rather than
Moscow first extended recognition of the Algerian FLN,
the PLO, and the Sahara Polisario Front. The
diplomatic consequences for Yugoslav anticolonialism
were manageable as long as Belgrade was not perceived
as a vehicle of Soviet influence.

Until the 1979 Havana Conference, the Yugoslavs
were loath to admit the existence of any challenge to
the "original principles" of the nonaligned movement.
In fact, however, an alternate concept of nonalignment
was emerging as a result of increasing complexity
within the movement and the changing composition of its
leadership. The first evidence of Cuban rivalry with
Yugoslavia emerged at the Algiers Summit in 1973.
First, the summit created a permanent bureau, later a
"coordinating bureau," charged with "making
preparations" for the next summit and "preparations on
matters of substance" for the Foreign Ministers
Conference preceding the Fifth Summit.(42) Although
the Bureau (17 members) included a number of "moderate"
members such as Yugoslavia and India, it also included
"radicals" such as Cuba and Syria. The balance of the
membership, the majoritarian principle of the Bureau's
operation, and the role of the host government as
Bureau chairman all served to the detriment of
Yugoslavia's traditional bilateral approach to
nonaligned diplomacy. Second, the Algiers Conference
adopted a "Program of Economic Action" advocating OPEC-
modeled "producer associations" to halt "degredation of
[nonaligned] terms of trade....to prevent harmful
activities by multinational corporations, and to
reinforce their negotiating power."(43) Yugoslav
economic interests involving bilateral agreements with
COMECON, the EEC and other market economies could gain
nothing from Algiers' strategy to resist "economic
aggression and political pressure." Yugoslav comment
insisted on the value of United Nations bodies, such as
the United Nations Conference on Trade and Development
(UNCTAD) and regional economic commissions, as the
appropriate forum for economic negotiations between
developed and developing countries. Far from accepting
a simple identity of interests between developing
countries and the nonaligned, one authoritative source
considered there to be nothing "automatic" about the
"unity" of the two.(44)

Finally, Algiers marked Cuba's emergence as an
active nonaligned member. At his first nonaligned
summit Fidel Castro rejected any reference to Soviet
"social imperialism" put forward by Libyan President
Muammar al-Qaddafi as "an attempt to pit the nonaligned
countries against the socialist camp [which] means

weakening and exposing ourselves to the mercy of the still powerful forces of imperialism."(45) Between 1973 and 1976 Cuba's viewpoint gained impetus as a result of several developments confirmed at the Fifth Summit in Colombo. Portuguese decolonization not only added three new "progressive" nonaligned members but brought Cuba a nonaligned "commendation" at Colombo for its military role in Africa. Second, Cuba was joined by Vietnam, Democratic Yemen, and Ethiopia among other "progressives" who succeeded in omitting any reference to [Soviet] "hegemony" as a companion to "imperialism" at Colombo. Unlike Yugoslavia, the "progressives" were willing to polarize the movement for the purpose of isolating or silencing "moderates." By contrast Yugoslavia avoided confrontation.

At the 1979 Havana conference, Cuba experienced its first major defeat as a "progressive" nonaligned state. Reference to the socialist bloc as a nonaligned "natural ally" was eliminated from the final document despite its inclusion in the original draft. Instead, the political Declaration "reaffirmed....the quintessence of the policy of nonalignment in accordance with its original principles and essential character, [which] involved the struggle against imperialism, colonialism....domination, interference or hegemony, as well as against great-power and bloc policies."(46) On other issues, particularly those concerning Latin America and the Economic Declaration, the Anti-Western or Anti-American impact of the "progressives" was apparent. However, Cuba had lost valuable prestige for several reasons in the contest with Yugoslavia.

First, the "natural allies" phrase had been unfortunate because it demanded not a coincidence of nonaligned-Soviet interests, but an outright commitment to Soviet purposes.

Second, the Cubans' choice of language clearly identified nonalignment as a vehicle for communist purposes. Moreover, the Cubans were willing to undertake measures that divided the movement. At Havana, the Cuban delegates led particularly violent quarrels over the question of Cambodian representation and condemnation of Egypt for its settlement with Israel, even though a majority of the nonaligned states preferred to avoid controversy. Indeed, the Coordinating Bureau, including both Cuba and Yugoslavia, had recommended that "open confrontations between opposing points of view should be avoided."(47) While the "progressives" were able to prevent the seating of the Pol Pot regime's representatives, they alienated potential supporters. Similarly, the Political Declaration had "condemned the Camp David Agreements and the treaty between Egypt and Israel," but it was unable to expel Egypt from the movement. Finally, Cuban attempts to organize the progressives as a reliable bloc within the movement evoked accusations of "Comintern" tactics, while attempts to exploit Cuba's position as a conference host brought protests from India and Singapore.(48)

The "progressive" challenge was contained at nonaligned summits, but Yugoslavia faced a persistent dilemma. First, the Soviet Union had shown up the weakness of the nonaligned response to the invasion of Afghanistan and Vietnam's continued occupation of Kampuchea. Soviet policy was no less interested in dominating the movement. Prior to the 1981 New Delhi Conference of Nonaligned Foreign Ministers, a Soviet writer separated "conservative" from "progressive" regimes. The former, apparently including Yugoslavia, were held accountable for the "groundless" theory that the nonaligned should maintain "equidistance" between the blocs. The "progressives," however, "do not allow the enemies of the movement--imperialism and Peking--to reduce it to a state of political prostration....Though the progressive-oriented regimes are in a minority, their weight and political prestige are very high."(49) Confrontation at the New Delhi Conference between Yugoslavia and pro-Soviet elements did not prevent the final statement from calling for the withdrawal of foreign troops from Afghanistan and Kampuchea. The "progressives" disassociated themselves from these positions.

Having failed in its bid for domination, Moscow turned to Bulgaria and the German Democratic Republic as proxies to bind the "progressives" more closely to the socialist bloc. Bulgaria's foreign policy initiatives were especially disturbing for Yugoslavia. During 1981, Bulgaria entertained more than a dozen nonaligned heads of state or foreign ministers, including all of the "progressives." Some, including Angola and the Democratic Republic of Yemen, the People's Republic of the Congo, and Mozambique, signed a series of technical and economic treaties with Bulgaria. Joint communiques lauded Bulgaria's "policy of peace in the Balkans." Typically, the Congolese communique "highly evaluated the principled and consistent policy of peace, good neighborliness, understanding, mutually beneficial cooperation conducted by the People's Republic of Bulgaria in the Balkans, Europe and the World."(50) Exactly what was being endorsed could not have been more apparent to Yugoslavia, for a few months earlier, Todor Zhivkov had announced his support of the CPSU Peace Program's "concretization in the Balkans" at the Twelfth Bulgarian Party Conference.(51) Ironically, Sofia had found more interest in Africa for its proposals than among its immediate neighbors. However, the Bulgarian diplomatic offensive did not lose momentum. Bilateral reactions continued with most nonaligned states. In late 1984, Zhivkov praised a newly signed Treaty of Friendship and Cooperation signed with Mozambique as an embodiment of the "principle of Marxism-Leninism and proletarian internationalism."(52)

In the autumn of 1984, Foreign Minister Petar Mladenov spoke at length about Bulgaria's "economic cooperation" with 80 developing countries and "treaties of cultural cooperation" with 40. He added that some 10,000 Third World students were in Bulgaria and the 11,000 "had already been trained." He emphasized the "particularly intense" cooperation with "countries with a socialist orientation."(53) Thus, Bulgaria not only became a means of extending Soviet influence, but an active force alienating other nonaligned states from Yugoslavia. Because Yugoslavia had never questioned publicly the compatibility of nonalignment with bilateral treaties, it was impossible to criticize Bulgaria or its partners as practising "bloc" politics.

The problem of Bulgaria's relations with Third World countries represented a less immediate threat compared with the opportunities Yugoslavia perceived for the Seventh Nonaligned Summit in 1983. The decision-making mechanism created before the Havana Summit remained intact, but in addition, Belgrade embarked on an extensive diplomatic offensive through a series of bilateral meetings intended to affirm the movement's "original principles." Perhaps the most important of these occurred in the fall of 1982 during President Hosni Mubarak's visit in Belgrade. Ideally the objective was to coordinate a joint approach with Egypt and India. Petar Stambolić, President of the State Presidency, and the Egyptian Head of State reaffirmed a common commitment to the New Delhi Summit through an "identity" of viewpoints and a common dedication to "tripartite economic cooperation among Yugoslavia, Egypt and India."(54) The meeting marked a change from earlier Egyptian objections that Yugoslavia had been guilty of "vacillation" at Havana in the face of various "pressures within the movement."(55) Supposedly, pressures from "rejectionist" Arab states had resulted in Yugoslavia's failure to defend Egypt's "peace initiative" in the Middle East. The Mubarak-Stambolić talks overlooked Yugoslavia's reluctance to endorse the Camp David peace process and probable differences on the Palestinian issue. Clearly a Yugoslav-Egyptian rapprochement was now more acceptable to other Arab states than any prior understanding with President Sadat. For Mubarak, nonalignment afforded a convenient opportunity for realizing greater East-West balance than his predecessor had sought.

Relations with India were more challenging for Yugoslavia than those with Egypt. India's concept of nonalignment differed from Belgrade's. In a 1981 speech to the Friends of the Soviet Union Society, Prime Minister Indira Gandhi explained why nonalignment could never mean "equidistance" between the superpowers for India. Specifically, she contrasted Soviet and American policy with respect to a series of Indian concerns, including the question of conflict with Pakistan, Goa, economic development as well as the expansion of American military facilities at Diego Garcia. India's "national interest model" was perfectly consistent with nonalignment and the 1971 Treaty of Peace, Friendship and Cooperation signed with the Soviet Union. In fact, the initial Indian draft for the New Delhi Summit called for "early normalization of relations" with the Soviet-backed Afghan regime of Babrak Karmal. But despite Prime Minister Gandhi's endorsement of "normalization" for Afghanistan, India was not "progressive" in the nonaligned sense. Over the objections of Afghanistan, an Indian-sponsored draft approved a "political settlement" for the country "on the basis of the withdrawal of foreign troops" and respect for its "independence, sovereignty, territorial integrity and nonaligned status."(56) Yugoslavia could not have been more satisfied, but India refused to endorse directly the theme of "original principles." In late August of 1984 President of the Collective Presidency Veselin Djuranović and Prime Minister Gandhi acknowledged "a pressing need for Indian-Yuguslav dialogue."(57) For her part, Gandhi perceived that the "biggest worry" of the nonaligned centered on the issue of a Middle East peace and the Palestinian problem, the "tragedy" of the Iran-Iraq war, and global economic problems.(58) For Yugoslavia, achieving "nearly identical views" with India represented an important diplomatic achievement, but it was entirely obvious that the Indian government had not wished to displease the Soviet Union for the sake of "original principles."

The New Delhi summit was generally considered a triumph for Yugoslavia and for the cause of a "nonbloc" approach to nonalignment. "Progressive" viewpoints were evident, particularly with respect to the section on Latin America criticizing the United States by name, but Yugoslav spokesmen were evidently pleased by the conference's relatively "moderate" stand on economic matters, reaffirmation of the movement's "nonbloc" orientation, and the call for withdrawal of foreign troops from Afghanistan and Kampuchea. However the problem of nonalignment for Yugoslavia was not entirely resolved. First, Yugoslav diplomacy simply had to accept different approaches to the meaning of nonalignment. For India such themes as "original principles" or bloc "equidistance" were an unnecessary affront to the Soviet Union--as indeed may have been too close an association with Yugoslavia. In early 1985 the new Indian Prime Minister, Rajiv Ghandhi, met with heads of state or government from Sweden, Argentina, Tanzania, Mexico, and Greece to call for a halt to the production, testing, and deployment of nuclear weapons and the "militarization of space."(59) Yugoslavia's conspicuous absence from the meeting signalled India's refusal to recognize a successive accord with Yugoslavia and Egypt modeled on the principle of a nonaligned founding triumvirate of Tito, Nehru, and Nasser.

The problem of the "progressives" would not simply go away, regardless of their New Delhi setback. Nicaragua, the latest "progressive" recruit clashed with Yugoslavia at the 1983 Nonaligned Coordinating Bureau meeting in Managua. Later Yugoslav commentary criticized Nicaragua for having circulated a pamphlet at the meeting advocating a "natural alliance" of nonalignment and communism. The commentary went on to criticize Nicaragua's rejection of "realism and moderation" over the Central American issue as "yielding" to United States' pressure.(60). However worthy Nicaragua might be to host the Coordinating Bureau's meeting, many delegates could also have concluded that some sort of "natural alliance" with the communist countries represented Nicaragua's best prospect against the United States-backed "contras." Similarly, "progressive" African states might desire "original principles" for nonalignment, but they could also understand the price of Soviet support for SWAPO or other African states against South Africa. Thus, conditions of intervention (Afghanistan, Kampuchea, Central America), nonaligned conflicts (Iraq-Iran, Syria-PLO), and different diplomatic priorities (India, Egypt) had created a more dynamic and less coherent nonaligned movement whose summits could have much less relevance of the foreign policy behavior of member states other than Yugoslavia.

THE ADAPTATION OF NONALIGNMENT OUTSIDE THE NONALIGNED MOVEMENT

Perhaps the most basic difference between the Yugoslav approach to nonalignment and that of other states concerns the relation of nonalignment to foreign policy outside the movement. While other nonaligned states may be unencumbered by nonaligned principles in their foreign policy choices, Yugoslavia has chosen to interpret all major questions of foreign policy as a function of its nonaligned and "self-managing" socialist character. Acknowledging such principles as respect for "territorial integrity, nonintervention and noninterference"--all nonaligned principles--has been a chief concern in Yugoslav relations with the superpowers. Other policy areas have a more complex relation to nonalignment. In this final section I wish to consider several foreign policy questions that remain distinct from the "issue area" of nonalignment. They include Yugoslav attitudes toward the European Conference on Security and Cooperation (CSCE), relations with the People's Republic of China, and Yugoslavia's position within UNCTAD. I do not intend to examine in detail Yugoslav policy with respect to the three areas, but to suggest how Yugoslav nonalignment serves as an approach to each. While these three are not exclusive, they do reveal Belgrade's aspirations as a "medium power." For example, Yugoslavia has attempted to organize Cyprus, Malta, and European neutrals within the CSCE as diplomatic intermediaries between the blocs. China has actively supported Yugoslavia's role within the Balkans since 1969. And UNCTAD has proven a forum for Yugoslav viewpoints on North-South economic issues independently of the politics of nonaligned summits. The three policy areas also provide needed alternatives to express nonaligned attitudes as Yugoslavia's influence waned within the movement.

Yugoslav spokesmen claim that since its inception, nonalignment has viewed world peace and by implication European security as central concerns, that Europe and the nonaligned are linked by economic interests, and that European security requires consideration of the interests of neutral and nonaligned states.(61) To the extent possible, Yugoslav formulations affirm a common normative set of "principles" that apply to Europe and nonaligned countries alike. Yugoslav proposals for European security are consistent with this viewpoint to the extent that they restate general nonaligned principles such as respect for "sovereign equality," "noninterference in internal affairs," "abstention from any threat or use of force and resolution of conflicts by peaceful means."(62) European security for Yugoslavia is a specific application of what Yugoslavia's Permanent Representative to the United Nations, Miljan Komatina, describes as nonalignment's content, as a "doctrine of international relations."(63) Nonalignment provides a distinctive Yugoslav orientation toward European security, including acceptance of principles which, by implication, would rule out interference in Yugoslavia's internal affairs, the extension of European security to the Mediterranean and the Middle East, and the promotion of a nonaligned-neutral group within CSCE that would prevent its becoming a bloc confrontation or collusion. In addition, Yugoslavia has actively promoted "confidence-building measures." During preparations for the Madrid follow-up meeting to CSCE, Yugoslavia urged stricter limits on the Final Act's provision requiring advance notification of maneuvers involving more than 25,000 troops.(64) Instead it sought actual limits on military activities. Yugoslav concern was especially evident during the Warsaw Pact's operation "Shield-82" held in Bulgaria.(65)

Yugoslav sources have insisted on a number of issues that facilitate neutral-nonaligned cooperation at the Helsinki follow-up conferences in Belgrade and Madrid. The group has submitted a conciliatory final draft supposedly to avoid bloc confrontation at the follow-up conferences as well as a number of specific proposals, including disarmament. Although Yugoslavia avoided any direct challenge to the Warsaw Pact during the Polish crisis, the neutral-nonaligned document referred to the problem of "non-implementation" of the Final Act's provisions on human rights. Yugoslavia has insisted that the language of nonaligned summits is fundamentally the same as that of the neutral-nonaligned group at CSCE. In fact the 1983 New Delhi Nonaligned Summit did endorse a Maltese proposal for a conference on Mediterranean security. The superpowers and most other participants opposed Malta's wish for "Mediterranean experts" to discuss security issues at the 1977 follow-up conference in Belgrade because they opposed discussion of such matters as Cyprus and the Middle East. While Malta and Yugoslavia won a concession promising a discussion of Mediterranean security in Madrid, they remained frustrated. Yugoslavia succeeded by late 1984 in organizing a group of "nonaligned Mediterranean states" (notably excluding Syria) for the purpose of a ministerial conference. The conference registered consensus on "a just and lasting solution of the Middle East crisis and the Palestinian question," the "integrity of nonaligned Lebanon," and an "end to the Iran-Iraq war." Such agreement cost the participants very little, and offered a more precise forum for Yugoslav interests than CSCE as well as a bolder alternative to Bulgaria's Balkan "nuclear-free zone."

Yugoslav efforts to advance nonalignment through European security have been limited by events outside Yugoslav control, viz., by the state of relations between NATO and the Warsaw Pact. The deterioration of relations between the Soviet Union and the United States at once restored the relevance of a "nonbloc" solution to European security while reducing the prospects of CSCE being of value to Yugoslavia.

Yugoslavia's relations with China have developed inversely to Yugoslavia's relations in Europe. The success of Yugoslav efforts to improve relations with China had depended less on Belgrade's efforts than on China's perception of nonalignment; and the improvement of Soviet-American relations has accelerated China's appreciation of Yugoslavia.

Following China's diplomatic isolation during the Cultural Revolution, Yugoslavia was one of the first countries with which China established relations. Following the Sino-Soviet clash on the Ussuri and early evidence of a Soviet-American rapprochement, Beijing resumed commercial relations with Belgrade in the Spring of 1969. Following the death of Mao Zedong in 1976, Tito was welcomed in Beijing in 1977; and in November 1981 party relations were reestablished. Tito's lavish reception in Beijing provided Yugoslavia with valuable support in its resistance to Soviet requests for Adriatic port facilities. In the 1980s, Sino-Yugoslav relations reached a level of particular value for both sides. Cultural and commercial relations complemented an annual exchange of Chinese and Yugoslav heads of party and state. Besides vigorously encouraging Yugoslav nonalignment and resistance to "hegemony," China also coordinated its stands on the occupation of Afghanistan and Kampuchea with Yugoslavia. Relations with the Soviet Union, however, remain sensitive, for Yugoslavia can have no assurance that Beijing would not sacrifice Sino-Yugoslav relations should there be a dramatic Sino-Soviet understanding. The Chinese have shown limited caution about the danger of an anti-Soviet provocation for Yugoslavia.

In 1983, China's Deputy Foreign Minister Qian Qichen, who was chief negotiator in talks with the Soviet Union, offered an interview to the Belgrade magazine, Start. He questioned Moscow's "real intentions" for the talks, advised the Soviet Union to destroy any missiles removed from Europe, and in a nod to nonalignment doubtlessly pleasing to the Yugoslavs, added that both the Soviet Union and the United States were hegemonistic. "The Soviet Union and the United States have been practising a hegemonistic policy: the former invaded Afghanistan, while the United States helps Israel and South Africa."(66) However, the following year, when Chinese Foreign Minister Wu Xuengian paid an official visit to Belgrade, he took the opportunity to discuss "some areas of Chinese-American relations" with Undersecretary of State for Political Affairs, Lawrence Eagleburger. The Foreign Minister's visit to Belgrade was given little attention in the Yugoslav press, possibly because of embarrassment about the Sino-American meetings or perhaps because it involved coordination of aid to Afghan or Cambodian resistance. Past efforts on the part of China and other nonaligned countries for a United Nations Conference on Kampuchea have met determined Soviet opposition.

UNCTAD AND THE GROUP OF 77

UNCTAD and the Group of 77 afford Yugoslavia the opportunity to coordinate an approach to the market economies and international economic institutions. Initially, Yugoslavia enjoyed a position of dominance within the "Group of 77" and UNCTAD, its main point of contact with the developed countries. At the first UNCTAD Conference in 1964, Yugoslavia established a valuable reputation for the superior competence of its representative, Dr. Janez Stanovnik, and his skill as a constructive negotiator.(67) Since the rise of economic concerns within the nonaligned movement following the 1972 Georgetown Conference of Foreign Ministers and the Algiers Summit, Yugoslavia's relations with the Group of 77 have been severely tested.

The Nonaligned Movement is an association both of fewer states than the Group of 77 and of higher diplomatic weight. Initially, UNCTAD was envisioned as a relatively specialized "technical" group designed to promote more equitable global economic relations. But as one American career diplomat has noted, "outside New York the distinction between the [Nonaligned Movement] and the [Group of 77] becomes less clear-cut, with little differentiation in positions on technical issues within the specialized agencies.... The nonaligned have often prevailed, even in the more technical agencies, in injecting [nonaligned] positions, and to a certain extent, political issues."(68) The danger for Yugoslavia was twofold: first, that "progressive" influence within the nonaligned movement would divide or radicalize the larger Group of 77; and second, that the themes of economic "self-reliance" at Algiers and implied confrontation at Havana would disqualify UNCTAD as a vehicle for Yugoslav interests. Moreover, the Cuban-Yugoslav struggle had directly affected the Group of 77. The Havana Summit "Economic Declaration" supported Cuba's offer to host the Sixth UNCTAD Session and recommended that the UNCTAD Trade and Development Board consider Cuba's offer favorably.

While the Cuban-Yugoslav conflict over political questions was resolved in Belgrade's favor by 1981, the economic conflict was not decided until 1982: UNCTAD's governing board did not accept Cuba's offer. After facilities at an alternate site in Gabon were judged inadequate, a majority of the board's members accepted

Belgrade as host for the Sixth UNCTAD Summit. The Economic Declaration adopted at New Delhi reflected Yugoslavia's more moderate approach in recognizing "the futility of any one country or group of countries attempting to find solutions to contemporary global economic problems between developed and developing countries in isolation."(69) Yugoslav success within the Group of 77 was not dependent on influence within the nonaligned movement but on enlisting Latin American countries to support its economic realism. In early 1983, Yugoslavia and Mexico cosponsored a symposium on nonalignment and the New International Economic Order. Following 1984 visits to Mexico, Venezuela and Ecuador, Federal Vice Premier Mijat Suković revealed that "it was mutually assessed. . . that conditions now exist for an international coordination of the developing countries' debt rescheduling efforts. The common stands and efforts of the developing debtor countries would considerably strengthen the negotiating position of each individual debtor country in relation to the creditors."(70) The support of "common stands" neither threatened northern economic support institutions, nor indicated impotence of inaction. The Belgrade UNCTAD Session devoted particular attention to the "unbearable problem of debts" recognized by President Mika Špiljak in his opening address, and ultimately to concerted and cooperative efforts towards debt rescheduling for Yugoslavia and Latin American debtors alike.

CONCLUSION

Nonalignment imposes some specific domestic discipline on the system, specifically in the area of economic austerity, and thus has a value also in justifying specific domestic policy decisions. Both the Eighth LCY Plenum in 1983 and the broader "social verification" of foreign policy carried out through the Socialist Alliance the same year indicate that Yugoslav authorities are sensitive to the popular value of nonalignment as source of federal legitimacy.

The nonaligned movement and other questions of Yugoslav foreign policy outside it are problematic for Yugoslavia. Yugoslavia may have wrested the nonaligned movement from "progressive" control but its success hardly guarantees the relevance of nonalignment to Yugoslavia's "global aspirations as a medium power." The "original principles" and stands initially valuable both to Yugoslavia and to other nonaligned states have become less valuable as a basis for diplomatic action than as a means of resisting Soviet domination. The nonaligned movement must be more for Yugoslavia to be effective.

The relation of nonalignment to other areas outside the movement will depend on factors outside Yugoslavia's control. In the three areas considered, Yugoslavia was able to bring to bear considerable diplomatic bargaining skill to gain relatively favorable outcomes, and to do so at a time when superpower relations were at their nadir. It appears that Yugoslav nonalignment has won an enduring if grudging respect and that neither superpower is willing to create conditions impossible for Yugoslavia's continued presence outside the Balkans.

NOTES

1. Branko Pribičević, "Socializem in Neuvrščenost," in <u>Teorija in Praksa</u>, Vol. 19 (1982), No. 3, pp. 362-380.
2. Momir Stojković, "Načela spoljne politike u novom ustavu," in <u>Socijalizam</u>, Vol. 17, No. 3 (March 1974), pp. 170-186.
3. <u>Program Saveza Komunista Jugoslavije</u> (Belgrade: Komunist, 1973), pp. 40-73, 106-127.
4. <u>Review of International Affairs</u> (February 20, 1982), p. 9.
5. B. Savić, <u>Yugoslavia in the Struggle for Action Unity in the Nonaligned Movement</u> (Belgrade: Socialist Thought and Practice, 1979), p. 34, as quoted in Peter Willets, <u>The Nonaligned in Havana</u> (New York: St. Martin's Press, 1981), p. 11.
6. Raymond Aron, <u>Peace and War: A Theory of International Relations</u> (Garden City, N.Y.: Doubleday, 1966), p. 83.
7. Robert O. Keohane, "The Big Influence of Small Allies," in <u>Foreign Policy</u>, No. 1 (Summer 1971), pp. 161-181; and Carsten Holbraad, <u>Middle Powers in International Politics</u> (New York: St. Martin's Press, 1984), pp. 67-91.
8. Rouhollah K. Ramazani, "Emerging Patterns of Regional Relations in Iranian Foreign Policy," in <u>Orbis</u>, Vol. 18, No. 4 (Winter 1975), p. 1050.
9. The problem of defining a "middle power" is discussed in Holbraad, <u>Middle Powers</u>, pp. 68-75, 86. Holbraad explicitly excludes Yugoslavia from the list of middle powers.
10. The impact of the Soviet invasion of Afghanistan is treated in chapter 12.
11. See Lars Nord, <u>Nonalignment and Socialism: Yugoslav Foreign Policy in Theory and Practice</u> (Stockholm: Raben & Sjorgren, 1972), pp. 285-286.
12. The treaty provided that "armed aggression against one [state]...on any part of its territory shall be considered as aggression against all." See <u>New York Times</u> (August 10, 1954).
13. <u>Ibid</u>. (September 20, and October 17, 1954).
14. Tanjug (September 14, 1981 and April 20, 1981), trans. respectively in FBIS, <u>Daily Report</u> (Eastern Europe), September 18, 1981, p. I6, and April 21, 1981, p. I16
15. Agerpress (July 10, 1981), trans. in FBIS, <u>Daily Report</u> (Eastern Europe), July 13, 1981., p. H1.
16. "Joint Yugoslav-Rumanian Communique," in <u>Review of International Affairs</u> (May 5, 1981), p. 34.
17. See Dobrivoje Vidić, "The International Situation Trends in the Workers and Other Progressive Movements in the World and the International

Position of the Socialist Federal Republic of Yugoslavia," in Socialist Thought and Practice, Vol. 23, Nos. 7-8 (July-August 1983), p. 32.

18. Although Yugoslavia has accepted a Greek proposal to convene a meeting of "experts" to consider nuclear-free zones prior to a summit, Yugoslav spokesmen have recognized "evident difficulties" with a summit.

19. James N. Rosenau, "Pre-Theories and Theories of Foreign Policy," in R. Barry Farrell (ed.), Approaches to Comparative and International Politics (Evanston, Ill.: Northwestern University Press, 1966), p. 81.

20. Holbraad, Middle Powers, p. 140.

21. Ibid., p. 151.

22. Quoted in "Bakaric Calls for Intensified Ideological Struggle against Cominformists," Radio Free Europe Research (October 28, 1975), p. 1

23. Ibid., p. 2.

24. George and Patricia V. Klein, "Nationalism vs. Ideology: the Pivot of Yugoslav Politics," in George Klein and Milan Reban (eds.), The Politics of Ethnicity in Eastern Europe (Boulder, Colo.: East European Monographs, distributed by Columbia University Press, 1981), pp. 258-259.

25. Tanjug (September 18, 1984), trans. in FBIS, Daily Report (Eastern Europe), September 19, 1984, p. Il.

26. Radoslav Stojanović, Jugoslovenski federalizam i spoljnopolitičko odlučivanje (Belgrade: Centar za publikacije pravnog fakulteta u Beogradu, 1981), pp. 85-89.

27. Radio Belgrade (May 27, 1982), trans. in FBIS, Daily Report (Eastern Europe), May 28, 1982, p. Il2.

28. Quoted in Slobodan Stanković, "The Aftermath of the Slovenian Party Congress," Radio Free Europe Research (April 28, 1982), p. 4.

29. Tanjug (May 26, 1982), trans. in FBIS, Daily Report (Eastern Europe), May 27, 1982, p. I5.

30. Muslim nationalism is discussed in chapter 6.

31. Glasnik Vrhovnog Islamskog Starješinstva, Vol. 7, Nos. 10-12 (October-December 1956), p. 297.

32. Oslobodjenje (December 5, 1973).

33. Start (November 28, 1979), p. 15. See also Zachary T. Irwin, "The Islamic Revival and the Muslims of Bosnia-Hercegovina," in East European Quarterly, Vol. 17, No. 4 (January 1984), pp. 453-454.

34. On August 14, 1984, the Libyan news agency announced the creation of a "Libyan-Arab-Yugoslav joint commission" on military cooperation. See

JANA (August 14, 1984), trans. in FBIS, Daily Report (Eastern Europe), August 15, 1984, p. I2.

35. Tanjug (February 22, 1983), trans. in FBIS, Daily Report (Eastern Europe), February 25, 1983, p. I9.

36. Borba (August 16, 1981).

37. Tanjug (October 23, 1981), trans. in FBIS, Daily Report (Eastern Europe), October 26, 1981, p. I9.

38. Ibid. (August 27, 1981), trans. in FBIS, Daily Report (Eastern Europe), August 28, 1981, pp. I2-I13.

39. Quoted in Willetts, The Nonaligned in Havana, p. 160.

40. Tanjug (July 15, 1981), trans. in FBIS, Daily Report (Eastern Europe), July 16, 1981, p. I4.

41. Miloš Minić, "Lasting Components of the Political Orientation of the Policy of Nonalignment," in Review of International Affairs (August 5-20, 1979), p. 27.

42. "Decision regarding the Mandate of the Bureau of the Conference," quoted in Willetts, The Nonaligned in Havana, p. 264.

43. New York Times (September 11, 1973).

44. Augustin Papić, "Od Lusake do Alžira," in Socijalizam, Vol. 16, Nos. 7-8 (July-August 1973), p. 883.

45. William M. LeoGrande, "Evolution of the Nonaligned Movement," in Problems of Communism, Vol. 29, No. 1 (January-February 1980), p. 42.

46. Quoted in Willetts, The Nonaligned in Havana, p. 81.

47. Recommendations of the Ministerial Meeting of the Coordinating Bureau, Colombo, June 1979, quoted in Ibid., p. 279.

48. An unnamed "Caribbean official" reportedly shouted at the Cuban Foreign Minister, "This isn't the Comintern!" Objections from Singapore and India to Cuba's behavior were more substantive. See New York Times (September 7, 1979).

49. Ibid. (February 6, 1981).

50. Rabotnichesko Delo (Sofia, September 26, 1981), trans. in FBIS, Daily Report (Eastern Europe), September 30, 1981, p. C3.

51. Grisha Filipov, "Effort and More Effort," in World Marxist Review, Vol. 24, No. 6 (June 1981), p. 34.

52. Rabotnichesko Delo (August 26, 1984), trans. in FBIS, Daily Report (Eastern Europe), August 30, 1984, p. C2.

53. Ibid. (September 6, 1984), trans. in FBIS, Daily Report (Eastern Europe), September 12, 1984, p. C10.

54. Tanjug (September 8, 1982), trans. in FBIS, Daily Report (Eastern Europe), September 9, 1982, pp. I1-I2.

55. Cited in Zdenko Antić, "New Polemics over Nonalignment," Radio Free Europe Research (August 8, 1979), p. 1.
56. New York Times (March 11, 1983).
57. Radio Zagreb (August 23, 1984), trans. in FBIS, Daily Report (Eastern Europe), August 24, 1984, p. I3.
58. Tanjug (August 25, 1984), trans. in FBIS, Daily Report (Eastern Europe), August 27, 1984, p. I4.
59. New York Times (January 29, 1985).
60. NIN (January 23, 1983), p. 40.
61. Ranko Petković, "Pokret Nesvrstanosti i evropska bezbednosti i saradnja," in Socijalizam, Vol. 23, No. 4 (April 1980), pp. 36-38.
62. Borba (July 6, 1973), as quoted in Slobodan Stanković, "Yugoslavia: Ideological Conformity and Political-Military Nonalignment," in Robert R. King and Robert W. Dean (eds.), East European Perspectives on European Security and Cooperation (New York: Praeger, 1974), pp. 192-193.
63. Miljan Komatina, "Nonalignment--Doctrine of International Relations," in Review of International Affairs (March 5, 1982), pp. 9-12.
64. Nils H. Wessell, "Yugoslavia: Ground Rules for Restraining Soviet and American Competition," in Journal of International Affairs, Vol. 34, No. 2 (Fall-Winter 1980-81), p. 320.
65. In September 1982, Warsaw Pact forces conducted an extensive military exercise in Bulgaria. Milenka Sundić, a Yugoslav observer, noted that this exercise was conducted on "Bulgarian territory, which does not lie in the immediate vicinity of the zone in which the NATO Pact's main forces are concentrated." Radio Zagreb (September 14, 1982), trans. in FBIS, Daily Report (Eastern Europe), September 15, 1982, p. I2.
66. Quoted in Slobodan Stanković, "China's Chief Negotiator with Moscow Talks to Yugoslav Magazine," Radio Free Europe Research (February 21, 1983), p. 4.
67. Alvin Z. Rubinstein, Yugoslavia and the Nonaligned World (Princeton, N.J.: Princeton University Press, 1969), p. 177.
68. Richard L. Jackson, The Nonaligned, the UN, and the Superpowers (New York: Praeger, 1983), p. 174.
69. Economic Declaration No. 3, paragraph 24, as quoted in Review of International Affairs (April 5, 1983), p. 43
70. Tanjug (August 18, 1984), trans. in FBIS, Daily Report (Eastern Europe), August 20, 1984, p. I6.

12
Yugoslavia and the USSR in the Post-Tito Era

Othmar Nikola Haberl

It required no gift of prophecy to anticipate, even as Tito struggled on his deathbed, that Yugoslavia would face difficult internal and foreign-policy problems in the post-Tito era.(1) Hence certainly the temptation to give pessimistic answers to the questions, Can Tito's state have any stability without Tito?, Will the Soviet Union make a grab for Yugoslavia after Tito's death?, or to portray Tito's demise in 1980 as a "decisive turning point" in Yugoslavia's history. One observer even argued that "Tito's death changes the world. A new, highly explosive political climate has arisen--and not merely in the Balkans; in world politics as a whole, especially among Third World and nonaligned countries, the accents [of policy] must be set anew, now that the great Yugoslav statesman is gone."(2) That seems overdrawn. On the other hand, J. F. Brown is undoubtedly right to claim that Yugoslavia has had to deal with three problems simultaneously in the 1980s: the problem of political leadership, the economic crisis, and interethnic relations. Brown is also surely right in saying that Yugoslavia has not thus far solved any of these three complexes successfully.(3) In addition, the unrest in Kosovo has destabilized Yugoslavia also in the foreign policy arena, insofar as it has damaged the delicate relationship developed between Belgrade and Tirana in the 1970s.(4) In this respect one can agree with Aleksa Djilas' thesis of Yugoslav instability in the 1980s, even if his hopes for a fundamental democratization of Yugoslavia(5) must be seen as politically unrealistic in the extreme. The analysis of recent political events in Yugoslavia gives one the impression, even more, that Yugoslav politicians are becoming conscious of the overperfection and unnecessary complication of their political system-- which allows at least the glimmer of a fundamental

political and economic reform to appear on the
horizon.(6)

YUGOSLAVIA'S POSITION BETWEEN THE BLOCS

In the first years of the post-Tito era, foreign
policy did not play an especially big role for
Yugoslavia. Yugoslavia's weight in world politics in
the post-Tito era is not as great as it was in Tito's
time. If, under such foreign policy conditions, only
relatively experienced politicians took over the
leadership of the Foreign Ministry in Belgrade (Josip
Vrhovec(7) in the transition phase and currently Raif
Dizdarevic,(8) once responsible for the Yugoslav Trade
Union's international contacts), that signifies that
the post-Tito political leadership has been fully
conscious that it could not continue Tito's centerstage
performance in foreign policy. The leadership has,
rather, had to focus its attention on internal
political and economic problems. Be that as it may, it
seems to me that the continuation of Yugoslavia's basic
policy vis-à-vis the superpowers, and also within the
nonaligned movement, would have been more effective, if
the foreign policy reins had been monopolized by the
narrow circle of better known politicians for more than
a few years in the immediate post-Tito period. (Lazar
Mojsov, the onetime Yugoslav ambassador to Moscow,
1958-1961, and Yugoslav ambassador to the UN, 1977-
1978, only became known worldwide during his term as
Yugoslav Foreign Minister, 1982-1984.(9)) That means
that the unavoidable descent on Yugoslavia's part from
a leadership function within the nonaligned movement
could have been softened considerably.(10) In sum, the
first years of the post-Tito era represent a kind of
transition to normality for Yugoslavia, after the
foreign policy euphoria of the 1970s.(11)
In spite of the necessity of this transition to
normality, one might say to "business as usual," the
preparation and execution of foreign policy decisions
is made more difficult by the constant rotation of
officials. But this rotation is an essential feature
of Yugoslavia's federal solution. It was Mitja
Ribicic, briefly party chief, who confronted the
Yugoslav public, in early 1984, with the challenge that
"equality cannot consist in a presumptive right to send
an incompetent deputy to an institution of the
federation...Take a look just at the cadres in our
diplomatic corps. I remember Foreign Minister
Mojsov...saying that some 30 of our ambassadors lacked
the training and experience for their jobs."(12)
Carl Gustav Ströhm concurs that the strategic goal
of the Soviet Union is "not a division of Yugoslavia,
but rather the ideological and foreign-policy

subordination of Yugoslavia as a whole, together with its leadership in Belgrade, to Moscow."(13)   On the other hand, there is no doubt that the West has "an interest in a stable Yugoslavia," so that "this country remains independent."(14)   American security guarantees to Yugoslavia in the 1950s provide evidence of this interest.   But the USSR has no less an interest in assuring that Yugoslavia does not drift too far toward America, i.e., the Soviet Union must also guarantee Yugoslavia's independence, without Yugoslavia's having to be accommodating to the USSR, let alone accepting some kind of "self-limiting sovereignty"(15) vis-à-vis the Soviet Union.   That means no less than that both superpowers have an equivalent interest in Yugoslavia's independence from each other--which is an ideal situation for Yugoslavia in the 1980s.   This circumstance has scarcely been better illustrated than at Tito's funeral, which both Soviet President Leonid Brezhnev and Chinese Party Chief Hua Guofeng attended, though the US sent a second-ranking delegation.(16) Moreover, American President Carter himself shattered the possible impression that his adherence at Tito's funeral signified that the US was less interested in Yugoslavia than was the USSR, or even China, by paying an official visit to Belgrade a few months later.(17)

POLITICAL RELATIONS BETWEEN YUGOSLAVIA AND THE SOVIET UNION

If the claim that Yugoslav foreign policy in the 1980s has returned to "normality" is to be sustained, then it must be shown that Yugoslavia's ostensible political omnipresence in the 1970s was built chiefly on the personality of Tito.(18)   That means, above all, that foreign policy "spectaculars" have become rarer and that Yugoslav participation in international conferences is often inked out.   In fact, it took some six months after Tito's death before it became obvious that the Yugoslavs were cutting back their foreign policy presence in order to save money.   Thus, for example, the Yugoslav delegation to the Nonaligned Conference in Delhi, in February 1981, consisted of only seven representatives; as a result, Yugoslavia could not be represented on all the working groups.(19) The problem of frugality in foreign policy was addressed by Central Committee (CC) member Dobrivoje Vidić, specifically with regard to the party's international contacts, in his introductory report to the Eighth Session of the CC on July 1, 1983:   "In order to save money, some international contacts which had been planned earlier had to be cancelled, and other similar measures are being put through."(20)   That means no less than that Yugoslavia's foreign policy has become too costly to bear.

The passage to foreign-policy "normality" was, at least at first sight, hindered by three events with which Yugoslavia was confronted in the early 1980s. The first of these, taking place April 22-23, 1980, on the eve of Tito's death, was the World Trade Union Conference on Development,(21) at the convocation of which the Yugoslavs took part.(22) The second of these was the Sixth UNCTAD Conference,(23) held in Belgrade from June 6 to July 3, 1983, for the institutionalization of which, at least, the Yugoslavs claimed for themselves a kind of copyright.(24) Finally, one must mention the Fourteenth Winter Olympics of 1984, held in Sarajevo.(25) All of these events recalled Yugoslavia's days of foreign policy euphoria in the 1970s.

Naturally, the renunciation of spectacular actions does not automatically mean the renunciation of the basic principles of foreign policy. But within the context of Yugoslavia's narrower foreign policy activity, the Soviet Union, conscious of the improbability of drawing Yugoslavia into the Soviet sphere of influence within the foreseeable future, decided on a strategy of pin-pricks, as if to test the limits of Yugoslav endurance. This strategy was not cleverly chosen, in that after the Soviet invasion of Afghanistan and the resultant shambles it made of nonalignment, Moscow's pin-pricks were not the most appropriate means whereby to combat the newly aroused mistrust. On the other hand, the Yugoslavs also disposed of a well tested instrument for arousing Moscow's allergies--which stirred unpleasant recollections, on Moscow's part, of the political outcome of the East Berlin Conference of European Communist parties in summer 1976.

THE POLITICS OF RECIPROCAL PIN-PRICKS

A mere month after Tito's passing, the 25th anniversary of the Belgrade Declaration, in which CPSU First Secretary Nikita Khrushchev had officially sanctioned Yugoslavia's maverick socialism, provided a good opportunity for controversy. V. Shafazhev was responsible for writing the Soviet assessment, which appeared in Pravda on June 1. On the one hand, in that the USSR had neither hushed up the Belgrade Declaration nor formally distanced itself from that declaration, Shafazhev wanted to underline its meaning for Soviet-Yugoslav relations, after the Afghanistan invasion. On the other hand, this was an occasion to reaffirm Soviet interest in drawing Yugoslavia closer. Hence, Shafazhev did not stress the fundamental significance of the Belgrade Declaration for Soviet-Yugoslav relations since 1955--as did the Yugoslavs--but rather tried to set this declaration in the context of Soviet-Yugoslav relations in the Khrushchev-Brezhnev era taken as a whole. In Shafazhev's construal, the Belgrade Declaration should be seen as an "enduring foundation for tight cooperation between our two countries."(26) Moreover, Shafazhev's reference to the "unshakable principles of Marxism-Leninism and the broad international solidarity" of communists, with its associations with Moscow's "selfless fraternal assistance" to Czechoslovakia in 1968, drove home to the Yugoslavs that _Pravda_ was by no means recognizing the independence or nonalignment of Yugoslavia. Indeed, it was clear that in Soviet eyes, Yugoslav nonalignment was, or should be, circumscribed by the common goal of "building socialism." In short, for _Pravda_'s writer, Shafazhev, there was no doubt "that the dominant tendency in relations between the USSR and Yugoslavia--countries with the same social formation--lies in what objectively unifies us and welds us together; this tendency is a regular feature of the development of socialism, discovered by Marx and Lenin and confirmed by the experience of many fraternal parties."

The very contrary thesis was developed by Zdravko Mičić, the editor of the Yugoslav party weekly, _Komunist_.(27) For him, it was beyond question that the Belgrade Declaration constituted the foundation for Soviet-Yugoslav relations, i.e., that the Belgrade Declaration had a much higher significance than all later joint Soviet-Yugoslav documents. Naturally, the Belgrade Declaration did not represent, for Mičić, an exception in Yugoslav foreign policy; on the contrary, it was more or less the point of departure for Yugoslavia's policy toward all other countries in the world. Moreover, under the Belgrade Declaration, the Soviet Union committed itself to noninterference "in questions of the internal order of different social systems and of different forms of the development of socialism, which are exclusively the concern of the people of the respective countries." Shafazhev did not, however, make even a single reference to this commitment. Unhappily, US President Jimmy Carter did not attend Tito's funeral in May 1980; however, his official visit to Belgrade shortly thereafter provided the Yugoslavs with the chance of documenting their independence of Moscow. Hence also Yugoslav attempts to deny that their relations with the Soviet Union had any special character, to the extent of using almost word-for-word the same formulations to characterize their relations with the US and the USSR.(28)

A year later--in April 1981--the foreign policy commentators of Borba and Pravda locked horns over the logic or illogic of nonalignment. Taking up the subject of the worsening of inter-bloc relations, Borba commentator Vlado Teslić noted that "an ever greater number of countries of different social systems are being subjected to psychological pressure, attempts at destabilization, and even the threat of open military intervention."(29) The goal of these threats was to form the nonaligned countries under the umbrella of the blocs. To this effect, the Soviets were developing theories about "special interests," about the "class character" in international relations, about the "special role of the countries of the socialist camp." In other words, some countries and people would have to be forced to be (socialistically) happy. The target of this policy was not just Yugoslavia, and not just the Balkans, but embraced the entire nonaligned world, because "independent and nonaligned Yugoslavia, through its principled policy and its overall activity on the international scene, but especially through its role within the nonaligned movement, puts up a determined resistance against all forms of power politics, of hegemonism, and of interference in the internal affairs of others."(30)

In his reply to Teslić, Pravda's commentator, V. Belyshev, noted that Teslić "equated the peaceful policy of the countries of the socialist community with the aggressive, imperialist policy of interference in the internal affairs of other states."(31) But, according to Belyshev, the very opposite is true: on the one side, there is "the defense of peace and of détente, the protection of the sovereign rights and freedom of peoples; and on the other side, there is the undermining of détente, the acceleration of the arms race, the politics of threats and interference, and the repression of the liberation struggle."(32) Teslić, in other words, compared policies which are not comparable, viz., "proletarian internationalism and the imperialist policy of spheres of influence." Finally, according to Pravda, Yugoslavia is threatened only "by the hostile actions of the imperialist powers," while Borba "falsely" suggested that the "anti-imperialist" bloc posed the same threat. Borba's "groundless" attack on Soviet foreign policy therefore served only the foes of socialism.

Teslić's reply, a week later, was correspondingly sharp. In contrast to Belyshev's by no means new or original two-camp theory, Teslić advanced the Yugoslav position, which is that a true alternative exists outside the two blocs.(33)

The most recent Soviet-Yugoslav political controversy (in 1984) had no immediate cause. But

through the publication of the Soviet attack in
Mezhdunarodnaia zhizn, the official organ of the Soviet
Foreign Ministry, the Soviets gave what was ostensibly
a disagreement between historians a direct political
significance. Through a scientifically untenable but
politically devastating discussion of the voluminous
Yugoslav documentation of the political history of the
Partisan resistance against German occupation and the
"socialist   revolution"   in   Yugoslavia,(34)
Mezhdunarodnaia zhizn almost completely repudiated
Yugoslav historiography of the Second World War and of
Soviet-Yugoslav relations during that war.(35)   The
Yugoslavs lent the greatest publicity to their
counterattack; the reply by Nešović and Petranović was
submitted, as an alternative view, to Mezhdunarodnaia
zhizn--though the authors could scarcely have hoped
that the Soviets would actually publish their reply.
It is symptomatic of the importance the Yugoslavs
attached to this controversy that they published it in
the popular weekly newsmagazine, NIN,(36) rather than
in the Foreign Ministry organ, Medjunarodna politika,
which reaches a largely foreign audience.
To the embarrassment of their Soviet colleagues,
the Yugoslavs disposed of stronger arguments, which are
generally accepted outside the Soviet bloc. Petranović
and Nešović claimed, for example, that the Yugoslav
resistance movement, under the leadership of the
Communist Party of Yugoslavia (CPY), had to deal with
attempts by Moscow to control its foreign policy. For
the Soviet leadership could "not reconcile itself to
the revolutionary innovation, which the CPY had
introduced in its struggle against fascism," viz., the
independence of the Yugoslav revolution.(37)   It was
clear that this reply was an indictment not merely of
the Comintern, and of the wartime Soviet leadership,
but also of Soviet foreign policy in 1984, for which
Yugoslavia's independent course remains a thorn in its
side.
In contrast to the Soviet "pin-pricks," of which
the Yugoslavs had no trouble disposing, the Yugoslavs
themselves chose more deadly ammunition in their ongoing polemics with the CPSU, choosing a context   in
which no direct Soviet reply was possible. The issue
at hand was the joint resolution adopted at the East
Berlin Conference of European Communist parties in
1976, which had declared that the communist parties
should
    develop their international, comradely, volun-
    tary cooperation and solidarity on the basis
    of the great ideals of Marx, Engels, Lenin, and
    with strict observance of the equality and
    sovereign independence of every party, the
    noninterference in each other's domestic af-

fairs, respect for the free choice of different roads in the struggle for progressive social change and for socialism.(38)

In view of this far-reaching concession on the part of the CPSU to essentially all (not merely the European) communist parties and in view of the previous and subsequent provable influence of the CPSU on other communist parties, it is scarcely surprising that this resolution, in the more than eight years that have passed since its adoption, has been totally "forgotten" in the USSR. On the other hand, for precisely the same reason, the Yugoslavs point to the historical significance of this conference. In his ceremonial address on the occasion of the 60th anniversary of the founding of the CPY, April 19, 1979, Tito described this conference as a touchstone of Yugoslav foreign policy, though he saw tendencies "to call every democratic achievement, which the European communist parties hammered out in the Berlin conference resolution, into question. We cannot come to terms with such tendencies."(39)

Nor was Soviet Foreign Minister Gromyko spared the uncomfortable recollection of the Berlin conference when he paid an official visit to Yugoslavia in April 1982. Upon meeting with Dušan Dragosavac, the Chairman of the CC Presidium, Gromyko was expressly reminded of "the significance of the principles which were enshrined in the document of the Berlin Conference of Communist parties of Europe"(40)--a point naturally omitted from _Pravda_'s reportage of the meeting, which mentioned, without more precise elaboration, only that "questions of the international communist and workers' movement" were discussed, (41) and from the final joint communique.(42)

The Yugoslav version of their bilateral relations reached the Soviet public during the funeral ceremonies for Leonid Brezhnev in November 1982. Petar Stambolić, at that time President of the Collective Presidency, and Mitja Ribičič, party chief, had sent separate messages of condolence to Moscow, which _Pravda_ could publish only with difficulty.(43) While Stambolić, without going into the concession about different paths in the building of socialism, praised only Brezhnev's endorsement of the "principles of nonalignment, sovereignty, territorial integrity, equality, and noninterference" in Soviet-Yugoslav relations, and thus raised a ticklish point, Ribičič did not have the slightest hesitation about embroidering his condolence telegram at what was surely, for the Soviets, a most inopportune moment. Ribičič praised the creator of the "Brezhnev Doctrine," not least because it was thanks to him that it had been possible to convene the Berlin Congress, which recognized the importance of equality and free cooperation in relations among communist parties. On the day his condolences appeared in Pravda, Ribičič, together with Stambolić, met the new Soviet party chief, Yuri N. Andropov.(44)

A new Party Program of the CPSU, announced since 1981, characterized the relations among socialist states and among communist parties somewhat differently from heretofore. For the Yugoslavs, it was above all noteworthy that "the principle of socialist internationalism is introduced in the program,...under which is understood the obligation to protect the achievements of socialism."(45) As a commentator in Komunist pointed out, this formulation was inconsistent with the resolution of the East Berlin Conference.(46) Komunist added, however, that the new program of the CPSU was "a program of continuity in the domestic and foreign policy of the CPSU," suggesting to the reader that with this new program the CPSU wanted to officially distance itself from the decisions of the Berlin Conference. And for the Yugoslavs, that is an indefensible position.(47)

YUGOSLAVIA, THE SOVIET UNION, AND NONALIGNMENT AFTER AFGHANISTAN

Yugoslavia was nearly invaded in 1949-1950,(48) and reacted with shock to the Warsaw Pact invasion of Czechoslovakia in August 1968.(49) But although Yugoslavia has been spared a military engagement which it has, not without some justice, feared, the Soviet military intervention in Afghanistan in December 1979 (50) showed that the Soviet Union was by no means unconditionally resolved to respect the political independence of nonaligned states.(51) In the context of the foreign policy controversy at the Seventh Summit Conference of the Nonaligned Movement in Havana in September 1979, the intervention in Afghanistan could only arouse conflicting reactions. Tito succeeded, only with great effort, in preventing the Havana Conference from adopting a formulation describing the Soviet Union as the "natural ally" of the nonaligned states and thus of causing a split in the nonaligned movement.(52) Instead, Tito advanced the Yugoslav thesis that the Soviet Union is a natural enemy of the nonaligned. Thus, the cement so necessary to the nonaligned movement, if it were to preserve its external unity, if not an actual ability to act, could have been provided by the Soviet intervention in Afghanistan. On the other hand, Soviet pressure on pro-Soviet nonaligned states could lead to a split in the movement. That the first of these alternatives resulted was due less to any failure in Soviet pressures on Cuba, which is scarcely demonstrable,

285

however, than to general revulsion felt toward this Soviet aggression.

It is true that Tito threatened to boycott the conference in Havana, if Cuba should "transform this meeting into a pro-Soviet rally."(53)   However, when Indian Premier Desai visited Belgrade, Tito and Desai agreed on the necessity of going to Havana under any conditions, in order to oppose Cuban influence on the nonaligned. Tito warned Castro in unmistakable terms, that "attempts...to divide the [nonaligned] movement, and to draw individual members to one bloc or the other, are regrettable, and are objectively contrary to the broad interests of the international community and to the aspirations of peoples for peace, security, and general progress."(54)

The danger of a split in the nonaligned movement was, with great effort, averted in Havana, and the Soviet incursion into Afghanistan later that year temporarily weakened this impulse. But the danger is still there. In January 1984, for instance, Ranko Petković, a commentator for Medjunaroda politika and for NIN, said quite openly that there were still claims being made that the Soviet Union was the "natural ally" of the nonaligned countries, which, as Petković noted, would divide the nonaligned states into two "fairly clear" camps: "those which adhere to the basic principles of nonalignment, and those which subscribe to the concept of 'natural affiliation' with the East bloc."(55)

Although Yugoslavia condemned the Soviet intervention in Afghanistan immediately,(56) it took more than a year before the nonaligned states issued a collective condemnation. While the Yugoslavs battled against this long delay,(57) Cuba's Castro was determined not to permit any condemnation of the Soviet Union as long as he was chairman of the nonaligned movement.   In any case, as the movement's chairman, Castro was supposed to convene a special conference of foreign ministers of the nonaligned states in Havana in mid-June 1980, at which it could be expected that there would be difficulties with the proposed condemnation of the Soviets.(58)   As it turned out, it was only in February 1981 that the special conference was convened in Delhi. Here, with the understandable exception of the Afghan representative, there was unanimous agreement on "an all-round political solution on the basis of the withdrawal of foreign troops and a complete respect for the independence, sovereignty, territorial integrity, and nonaligned status of Afghanistan, and a strict observance of the principles of nonintervention and noninterference."(59)   This resolution, to which even the "less nonaligned" states (Cuba, Vietnam) agreed, proved that the nonaligned movement was still capable of virtually unanimous verbal protests, in spite of the experience in Havana.

Naturally, Soviet-Yugoslav joint documents could not reflect a similar agreement, and indeed the joint communique of April 1982, issued on the occasion of Gromyko's visit to Belgrade, contains no reference to Afghanistan at all.(60) Similarly, there was no mention of the subject in the Soviet-Yugoslav joint statement of March 25, 1983, which excluded all points of disagreement.(61) However, contrary to the Soviets' usual practice, Pravda itself, in reporting a comment by Milka Planinc, chair of the Federal Executive Council, condemning American "power politics", left in a passage in which she also described "interference, suppression, intervention, and aggression" as the reasons for international crises.(62) Of course, the editors of Pravda could hope that the Soviet reader would interpret the entire sentence as a comment on American policy; but after the Soviet aggression in 1968 and 1979, the term "intervention" was, in Yugoslavia, not restricted to anti-American usage.

Yugoslav Foreign Minister Mojsov explained the accomplishments of the Seventh Summit of the Nonaligned States to the Yugoslav Federal Assembly in Belgrade in 1983. He underlined, in particular, the demand registered by the nonaligned states for the unconditional withdrawal of Soviet troops from Afghanistan and the creation of conditions for Afghan self-determination.(63) That the nonaligned movement had no political means of resolving the problem in Afghanistan was not at once clear to the Yugoslavs.(64)

If the Yugoslavs can, out of foreign policy considerations, polemicize much more clearly against the Soviets, it may seem trivial to recall that both sides have had to make great efforts to ensure that their relations, already enormously damaged by the intervention in Afghanistan, would not get even worse. In the context of the aforementioned policy of mutual "pin-pricks," this is complicated by the fact that each side has to save face: the Soviets being concerned about the domination of the Eastern Europoean states, and the Yugoslavs, about their nonaligned policy. That means no less than that the basic controversies have had to be dealt with indirectly. The bilateral relations between Yugoslavia and the Soviet Union can therefore be maintained or even developed, without either side having to concede any of its positions to the benefit of the other, as long as both sides agree to avoid conflict-laden issues. Yet the Brezhnev Doctrine remains valid for the Warsaw Pact members of Eastern Europe. So too does Yugoslav fear of Soviet military might and the specter of war, as suggested by

Tito's warning, in his political testament of April 1979, that

a war which does not have a defensive character, and military interventions, cannot be means whereby socialist countries advance themselves. We have never agreed with the idea that socialism might be spread through war or with the theory of the conquest of power through world war. Such ideas and practices are foreign to socialism. We shall therefore resolutely oppose all of this into the future.(65)

THE NEW NORMALIZATION OF SOVIET-YUGOSLAV RELATIONS

For all of that, neither their fundamental differences of opinion nor even the Soviet invasion of Afghanistan could produce a freezing of Soviet-Yugoslav relations--just as the crisis in 1968 did not either. It is true that between Yugoslavia's more frugal foreign policy and the successive illnesses and deaths of Brezhnev and Andropov, political-diplomatic contacts between the two countries became less frequent in the first half of the 1980s. In the transition from Brezhnev to Yuri Andropov and from Andropov to the late Konstantin Chernenko, five years passed without any contacts at the highest level, whether on the state level or on the party level, i.e., since the meeting between Tito and Brezhnev in May 1979.(66) Moreover, when Soviet Foreign Minister Gromyko came to Yugoslavia on an official visit in April 1982, this was the first occasion for contact between the respective foreign ministers in more than 12 years.(67) If this signalled a "normalization" of Soviet-Yugoslav relations, Yugoslav press organs did not reveal what the Soviet price for normalization was. Although foreign policy considerations prevented Yugoslav Foreign Minister Vrhovec from explicitly touching on the problem of Afghanistan, he used the occasion of the dinner speech to point out that "between us there are certain differences of opinion about some international questions."(68) While Gromyko had, of course, no reason to deal with this, it is surprising to note that the Soviet reportage of Vrhovec's speech did not remove this passage, which also appeared almost word for word in the final joint communique, and thus could not be excised from the Russian translation either.(69) For their own readers, Soviet writers quickly returned to the usual formulations. V. Kharkov, correspondent for <u>Novoe Vremya</u>, for instance, appraised Gromyko's visit as geared to a very contrary goal, viz., that "the Soviet Union and Yugoslavia should draw ever closer

together, because they both have the same social
system."(70)

At any rate, talks conducted during Premier N. A.
Tikhonov's visit to Yugoslavia March 21-25, 1983 showed
that Soviet foreign policy had resumed its pace quickly
after the first succession and that with the avoidance
of basic controversies, concrete agreements were
possible. In reality, precisely this visit above all
was relevant for longterm Soviet-Yugoslav economic
relations. Tikhonov and Planinc signed a document on
Bases for the Longterm Program of Economic and
Scientific-Technical Cooperation for the period up to
1990--a document which is even now not published. It
would be rash to divine in this economic cooperation an
incipient political dependence; after all, the Soviet-
Yugoslav credit agreement of 1971 did not produce any
such dependence.

Yet, despite these economic bonds, when Andropov
was laid to rest in February 1984, the Yugoslav
delegation had to return home without having met the
new Soviet party chief, Chernenko--in contrast to the
representatives from the other East European countries.
It may well be that in making the Yugoslavs an
exception, the Soviets were only getting even for
Ribičič's earlier statement, in November 1982, about
the significance of the decisions of the East Berlin
Conference of Communist parties. The Yugoslavs only
conceded their anger at this snub after Chernenko's
eventual meeting with Vidoje Žarković in late March
1984.(71) Nevertheless, correcting this snub was
superfluous, since ceremonial President Mika Špiljak
had, in the meantime, demonstrated Yugoslav flexibility
in the international arena by making an official visit
to the US, February 1-4, 1984. It is probably a matter
of the American side not sharing the Soviet/East
European/Yugoslav partiality for long-winded
documents--to the regret of the historian--that
accounts for the unavailability of a final communique
at the end of Špiljak's visit to the US. Yugoslav
commentators, however, comforted themselves with the
thought that even President Reagan had guaranteed that
"the US supports the independence, unity, and
territorial integrity of Yugoslavia, and respects its
nonaligned status."(72) In their rivalry for
Belgrade's favor, Moscow and Washington stand, once
again, at a draw.

INCREASED ECONOMIC DEPENDENCE ON THE USSR

This generally reassuring foreign policy
situation, as of the 1980s, has been sharply
complicated for Yugoslavia by the world economic crisis
of the 1970s and 1980s, which has impaired Yugoslav

efforts to maintain also economic independence of the USSR. On the one hand, the world economic crisis thwarted Yugoslavia's intention of according priority to trade with the nonaligned world--thanks to the institutionalization by UNCTAD of foreign trade relations in the Third World.(73) On the other hand, the strangulation of petroleum imports from Iraq (74) forced Yugoslavia to increase imports of Soviet petroleum, because only the Soviets were willing to sell petroleum without requiring payment in hard currency. The simultaneous climb, by leaps and bounds, of the world market price for crude oil further deepened Yugoslavia's dependence on Soviet supplies. Well known problems of convertibility and not least the bilateral character of intra-East European trade made Yugoslavia's foreign trade position yet more difficult, because the relatively competitive edge enjoyed by Yugoslavia's industrial products in the East European markets could not compensate for Yugoslavia's growing deficit vis-à-vis the Western countries.

Under these conditions, Yugoslavia was faced with a double dependence in its foreign trade: a debt of more than $20 billion toward hard-currency markets, which Yugoslavia still seems intent on amortizing, combined with energy dependence on the Soviet Union, which can only be paid through increased production, thus cancelling potential hard currency earnings in Western export markets. In consequence of the first factor, the International Monetary Fund can force the opening of Yugoslavia's economic doors; but on the other hand, the USSR is in a position to compel Yugoslavia to cover its petroleum purchases with counterpayments in kind. Given this situation, one is entitled to take issue with Reuter's claim that "fears of economic pressures in a grand style are uncalled-for."(75) For in the face of Yugoslavia's relatively greater petroleum imports from the Soviet Union, the USSR had to increase its imports of machines and equipment from Yugoslavia already beginning in the mid-1970s,(76) and of foodstuffs and consumer goods beginning in the early 1980s. The USSR could, of course, have obtained these items, in higher quality, from Western countries, but this would have cost the Soviets hard currency.

Table 12-1 documents the bilateral interest in intensive trade relations. Of particular interest is the fact that in contrast to the planned volume of Soviet-Yugoslav trade in these five-year periods, the actual volumes of trade were tangibly greater. And the available data for the current five-year plan period (reflected in Table 12-2) suggests that the current volume planned will also be exceeded.

Looking at the data in Table 12-2, one can also detect, quite clearly, the two sharp increases in Soviet-Yugoslav trade--1973-1975 and 1979-1981--due not the least to the increased and more costly Yugoslav imports of energy. Further examination of the data on exports and imports shows that occasional foreign trade surpluses on one side or the other are subsequently balanced on a bilateral basis.

The real dependence of Yugoslavia on Soviet supplies and the sheer impossibility of a reciprocal dependence is made clear in the data in subsequent tables. In recent years the Soviet Union has been absorbing a good third of Yugoslav exports, while about a fifth of Yugoslav imports came from the USSR, making the Soviet Union easily Yugoslavia's most important trading partner.

Despite Yugoslavia's importance for the Soviet Union as a supplier of certain commodities--it currently ranks as the USSR's eighth or ninth most important trading partner (77)--the proportions are not at all comparable. Yugoslavia conducts a quarter of its trade with the Soviet Union, while the Soviet Union conducts only a twenty-fifth of its trade with Yugoslavia. Certainly the bilateral pursuit of the principle of "business as usual," despite the Soviet invasions of Czechoslovakia in 1968 and of Afghanistan in 1979, shows that the Soviet Union is determined to keep its foreign trade relations free of direct political implications.(78)

Further, a detailed analysis of the actual purchases (Tables 12-5 through 12-9) shows that Yugoslavia must necessarily react more sensitively to variation in supplies or purchases. Exports of machines and equipment, for example, amount to a third of Yugoslavia's total exports to the Soviet Union, while clothing and shoes account for a good quarter. Indeed, the fact that the USSR takes in the lion's share of Yugoslavia's total exports (in machines and clothing, for example) or commands an import monopoly (as in the import of Yugoslav shoes)--Table 12-6--shows how sensitive the Yugoslav producer must be to fluctuations in Soviet purchases. This claim is ostensibly contradicted by the data in Table 12-7. For with a one-third share in total Soviet imports of shoes and clothing, Yugoslavia has essentially no competition in these areas. Yet these commodities are scarcely of existential significance for the Soviet Union, and hence Yugoslavia cannot exert pressure on the Kremlin through these exports. On the other hand, the similarly high proportion of Yugoslav exports of machines and equipment to the USSR could put Yugoslavia in a relatively strong position, if Yugoslavia's share had a corresponding significance as a proportion of

Soviet imports. The data in Table 12-7 show in reality that Yugoslavia has been able to increase its share in the 1980s to more than 4 per cent; that this would be a significant share for the Soviet Union can, however, scarcely be claimed.

Yugoslavia's dependence becomes even clearer when the structure of Yugoslav imports from the Soviet Union is analyzed. In 1980, petroleum accounted for almost half of Yugoslavia's imports from the Soviet Union, though that proportion has sunk to about a third since then (Table 12-8). At the same time, corresponding Soviet supplies have accounted for almost half of Yugoslav oil imports. In addition, where coal is concerned, in spite of the relatively slight importance of Soviet coal supplies for Soviet-Yugoslav foreign trade overall (5-6 per cent in the 1980s), half of Yugoslavia's coal imports come from the USSR (see Table 12-9). The effect of Yugoslavia's economic dependence was shown after the outbreak of the Polish crisis. Since 1980, Soviet petroleum shipments to Yugoslavia have sunk by about 10 per cent each year, thus forcing Yugoslavia to double its imports from hard-currency countries between 1980 and 1981, though it was able to trim the latter in 1982, by increasing markedly its imports from Libya.(79) It is quite obvious that Yugoslavia is, for currency reasons alone, not in the position to replace much more of the Soviet share through purchases in hard-currency countries. Naturally, the Yugoslavs have long been aware that this dependence on Soviet supplies has to be confronted. Hence, since 1979, total oil imports have been steadily reduced—less in consequence of the reduction of Soviet supplies than, much more, as a result of the drastic curtailment of Iraqi shipments that followed the outbreak of the Iran-Iraq war. From a total of 11.8 million tons in 1979, Yugoslavia's total oil imports fell to 8.5 million tons in 1982.(80) Nonetheless, one can still maintain that among Soviet imports from Yugoslavia, none may be found which could even approximate a potential counter against Soviet attempts to pressure Yugoslavia.

Under these conditions it was sheer political rationality that led the Yugoslavs to advise Soviet Prime Minister N. A. Tikhonov, during his March 1983 visit, that Soviet-Yugoslav commodity exchange could not enjoy "so dynamic a growth" in the 1985-1990 period as it had in the recent past.(81) That means no less than that the Yugoslavs are concerned to safeguard their economic, as much as their political, independence.

CONCLUSION

In sum, several points may be noted. First, when
one considers that Tito was one of the driving forces
of the nonaligned movement, one may say that Yugoslavia
has managed its transition to the foreign policy era,
despite an unavoidable contraction in its foreign
policy, with surprisingly little damage. This
certainly is not entirely due to Yugoslavia's own
efforts; the Soviet intervention in Afghanistan
contributed quite a bit to this result.

Second, the prospect of a strong Soviet influence
on Yugoslavia in the after-Tito era, which in 1980 was
not in principle excluded, did not come to pass.

Third, as a nonaligned state, Yugoslavia is not
interested in the longterm deterioration in relations
with either of the superpowers. In consequence, the
USSR and Yugoslavia can only try to overcome the shadow
of Afghanistan. That means the exclusion of
conflictual points from their bilateral agenda in order
to develop their common interests--and this concerns,
above all, their economic relations.

Fourth, the world economic crisis in general and
the Iran-Iraq war in particular have deepened
Yugoslavia's energy dependence on the Soviet Union.
Undoubtedly, some political influence can come of this,
if the Soviet Union were, under the right
circumstances, to threaten to withhold oil shipments.

Fifth, against this one sees, on the one hand, the
Yugoslav hope for an end to the war in the Middle East
and a consequent rediversification of oil suppliers,
and on the other hand, underlying Western interests in
the independence of Yugoslavia. Finally, in this
connection one may mention the necessity of Western oil
supplies to Yugoslavia in the event of a Soviet cut-
off--regardless of Yugoslavia's standing payment
problems.

Sixth, this albeit optimistic perspective depends
on a situation which cannot be described here and whose
resolution would not seem to be foreseeable.
Yugoslavia's enormous foreign debt has, not least,
involved the IMF in Yugoslav economic planning and the
IMF in fact demanded that Yugoslavia adopt drastic
austerity measures. While Yugoslavia may well have
handled all its difficulties up to now, honoring its
debts, a sharp reversal in the future cannot be ruled
out. Were the IMF to demand even broader intervention,
it cannot be excluded that Yugoslavia might simply
declare bankruptcy. That would result, without
question, in Yugoslav dependence on the Soviet Union
for the foreseeable future. It is therefore in the
Western interest to come to an agreement with
Yugoslavia for a longterm rescheduling of its debts,

not the least in order to strengthen that country's independence vis-à-vis the Soviet Union.

And seventh, if over the long term, Yugoslavia's nonaligned policy seems to enjoy Western support, there would also seem to be reason for optimism that the foreign policy preconditions may exist for Yugoslavia's being able to tackle the most important problems on its agenda in the late 1980s, viz., its economic crisis and the "national question."

(Translated from German by Pedro Ramet.)

Table 12-1

The Development of Soviet-Yugoslav Trade, 1971-1985 (in billions of dollars)

	Planned	Actual
1971-1975	3.7	5.1
1976-1980	14.2	15.7
1981-1985	32	n/a

Sources: M. Beljakova, "SSR-SFRJu. Dal'neishee razvitie ekonomicheskikh otnoshenii," in *Mezhdunarodnaia zhizn* (1981) no. 8, p 125; L. Harkov, "Bedgradskii dialog." in *Novoe vremya* (1983), no. 14, p.6; and M. Marinkovic et al. "Odnosi Jugoslavije i Sovjetskog Saveza 1970-1980," in *Jugoslovenski pregled* (1981), nos. 7-8, p 329f. Harkov and Marinković give the actual trade for 1976-1980 variously at $18 billion and $17 billion.

Table 12-2

The Development of Soviet-Yugoslav Trade, 1971-1983
(in millions of dollars)

	Exports	Imports	Total
1971	268.1	181.2	449.4
1972	329.4	283.0	612.4
1973	408.5	406.7	815.3
1974	671.8	751.8	1,423.7
1975	1,012.3	806.5	1,818.9
1976	1,141.8	1,001.9	2,143.7
1977	1,138.4	1,301.0	2,439.4
1978	1,393.9	1,374.5	2,768.5
1979	1,401.4	1,793.5	3,194.9
1980	2,489.2	2,697.9	5,187.1
1981	3,638.9	2,896.5	6,535.4
1982	3,423.7	2,736.7	6,160.5
1983	2,699.1	2,463.2	5,162.3

Sources: M. Marinković et al, "Odnosi Jugoslavije i
Sovjetskog Saveza 1970-1980," in
Jugoslovenski pregled (1981), Nos. 7-8, p.
329; I. Reuter-Hendrichs, "Jugoslawien und
der Rat fuer Gegenseitige Wirtschaftshilfe
(RGW)," in K.-D. Grothusen, Othmar Nikola
Haberl, and Wolfgang Höpken (eds.),
Jugoslawien am Ende der Aera Tito, Vol. 1:
Foreign Policy (Munich: Suedost-Institut,
1983), p. 128f; and Statistički godišnjak
Jugoslavije 1983 (Belgrade: Savezni Zavod za
Statistiku, 1983), p. 314; and Statistički
godišnjak Jugoslavije 1984, pp. 301 and 314.

Table 12-3

Soviet Share in Yugoslav Foreign Trade, 1971-1983
(in percentage)

	Exports	Imports	Overall
1971	15.1	8.5	10.8
1972	14.7	8.7	11.2
1973	14.3	9.0	11.0
1974	17.6	9.9	12.5
1975	24.8	6.8	15.4
1976	23.4	13.6	17.4
1977	21.6	13.5	16.3
1978	24.5	13.7	17.6
1979	20.6	12.7	15.3
1980	27.7	17.9	22.0
1981	35.7	19.9	26.4
1982	35.7	20.5	26.1
1983	27.2	20.3	23.4

Sources: Calculations from materials cited in previous
tables.

Table 12-4

Yugoslav Share in Soviet Foreign Trade, 1973-1983
(in percentage)

	Exports	Imports	Overall
1973	2.1	2.1	2.1
1974	3.3	3.0	3.1
1975	3.3	2.9	3.1
1976	3.3	3.1	3.2
1977	3.3	3.2	3.2
1978	3.1	3.1	3.1
1979	3.3	2.9	3.2
1980	4.2	4.0	4.1
1981	3.9	5.3	4.5
1982	3.9	5.0	4.4
1983	3.9	3.9	3.9

Sources: Calculations from data given in Vneshnaya
torgovlya SSSR za 1974 god. Statisticheskii
zbornik (Moscow, 1975)--hereafter VT SSSR
with year of publication--p. 13f; VT SSSR
1975, p. 9f; VT SSSR 1977, p. 9f; VT SSSR
1979, p. 9f; VT SSSR 1981, p. 9f; and VT SSSR
1983, p. 9f.

Table 12-5

Specific Commodities as % of Overall Yugoslav Exports to the USSR, 1974-1983
(in percentage)

	Bauxite	Non-electric machines	Electric machines	Clothing	Shoes
1974	1.0	n/a	6.1	9.0	13.8
1975	1.7	n/a	5.7	10.5	11.9
1976	1.3	13.1	2.0	10.2	12.6
1977	1.1	22.7	7.8	15.4	12.2
1978	0.8	22.4	9.4	8.7	15.3
1979	0.5	22.9	7.2	5.6	10.8
1980	0.0	15.1	7.2	8.8	12.7
1981	0.1	14.3	7.0	10.5	13.1
1982	0.4	18.1	8.1	8.0	13.4
1983	0.3	23.2	9.3	n/a	n/a

Sources: Statistički godišnjak Jugoslavije, issues for 1979 (pp. 313 and 317), 1980 (pp. 314 and 328), 1981 (pp. 311 and 315), 1983 (pp. 314 and 317), and 1984 (pp. 301 and 317).

Table 12-6

Soviet Share of Total Yugoslav Exports of Certain Important Commodities, 1974-1983
(in percentage)

	Bauxite	Non-electric Machines	Electric machines	Clothing	Shoes
1974	35.3	n/a	18.0	40.5	63.6
1975	69.0	n/a	21.6	52.1	68.9
1976	60.2	36.8	7.5	49.6	65.1
1977	63.7	46.8	25.0	77.8	64.2
1978	56.3	44.2	24.9	37.9	63.6
1979	46.1	44.6	20.9	31.0	54.8
1980	3.0	44.6	28.0	51.9	47.8
1981	20.5	49.0	34.5	76.9	80.5
1982	49.0	54.2	35.2	52.2	76.0
1983	32.0	54.7	31.0	n/a	n/a

Sources: Same as for preceding table.

Table 12-7

Yugoslavia's Share of Total Soviet Imports of Certain Important Commodities, 1973-1983
(in percentage)

	Machines and equipment	Clothing and shoes
1973	1.4	15.2
1974	2.0	20.6
1975	2.3	18.0
1976	3.1	27.4
1977	3.7	21.5
1978	3.6	22.7
1979	3.3	20.9
1980	3.5	24.3
1981	4.3	35.3
1982	4.5	33.4
1983	3.8	30.6

Sources: Calculations from data given in VT SSSR 1974, pp. 39, 51, 221-223; VT SSSR 1975, pp. 35, 47, 216-218; VT SSSR 1977, pp. 33, 43, 195f; VT SSSR 1979, pp. 33, 43, 194f; VT SSSR 1981, pp. 33, 43, 195-197; and VT SSSR 1983, pp. 33, 44, 195-197.

298

Table 12-8

Specific Commodities as % of Overall Yugoslav Imports from the USSR, 1974-1983
(in percentage)

	Machines and equipment (non-electric)	Petroleum	Coal
1974	5.0	24.8	5.3
1975	11.1	19.0	9.9
1976	13.6	30.0	9.7
1977	8.2	32.1	7.0
1978	10.6	37.9	7.1
1979	7.9	35.1	5.3
1980	4.6	44.5	4.4
1981	3.9	41.4	4.8
1982	4.4	37.8	5.9
1983	4.7	30.4	6.1

Sources: Calculations from data given in Statistički godišnjak Jugoslavije, issues for 1979 (pp. 313 and 320f), 1980 (pp. 314 and 321f), 1981 (pp. 311 and 318f), 1983 (pp. 314 and 320f), and 1984 (pp. 301, 314, 318, and 320).

Table 12-9

Soviet Share of Total Yugoslav Imports of Certain Important Commodities, 1974-1983
(in percentage)

	Machines and equipment (non-electric)	Petroleum	Coal
1974	3.6	27.4	65.0
1975	5.8	23.7	63.9
1976	8.5	36.1	63.9
1977	5.4	42.7	64.6
1978	6.3	49.5	60.8
1979	4.5	37.2	47.0
1980	4.7	44.4	49.7
1981	5.0	45.2	44.6
1982	5.7	47.2	54.1
1983	6.8	34.3	51.2

Sources: Same as for table 12-8.

NOTES

1. This general observation may be given more pessimistic or more optimistic variations, as seen in a conference on Yugoslavia organized by the Bundesinstitut fuer ostwissenschaft und internationale Studien, Cologne, in April 1980.
2. Quoted in Carl Gustav Ströhm, _Tito_ (Graz: Verlag Gustav Lubbo, 1980).
3. See J. F. Brown, "The Balkans: Soviet Ambitions and Opportunities," in _The World Today_, Vol. 40, No. 6 (June 1984), p. 245.
4. See Jens Reuter, _Die Albaner in Jugoslawien_ (Munich: R. Oldenbourg, 1982).
5. Aleksa Djilas, "Jugoslavia since the Death of Tito," in _Political Quarterly_ (1981), No. 2, p. 224. See also Vane Ivanović and Aleksa Djilas (eds.), _Demokratske reforme_ (London: Pika Print, 1982). In the former work, A. Djilas expressed the hope that "an attempt to democratize Jugoslavia might not be an endeavour so devoid of political wisdom after all."
6. See Jens Reuter, "Ziele und Aussichten einer Wirtschaftsreform in Jugoslawien," and Wolfgang Höpken, "Bewaehrung und Reformpotential des jugoslawischen Selbstverwaltungssystems unter erschwerten Bedingungen"--both talks presented at a symposium on "Reform and Change in Southeast Europe," organized by the Suedost-Institut in Munich, October 17-18, 1984.
7. The remarkable rise of Josip Vrhovec during Tito's lifetime, above all thanks to Tito's own support, whose power position within the Croatian party after the death of Bakarić was nearly uncontested, can best be documented in the fact that Vrhovec was not mentioned at all in the 1970 edition of the Yugoslav "Who's who?". See _Jugoslovenski savremenici: Ko je ko u Jugoslaviji_ (Belgrade: Hronometar, 1980).
8. See _Ibid._, p. 210; and _Ko je ko u Jugoslaviji: Biografski podaci o jugoslovenskim savremenicima_ (Belgrade: Sedma sila, 1957), p. 142.
9. Biographical information in _Sueddeutsche Zeitung_ (May 15-16, 1982); _Jugoslovenski savremenici_, p. 688f; _Ko je ko_, p. 473; _Neue Zuercher Zeitung_ (October 22, 1980); and _NIN_ (May 20, 1984), p. 24.
10. Although the murder of Indira Gandhi reopened the question of the leadership of the nonaligned movement, it seems unlikely to me that Cuba could regain such a role after its futile attempt, at the Havana Conference in September 1979, to have the Soviet Union acknowledged as the "natural ally" of the nonaligned states.

300

11. See Klaus-Detlev Grothusen, Othmar Nikola Haberl, and Wolfgang Höpken (eds.), *Jugoslawien am Ende der Aera Tito*, Vol. 1 (Munich: R. Oldenbourg, 1983).

12. Quoted in *NIN* (October 14, 1984), p. 17. See also *Ibid*. (November 4, 1984), p. 18.

13. Ströhm, *Tito*, p. 349.

14. *Ibid*., p. 351.

15. Hans Peter Rullmann, *Tito, vom Partisan zum Staatsmann* (Munich: Wilhelm Goldmann, 1980), p. 176.

16. See Vladimir Bakarić, *Josip Broz Tito* (Zagreb: Jugoslovenski leksikografski zavod, 1983), p. 78f.

17. For the joint communique issued at the end of President Carter's visit to Yugoslavia, see *Internationale Politik* (1980), nos. 726-727, pp. 25-27; and *Ibid*., pp. 5-7.

18. Between 1976 and mid-1979, Tito visited, *inter alia*, the USSR, the US, China, Great Britain, France, North Korea, and Portugal, as well as a number of Arab countries. During the same period, he hosted Brezhnev, Giscard d'Estaing, Honecker, Kadar, Gierek, Hua Guofeng, Ceausescu, and others. See *Die jugoslawische Innen- und Aussenpolitik. Bericht des Praesidiums der SFRJ, Darlegung des Praesidenten der Republik, Josip Broz Tito und Debatte in der Versammlung* (Belgrade: Jugoslovenski stvarnost, 1979), p. 76.

19. See *Neue Zuercher Zeitung* (February 3, 1981).

20. *8. sednica CK SKJ. Medjunarodna situacija, kretanja u radničkom i drugim naprednim pokretima u svetu i medjunarodni položaj SFR Jugoslavije* (Belgrade: Komunist, 1983), p. 37.

21. See *World Trade Union Conference on Development-- Belgrade, April 22 to 25, 1980* (Belgrade: Radnička Štampa, 1980).

22. See *8. sednica*, p. 36.

23. Roland Wartenweiler, "Die UNCTAD VI im Evolutionsprozess der internationalen Wirtschaftsbeziehungen," in *Europa Archiv*, Vol. 38, No. 16 (August 25, 1983), pp. 461-468.

24. See *Politicka enciklopedija* (Belgrade: Savremena administracija, 1975), p. 1432.

25. About this time, the following joke began to circulate in Yugoslavia: "Question: In what city were the Austro-Hungarian heir apparent and his royal spouse assassinated on June 28, 1914. Immediate answer, from a status-conscious Sarajevan: In the Olympic city, Sarajevo!"

26. *Pravda* (June 1, 1980).

27. *Internationale Politik* (1980), No. 725, pp. 9-12.

28. The US-Yugoslav assessment read: "We assess this visit very positively, since it shows that our

entire bilateral relations, as well as our useful cooperation in the international arena, can be pursued successfully on the basis of independence, equality, and mutual respect." The Soviet-Yugoslav joint communique used very similar language. See the report by Josip Vrhovec in _Internationale Politik_ (1980), Nos. 726-727, p. 20.

29. _Borba_ (April 12, 1981).
30. _Ibid._
31. _Pravda_ (April 19, 1981).
32. _Ibid._
33. _Borba_ (April 26, 1981).
34. See Slobodan Nešović and B. Petranović (eds.), _AVNOJ i revolucija. Tematska zbirka dokumenata 1941-1945._ (Belgrade: Narodna knjiga, 1983).
35. N. Semenov, "Za nauchnuiu ob'iektivnost. K izdaniiu zbornika dokumentov 'AVNOJu i revolucija'," in _Mezhdunarodnaia zhizn_ (1984), No. 10, pp. 123-132.
36. _NIN_ (October 28, 1984), pp. 34-36.
37. See my study, _Emanzipation der KP Jugoslawiens von der Kontrolle der Komintern/KPdSU 1941-1945_ (Munich: R. Oldenbourg, 1974).
38. _Konferenz der kommunistischen und Arbeiterparteien Europas, Berlin, 29. und 30. Juni 1976. Dokumente und Reden_ (Berlin: Dietz, 1976), p. 25.
39. Josip Broz Tito, _Sechzig Jahre des revolutionaeren Kampfes des Bundes der Kommunisten Jugoslawiens_ (Belgrade: Sozialistische Theorie und Praxis, 1979), p. 49.
40. _Politika_ (April 6, 1982).
41. _Pravda_ (April 6, 1982).
42. _Ibid._ (April 7, 1982); and Soviet-Yugoslav Joint Communique, in _Internationale Politik_ (1982), No. 769, p. 15.
43. _Pravda_ (November 15 and 16, 1982).
44. _Politika_ (November 17, 1982).
45. _Vjesnik_ (July 10, 1983).
46. _Komunist_ (September 7, 1984); and _Neue Zuercher Zeitung_ (November 6, 1984).
47. See Čedomir Štrbac, _Jugoslavija i odnosi izmedju socijalističkih zemalja. Sukob KPJ i Informbiroa_ (Belgrade: Institut za medjunarodnu politiku i privredu, 1975).
48. Re. 1948-1949, see Milovan Djilas, _Vlast_ (London: Naša reč, 1983), pp. 215-217.
49. See Othmar Nikola Haberl, "Jugoslawien und die Sowjetunion seit der tschechoslowakischen Krise. Zu einigen Aspekten ihrer Beziehungen," in Grothusen, Haberl, and Höpken (eds.), _Jugoslawien_, Vol. 1, p. 12.

302

50. Re. Soviet policy in Afghanistan, see Heinrich
Vogel (ed.), _Die sowjetische Intervention in
Afghanistan. Entstehung und Hintergruende einer
weltpolitischen Krise_ (Baden-Baden: Nomos, 1980);
and Karlernst Ziem, "Die Sowjetunion und
Afghanistan," in _Osteuropa_, Vol. 34, No. 9
(September 1984), pp. 723-733.

51. A recent assessment of Soviet policy toward the
nonaligned states can be found in Klaus Fritsche,
"Die Bewegung Blockfreier Staaten in Sowjetischer
Sicht," in _Osteuropa_, Vol. 33, No. 2 (February
1983), pp. 125-140.

52. On the other hand, Wilhelm Heiliger claims that
Yugoslavia "was hardly in the position any longer
to effectively challenge Cuba's position as
coordinator of the nonaligned or to prevail over
the opinion of those member states who hold that
the nonaligned movement should be simply a club,
which does not oblige its members to anything."
See W. Heiliger, "Die unsichere Zukunft
Jugoslawiens," in _Frankfurter Hefte_ (1983), No.
11, p. 12.

53. Quoted in _Sueddeutsche Zeitung_ (May 11, 1979).

54. _Die jugoslawische Innen- und Aussenpolitik_, p.
17f.

55. _Komunist_ (January 27, 1984).

56. _Internationale Politik_ (1980), No. 715, p. 14.

57. _Ibid_. (1980), No. 732, pp. 5-7.

58. _Die Zeit_ (August 22, 1980).

59. _Internationale Politik_ (1981), No. 741, p. 27f.

60. _Pravda_ (April 7, 1982); and _Politika_ (April 7,
1982).

61. Soviet-Yugoslav Joint Communique, in _Pravda_ (March
26, 1983); and _Politika_ (March 26, 1983). See
also _Internationale Politik_ (1983), No. 793, pp.
7, 15f.

62. _Pravda_ (March 23, 1983).

63. _Internationale Politik_ (1983), No. 790, p. 17.

64. _Politika_ (August 16, 1984).

65. Tito, _Sechzig Jahre_, p. 49.

66. There were, of course, a number of reciprocal
invitations to make such visits.

67. _Politika_ (April 4, 1982).

68. _Pravda_ (April 5, 1982).

69. _Ibid_. (April 7, 1982).

70. "SSSR-SFRYu. Traditsii druzhby," in _Novoe vremya_
(1982)n No. 15, pp. 8-9.

71. _Internationale Politik_ (1984), No. 815, p. 14;
Pravda (March 2, 1984); _Politika_ (March 2, 1983);
and _Komunist_ (March 23, 1983).

72. Quoted in _Internationale Politik_ (1984), No. 813,
p. 7.

73. See Branko Čolanović, "Balance-of-Payments Policy," in Radmila Stojanović (ed.), The Functioning of the Yugoslav Economy (New York: M.E. Sharpe, 1982), p. 138.
74. Between 1976 and 1979, Yugoslav oil imports from Iraq rose from 4.8 to 5.8 million tons, but sank to 1.3 million tons by 1982. See Statistički godišnjak Jugoslavije 1981 [hereafter SGJ and year of issue], (Belgrade: Savezni zavod za statistiku, 1981), p. 319; and SGJ 1983, p. 320.
75. Jens Reuter, "Jugoslawisch-sowjetische Wirtschaftsbeziehungen," in Suedost-Europa, Vol. 31, No. 9 (September 1982), p. 497.
76. Ibid., p. 489; and Milan Marinković, "Odnosi Jugoslavije i Sovjetskog Saveza 1970-1980," in Jugoslovenski pregled, Vol. 25, Nos. 7-8 (July-August 1981), p. 330.
77. Internationale Politik (1983), No. 793, p. 8; and Marinković, "Odnosi," p. 329.
78. Cf. the corresponding data in "Odnosi SFR Jugoslavije i SSSR (1955-1969)," in Jugoslovenski pregled, Vol. 14, No. 5 (May 1970), p. 219.
79. The Soviet Union supplied 4.8 million tons in 1980, 4.3 million in 1981, 4.1 million in 1982. See SGJ 1983, p. 320.
80. Within Yugoslavia, the throttling of oil imports was accomplished by rationing gasoline and raising prices. At the end of 1984, Yugoslavia announced it would end rationing January 1, 1985. See Westdeutsche Allgemeine Zeitung (Essen, December 28, 1984).
81. Internationale Politik (1984), No. 815, p. 8.

Part 4

Systemic Views

13
Political Decay in One-Party Systems in Eastern Europe: Yugoslav Patterns

George Schöpflin

The East European political experience since the communist revolution has had one extraordinarily paradoxical and contradictory aspect. Despite the fact that communist parties seized power in the name of an ideology that would bring about a secular utopia and set about transforming the societies under their rule into what they believed would foster the emergence of that utopia, the overall result of their efforts has been to create a strikingly anti-innovative political order. Communist-ruled states have proved resistant to change, above all, and, in consequence, their political systems have begun to suffer a process of erosion, of political decay.

Political decay is to be seen, in the first place, as a process where the formal institutional order has less and less to do with the distribution of power, the structure of interests, and the articulation of aspirations. Second, because there exists a serious maldistribution of power, all attempts to bring about change run into an immoveable obstacle--the refusal of the existing holders and beneficiaries of power to countenance changes which would diminish their power. Third, the process of erosion is a dynamic one in both directions between state and society. The modernising changes engendered by the communist revolution--the movement towards greater complexity, choice and continuous change--repeatedly come up against the barriers of power and thereby find alternative channels of articulation, which are inevitably informal, and thus the gap between the institutional framework and the realities of power are further widened. But equally, this frustration of change produces yet more decay, makes the resolution of political, economic and social problems increasingly more difficult. Value systems grow more and more divorced from the formal system, both among the haves and the have-nots of power. And that similarity points towards an ever

greater gap between shadow and substance, between the
formal and real aspects of politics. One of the more
striking features of communist politics in the 1970s
and 1980s has been the accelerating growth of
informalism in political, economic and social
interaction. The fourth outcome of this is that the
need for reform likewise increases and looks ever less
likely to be achieved, so that change requires a major
upheaval and thereby in the eyes of many, all change
becomes associated with upheaval. Orderly, incremental
change weakens or disappears as an alternative from the
mental map of politics.

At the core of the problem is the maldistribution
of power. The fact that power is vested in and is
retained by a political organisation that calls itself
a "party" and tries to legitimate its hold on power by
reference to a variety of formal and informal devices
remains the central political reality of East European
politics.(1)

The word "party" is, of course, a complete
misnomer for the neo-Leninist organisations that rule
in Eastern Europe, for they are in no sense a "part" of
anything nor do they seek to represent a partial
interest in society, but on the contrary arrogate to
themselves the role of being the aggregator of most, if
not all, interactions. Over time, the original
ideological impulse driving these parties has been
diluted and they have become, to use a word favoured by
many Western observers, more "pragmatic". In a word,
they are increasingly likely to profess one course of
action in terms of the ideology, but act entirely
differently, by other criteria. In this respect, the
word "pragmatic" is potentially misleading if it is
taken to mean something positive from the standpoint of
East European societies--the criteria by which
decisions are taken may no longer be "ideological", but
are still just as far outside the control of society as
ever. If anything, because the ideology theoretically
provided fixed points, action based on the canons of
this ideology could provide some consistency and
predictability; from this angle, "pragmatism" appears
very largely to be the self-serving pursuit of the
interest of the holders of power only.

Maldistribution of power means, therefore, that
some sections of society have excess power and others
suffer from a scarcity of it. In such circumstances,
those without or those who feel that the power they
have is insufficient (and this perception will depend
on a variety of factors, notably political culture)
will generally attempt to remedy the situation by
attempting to maximise whatever power they do possess.
The central method in this connection is to ignore the
formal, ostensible institutional structures, which are

(usually rightly) regarded as serving the interests of the power elite only and to create alternative channels and instruments for the exercise of power. It is in this respect that the decay of institutions is an accelerating trend.(2)

The remedy for this state of affairs is, self-evidently, reform. The word reform, like pragmatism, demands careful definition. Neo-Leninist systems may be (and frequently are) subjected to a process termed "reform". This, however, need not be much more than improvements in the existing dispensation in the relationship between the locus of power and the instruments for exercising it. It may involve some deconcentration of power or some redistribution of it within the elite, as say between the political elite and the technocrats. Edward Gierek's much vaunted reforms of the early 1970s in Poland were a classic of this kind of reform. Often reform (in this sense) can signify the ostentatious, public recasting of facades while leaving the basic reality unchanged--Nicolae Ceauşescu's rotation of cadres in Romania is a good illustration.(3)

This type of reform suffers from the further disadvantage that, given the pivotal reality of these systems--the centralisation of power--deconcentrations of power will tend to be followed by later reconcentrations, as there is no way of entrenching the redistribution of power in any institutional form.(4) Hence any change in the distribution of power will be temporary, contingent, and dependent on informal, ad hoc, and unenforceable factors (like the personality of the leader, the degree to which the elite respects or fears the will of society, the experience of society in taking on the state, and so on).

The real remedy for the maldistribution of power is not "reform" but democratisation. This involves the major and by implication irreversible redistribution of power; the recasting of the institutional structures carrying it; and ultimately, the ideology by which the elite sustains itself must also become the subject of open debate. Above all, democratisation must involve the acceptance of entrenched autonomy of institutions, the autonomy of some code of rules by which conflicts of interest may be regulated, and the recognition that the autonomy of the state over society must be moderated by the introduction of regularised social and political control over power. Given the extent and depth of the transformation in Eastern Europe since the communist revolution, changes of this kind must of necessity include the extension of the right of participation to ever wider sections of society and the acceptance of autonomous sources of legitimacy for social institutions, that is, freedom from political control through the doctrine of the leading role of the party. By the same token, a change of this kind must bring about a pluralism of ideologies, as well as of institutions. Self-evidently, a transformation along these lines is far outside the realm of political possibility in Eastern Europe currently. Failure to move in this direction creates the preconditions for political decay.

Political decay has been accelerated by yet another development, the decay of ideology.(5) When the communist parties seized power in the aftermath of the Second World War, they counted among their ranks at least a minority of genuine believers, who were motivated by their sincere belief in the idea that the secular utopia inherent in the Marxist ideal (full communism) was realisable. While this belief made them reject all compromise, it also acted as control over their own aspirations in the political realm. It created a sense of discipline within the party and subordinated day-to-day actions and desires to a longer-term futurity. However, inherent in the effectiveness of the ideology to mobilise individuals was the proposition that change derived from the canons of the ideology was within the possibilities of the system. It was this belief in change which underlay the revisionism and national roads to communism of the 1950s and 1960s.(6) With the effective termination of the possibility of change by the Soviet-led invasion of Czechoslovakia in 1968, an ever growing number of Marxist believers grew disillusioned and concluded that what they had taken to be a viable, living doctrine from which they could draw a guide to future action was in reality a facade, a set of empty formulae used to shield the ruling elite from challenges to its power.

Eastern Europe has been the scene of yet one further development with significant political implications. One of the consequences of the inability of the system to accept the redistribution of power has been the transformation of the party itself. Once the initial ideological impulse had gone and once the party accepted that it ruled over societies which were not homogeneous, but in which conflicts of interest could and did occur, it had to redefine the leading role of the party. Under monolithism this was straightforward: all power, action, and initiative were in the hands of the party. After the abandonment of the monolithic concept of society, the party gradually accepted that its own organisation should, at any rate in practice, be looser and less centralised. By the 1980s, this process had gone so far that the East European parties were no longer recognisable as adhering to the original Leninist model of organisation. Instead, local or functional interest groups within the party acted to a greater or less extent autonomously of the centre, sometimes in combination with bodies outside the party (like enterprises). This process, which varied in its intensity from state to state, meant that central control over the party, above all in the crucial area of cadres through the nomenklatura, had become much weaker than it appeared from the outside.(7)

YUGOSLAV SPECIFICITIES

The application of this model of political decay to Yugoslavia poses certain problems. In particular, has the Yugoslav path been similar enough to the overall East European experience for the pathologies suffered by the latter to be applicable to the former? The contention that I would like to argue first is that despite key differences between Yugoslavia and the rest of Eastern Europe, there is sufficient shared ground between them to make the model valid, always provided that the differences are taken into account in the analysis.

The central features of the Yugoslav experience may be summarised in these terms. (a) The Yugoslav party seized power independently, with only limited support from the Red Army. (b) The foundations of this seizure of power had been the Yugoslav communists' wartime programme of an end to conflict among the Yugoslav nations, of resistance to the foreign occupier, and of the satisfaction of some of the aims of the pent-up peasant radicalism that was left frustrated by the pre-communist regime. (c) This gave the Yugoslav communists a measure of domestically generated legitimacy. (d) In Tito, the Yugoslav party was fortunate in having a leader of genius who attracted genuine political support even to some extent independently of the party that he built up--a factor of considerable relevance in a politically somewhat illiterate community. (e) The break with Stalin constrained the Yugoslav leadership to reexamine the basis of its power and, by opting for a road that simultaneously emphasised independence and socialism, it could capture the support of much of Yugoslav opinion. (f) Given the inherently fragmented and fissiparous nature of Yugoslavia--geographically, historically, politically, and in terms of religion--the party accepted fairly early on that some aspects of Yugoslav power would have to be decentralised; how far this should go has been one of the central sources of tension in the whole history of the country. (g) The strategy of modernisation, concentrated on economic change and advancement, was attractive to the large sections of the population which benefited from it.(8)

Some of these factors were peculiar to Yugoslavia;
others, above all, the last, were common in some form
or another to the whole of Eastern Europe. Even more
significantly, the Yugoslav party lined up with the
other communist parties of Eastern Europe in adhering
to the one-sided distribution of power, refusing to
countenance political pluralism. The Yugoslavs were
evidently different in accepting virtually from the
outset that the economy could not be run on strictly
centralised, Stalinist lines, so that some devolution
of economic decision-making from the centre was
desirable and in recognising that theirs was not a
socially homogeneous, let alone monolithic state;
likewise, self-management signalled the acceptance of
some (guided) control and representation from below;
and the introduction of a federal system was similarly
evidence of the Yugoslavs' readiness to tackle the
national question at the level where they thought it
mattered, in culture. Yet none of these measures,
sensible though they were, served to stave off the day
when the question of the redistribution of political
power returned to the agenda. On this issue, there has
been virtually no movement within the Yugoslav system.
The Yugoslav communists continue to insist that they
must hold onto power by right of having seized it in
the first place and that real political power cannot be
shared with other political actors. In that respect,
the Yugoslav experience does not differ substantially
from the rest of Eastern Europe.

The problem with all of these specific Yugoslav
strengths is that they are all ultimately contingent on
factors outside the control of the holders of power.
The power relationship between rulers and ruled tends
to be determined by one-directional flows deriving from
the elite's control of most of the instruments of
power. In certain circumstances, the power elite loses
that control and, unwilling to accept new sources of
stabilisation because these would involve a
redistribution of power, it discovers that the system
as it exists has begun to undergo a process of decay.
At the same time, by reason of the party's
unwillingness to accept the redistribution of power
through democratisation, the systemic crisis
accelerates and is expressed in new, and potentially
more damaging forms.

Taking the above noted factors of stability one by
one, we find that the legitimating effect of the
wartime liberation is less effective for those for whom
that war is no more than the memory of their parents'
generation. They may accept the experience as the
historical origin of the present system and even
approve of it in these terms, but they reject it as an
instrument justifying their own exclusion from power.

The relevance of the liberation, and even of the satisfaction of peasant radicalism, has decreased in effectiveness with time. In the 1980s, Yugoslavs defined new needs and they have found it difficult to satisfy them within the framework of the system. The reluctance of the party to innovate in this area is, thus, explained by the pressure to redistribute power and to accept that the gains in legitimacy from being the liberator function in this way only for a time and cannot guarantee the holding of power forever.

Again, the system appeared to function reasonably effectively as long as Tito was alive. He acted as the ultimate aggregator through his ability to transcend politics and to enforce compromises in which all acquiesced, whether they liked them or not. But with his death, his pivotal charisma and prestige were irreplaceably removed from the equation, which thereafter began to fall apart. In practical terms, this meant that there was neither the instrumentality nor agreement on the criteria for the resolution of conflicts. If anything, this was exacerbated by the way in which the 1974 Constitution introduced the principle of unanimity into decision-making in certain key areas, for these were gradually extended to cover a wide range of political issues. The institutions established to cope with the running of Yugoslavia after Tito's death could not cope with the situation because in essence they had been created to deal with a system which actually had a Tito-like figure at the top. In other words, the efficient functioning of the system was contingent on a factor outside the control of the party.

Much the same applied to economic legitimation. This device, which was well known from Eastern Europe as a whole, depended on the availability of domestic and international resources of an extensive kind (cheap labour, cheap raw materials, cheap foreign loans), which these economies could rely on to provide the steady improvement in living standards, rather than resources generated by intensive growth. The Yugoslavs, in common with other East European planners, have proved to be rather inefficient in generating resources through higher productivity and intensive growth. Hence when their country was hit by the two oil shocks and the consequent decline in the world economy, the Yugoslavs had very few answers with which to meet the new conditions. Indeed, if anything the deconcentration of economic powers to the republics and provinces (to be termed "republics" hereafter) but without any devolution of political responsibility for the use of those powers made matters worse. Economic decisions, notably in investment, were made without any serious reference to economic criteria on the unspoken

assumption that Yugoslavia's foreign creditors would
continue to offer finance forever. In this sense, the
decision-makers were subject to neither political
(accountability) nor economic (market) disciplines and
acted accordingly, to make their choices by the
criteria of prestige or the enhancement of local power.
Understandably, the result has been to accentuate
waste, inefficiency, and the relative ineffectiveness
of the Yugoslav strategy of development. Economic
legitimation has been the loser.(9)

Nor have matters been any better in the realm of
ideology. While the distinctiveness of the Yugoslav
ideology of self-management and nonalignment has always
attracted a measure of support from Yugoslav opinion,
some of this support began to fray at the edges after
the 1971 crisis, not least because the prospect of
potential redistribution of power represented by the
reforms of the 1960s (like open elections) had been
foreclosed. The partial recentralisation of the mid-
1970s initiated a process whereby some, if not all, of
the attractiveness of self-management was lost by the
enhancement of the power of local political figures.
They tended to use this power to interfere in the self-
managing process and thereby undermined it.
Nonalignment also lost some of its allure, particularly
in that many Yugoslavs regarded it primarily as a
concept with the aim of underpinning Yugoslavia's
autonomy vis-à-vis the Soviet Union. Thanks to a set
of chance events—the preoccupation of the Soviet Union
with other issues, like Afghanistan and Poland and the
decline of nonalignment as a world movement—coupled
with the sense that perhaps too much of nonalignment
was directed against the West with which Yugoslavia had
ever more intimate contacts, the force of nonalignment
as a legitimating instrument began to decay.

It is conceivable that the Yugoslav system could
have weathered the decay of one of these instruments of
legitimation, including the death of President Tito.
But their simultaneity has resulted in an accumulating
systemic crisis, affecting a variety of areas at a
variety of levels made worse by the way in which they
interlocked causally, so that a remedy for one problem
immediately raised the solution of others. There is a
further argument in this, namely that the emergence of
one problem into the open can frequently bring to light
others hidden until then.(10) Thereby, the situation
is made to appear even worse. In this respect, earlier
decisions not to tackle problems but to ignore them or
suppress them can be said to have contributed to the
present multifaceted nature of the crisis and, hence,
to have added to the difficulty of finding acceptable
solutions. The recentralisation launched in the early
to mid-1970s was clearly a crucial nodal point in this

respect and, arguably, represented a major wasted
opportunity for avoiding the decay subsequently
experienced by Yugoslavia.

At the same time, even as these ideological
instruments were losing their effectiveness, other
competing ideologies emerged or reemerged into the
political arena. Nationalism proved to be the most
tenacious of these. Far from having settled the
national question by the measures introduced after
1945, which were generally assumed to have resolved the
problem for good, the politicisation of cultural traits
(the essence of nationalist ideologies (11)) persisted
overtly or covertly. The party's initial analysis,
that nationalism would fade away once the economic
inequality that had given rise to it was eliminated,
was faulty. The roots of nationalism were deeper and
lay elsewhere. Uneven development was, at most, one
factor among many accounting for the survival and
recrudescence of nationalism. By the time of Tito's
death, the fusion of latent nationalism with republican
institutions was far-reaching and probably
irreversible.

THE RISE OF THE REPUBLICS

The most serious consequence of this concatenation
of circumstances--the strengthening of the republics,
the de facto introduction of the principle of unanimity
and the removal of the aggregator through the death of
Tito--was the disarray in which the all-Yugoslav
institutional framework suddenly found itself. Whereas
previously Tito had been powerful enough to enforce a
common concept of what Yugoslavia meant and a common
strategy, albeit with occasional hiccups, this now
proved impossible. The republics had had a vital
constraint over their freedom of action removed and
rapidly emerged as full-fledged centres of political
power. But there was one gravely weakening factor in
the republics' new-found power: the relationship
between the republican elites and republican societies
continued, by and large, to be governed by the same
rules as obtained for Yugoslavia as a whole. There was
to be no distribution of power. This left the
republican leaderships in a dilemma. They had to pay
some heed to republican opinion--otherwise their
domestic power bases would be undermined--but the
mechanisms for ascertaining this and for mediating the
power flows were underdeveloped. On the whole, the
leaderships preferred it this way. The exclusion of
republican societies from the centre of the political
arena allowed the elites to hang onto more power (and
the accompanying privileges) than would otherwise have
been possible. But in the overall Yugoslav framework,

this unsettled relationship between rulers and ruled has led the republican elites to glance continually over their shoulders at their home republics, for fear that too great a concession to the overall Yugoslav interest might prove unacceptable and thereby undermine their positions in the eyes of republican opinion.

This "republicanisation" of Yugoslav politics has been one of the most significant developments in the country's history since the war. Whether this significance is to be interpreted positively or negatively depends entirely on one's initial standpoint. Thus, if one places the emphasis on the well-being of the Yugoslav polity as a whole, then republicanisation is the clearest possible evidence of accelerating decay. If, as against this, one takes a neutral view of Yugoslav unity, then the decay of federalism may be regarded as nothing more than the further evolution of Yugoslavia along its natural cleavage lines. Or, again, by the criterion of redistribution of power, republicanisation has both positive and negative sides. It can be said to be positive because it takes power away from the federal centre and brings it closer to the republics which are the political institutions with which most Yugoslavs have to deal and with which they identify closely. But equally, the development has its negative aspect because the republicanisation of power has eliminated central control over the republics--and this could operate in favour of society as well as against it--and has thereby made it easier for local coteries to entrench their power and exercise it without responsibility.

The fact that different republican elites create very different types of political climates, ranging from the liberalism of Serbia to the hardline neo-Stalinism of Bosnia-Herzegovina (12), is not in itself a source of weakness; on the contrary, it could actually function as a positive factor both by offering greater choice and as a demonstration effect. What republicanisation has brought about, however, is the fragmentation of Yugoslavia and given that Yugoslavia remains an international actor with international responsibilities, this has repercussions on the fate of the republics too. Above all in the realm of economics, the republics continue to use the creditworthiness attaching to Yugoslavia as a whole (and this is as much a function of political as of economic considerations), even while they no longer pursue Yugoslav objectives. From this viewpoint, republicanisation has been a disaster. It has permitted the republican elites to dodge their responsibilities and has contributed to their ability to legitimate their non-responsible actions. Thus, it has become relatively straightforward for republican leaderships to avoid taking a certain range of hard decisions by claiming that these decisions are Yugoslav and not republican issues.

A very real difficulty in this complex is how the definition of what is "Yugoslav" is to be arrived at. In theory, the all-Yugoslav interest is, presumably, to emerge from the shared interest of the republics in maintaining Yugoslavia as a single polity. In practice, this has not proved strong enough and the post-Tito collective leadership has for all practical purposes functioned without the criteria for determining what is Yugoslav, let alone the degree of consensus for making any decisions stick. The fate of the Long Term Stabilisation Programme of 1983 illustrates this clearly. Although the Programme was adopted centrally, there was little real commitment to making it work, because that would have demanded the sacrificing of republican interests deemed important by the republican elites, like cutting back on investment in unprofitable areas and letting loss-making enterprises go under. Hence, the federally determined Programme has simply been flouted by the republics, even where its provisions may actually have been backed up by legislation. Federal legislation, whatever its legal status, no longer has the political weight which would make it enforceable at the republican level.

The extent and intensity of republicanisation has been so far-reaching that neither of the institutions regarded by Tito as his successors to the aggregator function--the party and the armed forces--has been able to carry this out. The party, as already argued in the foregoing, has become republicanised and at the federal level its existence is tenuous. The armed forces, on the other hand, were expressly entrusted with the role of being the guardians of "brotherhood and unity" by Tito himself. Yet they have found it difficult to make much of an impact.

The explanation for this should be sought in the structure of the armed forces, which still have the image of being a Serbian institution in the eyes of non-Serbs, in the perception of the military leaders of their own relatively weak legitimacy to take direct political action, and in their helplessness in the absence of any political consensus as to what the future strategy of running the country should be. In many respects, the position of the Yugoslav armed forces (in the context of domestic politics as distinct from internationally) is somewhat anomalous. In as much as "Yugoslav" politics is becoming more of a fiction than a reality, the armed forces' political role must be equally fictive. Any attempt to transform that role into something real would rapidly run into serious republican opposition with far-reaching repercussions. Only on the issue of Kosovo, which is itself more than a little contradictory in the context of Yugoslav politics, is there enough agreement to use the armed forces to buttress "brotherhood and unity". If the armed forces lack the underlying consensus to impose unity on Yugoslavia, then any attempt to act as integrator would create more problems than it would resolve. In these circumstances, the lesser integrative factors working for the maintenance of unity--like habits formed by having lived together in the same state, attachment to Yugoslav symbols, a loyalty to a concept of Yugoslavia as a single polity-- have inevitably tended to suffer erosion. This does not mean that they have disappeared altogether, but they did seem to be weaker than they were formerly.

WHAT IS YUGOSLAVIA?

A pivotal aspect of the problem rests on the proposition that the terms on which Yugoslavia was reconstituted under Tito are no longer as readily accepted as they were after 1945. After the war and the horror of the wartime bloodletting, the majority of Yugoslavs were ready to accept a high degree of centralisation and central rule. This was underpinned by the promise of rapid economic progress directed by the party. Gradually, this system came to be regarded as counterproductive and as working against strongly held beliefs in ethnic identities. As these ethnic identities slowly reemerged into the political arena-- sometimes helped by the federal party (e.g., Macedonia), sometimes not--subsequent attempts to redefine these terms by raising the required level of commitment to a Yugoslav ideal have met stiff resistance from the republics which came to feel that they had too much to lose.

It could be argued that the present process of republicanisation is, in effect, a substitute for this redefinition of the agenda and purposiveness of the Yugoslav ideal. But this proposition does avoid the underlying lacuna, namely that in general the republican elites have given up doing anything more than paying lip service to an all-Yugoslav ideal and that there is a strong current which seeks to delegitimate all such arguments as "unitarist" and "hegemonist." In this respect, the Tito years must be regarded as a wasted opportunity, for while Tito was alive, the political, economic, ethnic, and social agendas of Yugoslavia could have been subjected to a debate at a time when the situation was stable. Instead, the various different identities by which individuals and collectivities define themselves in politics tended to be narrowed down to a confrontation between a derivative of the classical Marxist view that economic interest and rationality were paramount and the ethnonationalist argument, that ethnic loyalty was the overriding imperative. This oversimplification of the argument was unavoidable in a system ruled by a single party using a single ideology to sustain its rule. Other definitions of political identities would have cut across the party's central political purposiveness--the maintenance of its power.

THE MANIFESTATION OF THE CRISIS

The crisis in Yugoslavia is widely acknowledged inside the country. But analyses of the nature of the crisis and possible ways out of it are subject to the most fierce disagreement. For some time in the 1980s, the existence of an economic crisis was acknowledged; by 1984, so was the existence of a political crisis. The debate threw up three positions: those who argued that no reform was needed, those who claimed that the existing system was adequate to the occasion but required improvement, and those who insisted that only a radical reshaping of institutions would suffice.(13)
Much of the discussion centred on the powers of the republics. The argument was that these were too extensive to permit the implementation of any reform because meaningful reform would cut across republican interests.(14) In one crucial sense, this argument missed the point. The first question which should be reexamined is whether the republican elites retain enough of a commitment to Yugoslavia in real terms to maintain it as a single state. Following on from this, the next question is whether republican societies retain a similar commitment. These questions could not, however, be asked openly in Yugoslavia and as long as there was a lack of clarity concerning the terms on which the republics remained a part of Yugoslavia, the various obfuscations which bedevilled the situation in the early 1980s would persist.
Without clarity on this issue, the other problems of political decay affecting Yugoslavia were unlikely to find an acceptable resolution, however fundamental and damaging they might be. Yet most, if not all, the indicators were beginning to show red. Attitudes towards the self-managing system, long seen as a barometer of the level of popular acquiescence in the existing order, showed a sharp downward trend between the mid-1970s and the early 1980s, notably in the younger age groups (falling from roughly two-thirds to just over half, according to NIN).(15) Even in prosperous Slovenia, the proportion of the population that expressed complete confidence in the policy of the

party had dropped from 49.8 per cent in 1980 to 22.9 per cent in 1982.(16) The early 1980s appeared to be marked by a lack of confidence not just in the party itself, but generally in the future. This suggested that Yugoslav opinion had a low level of expectation of being able to improve matters and of being able to influence policy. Passivity of this kind may have been helpful in sustaining elite hegemony, but it was not fruitful soil for the launching of new initiatives.

Other aspects of the political crisis have received extensive treatment in the writings of Neca Jovanov, Najdan Pašić, Jovan Mirić, Dušan Bilandžić, and others. They include overregulation and the creation of a complex and opaque system of governance; the de facto voiding of elections through manipulation like lateral rotation to perpetuate elite power; immobility resulting from apathy and absenteeism; the usurpation of collective property and goods by particularistic groups; the rise of localism and the latent reemergence of familial patterns of politics; the fragmentation of the system through overlapping competences and powers, resulting in the thoroughgoing ineffectiveness of the system; the opting for short-term advantage over long-term interest (this has proved to be one of the crucial weaknesses of neo-Leninist political systems throughout Eastern Europe and is manifested, for instance, in the ignoring of ecological damage in favour of the short-term gains of economic activity); and, finally, a phenomenon not usually stressed by Yugoslav analysts, but familiar from other East European states, is the extraordinary decay of the language of Yugoslav politics, the heaping up of meaningless phrase on meaningless phrase--a kind of primitive accumulation of vocabulary.(17)

The upshot of all this is that as things stand in 1985, it is hard to put forward a convincing argument that Yugoslavia is still a single state in the usually accepted sense. Real power lies with the republics and is controlled to a greater or lesser extent by republican elites. The degree of popular control over these elites varies greatly, adding to the already anomalous and contradictory situation if one accepts that there should exist a homogeneous Yugoslav concept. The policies of the different republics vary greatly, so that it was perfectly possible to ban a play like Golubnjača in Novi Sad and stage it in Belgrade, to give only one instance. But it should also be stressed that this can only be regarded as a contradiction if it is assumed that the same cultural (or economic or social or whatever) policies should operate across the entire Yugoslav polity. This would demand a degree of homogenisation that few Yugoslavs would tolerate in the long term. The tension between unity and diversity is inherent and unavoidable in the make-up of Yugoslavia and the pulls of the two in different directions have affected the country from December 1, 1918 onwards, when the new state was constructed out of ethnically, culturally, economically, socially, and politically very different components. The underlying problem is that none of the various solutions tried since that date have satisfied a decisive majority of Yugoslavs. For the time being, it does not look as if any more persuasive solutions are in the offing. Hence the outlook for Yugoslavia at this writing (March 1985) appears rather bleak. The country will continue to be beset by an accumulation of causally interlocking political, economic, and social dilemmas for which the political leadership will not be able to find adequate answers.

322

NOTES

1. I have looked at the instruments of legitimation in greater detail in George Schöpflin, "The Structure of Power," *EIU Regional Review: Eastern Europe and the USSR 1985* (London: Economist Intelligence Unit, 1985), pp. 9-13.
2. The literature on political decay in Eastern Europe is growing and includes: Michael Vale (ed.), *Poland: the State of the Nation* (London: Pluto Press, 1981); Janos Kenedi, *Do it Yourself: Hungary's Hidden Economy* (London: Pluto Press, n.d.); and László Bogár, *A fejlödes ára* (Budapest: Közgazdasagi és Jogi, 1983).
3. There is a wealth of literature on Poland, including Vale (ed.), *Poland*; Adam Bromke and John W. Strong (eds.), *Gierek's Poland* (New York: Praeger, 1973); Maurice D. Simon and Roger E. Kanet (eds.), *Background to Crisis: Policy and Politics in Gierek's Poland* (Boulder, Colo.: Westview Press, 1981). On Romania, see Robert R. King, *History of the Romanian Communist Party* (Stanford, Calif.: Hoover Institution Press, 1980); Daniel N. Nelson (ed.), *Romania in the 1980s* (Boulder, Colo.: Westview Press, 1981); and Michael Shafir, *Romania--Politics, Economics, Society: Political Stagnation and Simulated Change* (London: Frances Pinter, 1984). Also relevant is: Milan Šimečka, *The Restoration of Order: the Normalization of Czechoslovakia* (London: Verso, 1984).
4. See, for example, Ray Taras, "The Process of Reform in Post-1970 Poland: the Case of the People's Councils System", in Jane P. Shapiro and Peter J. Potichnyj (eds.), *Change and Adaptation in Soviet and East European Politics* (New York: Praeger, 1976), pp. 58-76.
5. Leszek Kołakowski, "Theses on Hope and Hopelessness", in *Survey*, Vol. 17, No. 4 (Summer 1971), pp. 37-52.
6. György Márkus, "Debates and Trends in Marxist Philosophy", in Frantisek Silnitsky et al. (eds.), *Communism and Eastern Europe* (New York: Karz Publishers, 1979), pp. 104-132.
7. In Poland, it is clear that the traditional core of the party has been to a large extent replaced by the uniformed section of the party, with far-reaching consequences for the Leninist model. See the argument by Jan de Weydenthal, Bruce Porter, and Kevin Devlin, *The Polish Drama 1980-1982* (Lexington, Mass.: D. C. Heath, 1983). In Hungary, over the last decade or so, only one county party first secretaryship has been filled

from centre and this concerned someone who had
originally come from that county in the first
place—this implies that central control of county
level nomenklaturas is very weak. In Romania, the
Leninist model has been explicitly abandoned by
Ceauşescu in favour of a mass, as distinct from a
cadres, party, and the "intertwining" of party and
state institutions. Around one-fifth of the adult
population of Romania has party membership.
"Intertwining" occasionally subordinates party to
state bodies.

8. This interpretation of Yugoslavia is based on,
    among other writings: Dennison Rusinow, The
    Yugoslav Experiment, 1948-1974 (London: C. Hurst,
    1977); Stevan K. Pavlowitch, Yugoslavia (London:
    E. Benn, 1971); April Carter, Democratic Reform in
    Yugoslavia: the Changing Role of the Party
    (London: Frances Pinter, 1982); Steven L. Burg,
    Conflict and Cohesion in Socialist Yugoslavia
    (Princeton, N.J.: Princeton University Press,
    1983); Lenard Cohen and Paul Warwick, Political
    Cohesion in a Fragile Mosaic: the Yugoslav
    Experience (Boulder, Colo.: Westview Press,
    1983); Sharon Zukin, "Beyond Titoism", in Telos,
    No. 40 (Summer 1980), pp. 5-24; and Sharon Zukin,
    "Yugoslavia: Development and Persistence of the
    State," in Neil Harding (ed.), The State in
    Socialist Society (London: Macmillan, 1984), pp.
    249-276.

9. Ljubo Sirc, The Yugoslav Economy under Self-
    Management (London: Macmillan, 1979); and Attila
    Károly Soós, "Gazdasági reformok bevezetése es
    részleges visszavonása: a Jugoszláv példa," in
    Medvetanc (1981), No. 2-3, pp. 117-129.

10. This particular argument is derived from Csaba
    Gombár, "Bukás vagy vereség? Megjegyzések a
    magyar reform politikumához," in Új Forrás, Vol.
    15, No. 4 (August 1983), pp. 46-55.

11. On nationalism, my own (latest) ideas are set out
    in George Schöpflin, "Nationalism, Politics and
    the European Experience", in Survey (in press).

12. Aleksa Djilas, "Communists and Yugoslavia", in
    Survey, Vol. 28, No. 3 (Autumn 1984), pp. 25-38.

13. Jens Reuter, "Braucht Jugoslawien politische
    Reformen? Kontroverse Diskussion ueber ein
    zentrales Thema", in Suedost-Europe, Vol. 33, No.
    11-12 (November-December 1984), pp. 632-640.

14. Borba (October 13-25, 1984).
15. Ibid. (September 26, 1982).
16. Danas (July 24, 1982).
17. I have dealt in greater detail with some of these
    issues in George Schöpflin, "Yugoslavia's
    Uncertain Future", "The Yugoslav Crisis", and

"Yugoslavia's Growing Crisis", in, respectively, <u>Soviet Analyst</u>, Vol. 11, No. 13 (June 30, 1982), Vol. 12, No. 2 (January 26, 1983), and Vol. 14, No. 25 (December 19, 1984).

14
Contradiction and Reform in Yugoslav Communism: A Conclusion

Pedro Ramet

Yugoslavia's effort to adapt communism to its own needs has been beset with internal contradictions from the start. The crux of the matter is that instead of jettisoning a doctrine concerning which they themselves were having second thoughts, the Yugoslavs endeavored to refine it and reform it. Part of the explanation for their retention of Marxism as the centerpiece of their system is the fact that Yugoslavia's evolution away from Soviet-style communism was incremental: the open rift in 1948 deprived them of external poles of legitimacy; the development of self-management between 1950 and 1952 provided a new ideological bedrock for the system; the emergence of a nonaligned movement in the mid-1950s gave Yugoslavia a new foreign policy doctrine; and the economic and political reform of the mid- and late 1960s scuttled political centralism and moved Yugoslav communism far afield from the bloc applications. At no time did the Yugoslavs have to confront all the great questions at once: hence, there were always some which were assumed to have been adequately answered within the scope of Marxism and hence also the issue of abandoning Marxism was never seriously raised.

But in the process of their incremental adjustments and readjustments of the system, the Yugoslavs managed to invert the original contradictions of communism between control and efficiency on the one hand and between planning and democracy on the other, so that, in the Yugoslav "inversion," planning and democracy become compatible in a self-managing process that makes sacrifices in both control and efficiency. The Yugoslavs also created qualitatively new contradictions of their own. Political power and economic jurisdiction were decentralized to the eight

*I wish to thank Robin Alison Remington for her comments on an earlier draft of this chapter.

component federal units in order to satisfy the
autonomist strivings of the diverse nationality groups
that make up Yugoslavia, thus repudiating the
traditional Leninist ideal of strict centralism. In
the far-reaching program of devolution, only the party
itself was exempt from reorganization along the federal
principle (though even here, some Yugoslavs fear a
creeping federalization of the party itself). The
argument was rightly made that the Yugoslav system
could not function peaceably and efficiently unless the
component nationalities were allowed to run their own
affairs. Political efficiency demanded decentralization.

But although the Yugoslavs had, from one
perspective, inverted the Soviet political formula,
they have remained impaled upon a contradiction between
the imperatives of political efficiency and the
imperatives of economic efficiency. For while
decentralization mollified the nationalities and
allowed local elites to rise within local hierarchies,
it also provided institutional instruments for the
economic isolation of the federal units from each
other. As a result, the economic plans made by the
respective federal units have regularly been at odds
both with each other and with the supposed goals of the
federation (whether one speaks of their inability to
cut back on imports--this concerns Croatia especially--
or of the perennial duplication of factories and
services, even in the transport sector).
Decentralization has also meant that controlled prices
(and not all prices in Yugoslavia are controlled) are
controlled by the federal units and not by the
federation; as a result, prices vary from unit to unit
and local shortages have repeatedly flared up when
local merchants have preferred to fetch a better price
by selling elsewhere in the country. Decentralization,
the underpinning of Yugoslav politics, has proven to be
the guarantee of economic inefficiency.

The Yugoslav system has also managed to alter the
terms of another dilemma which confronts all political
systems in one form or another, viz., the dilemma of
political participation vs. political orchestration.
For, much more than their fellow communists elsewhere
in Eastern Europe, the Yugoslavs seem to take the issue
of political participation most seriously. But while
genuinely aspiring to create political democracy within
communism, the Yugoslavs have been unwilling to open
the floodgates to noncommunist forces and have engaged
in the Sisyphean attempt to foster genuine democracy
within fixed boundaries, i.e., to orchestrate genuine
political participation. Because the Yugoslav
political formula entails genuine liberalization in
several spheres (including culture, media, economics,

migration, nationalities issues, and even, to some extent, religious policy), it has been natural for critics and skeptics within the system to speak openly. As a result, in the five years since Tito's death, Yugoslavia has witnessed one of the liveliest political debates in postwar East European history. If Yugoslavia has thus far demurred from restructuring or revamping the system bequeathed by Tito, it is not for any shortage of ideas. The problem is rather that change in one term of the equation necessarily affects the other terms as well: moves to improve economic efficiency may threaten vested political interests; attempts to impose a clear party line in culture and media come up against the resistance of party liberals, who nonetheless join with party conservatives in resisting any democratization which would create noncommunist alternatives. One Yugoslav described this political formula as the combination of impotence in important decisions and permissive anarchy in everyday life.(1)

The "republicanization" of Yugoslav political life noted by George Schöpflin and documented by other contributors to this volume has served certain vital political functions, thus. But it has also entailed tangible costs, both in economic and political terms. Dennison Rusinow argues that rival factions in the Yugoslav political spectrum are searching for a common denominator for a broad coalition to overcome the crisis. For this there are both incentives and obstacles.

The contributors to this volume differ as to the prospects for Yugoslavia's successful handling of the crisis. Wolfgang Höpken believes that the political status quo is the outcome of untenable compromises and that the party must ultimately choose between organizational recentralization and complete confederalization. The problem in his view lies in the appearance of "a polycentrism of decision-making centers." Rusinow, by contrast, considers the "optimal" scenario to be a continued "muddling through" on the basis of "existing constitutional and statutory arrangements." Skeptical of the chances of major structural or organizational transformation ("reform," as the Yugoslavs always call it), Rusinow nonetheless considers it likely that economic and political pressures will produce a new spirit of cooperation among the major "tendency groupings" in the political system. Chris Martin, Laura Tyson, and George Schöpflin, however, tend to be more pessimistic, describing the outlook for Yugoslavia as "bleak." The trouble, according to Schöpflin, is that "the formal institutional order has less and less to do with the distribution of power, the structure of interests, and the articulation of aspirations." The result, says Schöpflin, is political decay. Yet, as I note in the introduction, there are important regenerative processes at work in Yugoslav society, the outcome of which cannot be predicted.

Only one contributor to this volume (Rusinow) explicitly calls himself an "optimist" where Yugoslavia's future evolution is concerned, and he qualifies this by calling it "perverse optimism." This "optimism" is derived as much from the fact that Yugoslavia's biggest "question"--the "national question"--has been at the same time the central force for what Höpken calls the "pluralization" of the Yugoslav political system. As such, this optimism must remain "perverse," because it links the strengths of the system organically with its weaknesses.

Yugoslavia has always seemed to be in one "crisis" or another. This should not be permitted to blind one to the fact that popular perceptions and orientations have changed. Robin Remington's reference to the post-Tito period as Yugoslavia's "Time of Troubles"--which recalls the Russian "Time of Troubles" of the early seventeenth century--aptly captures the distinctive mood of the 1980s. More specifically, the basic formulae of the system--reflected in the slogan, "nonalignment, self-management, brotherhood and unity"--are no longer working even as well as they did in the troubled 1960s and 1970s.

Nonalignment, to begin with, was originally designed to serve three functions: to protect Yugoslavia from the USSR, to give Yugoslavia a world role, binding it to the developing world, and to serve as a vehicle of socialization. As Othmar Nikola Haberl observes, there has been an erosion of the first two functions, which spill over into the third realm. Certainly, the nonaligned movement has lost some of its dynamism and vitality. Badly split between those who, like Cuba, wish to see the movement serve Soviet interests, and those who, like Yugoslavia, prefer to see nonalignment remain, in some sense, equidistant from both blocs, the nonaligned movement experienced a crisis in December 1979, when it suddenly discovered that one of the superpowers did not respect the nonaligned status of one of the movement's members: it is perhaps ironic that the Soviet invasion of Afghanistan that month came only three months after the clash between Tito and Castro at the Havana Conference.

But it is necessary to distinguish between the nonaligned movement and nonalignment as a policy. However weakened the nonaligned movement may become, it is hard to conceive of any foreign policy which would serve Yugoslavia's foreign and domestic interests better.(2) Moreover, as Zachary Irwin notes, it is doubtful whether a domestic consensus could be achieved on a policy which would align Yugoslavia with either East or West.

Self-management was likewise designed to serve three functions: to distinguish the Yugoslav system from the Soviet, to legitimize the system and develop loyalty to it, and to provide a starting point for a radically new form of political development. It is arguable how much erosion there has been on the first count, but, as Sharon Zukin notes, public confidence in self-management has plummeted, and even party officials criticize the implementation of self-management. Where the third point is concerned, moreover, it is clear that the Yugoslavs themselves are frustrated at their inability to move faster toward new solutions, at their admitted failure to implement self-management as legislated, and at the inefficiency that has come with massive decentralization.

Finally, brotherhood and unity encompasses three chief functions: to convince the peoples of Yugoslavia that without the communist party, the only choice would be between fratricidal war and foreign domination, to legitimize the principles of proportionality in representation and ethnic-based federalization, and to convince people that the system is just to all peoples of Yugoslavia. After the Croatian crisis of 1971 and the April 1981 riots in Kosovo, the third function has been badly damaged. But the first two principles are still widely accepted in Yugoslavia.

The Damocles' sword of fratricidal civil war, which is often linked with proposals to restore multi-party democracy, is a central raison d'être for the LCY monopoly. In seeking to buttress this argument, the party has magnified and mythologized the Partisan struggle and has correspondingly given short shrift to other aspects of Yugoslav history. The recent reawakening of interest in interwar and early postwar history is a symptom of the dissatisfaction engendered by this policy. One participant in a recent discussion arranged by the ideological and information commission of the Central Committee of the LC Croatia was moved to comment:

> We often underestimate or completely forget our past. I am speaking about the history of the Croats, but this is equally true of the history of the Serbs and other nationalities in our country. During the last forty years we have wiped out many important pages [of our history]. Significant names and testimonies have disappeared. One thing today, another tomorrow. Our great minds in science, literature, politics, creative arts, and the struggle for national survival are losing the battle with names of

Partisans and with contemporary events. I am
speaking as a Croat, a communist, and a Partisan.
I wish to draw your attention to the fact that we
must all strive to halt this process.(3)

Reading between the lines of the internal debate
of the last five years, it seems evident that the
Yugoslavs themselves have come to realize that while
many of their problems are caused by the internal
contradictions within their system, these contradictions are necessary insofar as they reflect and
serve opposing interests. And hence, the resistance to
reform is imbedded in vested interests. The
implication is that reform in Yugoslavia is apt to
remain a politically divisive question in which, as in
the 1960s, draft recommendations and resolutions, such
as the recommendations of the Krajgher commission, are
apt to encounter ritual acquiescence, obstruction, and
open doubt. However, this is not to say that further
reform is impossible. After all, the Yugoslavs have
long been in the forefront of innovative reform among
one-party systems, and indeed, the development of an
apocalypse culture in contemporary Yugoslavia is a sign
of the growing conviction that the system is in need of
reform.

NOTES

1. Marko Konstantinović (pseud.), "Samoupravljanje kao barijera demokratskim reformima," in Vane Ivanović and Aleksa Djilas (eds.), <u>Demokratske reforme</u> (London: Pika Print, 1982), p. 98.
2. See Robin Alison Remington, "The Function of Nonalignment in Post-Tito Yugoslavia: Domestic/Foreign Policy Linkages," in <u>The Nonaligned World</u>, Vol 2, No. 2 (April-June 1984).
3. <u>Vjesnik</u> (May 29, 1984), as quoted in <u>AKSA</u> (June 1, 1984).

Index

Bulgaria (cont.)
and Nonaligned Movement,
262-263
and Yugoslavia, 252
in Yugoslav press, 104,
105
Bureaucratization, 80
Burg, Steven L., 143, 156,
157
Burma, 251
Buses, 225

Cadres policy, 39, 43, 47,
48, 137, 138
Cambodia. See Kampuchea
Camp David Agreements
(1979), 261, 263
Canada, 242
Capital
accumulation, 86
allocation, 186, 192, 196
-intensive projects, 8
Car, Marija, 175, 179
Carter, Jimmy, 278, 280
Castro, Fidel, 260, 285,
328
Catholic Church and the
Croatian People, The
(Sagi-Bunić), 172
Catholics. See Roman
Catholicism
CC. See Central Committee
Ceauşescu, Nicolae, 251,
309
Censorship, 100, 106, 240
Census
1971, 10, 11, 160, 224
1981, 10, 11, 159-160
Center of High Military
Schools, 61
Central America, 265
Central Committee (CC)
(LCY), 33, 34-35,
36-38, 39, 48, 58, 63,
69, 154, 155, 278
Commission for Appeals
and Complaints, 6
grassroots organizations,
7
membership, 44, 58, 59
Presidium, 7, 33, 35,
36, 37, 38, 58, 59, 63,
67, 68, 157, 204
Presidium age structure,

73-74(n38)
and provincial organiza-
tions, 40, 41
representation, 59, 68,
204
Centralization. See
Democratic centralism;
Federalization
Centralized autocracy, 161
Chad, 257
Chamber of Republics and
Provinces, 233, 238, 240
Chernenko, Konstantin, 56,
287, 288
Chetniks, 4, 10, 15, 105
Chief Inspector of National
Defense, 62
Chief of Staff, 62
China, People's Republic of,
254
and U. S., 268
and Yugoslavia, 266,
268-269, 278
in Yugoslav press, 104, 268
Christianity Today (pub-
lishing house), 106, 170,
172
Church of the Brethren, 178
Čičak, Ranka, 108
Čik-Ekstra (weekly), 101
Classical bureaucratic
theory, 167
Classless society, 93
Clericalists, 150, 151
"Clerico-nationalism," 170
"Club of 1941," 68
CMEA. See Council for Mutual
Economic Assistance
Coal, 226, 230, 231, 238,
291, 298(tables)
"Code phrases," 154
Collective entrepreneurs,
186
Collective past, 78, 79,
95, 329-330
Collective work, 63-65
Comecon. See Council for
Mutual Economic Assistance
Comisso, Ellen, 87
Communism, 5, 325. See also
Communist-ruled states;
League of Communists of
Yugoslavia; Socialism
Communist militaries, 56-57